COUNTRY

Pickers, Slickers, Cheatin' Hearts & Superstars

COUNTRY

THE MUSIC AND THE MUSICIANS

The Country Music Foundation

Abbeville Press • Publishers • New York

EDITORS: Paul Kingsbury, Country Music Foundation
Alan Axelrod, Abbeville Press

DESIGNER: Molly Shields

PRODUCTION SUPERVISOR: Hope Koturo

JACKET FRONT: Earl Scruggs and Lester Flatt, photo hand painted by Curtice Taylor
JACKET SPINE: Dolly Parton
JACKET BACK (CLOCKWISE): Willie Nelson; Randy Travis; Elvis Presley;
Linda Ronstadt, Emmylou Harris, and Dolly Parton
FRONTISPIECE: Porter Wagoner
FOLLOWING CONTENTS: Tammy Wynette and George Jones

Library of Congress Cataloging-in-Publication Data

Country : The Music and the Musicians
        p.   cm.
    Published for the Country Music Foundation.
    Bibliography: p.
    Includes index.
    ISBN 0-89659-868-3
    1. Country music—History and criticism.   I. Country Music
Foundation.
ML3524.C66   1988
784.5′2′00973—dc19

First edition

Published in the United States of America in 1988 by Abbeville Press, Inc.

CONTENTS

FOREWORD

Country music, as we now know it, began to take shape in the nineteenth century. From traveling entertainer to townsfolk, friend to neighbor, parent to child, scraps of ancient British airs, blues, minstrel songs, hymns, contemporary popular songs, and, later, jazz and ragtime passed back and forth, and mingled. Though this music was a cherished pastime for many, with the rare exception of early twentieth-century folk-song collectors like Cecil Sharp, no one considered the tunes themselves any more valuable than, say, nursery rhymes.

By the early 1920s, however, the phonograph was becoming a common household item, joined soon after by the radio. As sharp-eyed businessmen noticed the commercial possibilities of this simple rustic music, the old songs and instrumental numbers (which, for years, had been casually arranged and rearranged like so much small-town gossip) suddenly crystallized. A new musical genre was born and christened with various names, the most popular being "old-time music," for the tunes sounded old-fashioned and traditional even then.

Country: The Music and the Musicians begins in the 1920s, when country music began developing as a distinct commercial genre and as a (more or less) dependable source of income for struggling part-time musicians like Jimmie Rodgers and the Carter Family. Our story continues as far as printing schedules allowed, which is somewhere in mid 1988—at which point, after more than six decades of country, record executives, radio station programmers, performers, and fans still can't come to a consensus on just what country music is and what it isn't. In between these self-imposed limits, sixteen essays discuss country music's most influential performers and its leading historical developments. Interspersed throughout the essays are some 800 rare and remarkable photographs, including vintage publicity stills, candid snapshots from tours and recording sessions, reproductions of rare records and song folios, and many other related curios—all organized in roughly chronological order. They serve not only to illustrate the essays but also to expand upon them, conveying the myriad personal details that are, in fact, the brickwork of country's history.

The text and the photographs were compiled by the Country Music Foundation, the world's largest and most active research center devoted to a single form of popular music. Established in 1964, the CMF is perhaps best known for its nationally accredited Country Music Hall of Fame & Museum. Besides running this popular tourist attraction, the CMF operates a reissue record label, educational outreach programs, an oral history project, and the Country Music Foundation Press. The CMF's Library and Media Center is an enormous repository for material related to country music—recordings, books, periodicals, published music, and photographs.

Most of the images that appear here have come from the CMF archives. These archives owe their existence to the foresight and generosity of many individuals, among them country music performers, business people, and their families; collectors; record companies; trade magazines; photographers; and the boards of the CMA and the CMF. Two large collections that added substantially to the CMF's holdings in 1980–81 deserve special mention: the photographs and files of Thurston Moore, who had collected some 4,000 photos while publishing his popular *Country Music Scrapbook* for fans and *Country Music Who's Who* for the country music industry; and the prints and negatives of the late Walden Fabry, a Nashville studio photographer who worked with country performers from the late forties into the seventies.

A small cadre of generous photographers and collectors lent the CMF select photographs just for the purposes of this book; they include Colin Escott, Robert Dye, Alan Mayor, Gordon Stoker, Leonard Kamsler, Jon Sievert, Bob Pinson, and Chris Skinker. In addition, most of the color photographs of contemporary stars appear courtesy of the Nashville offices of the major record companies.

Though this illustrated history has been a CMF staff project—and could not have been completed without the hard work and support of the entire organization and board —certain individuals deserve special recognition for their contributions. Invaluable in the planning and shaping of this book has been the brain trust of Bill Ivey, Bob Pinson, Kyle Young, Charlie Seemann, John Rumble, Ronnie Pugh, Jay Orr, and Chris Skinker. This book owes its liveliness in conception, its accuracy, and its thoroughness to their efforts. Special thanks are also due Chris Skinker for the many days, nights, and weekends spent processing the photos that appear here; Francesca McLean, John Rumble, and Ronnie Pugh for compiling the index; Diane Roberts for administrative support; and Carolyn Tate for proofreading.

Special thanks also to Abbeville's Molly Shields for design and to Alan Axelrod for patient and judicious editorial work and shepherding this complicated book through its production. Finally, the CMF is indebted to John Morthland for giving sage advice when the book was still only an idea.

This illustrated history is intended to be a celebration of and a companion to the music. It is by no means a complete or definitive history of country; that task has been ably tackled by others, most notably Bill C. Malone in his landmark *Country Music USA*, first published by the University of Texas Press in 1968 and reissued in a revised and expanded version in 1985.

For most of seventy years now, country music has consistently managed to stay just out of step with what the "tastemakers" pronounce fashionable. Therein surely lies a great deal of its charm and durability. While we hope this book might tempt some new listeners to country music, we will be content if it measures up to the music and performers that inspired it.

Paul Kingsbury, Editor
Country Music Foundation

ORIGINS

The Singing Brakeman.

1

HEY, HEY, TELL 'EM 'BOUT US: JIMMIE RODGERS VISITS THE CARTER FAMILY

Nolan Porterfield

The girls are singing "My Clinch Mountain Home": *Far away on a hill, to a sunny mountainside, many years ago we parted, my little ol' Ruth and I . . .*

"Stop that noise!" says A. P. "There's a strange car coming up our road."

"Law, it may be the revenue officers."

"It has a Texas license."

"Why, that's Jimmie Rodgers."

The motor car with the Texas license is long and sleek, a new 1931 Chrysler, square-cut and massive in the grand style of the time. "Hey, hey," the driver calls out, "howdy folks. Dee-yodel-lay-ee."

"Get out and come right in, Jimmie—you're the first cowboy we've seen in a long time."

Handshakes all around, amid welcoming small talk. Jimmie is offered a drink—"Yeah, son, go get the ol' boy a little squirt," he says—and they all admire the view across the valley, in the shadow of Clinch Mountain. The girls sing a few bars of another old ditty "to make him feel at home while he's at Maces Springs."

The scene is thus set for The Spectacular Meeting of the Stars: America's Blue Yodeler has driven up from Texas to visit

Jimmie Rodgers, the Singing Brakeman: although he romanticized the life of the railroad man in song, Rodgers worked the trains only when he absolutely had to.

Grave as headstones, the Carter Family sit for a 1920s publicity photo, dressed in their very best. Maybelle holds the arch-top guitar, her cousin Sara the autoharp. A. P., the group's leader and Sara's husband, stands over them.

the famous Carter Family at their lofty mountain home in Virginia, where two of the most popular recording acts of the time will relax on the front gallery in the cool summer breezes, flouting the Prohibition laws, spinning yarns, and warbling a few tunes, oblivious, of course, to the Victor microphone that is recording it all.

Between idea and reality falls the shadow, as T. S. Eliot almost said. In truth, all of the above is taking place not in the cool Virginia mountains but in a sweltering, airless storefront building on East Main in Louisville, Kentucky, a dismal place rented by Ralph Peer for a week to record local performers, mostly black gospel or blues singers, for the RCA Victor company. The date is June 11, 1931, in the pit of the Great Depression. Scarcely two weeks earlier the Carters recorded seven sides for Peer in Charlotte, North Carolina, and, despite press-

14

ing family matters, sick children, and the heat, they have agreed to follow him to Louisville to meet Rodgers. The Blue Yodeler, for his part, has journeyed by car a thousand miles in two days. Remember: no interstates, no cruise control, no auto air conditioning in 1931; and he is suffering, as he has for seven years, the effects of advanced tuberculosis, less than two years from death, lung-ravaged and already traveling on little more than nervous energy, sheer grit, and morphine.

It's a wonder things went as well as they did. Overnight, in his suite at the Tyler Hotel, Rodgers had hastily sketched out a script. His material was thin at best, less than a page in length and littered with awkward gaps and non sequiturs. After a few rehearsals in the studio the following afternoon, three takes were attempted, each marred by bad timing and stiff, inept performances all around. A. P. in particular had trouble following the script without sounding as if he were declaiming from an elementary primer. Sara and Maybelle weren't much better, and even Rodgers contributed his share of the muddle, stumbling over lines, repeating himself, and ad libbing awkwardly. They were, in a word, flat.

The first three takes were promptly rejected, and takes 1 and 2 apparently destroyed; the third take, which came to light only a few years ago, shows the problems they were having. By that stage, after numerous rehearsals, many script revisions, and three takes, they had clearly struggled a long way from Rodgers's original version—and just as clearly were still short of an acceptable recording. As the day wore on, Rodgers grew increasingly tired and irritable. Tempers began to flare, and the spirit of Old Home Week—a thin veneer at best—wore off. Peer decided to call it a day while everyone was still on speaking terms. The next morning, rested and refreshed, they dug in and got it down in one take, along with a sequel they had also been struggling with.

Four months later, in October, "Jimmie Rodgers Visits the Carter Family" (Victor 23574) went on sale in music stores around the country. RCA prepared elaborate promotional materials for its dealers and announced the release with special ads in metropolitan newspapers, a rare move in those bleak Depression days. The sequel, "The Carter Family and Jimmie Rodgers in Texas," which is in many ways superior, unaccountably remained in the vaults until 1937 when it was issued on Victor's cut-rate Bluebird label.

While the Rodgers–Carter Family "reunion" recordings are cherished by die-hard fans (an ever-shrinking number of old-timers, whose loyalty to their country music idols was fixed long

15

Meeting of opposites: rambling Jimmie Rodgers with the stolid Carter Family in Louisville, June 1931.

ago), younger non-initiates find the records unintentionally hilarious or, more often, to use Ralph Peer's memorable phrase, "plu-perfect awful."

To the country music establishment in general, the Rodgers–Carters sessions are thought of, if at all, as little more than curiosities out of the old days—it wouldn't do to laugh of course, but my, weren't them old hillbillies a mess? Folks with a calmer view simply enjoy them, warts and all, for what they are: occasionally awkward but winning performances by the early movers and shakers of country music. As someone once said of Wagner's operas, they're not as bad as they sound. One of the more endearing rumors has it that, off-stage, Maybelle's daughter June (Mrs. Johnny Cash) and Eddy Arnold perform a grand send-up of "Jimmie Rodgers Visits the Carter Family." Otherwise, subscribing to the notion that you don't laugh in public about your ga-ga uncle locked in the attic, Music City apparently tries to keep a straight face about it all. The subject came up not long ago during a tribute to Rodgers on cable TV's Nashville Network, in the course of which the participants set a new record for garbling facts and blissfully offering up pure error as God's Own Truth. The most accurate comment of the evening came from Roy Acuff. Asked if Rodgers had been an influence on him in the early days, Acuff turned waspish, obviously irked by the suggestion that he'd ever looked up to anyone. "No!" said the aged King of Country Music, to the great relief of Jimmie Rodgers fans everywhere.

Although the Louisville sessions in 1931 marked the first time Rodgers and the Carters worked together, Ralph Peer's field sessions had brought them into hailing distance on previous occasions. Two years earlier in Atlanta they were in the studio on the same day, and—as almost every country music fan knows—they made their first records only a few days apart in Bristol, Tennessee, back in August 1927.

Music historians and others fond of dates and places have a special weakness for "Bristol, August 1927." As a sort of shorthand notation, it has. come to signal the Big Bang of country music evolution, the genesis of every shape and species of Pickin'-and-Singin' down through the years. Feed "Nashville Now" into the projector and run it backward: past Porter and Dolly; past "Heartsick Soldier on Heartbreak Ridge"; past Lefty and Hank; past the Dawn of 16th Avenue (look, there's Webb Pierce's guitar-shaped swimming pool!); back beyond The Golden Age and the yodeling cowboys and "There's a Star Spangled Banner Waving Somewhere"; past "Orange Blossom Special" (and God said, "Let there be Bluegrass!"); past Melody Ranch and Renfro Valley and the Light Crust Doughboys, the Swift Jewel Cowboys, the Tennessee Plowboy, and hundreds of Playboys; when you pass Al Hopkins and the Hillbillies and hit the hub, the place where it all started, you'll be at the vacant hat warehouse on State Street in Bristol in August 1927, with Jimmie Rodgers and the Carter Family.

The idea is oversimplified, but it works. When Rodgers first appeared on the scene, the music then becoming known as "hillbilly" was mostly string-band instrumentals and maudlin old stage ballads. To this Rodgers added authentic blues lyrics from Afro-American folk song, jazzy dance-band accompaniments, and a cool, catchy, vibrant vocal style that is still finding its way into the work of Nashville's young and restless (Randy Travis and Dwight Yoakam are only two that come readily to mind). The Carters, more traditional and less flashy, influenced the music in ways that were subtle but no less significant. If the path they steered was more in the mainstream of old-time music, it also made dazzling loops in mid-course and left in its wake some valuable cargo for others to pick up. Among the treasures bestowed by the Carters, you'll find: the simplest close harmony yet discovered, so pure it's scary; that famous, intricate Carter guitar lick, widely imitated but never improved on; and their ultimate gift to the world, a vast repertoire of true Anglo-Ameri-

17

A wellspring of country harmony: hymnals published by James D. Vaughan and the Stamps-Baxter Company—and the traveling gospel quartets they sponsored to promote the hymnals—were crucial to the development of country harmony singing.

can folk music, laboriously gathered in bits and pieces across the folkland, much of it masterfully arranged and restored ("worked up" was A. P.'s term) to fresh vigor, saved from oblivion and passed on to its rightful heirs, the grateful and ungrateful alike.

The names of those touched and influenced by Jimmie Rodgers and the Carter Family constitute nothing less than a roll call of popular music stars over half a century. Dividing them into two lists, one headed "Rodgers" and the other "Carters," serves like "Bristol, August 1927" as a convenient if simplistic means of tracing styles, defining movements, and identifying the complex elements in the music we hear today. On the "Rodgers" ledger at least three collateral lines emerge. One runs immediately to young Gene Autry and spreads through the singing cowboys of the 1930s and 1940s. A second leads off to western swing by way of Bob Wills and all those "hot string bands" in the Southwest who were recording Rodgers tunes in the same period. The third line stretches to Ernest Tubb, the Texas Troubadour, who after his own fling as a warbling saddle pal in the shoot-'em-ups, brought the Rodgers aura to the Grand Ole Opry, reinforced by Red Foley, Hank Snow, and Hank Williams. In the early 1950s, these artists, along with Lefty Frizzell, became the leading exponents of the genre sometimes known today as honky-tonk, that recombinant strain of cheatin' hearts and faded love that draws heavily on the style of Rodgers's heart songs and rowdy blues renditions.

These are only the pivotal names; others along the way who have acknowledged debts to Rodgers or demonstrated his influence include Cliff Carlisle, Bradley Kincaid, Floyd Tillman, Grandpa Jones, Merle Travis, Bill Monroe, Moon Mullican, Bill Boyd, Elton Britt, Johnny Bond, the Delmore Brothers, Jimmie Davis, Billy Walker, Johnny Cash, and more recently, Merle Haggard, Maria Muldaur, Leon Redbone, Crystal Gayle, and Razzy Bailey. Rodgers's music keeps cropping up in the rarest places—Dolly, Linda, and Emmylou's 1987 album *Trio* includes, of all things, a version of "Hobo's Meditation."

The Carter Family, with their emphasis on Mother-and-Home, the old country church, and the fundamental values of rural life, initially reached a smaller, more insular audience than Rodgers,

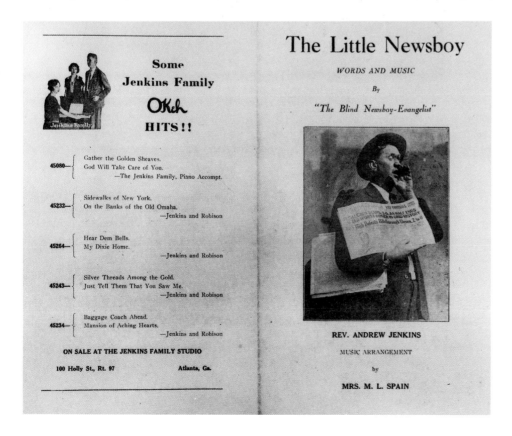

Atlanta's Rev. Andrew "Blind Andy" Jenkins is best known for his made-to-order ballads like "The Death of Floyd Collins" (a hit for Vernon Dalhart in 1925), written to cash in on the death of a young Kentucky spelunker. This 1920s song folio features some other favorites from Jenkins and his stepdaughter and collaborator, Mrs. Irene Spain.

19

but as the years passed they attracted an increasingly large and diverse following who looked upon them, as one writer put it, as "the patron saints of traditional music." By the 1940s, "Wildwood Flower" had acquired an almost mystical status as the prototypical string-band anthem, and dozens of Carter standards were forever embedded in the communal consciousness: "Little Darling Pal of Mine," "Wabash Cannonball," "Will the Circle Be Unbroken?" "Gold Watch and Chain," "I'm Thinking Tonight of My Blue Eyes," "Gospel Ship," "I'll Be All Smiles Tonight." Their tunes were recorded by performers as divergent as Roy Acuff and Woody Guthrie. Almost every country vocal group in the late 1930s—the Delmore Brothers, Mainer's Mountaineers, the Blue Sky Boys, the Dixon Brothers, and others —drew on the Carter harmony. Sara Carter was singing bluegrass before there was Bluegrass—indeed, the Carter Family

J. E. Mainer's Mountaineers were one of the Southeast's most popular hillbilly bands during the thirties and an important precursor of bluegrass. J. E. stands at the mike of station WBIG, Greensboro, North Carolina.

planted those "fields of bluegrass green" later harvested by Bill and Charlie Monroe, the Stanley Brothers, Don Reno and Red Smiley, Flatt & Scruggs.

The Carters acquired new fame and recognition in the folk revival of the 1960s, when yet a third generation of fans and performers—led by Joan Baez and Mike Seeger—recognized their true artistry and historical importance. The Carter influence is distinct in the work of the Phipps Family, Doc Watson, the New Lost City Ramblers, Jean Ritchie, and—as transmitted and adapted through Woody Guthrie—that of Bob Dylan and the many artists and writers whom Dylan in turn has influenced.

Foreshortened in this manner, the careers of Rodgers and the Carters seem clear-cut and their fame almost pre-ordained. It is sobering as well as instructive to see it otherwise, at the expense of a considerable, maybe even doomed, effort to go back and stand in the middle of, say, 1930 and look both ways.

Tony Alderman and Charlie Bowman both fiddled for Al Hopkins's string band, the Hill Billies. In this shot (ca. 1927), they play each other's instruments, a country stage gimmick that survives to this day in the live performances of the contemporary country band Alabama.

When Rodgers and the Carters went to Louisville in the summer of 1931, almost twelve million Americans were unemployed—nearly a third of the work force—and those who had jobs were grateful to earn ten cents an hour. At ninety-five cents a record, "Jimmie Rodgers Visits the Carter Family" cost roughly a day's wages for many people. (Some 24,100 bought a copy, eventually netting the artists about a thousand dollars at the standard royalty rate, spread over several quarterly statements.) In 1931 the national debt was $16,000,000,000, and you could buy a Hupmobile Century Six Sedan for $995 or sail to Europe on the White Star Line for $105, one way. Depression statistics are easy to come by; one could go on and on. But all the facts and numbers massed together can't really convey to our affluent, fast-food, gadget-ridden society just what a small, hard place the world was in those days, or how radically it has been changed by technology and money in the half century since.

Country music is an appropriate example. Think of everything the term represents today: platinum records, million-dollar stage productions, cable TV, fan clubs, Opryville, glitzy award ceremonies, a multi-billion dollar entertainment industry whose power to bedazzle and whose taste for wretched excess is second only to that of Hollywood. In 1931, none of this existed, nor did anyone imagine in their wildest dreams it ever would. String-band musicians and vocalists scrambled for work and recognition on the lowest rungs of the entertainment ladder, ignominiously labeled "hillbillies" and vastly outnumbered by guys in suits playing saxophones. There was nothing romantic or enviable about being country before country was cool.

When Rodgers and the Carters recorded in Louisville, they were fairly well established in their profession, but that in itself did not mean they were nationally known. The following they had was committed and intensely loyal—perhaps the most dedicated fans of all, as time has shown—but they comprised only a modest segment of the general population, concentrated mostly in rural areas of the South and Southwest. In those days, before the rising Sunbelt, even Dallas, Atlanta, and Phoenix were strictly podunk.

Counterparts to Rodgers and the Carters on the national scene were then-famous names like Johnny Marvin, Gene Austin, Billy Jones & Ernie Hare, the Ipana Troubadours, Correll & Gosden, the Knickerbockers, Ford & Glenn, Frank Crumit, Nick Lucas, the High Hatters—acts that performed more sophisticated material and toured the Big Time (i.e., cities in the North).

All those have faded, while the lives and careers of Jimmie Rodgers and the Carter Family have acquired increasing fame and attention. One curious indicator is the extravagant claims still made on their behalf, not only by well-meaning if uncritical fans, but by ardent historians as well. No, Jimmie Rodgers didn't sell twenty million records (or seventy million, as sometimes argued; the figure is more nearly ten million, over many years), and no, Mother Maybelle was not "the most influential instrumentalist in country music." (Exaggeration sometimes runs to the opposite extreme, as in Nick Tosches's witty but wrong-headed remark that "Mother Maybelle Carter's influence as a country music instrumentalist is equal to that of, say, Rudy Vallee.") Almost all of the recordings of Rodgers and the Carter Family have been reissued on LPs at some time or another by major companies, including elegant boxed sets of "complete works" by Japanese Victor. Small independent labels scramble to release their outtakes and ephemera, and only last year Rodgers's significant place in our cultural history was affirmed by no less an authority than the Smithsonian Institution, which issued a two-record set of the Blue Yodeler's best work, making permanently available many of the sides that RCA had allowed to slip from the catalog. None of the contemporaries of Rodgers and the Carter Family enjoys such prominence and continued attention today, more than half a century after their prime. What explains this curious circumstance? The answers, although they sometimes appear to be obvious, are not simple or easily formed.

While the Carter Family has been the object of considerable attention from writers and historians in recent years, some of the most intriguing questions posed by their lives and careers

STRINGS IN NUMBERS

Prior to the emergence of country vocalists like Jimmie Rodgers and the Carter Family, the most prevalent form of country music came from string bands, so called because they made music primarily on stringed instruments: the fiddle, the banjo, the guitar, and, occasionally, mandolin or autoharp—perhaps a harmonica as well. The origins of the string band date back to the American frontier. The first settlers in the South brought fiddles and ancestral fiddle tunes from Ireland, Scotland, and England. Because of the fiddle's portability and simple, fretless construction, it was by far the most popular instrument in rural areas and remained so well into the twentieth century.

By the mid-1800s, the banjo had become widely known as well. Orig-inally an African instrument brought to this country by slaves, the banjo evolved in the New World and eventually became a popular minstrel instrument. Rural white musicians began to play it in combination with the fiddle, thus creating the first string bands. In some areas of the southern Appalachians, particularly North Carolina and Virginia, the playing of fiddle tunes as fast, intricate fiddle and banjo duets developed into a high art (still practiced there today).

During the latter part of the 1800s and the early 1900s rural musicians began to discover the guitar (just then being mass produced), first in the flatlands, and later in the mountains, where traveling black railroad workers often introduced it to white

Young guitarist Ernest V. (later "Pop") Stoneman and his Dixie Mountaineers from Galax, Virginia, were already seasoned recording veterans of three years when Ralph Peer invited them to participate in what became the legendary Bristol sessions of 1927.

mountaineers. Combined with the fiddle and banjo, the guitar added rhythmic accompaniment; moreover, its chords provided a solid background for singing, thus encouraging string bands to include songs as well as instrumentals in their repertoires.

By the early 1920s, when the first rural musicians were beginning to play on the radio and make phonograph records, the string-band ensemble tradition was well established. Repertoires usually consisted of traditional fiddle tunes, southern folk songs, and popular nineteenth-century parlor and sentimental songs. Colorful names, calculated to reflect rural roots, became standard: the Skillet Lickers, Al Hopkins & the Hill Billies, Fiddlin' John Carson & His Virginia Reelers, Charlie Poole & the North Carolina Ramblers, Earl Johnson & His Dixie Clodhoppers, Pop Stoneman's Dixie Mountaineers, the Fruit Jar Drinkers, the Possum Hunters.

Old-time string-band music remained popular throughout the 1920s and 1930s. During the mid-1940s, when electric honky-tonk and western swing music were eclipsing the older styles, musicians like Bill Monroe and banjo player Earl Scruggs pioneered a new strain of string-band music, emphasizing instrumental virtuosity and close-harmony singing. Eventually called bluegrass, this "new" style transformed and popularized string-band music for a new generation attracted to its acoustic, traditional sound and the rural-flavored, "down-home" lyrics of its songs.

Today, enclaves of old-time string-band music still exist side by side with contemporary commercial country music and bluegrass. A visit to mountain towns like Mount Airy, North Carolina, or Galax, Virginia, will turn up many fine old-time fiddlers and banjo players of all ages, still performing for local dances, social events, and fiddle and banjo contests. That this music is still being passed along from generation to generation and is still being played by amateurs for the pure joy of it is powerful testimony to the enduring strength and beauty of one of our most venerable forms of country music.

25

Vernon Dalhart

Country music's first star originally sang light opera. Born Marion Try Slaughter, Vernon Dalhart took his stage name from two small towns in his native Texas. After persuading Victor to let him sing hillbilly, he recorded "The Wreck of the Old 97" and "The Prisoner's Song." The 1924 release became country's first million seller.

have not been answered—and perhaps never will be. Unlike Rodgers, who relished the limelight and often helped dress up his public images—railroader, cowboy, rake, and rambler—the Carters were apparently a stolid, unpretentious lot, little given to self-promotion, introspection, or reminiscence. Tragically, A. P. was dead by the time new audiences and country music scholars began to revive their music in the 1960s, but Sara and Maybelle were interviewed on several occasions. While they invariably tried to be helpful with dates and facts, their straightforward, unembellished answers offered scant evidence of their inner lives and emotions.

The questions and contradictions live on, unresolved. Working within a conservative, even hidebound musical tradition, they brought forth, quite suddenly, a very different, almost radical style. What inspired it, and how did they maintain and develop it over the years, seemingly immune to all the "new" (i.e.,

26

commercial) things that were happening in country music? As Bill Malone has observed, "The Carters never changed, they merely got better." Even more, one wonders: How were Sara and Maybelle—two young, frightfully shy and unworldly country women in a dominantly male society—first persuaded to leave their homes and small children to go with A. P. and undertake something so strange and unknown as making records? Later, apparently in the same silent, placid manner, they would follow him to New York, light-years from Poor Valley, and eventually even to Another Country (Del Rio, Texas, was surely as foreign to them as anything offered by Mexico, just across the river). What were the circumstances of A. P. and Sara's separation in 1932, and how were they able to work together so effectively for almost a decade after that? During their stay in Texas, certainly a stressful time for everyone, Sara married A. P.'s cousin, and they all lived in close proximity. What were the complications of that, and why did Sara, with one of the purest, most eloquent voices of any singer of her time, quit suddenly in her prime and retire to a small town in northern California? When Sara and A. P. left the business, what prompted Maybelle, the most reticent of the group, to form an act of her own and pursue an independent career in show business? As "Mother Maybelle," we're told, she rode motorcycles and was an avid fan of classical music.

Most enigmatic of all, however, is the leader of the group, that gaunt, handsome fellow who—in our mind's eye, at least—always seems to be in the background, head lowered, staring out impassively, pacing to and fro, ambling forward to announce a tune and "bassing in" occasionally, then walking away, sometimes disappearing from the stage entirely. All lives move in ways that sometimes seem strange and inconsistent, but A. P. Carter was a veritable swarm of mysteries, quirks, and contradictions. There is ample reason to feel that we will never know much about him beyond the mere biographical facts.

Alvin Pleasant Delaney Carter—known to the family simply as "A. P." or "Doc"—was born in 1891 near the hamlet of Maces Springs (since renamed Hiltons) in the Poor Valley of Virginia, a mountainous region in the far southwestern part of the state. His pioneer ancestors had settled there more than a century earlier, and one of the most powerful elements in his life, from childhood on, was an acute sense of the past, of belonging to a time and a place and people rich in tradition. Music was a central element of that tradition, part of everyday life in the community. As a boy, A. P. Carter absorbed the old familiar songs of the region and sang with a gospel quartet at local

A. P. Carter, dreamer: "If he felt like singing, he would sing, and if he didn't, he would walk around and look out the window," Maybelle once said of him. "So we never depended on him for anything."

churches. He even tried to learn the violin, although he apparently had little talent for it and was strongly opposed by his fundamentalist parents, who viewed the fiddle as "the devil's box." Dealing with the conflicting demands of the worldly and the sacred was an early and lifelong task, perhaps only symptomatic of other oppositions that pulled him to and fro.

It seems there was always something a little odd about A. P. Endlessly curious about the world, he was a lover of books and a seeker of knowledge all his life, yet he was taken from school at an early age because the other children laughed at his strange ways and trembling hands. Despite his close attachment to his family and his native region, as a young man he was forever on the go, roaming restlessly about the valleys and mountains, visiting, working at odd jobs, searching for something he couldn't quite find. His mother said he was "marked" by a bolt of lightning that frightened her not long before his birth; A. P. was "born nervous." Around 1910 he left home and went "up North" to Indiana or Detroit to work as a carpenter or railroad hand— the stories vary. A year later he was back home, walking the hills again and peddling fruit trees in the area around Maces Springs. It was this job that one day took him beyond Clinch Mountain to Copper Creek and the home of Milburn and Melinda Nickels, whose young niece—according to family tradition— was playing an autoharp and singing "Engine 143" as A. P. approached the house. She was Sara Elizabeth Dougherty, with raven black hair and brown eyes so piercing that, as her daughter later said, they "seemed to have gold stars in the middle." A. P. was in love with her instantly—and apparently forever. "She was the most beautiful girl I ever saw," he would say all of his life, long after they were divorced and a continent apart.

Sara was seven years younger than A. P. and quite unlike him in temperament and outlook. Music, however, was one of the things they had in common. She was not yet seventeen when A. P. persuaded her to marry him and move to Maces Springs, where he had a plot of farm land and all sorts of other plans and schemes for earning a livelihood. Over the years, he was a jack-of-many-trades: carpenter, farmer, salesman, blacksmith, grocer, miller, songwriter and collector—"a man who had more than one idea in his mind," said his daughter Janette. He was a hard worker but an inconsistent one, always starting one job, then wandering off to another, returning to finish the first only when the notion took him, sometimes months later, sometimes never. He had a great appetite for traveling, meeting people, absorbing the world, a kind of lively, brooding mountain genius, a character out of Thomas Wolfe, high strung and stern but also

28

a sensitive romantic, a dreamer. He tried his hand at almost anything he could imagine; there's the persistent notion that, except for it never having occurred to him to do it, he, like Wolfe, might also have gone off to some university, hurled himself at the world, and become a great raw-boned playwright, novelist, or poet. Instead, he stayed home and "worked up" songs and maneuvered an erratic but ultimately brilliant path to an immortality of his own.

One thing about A. P. Carter is certain: warring spirits were in him. Outwardly a kind and gentle man, he was also temperamental and quick to anger; gregarious, talkative and outgoing, he was given to moody silences and lonely walks about the countryside. Music was his great consolation, and long before the professional career of the Carter Family, he was spending more and more time collecting songs, searching out old ballads and bits of tunes here and there as he traveled about the region.

Like her husband, Sara had been involved with music all her life, and it was only natural that the newlyweds sang and played together, sharpening their talents and occasionally performing as a duet at church services and social affairs. Almost accidentally, they learned that people would pay to hear them perform;

Maybelle, A. P., and Sara, dressed for chores, at their Clinch Mountain home.

Opry favorite Fiddlin' Sid Harkreader toured vaudeville with fellow Tennessean Dave Macon for two years prior to the founding of Nashville's WSM radio and performed on Macon's recordings.

29

Under Ralph Peer's direction, by 1925 Okeh Records led the recording industry in signing southern rural talent. This ad from a 1925 record catalog features some of Okeh's early acts.

their car had broken down one day far from home, and when A. P. pondered ways to raise cash for repairs, Sara said, "Well, all I know to do is sing." They filled the local schoolhouse that night at ten cents a head, and A. P. had another money-making scheme to consider.

The Carter Family as a professional unit began to emerge a year or two later, when Sara's younger cousin, Maybelle Addington, moved into the community as the wife of A. P.'s brother Ezra ("Eck"). Like Sara, she had grown up in a family environment where making music was a part of everyday life and developed an early interest in the autoharp, banjo, and guitar. Although only a child when Sara and A. P. married, Maybelle was soon attracting attention as the family's most talented instrumentalist. Through the years, whenever Sara returned to Copper Creek to visit, the cousins had played and sung together for their own entertainment as much as for others.

Their opportunities for making music together were more frequent after Maybelle moved to Maces Springs in 1926. Whether Sara and Maybelle viewed these get-togethers as anything more than merely a continuation of an old family pastime is unclear. One thing is evident: A. P. took them seriously, and he quickly became the motive force behind the group, booking shows at school socials around the area, hanging around music stores in town for advice and word-of-mouth promotion, writing to record companies in faraway big cities to ask if they needed singers and musicians. There are varying accounts of how he arranged to record for Ralph Peer; Sara thought he'd answered an ad in the Bristol paper, but later research turned up no advertisement, only a small news story on the front page about Peer's recording activity. Peer himself recalled afterward that "I think the Carter Family came in as the result of a local [record] dealer. They'd gone in to see the local dealer; in fact, they'd had some corre-

Maybelle and Sara Carter looking more like the God-fearing country folk they were than trailblazing performers.

31

spondence with Brunswick or Aeolian or some small company, but they hadn't done anything about it. The dealer knew about it and he gave me the tip and I got in touch with them."

How it happened hardly matters. The important thing is that, almost instantly, Peer recognized the artistry in Sara Carter's voice, which says a great deal for both of them. Peer was the product of an urban, cultivated background, in an era when the lines between social classes were far more rigidly drawn than they are today. All his life he seems to have resented the fact that his money and his reputation derived from the work of crusty old fiddlers, rustic balladeers, and yodeling roustabouts. Over the years, he acquired a note of cheerful resignation about it all, somehow managing to sound noble and condescending at the same time. Jimmie Rodgers, he said, at the time of the Bristol sessions was just a "bus boy in a roadside cafe, singing nigger blues," and he remembered the Carter Family, even less accurately, as a shabby lot of hillbillies, dressed in overalls and calico (proud country people, they would suffer no shame so great as appearing in public in anything but their very best, as all of their publicity photos clearly show). Yet, to his credit, Peer found Sara Carter, and knew what he'd found, for us and all time, that wondrous homespun soprano voice, like gritted wind on a crystal chime. "As soon as I heard Sara," he said, "that was it. On that very first effort, why . . . I knew this was going to be wonderful."

So impressed was Peer that he stretched his usual rule that limited new artists to only one or two test records. The Carters cut six titles in Bristol and were called to Camden, New Jersey, the following spring for an extended session that more than tripled their recorded repertoire and produced such classics as "Little Darling Pal of Mine," "Keep on the Sunny Side," and "Wildwood Flower." During the next dozen years—spanning the worst of the Depression, when the record business was shrinking practically out of existence—they were in the studio annually, recording as many as forty titles a year, roughly equivalent to three or four modern-day LP albums, year in and year out. The Carter Family discography lists some three hundred recorded takes and more than 250 issued titles over fourteen years, a remarkable body of work matched in volume and endurance by few other artists in any era and all the more astonishing in light of the fact that it was achieved without a single verifiable hit in all those years. Like the Carters themselves, their recorded repertoire was steady, rock-solid, and durable—*every* Carter Family record found a wide audience, and their value continues to appreciate today. Ask any record collector.

After Bristol, Jimmie Rodgers began advertising himself as a "Victor Recording Artist" and headed for New York. Asked what the Carters did while waiting to learn when—and if—they would be called back to make more records, Sara said simply, "Why, we went home and planted the corn." For a number of years, that would be the standard routine—tending to the chores at home and going off once or twice a year to some large city to record for a day or two. In between, A. P. continued to book as many personal appearances as he could manage, mostly at school socials in the surrounding area.

Throughout their careers, the Carters held to a curious sort of professionalism. They were, on the one hand, perfectionists when it came to recording, yet, on the other, somehow lacking

Ralph Peer, a dapper gentleman of taste and refinement who made a name for himself—and a fortune— recording hillbillies. The music he tolerated; it was flowers and horticulture that he loved.

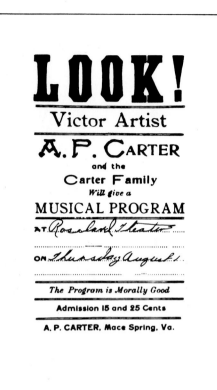

Advertising, Carter Family style, August 1, 1929.

the same flair and energy when it came to promoting themselves through public appearances. Despite the rigors of their daily lives and the demands of making a living apart from show business, once they had begun to make records, they practiced regularly and intensely, working out kinks and almost obsessively timing each selection to fit the three-minute limit of 78 rpm records. They went to the studio rigorously prepared, on several occasions recording as many as twenty titles in a single all-day session—all issued and each done in one take. Yet, in contrast to Jimmie Rodgers, they never undertook promotional tours or appeared on major vaudeville bills to capitalize on their recording success; their occasional stage appearances, although carefully rehearsed and presented, were rather casual affairs, with none of the showy staging of later country music acts.

Similar contradictions are revealed in A. P.'s songwriting and collecting. Between arranging show dates and pursuing his varied "business interests," he scoured the countryside for song lyrics—bits and pieces of folk poetry that he labored over endlessly, rewriting here and filling in there, rearranging and "working up" such now-classic songs as "Keep on the Sunny Side," "Grave on the Green Hillside," "Cyclone of Rye Cove," "Jimmie Brown the Newsboy," "Lonesome Valley," "Let the Church Roll On," and dozens of others that are attributed to him, although in many cases it is clear that earlier sources exist. Carter took this work seriously, as befits a chronicler and hander-down of human events, yet despite the loving care and intensity he devoted to it, there survived an abundance of clinkers, curlicues, puzzling allusions, and wonderful garble (the best example of which is probably "Wildwood Flower," with its Edward Lear-like "mingles and waving black hair," its "pale and the leader, and eyes looked like blue," which even the Carters didn't understand). But, of course, art is never held to be rational, and in its own rare fashion A. P. Carter's music is as rich and full of meaning as any we are likely to get.

It is another curious fact of the Carter Family's career that, although they continued to work together as late as 1943, they had ceased, at least in the legal sense, to be a family more than ten years earlier, when Sara and A. P.'s marriage broke up. From the beginning it had been a match of opposites, each suffering its own inner oppositions: soul-ridden Sara, quietly, stolidly in flames, a strong, handsome woman, gifted—and burdened—with a talent perhaps even she did not fully comprehend; all that paired to restless, talkative Doc, alternately given to fits of temper and a moody gentleness, the family oddball, always chasing any strange notion that hit him. Given Sara's

34

earth-mother tendencies, it is easy to understand Janette's re-mark that her father's antic behavior "drove my mother and Maybelle up a wall." Sweeping the porch one day, Sara heard a terrible racket echoing through the valley and looked up in shock to see A. P. at the wheel of their flimsy old car, dragging home behind him an entire sawmill—a task that normally required a railroad engine.

It seems inevitable that Sara would eventually feel she'd had all she could stand; it is also important to realize just how radical and traumatic her action was, in that time and place, when she ended the marriage of seventeen years, left her three children behind because she had little means of supporting them, and moved back to her aunt and uncle at Copper Creek. For a time, the only income she had was her meager one-third of their re-cording royalties, which A. P. scrupulously divided up as long as he lived.

Steady, rock-solid, and durable: for years the Carters mainly tended to the chores at home, going off only once or twice a year to record for a day or two.

Record sales were never a major source of income for early country music artists, but the volume of records turned out by the Carter Family brought spare cash from time to time. "After they got into the music business," said Janette, "there was more to eat, it seemed, more money, and we bought a car." Yet their standard of living changed little—the car was an old one, prone to flats and breakdowns—and A. P. went on dabbling at every odd job and enterprise that might turn a dollar. Maybelle and Eck were slightly better off, because Eck held a steady (and in the eyes of the community, prestigious) job as a mail-train clerk; they lived in the "biggest, prettiest home," said Janette, and had hired girls to clean and to look after the children. Still, these were Depression days, and no one took financial security for granted.

Money seems the logical, and perhaps only, reason that the Carters suddenly, in the late 1930s, pulled up stakes, left every friend and relative and familiar sight, and moved from their mountain homeland to the far dusty reaches of the Texas border. The social and cultural shocks could hardly have been greater had they gone to the moon. Janette, now fifteen, was "jerked up" and taken along, together with her younger brother, Joe; they lived alone with A. P. in a small house in Del Rio. Sara and her new husband, Coy Bayes, took an apartment nearby; May-belle was joined by her daughters, Helen, June, and Anita, who together with Janette now became part of the act, broadcasting over XERA, the 100,000-watt Mexican station across the border in Villa Acuna, with studios on the Texas side of the river.

Just how this improbable situation came about is still another mystery. It was apparently engineered by a Chicago advertising

35

agency, whose clients included a manufacturer of patent medicines that appealed to rural consumers. This agency had developed a working relationship with the Mexican border radio stations owned by Dr. J. R. Brinkley, the infamous "goat-gland doctor" from Kansas. Stripped of his broadcasting license in the United States, Brinkley, with the blessing of the Mexican government, had taken over a transmitter in Villa Acuna, boosted the power to 100,000 watts to blanket the North American continent, and began the lucrative business of beaming out to the hinterlands around-the-clock programs of hillbilly music and religious exhortations, heavily interlaced with ballyhoo for laxatives, baby chicks, garden seeds, glow-in-the-dark pictures of Jesus Christ, medicinal tonics, and other artifacts considered vital to the lives of rural Americans. By the mid-1930s, Brinkley was operating two additional border stations—XEG and XENT—and was hard put for enough program material to keep the commercials from overlapping.

The Carter Family, with their homey repertoire of old folk ballads and sacred songs and an established audience among country folk, were a natural for such an operation. In 1936 they

Sara and Maybelle Carter with the next generation: Maybelle's daughters June, Anita, and Helen, early 1940s.

In the 1950s, Sara and A. P. (at right; by this time divorced) and their daughter Janette (left) visiting with Kathleen and A. L. Phipps, musical disciples of the Carters who recorded as the Phipps Family.

had recorded a series of electrical broadcast transcriptions for the Associated Programming Service, possibly as a trial run to test radio markets and the Carters' suitability to that medium. In due course, arrangements were made for the group to begin broadcasting on XERA under the sponsorship of the Royal Chemical Company of Chicago, makers of the medicinal tonic Peruna and Kolor Bak, a hair tint. The Carters moved to Del Rio in 1938 and soon were so popular that they were recording program transcriptions to reduce their hours in the studio and provide material that could be shared with XERA's sister stations.

This arrangement ended in 1941, undoubtedly as the result of several factors: the Carters' increasing unhappiness with their strained living arrangements in barren Texas, the coming of the war, and new agreements between the governments of Mexico and the U.S. that began to restrict radio operations such as Brinkley's. In the fall of 1942 the Carters wound up in Charlotte, North Carolina, where for a brief time they were on the staff of WBT. Finally, in 1943, after more than sixteen years as a professional unit, they disbanded. Sara left show business for good and moved to California. Maybelle, who'd always been in the background, seemingly the shyest of the shy, now formed an act with her daughters and set out to enter the mainstream of emerging country music, joining WRVA's Old Dominion Barn Dance in Richmond, Virginia, as Mother Maybelle and the Carter Sisters. Soon they were attracting national attention, with recordings for Victor and Columbia and, in 1950, a permanent spot on the Grand Ole Opry, where Mother Maybelle became one of the Gray Eminences of Country Music.

A. P. went back to Maces Springs and opened a country store. The breakup of the Carter Family had taken its toll. According to Janette, "He seemed lonelier, he walked more, and his laughing blue eyes seemed sad." Music had become the central part of his life, and he was unwilling to relinquish it. Said his daughter later, "He tried the hardest of any man I ever knew to keep his music alive." In the 1950s he worked with his children, Joe and Janette, and even on occasion persuaded Sara to rejoin them to record for a small regional label, but nothing came of it. The odds were against him. He was an old man, in failing health, his work as a songsmith and recording artist mostly forgotten. When he died in 1960, there was no Country Music Hall of Fame, and rockabilly was all the rage. The only way you could hear the Carter Family was on 78 rpm records, which most major companies had stopped making by that time.

Only ten years later, record bins everywhere had Carter Family LP reissues from RCA, Columbia, and Decca. Scholars were tracing the sources of Carter Family songs, and one learned group searched out and issued a selection of their rare radio transcriptions, with annotations and exhaustive commentary. A. P. Carter, they said, was "one of the makers of modern music."

Curious as the results of their 1931 Louisville sessions may seem, there's little reason to question Ralph Peer's decision to pair the Carter Family with Jimmie Rodgers. They were, after all, the two most successful and best known acts in what was just then emerging as "hillbilly music." On the other hand, aside from the fact that they all played stringed instruments and performed songs that were old, or sounded old, America's Blue Yodeler and the Patron Saints of Traditional Music had surprisingly little in common.

The differences in their personalities and professional styles are captured by the newspaper ads that promoted their joint recordings: Jimmie wears his characteristic dapper grin while the Carters stare out solemnly, grave as headstones. Rodgers roamed far and wide, toured the big-time vaudeville circuits, tried his hand at movies and national radio, made fast friends

*The Hometown Boys, 1920s:
fiddlers Bill Helms and Gid
Tanner flank blind guitarist
Riley Puckett. Tanner and
Puckett were also charter
members of the Skillet Lickers,
the quintessential early string
band, which included fiddler
Clayton McMichen and
banjoist Fate Norris.*

everywhere he went, and left a trail of broken hearts behind, while the Carters for the most part stayed close to home, tended to business, and kept their own counsel. As recording stars, Rodgers was a genuine hit-maker, with two or three million-selling records, while the Carters were merely "steady."

The differences go back to their very roots. Rodgers was, as Snuffy Smith used to say, a "flatland furriner," born in the pine-lands of eastern Mississippi and raised mostly in towns and cities. In the time the Carters were growing up in their Virginia mountains, more or less isolated from other cultures and musical influences, Jimmie was railroading around the country, taking in the faraway places with strange-sounding names and the varied musical strains that would later find their way into his songs, producing, perhaps for the first time, a truly American music, the "varied carols" that Whitman heard, those ballads of the nation's streets that Emerson had called for.

Rodgers—again unlike the Carters—had his sights on a professional career almost from childhood. At twelve he won an amateur talent contest in his hometown of Meridian, and he was not yet fifteen when, in 1911, he ran away from home with a small-time medicine show. For another fifteen years he doggedly pursued the elusive grail of stardom, playing with pickup bands, singing on street corners for carfare, joining up with any scruffy touring show that came his way. In later years he encouraged the romantic notion that he was really a railroad man at heart

Looking the part of the young man about town: one of Jimmie Rodgers's first publicity poses, ca. 1921.

and had only been sidetracked into show business because illness had taken him off the high iron. But long before he contracted tuberculosis in 1924, his random railroad jobs had been little more than a means to an end, paying for room and board while he followed the carnivals and rep shows from one place to another. An early marriage in 1917 had lasted only briefly because, as his ex-wife said later, "he was always plunking on some old banjo or guitar and never had a dime to his name."

In these years he held all sorts of jobs, driving a truck, tending store, washing dishes in depot cafes. His occasional railroad work came mostly from the "extra board" (that is, with temporary crews on special runs). He railroaded in Florida awhile, then drifted west. In 1926 he was fired off the Southern Pacific out in Tucson for missing work to play for dances. A family man again

40

HOME OFFICE
KERRVILLE, TEXAS

"America's Blue Yodeler"

JIMMIE RODGERS
EXCLUSIVE VICTOR RECORDING STAR

ENROUTE:

Meridian Miss,
July 27th 1932

Mr Clayton McMichen,
℅ Radio Station W.H.K.
Cleveland Ohio.

Hello Clayton:

Well son heres the dope on Recording. I plan on leaving here about Sunday morning July 31st ariveing in Washington D.C. the nation,s Capital Wednesday evening the 3rd of August, and will expect you to meet me there then, or not later than Thursday or Friday Aug the 4th or 5th. We will meet at my Bro and Sister in Laws House Mr and Mrs Alex Nelson. The Adress is as follows 1148 Abbey Place North East. And Ole Fiddler and Violin playing fool I is Sho looking for you to be there.

I am driving through in the ole Cadalic Mrs Rodgers and my little Daughter Anita will be with me as far as Washington and we will go on to New York togather. I am planing on having A good Banjo Player to go with us. You may knew him his name is Oddie McWindows. And boy can he play A banjo? Ill say he can. Mac he plays A 5 string Banjo ole style and also plays all the popular stuff ███. I mean takes solos and playes leads. Well he beats any dam thing I ever heard of Playing A banjo Baring no body.

Mr Peer says he wonts me to do at least 10 numbers so if you have any thing of your own be sure to bring it along because Im pretty sure I can get several of your Songs Recorded. Then after the Recording is all finished we all go under the Hammer for the Audition with the N.B.C. which seams like A pretty good break as ther have been wonting me to work in Nwe York for the last 2 or 3 years. Now about this guitar player you spoke to me about on the Phone A few days ago. I will do all I can to get Mr Peer to use him but I would Rather Not guarané any thing for him. But I will pay his expensesif he cares to come along with you and take chances on working. I mean eating and sleeping expensesas long as he is with us. over Your Same Ole Pal Jimmie Rodgers

Hillbilly singers didn't have managers and agents in Jimmie Rodgers's day, so he just took care of business himself. With this letter, Rodgers asks Clayton McMichen to join him for August 1932 recording sessions in Camden, New Jersey.

by this time, he managed to get his wife and child back to Meridian, where he left them and took off for Asheville, North Carolina, supposedly to find another railroad job but in fact devoting most of his time to music, hooking up with local string bands to play on the city's new radio station. When that effort failed, he went on the road with his new band, the short-lived Jimmie Rodgers Entertainers, and worked a few weeks at a mountain resort—until he learned that the Victor Talking Machine Company had set up a portable studio to record local talent in the Tennessee-Virginia border town of Bristol, some ninety miles away. Lacking any real reason to believe they'd succeed—or even get in the front door of the studio—Rodgers gave notice on the spot and took his Entertainers off to Bristol to become famous recording artists.

HE WAS A SWELL GUY, YES SIR

Steel player Cliff Carlisle (1904–83) and his partner, guitarist Wilber Ball, had been performing together on the vaudeville and tent-show circuit for more than a decade in 1931 when Jimmie Rodgers heard the duo over Louisville's WHAS and invited them to record with him. Growing up in rural Kentucky, Carlisle had mastered the Hawaiian guitar (now known as the steel guitar) during a brief national craze for Hawaiian music at the dawn of the Jazz Age. Carlisle added yodeling as well to his repertoire when Rodgers became the Next Big Thing. In fact, Carlisle's own recording career began in 1930 on the Gennett label, when he demonstrated his ability to imitate Rodgers. Gennett was so eager to cash in on the Rodgers hit machine that no fewer than eleven of Carlisle's first twenty-five songs were covers of the Blue Yodeler's material. (Later, Carlisle would go on to find his own style, as a solo act and with his brother Bill.)

Cliff Carlisle, a spiffy man of many parts: ardent disciple of Jimmie Rodgers, raunchy country blues singer par excellence, and successful family musician with brother Bill, son "Sonny Boy" Tommy, and accompanist Shannon Grayson.

"One of ma boxcahs": at the height of his fame, Jimmie Rodgers poses with one of his several flashy cars.

Rodgers was probably aware of (and flattered by) Carlisle's imitative recordings when he invited Cliff and Wilber to participate in the 1931 Louisville sessions that resulted—among other recordings—in "Jimmie Rodgers Visits the Carter Family." Although Cliff did not perform on the Rodgers-Carter sides, he was present for them and his first-hand account of the proceedings gives us an unusually vivid impression of what Jimmie was like and how the sessions went.

I recorded with Jimmie and made a few personal appearances with him back in 1931 or 1932. He was a swell guy, yes sir. He was just real relaxed, an everyday guy and the same every time you saw him.

When you was with Jimmie, he'd want to take care of everything—any way in the world he could keep you from spending your money. He was an ol' skinny, bony kind of a guy. He was, I'd say, about six feet tall and lantern jawed, a long-like face and big eyes. Looked like a mouse—you know, a mouse's eyes are great big.

He had two or three Cadillacs, big ol' black ones. You remember the gangster pictures? They used to have them big ol' Cadillacs with the tops, you know. He called a Cadillac his "boxcar." He'd say, "I got ma boxcah." You know that long, drawly brogue he had.

You remember "When the Cactus Is in Bloom"? I done his steel work on that for him, that and "Lookin' for a New Mama." Those were made down in Louisville, down on West Main Street, 7th and Main.

Jimmie got in touch with me and Wilber Ball, a fellow that used to play with me, and we went down on Main Street there in Louisville. It was in one of them old-time buildings. It was a long narrow building.

They [Ralph Peer and his field recording engineers] used to carry these portable sets around and go in just anywhere they could find a vacant building, see? And they'd just take a whole big bunch of burlap and hang it up all around, and then they'd have a partition built in it, and they'd put their recording equipment in back, and they'd just go in there, boy, and start recording. They'd try to locate a central location, see, and they'd call people in from three or four hundred miles away, recording artists. That's the way Victor used to do it.

So Jimmie and the Carters were recording this together and, if you remember, it's "Jimmie Rodgers Visits the Carter Family." So they had cut and cut and cut and cut on that thing, and they just couldn't get it at all. Somebody would foul up somewhere. I mean, that happens so much. I've worked half a day a many a time on a song, and they finally just say, "Go on and take this twenty dollars, and go back to the hotel and come back tomorrow." Well, anyhow, they finally just worked and worked and worked and worked, and everybody was tired, and they just couldn't hardly go on, see, but they finally got one, boy, and it was perfect. Everything was perfect, and Jimmie rared back and said, "By God, I guess we got that one!" And that went on the record and messed that one up, see. Well, they quit for the day. I'll bet you Ralph Peer blowed his stack. Him and Jimmie argued all the time anyhow.

(Transcribed and edited from Cliff Carlisle's taped interviews in the Oral History Collection of the Country Music Foundation.)

43

The band that quit Jimmie Rodgers, May 1927: the Tenneva Ramblers met Jimmie Rodgers in Asheville, North Carolina, performed with him there for the summer, then split with the cocky singer during the Bristol sessions in August. Known for this brief period as the Jimmie Rodgers Entertainers, Jack and Claude Grant sit with banjos, Jack Pierce stands with guitar, and the fearless leader sports the funny glasses.

It didn't work out quite that way. Peer agreed to give them an audition, but before they got to the studio, the band members, who were experienced and capable musicians long before they heard of Jimmie Rodgers, had begun to feel they'd had enough of his harebrained schemes. They decided to revert to their former name—the Tenneva Ramblers—and use that billing on the records they were to make. Rodgers, of course, would have none of it, whereupon the newly reconstituted Tenneva Ramblers simply rambled away, leaving the bandleader bandless. It was clear they did not think much of him as a musician, and that was an opinion shared by just about everyone else at the time. A lesser man would have folded, but Jimmie had been riding on little more than sheer guts for a long time. He simply straightened his hat, took a deep breath in his fevered lungs, and strolled off to convince Peer that Jimmie Rodgers, all by himself, "just me and my old guitar," was one of the best things that had ever come down the pike. Indeed he was, as history has shown.

While the Carters went home to plant corn after Bristol, Rodgers headed for the bright lights and big cities. He had, as the old saw says, struggled for thirty years to become an overnight success. In November he recorded "Blue Yodel (T for Texas)," destined to be his biggest hit when it was released the following spring. Within the year he was broadcasting weekly from the nation's capital over WTFF and preparing to headline a major vaudeville tour on the Loew Circuit. From that time until the end, the pace rarely slackened. Rodgers headed another vaudeville tour in 1929, played with repertoire shows under canvas, broadcast from major cities in the South and Southwest, and somehow found time for as many as five extended recording sessions a year.

A comparison of Rodgers's recording activity with that of the Carters during this time indicates the nature of his flurried career, against the Carters' more steady and deliberate pattern. The Carters were in the studio only once or twice a year, usually in Camden, while Rodgers was all over the place—Camden, Atlanta, New York, Dallas, Hollywood. Although the Carters began with six sides to Rodgers's two, within a year he was ahead by seven, and through 1933—the year of his death—the Carters recorded only 87 titles to Rodgers's total of 110. Ironically, at the time they began their joint sessions in Louisville that summer of 1931, the figures were exactly even—each had 67 sides in circulation or waiting for release in Victor's vaults.

The Louisville sessions are significant for yet another reason. Except for those few sides with Rodgers in 1931, the original Carter Family, in all their years on major labels, recorded en-

44

tirely alone—just Sara and Maybelle, with A. P. bassing in occasionally and taking a solo here and there. In contrast, Rodgers was accustomed to all sorts of accompaniments, from creaky studio bands to Louis Armstrong. Beginning with his third session, in 1928, he'd sought out professional musicians to back him, and in later years he recorded with his own guitar only rarely, relying more and more on young Billy Burkes to copy the fluid if eccentric style he'd established. Rodgers was no doubt one of the first major white artists—and certainly the first "hillbilly" star—to record with black musicians. As early as 1929, he'd brought a black group into the studio to record "Frankie and Johnny," although the takes were never issued. In addition to Armstrong, Rodgers recorded with St. Louis bluesman Clifford Gibson on an unissued side, and with the redoubtable

Clayton McMichen (ca. 1931): founding member of the Skillet Lickers and the Georgia Wildcats, early studio musician in Atlanta, pal of Jimmie Rodgers and recording partner, national fiddle champion more than a dozen times, the fiddler's fiddler who preferred jazz to country and was known to call hillbilly music "swamp opera."

COWHAND'S LAST RIDE
Sung and Played by JIMMIE RODGERS
A 18-6000

Country's first picture disc was this 10 inch, 78 rpm laminated record. RCA Victor released the record in June 1933, one month after Jimmie Rodgers's death.

Louisville Jug Band on "My Good Gal's Gone Blues," which today ranks as one of his rarest and most avidly sought originals. Also included on Rodgers's sessions were Hawaiians Joe Kaipo and Lani McIntire, as well as Charles Kama, M. T. Salazar, and Mike Cordova, who were Americans of Mexican descent.

In the year following the Louisville sessions, Rodgers made every effort to keep up the pace, against increasingly bad health and the effects of the Depression. But sickness and hard living were taking their toll, and his final sessions in 1932 and 1933 produced only a few sides that rank among his best, notably "Peach Pickin' Time Down in Georgia," "Miss the Mississippi and You," and "Old Love Letters." Despite his desperate attempts to stay on his feet and get his work done, time was running out and he knew it. In early 1933, badly in need of money, he signed a deal with Peer to record twelve songs for a cash advance of $250 per side.

The moving story of Rodgers's last sessions in New York has been recounted many times. Too sick to stand up for long, he rested between takes on a cot set up in a rehearsal hall. A couple of studio musicians were called in to help with some sides, but on the last day Jimmie finished up alone, as he'd begun. Among the numbers recorded in those last days were such tragically prophetic titles as "I'm Free from the Chain Gang Now," "Yodeling My Way Back Home," and "Women Make a Fool Out of Me," released as "Jimmie Rodgers' Last Blue Yodel." It took eight hard, grueling days, but he had completed the contract and done what he set out to do. Less than thirty-six hours later, on May 26, 1933, he was dead of a massive lung hemorrhage in his room at the Taft Hotel.

It is difficult for many today to understand just what an impact Jimmie Rodgers had in his own time. A few people still recognize "T for Texas," but the once-familiar strains of "In the Jailhouse Now," "Waiting for a Train," "Treasures Untold," and "The One Rose" are all but forgotten by the general public. Rodgers's likeness is seen today only on a few cheap album covers, most of them wretchedly drawn, and in a single ten-minute movie, badly lit and shot on primitive sound stock. By his own admission, he never learned how to read music, and Ralph Peer accused him of knowing only "one or two" guitar chords. His records, lacking today's lush arrangements and multiple-track overdubs, sound decidedly flat coming through the stereolliptical

Jimmie Rodgers made one appearance on film, in the 1929 short "The Singing Brakeman." He sang three tunes—"Blue Yodel," "Daddy and Home," and "Waiting for a Train"—to actresses positioned on the low-budget train station set.

*Will Rogers and Jimmie
Rodgers (whom the humorist
referred to as "my distant son")
at Jimmie's home in Kerrville,
Texas, January 1931. At the
time, they were touring Texas
for the Red Cross.*

power channels of your kid's AlphaWarp Integrated Dyna-Amp.
Worst of all, he *yodels*. Finally, measured against the megasalaries of today's stars and their godlike status in the minds of millions, Rodgers's success certainly can't be demonstrated in terms of dollars or numbers of records sold.

What one has to remember is that when Jimmie Rodgers appeared on the scene, there simply were no others like him. In a few short years, there would be Crosby and a horde of radio crooners and matinee idols in the talkies. But looking back now, one sees a decided shortage of lasting personalities during the time Rodgers was coming to the fore. George M. Cohan was in his fifties and fading; Al Jolson's career, revived briefly by the specious novelty of *The Jazz Singer* in 1927, would shortly peak and go into decline; Harry Lauder had retired to Scotland, recording only sporadically. Just below, on the middle rungs of stardom, there were of course dozens of then-familiar names—but few caught the public so fast and with such lasting power as Jimmie Rodgers, the Singing Brakeman, America's Blue Yodeler, the Father of Country Music.

Whatever Rodgers lacked as a polished musician he made up for in the simple authenticity and intense emotion he brought to every performance. Whether the song was humorous or bluesy, sentimental or bawdy, Rodgers sang it like testament, as if he'd lived every line and suffered every change. Never an accomplished, orthodox guitarist, he simply overpowered the instrument and absorbed it as an organic extension, like the yodel, of his singing voice. Even in Rodgers's time, the yodel was a hand-

"Dance orchestra," as advertised in a 1927 Columbia Records catalog. Led by a rambunctious, chicken-farming fiddler, James Gideon Tanner, the Skillet Lickers first recorded for Columbia in Atlanta, in 1926. Though typecast as a bunch of backwoods moonshiners, this string band was as comfortable with pop standards as with fiddle tunes and breakdowns.

Like his friend (and eventual enemy) Vernon Dalhart, Carson Robison began his music career in vaudeville. During the twenties, he specialized in writing "event songs," based on tragic news stories. He wrote hundreds—some for Dalhart, some for himself, and some that have become standards.

icap, considered foreign and old-fashioned by many, and early in his career he'd borne the jibes of those who thought he should dress up like Farmer Brown or an Alpine warbler, in lederhosen and feathered cap. There's a lingering suspicion that Jimmie, a strong-minded soul if there ever was one, persisted in yodeling, in part, purely in defiance of those who said it wasn't the thing to do. In any event, soon no one was laughing: he had transformed the yodel into something uniquely his own, quite unlike any other before or after. As Bob Coltman has written, "He wore each yodel like an old shirt, supremely at ease [and] in his throat [the yodel] shed its Swiss starch and its black inversion . . . making other singers of the time sound as if they were standing at attention wearing tight-fitting tuxedos."

Although it has not always been easy to make the case, there is an increasing sentiment among critics and historians these days that Rodgers was, as a recent reviewer boldly put it, "the most important and influential popular singer of the '20s and '30s." He certainly has been the most enduring.

As Jimmie Rodgers's visit with the Carter Family draws to a close, he suggests that they all join in together for "a little old shore 'nuff ridiculously harmonizing" on "Hot Time in the Old Town Tonight." No one listening today pays much attention to what follows. The music runs only a few bars, and none of those gathered at the mike seems to know the words. But it's truly a group effort and the wildest, most audacious thing on the record —a scant twenty seconds of country scat, Sara in the lead, Maybelle solidly behind her, A. P. boldly bassing in, Rodgers filling the gaps with shimmering little yodels punctuated at the end by a big full one. "Hey, hey," says Jimmie, heading off for another snort. "Boy, tell 'em 'bout us." As if he needed any help.

In 1928 the Weymann Guitar Company of Philadelphia presented Jimmie Rodgers with this custom-made guitar— personalized with his name inlaid in mother of pearl—in exchange for his endorsement of their mass-produced "Jimmie Rodgers Special" model.

51

2

THE TRIUMPH OF THE HILLS: COUNTRY RADIO, 1920–50

Charles Wolfe

One evening in the fall of 1930 a strange procession made its way down a mountain trail in Putnam County, West Virginia. It was a family of skilled musicians—banjo players, fiddlers, guitar players—and they were well known in the hilly region for their work at square dances and fiddling contests. Yet tonight they carried no instruments—only blankets, a sack of cold biscuits, and a jug of drinking water. Crossing a stream, they began to climb up toward a ridge known locally as the Thornton place, and soon came out into an open clearing on top of the hill. The leader of the group was a man named Uncle Walter Bird, and the youngest was a boy of eight named Elmer Bird. It was Elmer who, years later, would recall the evening with special vividness.

"Uncle Walter had the first radio in that part of the country, and he had it rigged up to run off a car battery. As we got up to the top of the hill he would start hooking up the radio. Meanwhile, other people would begin arriving from other directions; some of them would walk three or four miles to get up there, up where we could really get the good reception. And we'd gather in. And at nine o'clock we'd start listening to the Grand Ole Opry. And the different ones of us that played different instruments liked the different acts. Uncle John, the fiddle player, he liked to hear Arthur Smith; Dad used to like Uncle Dave Macon;

The Cumberland Ridge Runners, WLS, Chicago. See page 56.

The Opry cast, ca. 1933. Back row: Blythe Poteet, Alton and Rabon Delmore, Lewis Crook, Dee Simmons, Nap Bastien, DeFord Bailey. Second row: announcer David Stone, Herman Crook, Kirk McGee, Arthur Smith, Sam McGee, Robert Lunn, Bill Etter, Staley Walton, Judge Hay. Third row: Oscar Stone, Oscar Albright, Dr. Humphrey Bate, Walter Ligget, Dorris Macon, Uncle Dave Macon, Paul Warmack, Roy Hardison, Burt Hutcherson. Front row: Buster Bate, Claude Lampley, Howard Ragsdale, Tommy Lefew, George Wilkerson, Charlie Arrington, Tom Andrews, Gale and Amos Binkley.

others liked the sound of the harmonica in the Crook Brothers, and some liked the Possum Hunters, and some just liked to hear the jokes of old Judge Hay, the man who ran it. All of us would sit up there under the stars and listen to it until it went off the air after midnight. It was fine."

Elmer Bird himself later went on to become a nationally known banjo player, the one member of his musical clan to make a mark beyond the confines of the West Virginia hills. Yet he never forgot those nights as a boy when he and his family sat on a lonely hill and heard the "miracle of radio" as it picked up a distant signal from three hundred miles to the southwest, from a town none of them had ever seen called Nashville. The proud, tough mountain musicians of the Bird family had nourished their fiddle and banjo music for generations, and now to hear this same kind of music flung out across the miles through this new marvel of modern technology, the radio—this was something. Not only did it offer a multitude of new songs and new styles,

In a 1930s publicity shot, the Crook Brothers assemble on the steps of a country store. Sitting on the top step are harmonica player Herman Crook and Lewis Crook on banjo. One of WSM's first string bands, the surviving members were still playing the Opry fifty years later.

In 1936, Pat Buttram was a dashing young man who played rube characters in comic routines for Chicago's WLS. Later he starred in dozens of westerns as Gene Autry's comic sidekick and as Mr. Haney on TV's "Green Acres." Today he co-hosts the Nashville Network's "Melody Ranch Theater," a cable program featuring classic Autry westerns.

With arm upraised, John Lair calls the tune as his Cumberland Ridge Runners lean into a fast number for WLS's exhibition square dancers. Making up the band in the back are Slim Miller, Hugh Cross, Karl Davis, and Harty Taylor

Looking every bit the proud patriarch, John Lair presides over an early morning broadcast from Renfro Valley, his birthplace and the home of the barn dance he founded. Lair called such slices of life "reality broadcasting" and thought them essential for establishing the down-home flavor of his radio shows.

but it was a validation: a strong statement that their music had meaning and that it was a part of a wider musical community across the South and, indeed, across the country.

From the very first, radio seemed ideally suited to rural America—even though most of the early radio stations in the South were located in urban centers and owned by urban interests. The big stations in Dallas, Atlanta, and Louisville were owned by the local newspapers, while WLW in Cincinnati answered to

56

the Crosley Radio Corporation, and WSM in Nashville was the brainchild of the National Life and Accident Insurance Company. Only WLS in Chicago had any formal connection to rural America, through its affiliation with Sears Roebuck's catalog sales and through its ownership by an organization called "Agricultural Broadcasting Company." Most of these stations started off seeing themselves as municipal public servants, with their prime clientele inside their city limits; soon, though, often within a period of months, the cards and letters from outlying areas began flooding in, and they realized that a vaster and more enthusiastic audience lay out there in the hills and plains. "I walked four miles and forded two streams just to hear your seven o'clock program," wrote a north Georgia farmer to WSB in Atlanta. It was not long after this that WSB borrowed its newspaper owner's slogan and began to brag that it "covered Dixie like the dew."

Country music soon became an integral part of this coverage. And some forms of country music had been on radio almost from the start of commercial broadcasting on KDKA (Pittsburgh) in 1919. Obscure firsts abound. First documented string band on radio: Berg's String Entertainers over KDKA, May 1922. First documented performance by a solo country artist: Fiddlin' John

Long before marketing focus groups and demographic studies became fashionable, radio stations gauged the popularity of their shows and singers by the sheer quantity of fan mail they inspired. Here cowboy singer and movie star Ray Whitley gazes in mock disbelief at a bumper crop of letters.

Karl & Harty—mandolin player Karl Davis and guitarist Hartford Connecticut Taylor—came to WLS in Chicago from their native Kentucky, as did their former schoolteacher, John Lair. They made their most lasting impression with country standards like "I'm Just Here to Get My Baby Out of Jail," "Kentucky," and "Prisoner's Dream."

Bradley Kincaid's clear tenor treatments of mournful folk songs and Tin Pan Alley favorites so charmed Chicago's WLS audience that he received more than 100,000 letters a year during his four years on the "National Barn Dance" in the late 1920s. He went on to perform on almost every major barn dance, including the Opry.

Lulu Belle & Scotty, WLS's "Hayloft Sweethearts," both came from North Carolina to Chicago, where they met and married. Sentimental numbers like "Have I Told You Lately That I Love You?" (written by Scotty) and their comic repartee endeared them to audiences; a 1936 national poll listed Lulu Belle as the most popular woman on radio.

58

Carson, over WSB, Atlanta, September 1922. First regular use of a barn dance (i.e., country music variety show) format: WBAP, Fort Worth, January 1923. First documented country song performed on radio: Ernest Rogers (no relation to Jimmie) doing "He's in the Jailhouse Now" on WSB, July 4, 1922. But it was WSB in Atlanta and WLS in Chicago that really made the first sustained efforts to use country music—or what would eventually be called country music—on the radio. Through 1923 WSB featured dozens of acts, from Sacred Harp singers to old-time fiddlers to twangers of musical saws, on its series of random but well-received programs. One witness has said that announcer Lambdin Kay, who ran this early station, used "anybody who could sing, whistle, play a musical instrument, or even breathe heavily." Fortunately, the hills around Atlanta were filled with talented folk musicians, and soon the station became a hotbed of all sorts of musical activity, including record making.

Up at WLS in Chicago the effort was more calculated and more deliberate. The station went on the air around April 12, 1924, and within a week a fiddler from Kankakee, Illinois, Tommy Dandurand, was standing on a small mezzanine in the Sherman Hotel, playing "Leather Breeches" for the radio microphone. Then, if later publicity can be believed, cards and letters poured in at an alarming rate, convincing WLS management to program more country music, and on a regular basis. (Similar yarns were to be told about the founding of almost every country barn dance program of the 1930s, from the Fort Worth WBAP barn dance to the Grand Ole Opry. The familiar story took on the qualities of a folk tale: Callous and sophisticated program directors, either by accident or due to some emergency, allow a country fiddler or singer to entertain briefly on the air. Cards, letters, telegrams, and phone calls inundate the station, celebrating the fine old-time music. Callous directors reconsider and start a country show. *Vox populi.*) For a time, the new WLS show was called "The Aladdin Playparty," in deference to its sponsor, the Aladdin Kerosene Lamp Company; then it was called "The Old Fiddlers' Hour," in deference to the national fad for old-time fiddling that Henry Ford had generated with the fiddling contests he sponsored; by 1926 it was christened "The National Barn Dance," and men like George Biggar, John Lair, and Edgar Bill were working behind the scenes to make it a national institution. Many of the early stars came from Kentucky: Walter Peterson, a thin, tall character who played guitar and a harmonica on a wire rack; Chubby Parker, a banjoist and songster whose "I'm a Stern Old Bachelor" was his trademark; the Cumberland Ridge Runners, a band featuring the vocal tal-

Lester McFarland and Robert Gardner, better known as Mac & Bob, met while attending the Kentucky School for the Blind. After getting their start on Knoxville radio, they became a successful act on Chicago's "National Barn Dance" during the thirties with a polished, polite approach to old-time songs.

Doc Hopkins came by his nickname honestly: he was christened "Doctor Howard Hopkins." His material consisted of faithful renditions of old folk songs learned in his native Kentucky. He was a comfortable fixture on WLS from 1930 to 1949.

59

ents of Karl Davis and Harty Taylor, who would later write "Kentucky"; and Bradley Kincaid, a sweet-voiced singer whose "Barbara Allen" was so popular that he sang it on the show every Saturday night for three years. By 1932 the "National Barn Dance" was on the NBC network and was heard over more than fifty stations coast-to-coast. It was the first real success in country radio, and by 1934 Barn Dance acts were showing up in the top ten favorites in national listener polls, ahead of the likes of Al Jolson, Fred Allen, and Guy Lombardo. (In 1936, in fact, Barn Dance singer Lulu Belle Wiseman was named the most popular woman on radio in a national poll conducted by *Radio Digest* magazine, the forerunner of today's *TV Guide*.)

Imitations were inevitable. On October 5, 1925, eighteen months after the "National Barn Dance" started, station WSM had its first broadcast from Nashville. It started off with 1,000 watts of power—not impressive by modern standards but

Hay fever in Chicago: the cast of the WLS "National Barn Dance" assembled onstage at the Eighth Street Theater, during the show's heyday, June 16, 1934.

Looking as sweet as the old-fashioned songs they sang are the Three Little Maids, one of several women's trios that appeared on WLS during the 1930s. The Maids—Eva, Evelyn, and Lucille Overstake —soon went their separate ways: Eva married Red Foley, and Lucille became a successful country songwriter in the 1940s under the pen name "Jenny Lou Carson."

Georgie Gobel, later known as TV comedian "Lonesome" George Gobel, was billed on WLS as the Little Cowboy. He came to the station in 1932 at age thirteen when the program director heard him in an Episcopal choir and asked if he could sing cowboy songs. He remained with WLS for eight years.

The Hoosier Hot Shots brought a vaudeville comedian's touch to country music at Chicago's WLS with zany novelty songs and a mess of uptown and backyard instruments, including clarinets, trumpets, washboards, and kazoos.

Rural Radio

THE ONLY MAGAZINE PUBLISHED EXCLUSIVELY FOR RURAL LISTENERS!

Vol. 1. No. 1.   FEBRUARY, 1938   Ten Cents

"THE *New* PARTY LINE"

CRAMMED FULL OF PICTURES,
GOSSIP AND NEWS OF RURAL
RADIO PERSONALITIES.

Lambdin Kay • Morse Salisbury • The Hired Hand Returns • Four Solid Pages of Pictures
How to Double The Range of Your Radio-set • Lulu Belle Fashions • and Other Exclusive Features

WORD FROM HOME

Before the advent of television, radio held millions in its spell, and probably nowhere more powerfully than in the countryside. In 1938, according to a national study sponsored by Tide *magazine, 9.4 million rural families in America owned radio sets (a whopping 69 percent of all rural families accounted for). On average, they tuned in for 5½ hours a day. Radio kept the home folks company, entertained and comforted them. And they responded: Chicago's WLS, home of the "National Barn Dance," reported receiving well over a million letters from listeners in 1934, and again in 1935.*

Catering to this large audience hungry for country programming were a variety of fan magazines—the down-home antecedents, if you will, of People. *In addition to feature articles and interviews with the stars, these magazines included often-lively letters columns that reflected how seriously country radio listeners took their pastime. The following letters originally appeared in two of the most popular of the country radio fan magazines—*Stand By, *a weekly published by WLS in Chicago, and* Rural Radio, *an independent monthly published in Nashville. Together, these letters suggest just how important country radio programs were to the home folks, wherever they might be.*

January 1939

I am really going to try to thank you for publishing RURAL RADIO. . . . I am a girl 19 years old who has been raised on a farm and believe me, you don't get any time to listen to the radio. I really like music but the only time I get to listen in the summer is on Saturday nights. As soon as I have finished with my work, I get hold of that radio dial and get the Grand Ole Opry. Believe me, that music brings fun into a tired, hard day's work. It puts pep into me, and I could listen to that swell music all night. During the winter months, I get to listen to more music, then I tune in on KMOX and get Pappy Cheshire and his gang.

I sure like Uncle Dave Macon. I have some smaller sisters and they just can't wait until he gets on the air. So you see, we were pleased to see his picture in RURAL RADIO a couple of months back. We still get out RURAL RADIO and look at him.

I just can't tell you in words how much we like your Magazine. I would like to see more pictures of the Grand Ole Opry so I am enclosing $1.00 to renew my subscription to RURAL RADIO and get the Picture Album free.

Yours truly,
Miss Winefrieda Steinnerd
Laflin, Missouri

January 18, 1936

Who can beat this record? I wonder how many listeners of the National Barn Dance can tell you the name of the artists and the songs they sang on each Barn Dance for the last five years? I have a record of the appearance of each artist and the songs they sang on 250 Saturday night Barn Dances out of 260 in the past five years. I have enjoyed all the Barn Dances but I especially enjoyed the New Year's Eve Party of this past year. . . .

Betty Wilkey
Maroa, Illinois

March 1938

We live on a ranch in the most remote part of Ontario, Canada. A beautiful part it is and we are surrounded by neighbors, both American and Canadians. Radios are not too plentiful here. I have seen as many as twenty or thirty gathered in our home on Saturday night to enjoy the Saturday Night Barn Dance. Since we have received RURAL RADIO we enjoy it all the more now. Thanks and good luck to your magazine.

Hugh and Ann MacNabb
Rothsay, Ontario

February 1, 1936

I live way up here in the "sticks" in northwestern North Dakota. . . . We're located in the drought-stricken area and so our radio is not the best, making it hard and oft-times impossible to tune in during the day. But believe you me, we are ardent listeners every morning and Saturday night. Saturday night is the affair of affairs up here. Those who have no radio congregate at the homes of those who have and what an enjoyable evening! Yes, enjoyable to the superlative degree. The only amusement we have is a show house 20 miles away and an occasional dance. So radio folks can't possibly know what glorious entertainment you render to us "shut-ins." . . . Last Saturday the louder Scotty sang, the louder the wind whistled around our cabin, as if it, as well as we, were shouting congratulations to Scotty and Lulu Belle [the singing duo had recently married]. . . . No, a thousand times no, don't put your swell old time programs on the shelf to make room for jazz! . . . All in our community wouldn't object if Saturday night programs came every night. . . .

Leone Neises
Raub, North Dakota

June 1, 1935

I feel that your music and songs are what pulled me through this winter. Half the time we were blue and broke. One year during the depression and no work. Kept from going on relief but lost everything we possessed doing so. So thanks for the songs, for they make life seem more like living. . . .

Chicago Listener

63

WLS program director George Biggar, looking like he means business, graces the cover of the station's feature magazine.

January 1939

I received my copy of RURAL RADIO, and I can't tell you how proud I was to get it. I can hardly wait to get my big album that I have subscribed for, and am waiting patiently to get it any day now. . . . Receiving pictures of radio stars is my hobby and believe me I sure have a large number of them and love them all. I paste each picture or group of pictures on great big cardboard, then tack the cardboard over my radio so I can see them. When you hear them over the radio it just seems like you are in their crowd watching them. I get a great kick out of the programs and the pictures hit the right spot.

Mrs. Ed Dalton
St. Francois, Missouri

June 1939

I've been a reader of your wonderful paper over a year and find myself looking forward to it each month. I enjoy the four pages of pictures, the stories, the Solemn Ole Judge's column. In fact, I'd never be able to tell which part of the magazine I like best. Our entire family, consisting of four children, all enjoy it. And when neighbors come in, we have real enjoyment looking over the past issues together. Radio programs are so much better since we have so many pictures of the stars. My hobby is collecting pictures of radio stars. I intend to make me a scrapbook with my RURAL RADIOS but haven't yet decided just how. Another hobby is collecting song books.

Mrs. Leo Kulp
Chicago, Illinois

Feb. 16, 1935

Submarine Division Twelve
U.S.S. Bass
At sea, enroute from Dutch Harbor, Alaska, to Pearl Harbor, T.H.

Manager,
Radio Station WLS,
Chicago, Illinois

Dear Sir:

At the request of the crew of the *U.S.S. Bass*, one of the U.S. Navy's largest and finest submarines, thanks is given for the wonderful program of last Saturday.

The *Bass*, on a cruise starting from San Diego, California on July 2nd, has been to San Francisco, Seattle and then on up to Ketchikan, Sitka, Juneau, Valdez, Seward, Kodiak and Dutch Harbor in Alaska. We are now headed for Pearl Harbor, Territory of Hawaii. During our trip we have at various times picked up your station but the National Barn Dance which we picked up yesterday afternoon, during daylight and at four in the afternoon, tops the list. The reception was excellent, the program was one to be remembered, and we appreciate it.

It may be of interest to you to know that we were, at the time of your broadcast, in Latitude 45-42 North and Longitude 161-25 West and, as near as can be estimated, 4,500–5,000 miles away from your station.

In closing we wish to express our appreciation of your station and of your programs in a Navy manner. YOKE WILLIAM RAY, W.L.S.

A well done from us all.

Yours very truly,
Ship's writer

stronger than 85 percent of the other stations in the country in 1925. The inaugural program attracted comments from the governor of Tennessee, and music by the Fisk Jubilee Singers, the Knights of Columbus Vocal Quartet, Ted Stover ("the Syncopating Pianist"), and others—but not a note of country music. Later that month the station let Dr. Humphrey Bate appear a few times. Bate was a country doctor from north of Nashville who led an excellent old-time string band; their distinctive sound, which featured a harmonica lead, two fiddles, and a bowed string bass, graced a repertoire of Civil War dance tunes like "Old Joe" and "Throw the Old Cow Over the Fence." But the real breakthrough did not occur until November 2, 1925, when WSM hired a young announcer named George Hay to direct their new station. Hay was only thirty years old, but had had a wealth of experience: a native of Indiana, he won his initial fame as a newspaperman and announcer in Memphis, then went to WLS, where he served as announcer for the "National Barn Dance" show. WSM hired him primarily because he had just won a gold cup from *Radio Digest* for being the nation's most popular announcer.

Seeking to expand the audience of this rather stodgy station, Hay noted the popularity of musicians like Dr. Bate, who appealed not only to the people of Nashville, but to folks in distant outlying areas as well. On November 28, 1925, Hay put on the air a seventy-seven-year-old champion fiddler from nearby Laguardo, Tennessee, Uncle Jimmy Thompson. Uncle Jimmy had

Harmonica-playing Dr. Humphrey Bate (playing with the hound) led the Possum Hunters, one of the first string bands to play on WSM. In 1933, WSM advertised Bate's services as follows: "Dr. Humphrey Bate and His 'Possum Hunters (Barn Dance Orchestra): One of the featured acts on the Saturday Night Grand Old [sic] Opry since its beginning. Noted for their unique way of playing the old time songs typical of the Tennessee hills. Available only for special program. Rate on request."

*Above, right
George D. Hay, the "Solemn Old Judge," in full regalia.*

65

Judge Hay with the press agent's dream: white-bearded, outspoken, hard-drinking Uncle Jimmy Thompson, who claimed he could "fiddle the bugs off a 'tater vine."

David Harrison Macon—known professionally as Uncle Dave Macon—was fifty-five and a vaudeville veteran when he first appeared on WSM. With his rollicking banjo playing and his exuberant comic style, he became one of the Opry's most popular performers and a living link to tradition years after his contemporaries had passed away. He died in 1952, aged eighty-two, three weeks after his last Opry appearance.

actually learned some of his tunes during the Civil War, and (though few realized it at the time) he was one of the oldest musicians ever to appear on radio. He was a press agent's dream: white-bearded, outspoken, hard-drinking, barking a challenge to the champion of the latest national fiddling contest sponsored by Henry Ford. "Let him come to Tennessee," Uncle Jimmy boasted, "and I'll lie with him like a bulldog." Who could resist this kind of style? Hay couldn't, nor could his listeners, and on December 26, 1925, he announced: "Because of the recent revival in the popularity of the old familiar tunes, WSM has arranged to have an hour or two every Saturday night." Though it wouldn't find its name for another eighteen months, the Grand Ole Opry was born.

Although it looks like a sparsely furnished parlor, this room was WSM's first studio, built the year the station began broadcasting (1925) and located on the fifth floor of the National Life and Accident Insurance Company building at Seventh and Union in downtown Nashville.

The Dixieliners with their arsenal, 1930s. Brothers Sam and Kirk McGee joined forces with Fiddlin' Arthur Smith, a railroad hand who worked on the Dixie Line, to form the popular Opry act in 1932. Although Smith left the McGees in 1938, all three continued performing until their deaths in the 1970s and 1980s.

Where the "National Barn Dance" was "soft" country—with a lot of vaudeville, barbershop quartets, polka bands, and ersatz cowboy songs—the early Opry was a heady mixture of hard-core string bands, traditional singers, down-home gospel quartets, and robust banjo players like Uncle Dave Macon, the first real star of the show. Like dozens of southern radio barn dance shows that were to follow it, the Opry went through a gestation period clearly divided into four stages. The first was the informal stage, when just about any picker could come down and get on the air for a few minutes, and when nobody got any money. The second was the addition of the live studio audience to the show; early audiences simply stood in the studio and watched, but as demand grew, the show moved to a theater, where it was broadcast

remote and took on the trappings of a stage show. The third (which, in the case of most barn dances, followed on the heels of stage two) was the conscious attempt to fix an image for the show, with the development of on-air personalities—colorful announcers, comedians, ad-libbing musicians, and entertainers with funny names. On the Opry, it was Judge Hay who gave the bands their names, like the Fruit Jar Drinkers, the Gully Jumpers, the Possum Hunters; it was Hay who made the musicians stop wearing suits and ties, and dress in overalls and floppy hats; and it was Hay who made them pose for publicity photos in cornfields and pig pens, even though many of the musicians were not from the boondocks, but were watchmakers, auto repairmen, railroad telegraphers, and even policemen. These early stars soon included Obed Pickard and the Pickard Family, from nearby Ashland City, the first singing stars of the show; DeFord Bailey, a remarkable harmonica player from Carthage who featured train imitations and became country music's first black star; Sam and Kirk McGee, wizards on the guitar and banjo who often accompanied Uncle Dave Macon; Sarie and Sallie, a team of wildly funny comediennes whose dialogues set the tone and pace for the later success of Minnie Pearl; the Vagabonds, a smooth-singing vocal trio who were the first fully professional act to join the show; and the Delmore Brothers, whose original southern songs and harmonies soon eclipsed the more formal efforts of the Vagabonds.

The fourth stage of barn dance program development was professionalization: the creation of a system whereby artists could earn enough by radio work to give up their day jobs. This happened with the Opry around 1933 with the creation of the Artist Service Bureau, which helped book group tours of Opry stars. By the mid-1930s, stations were able to charge for commercial time on barn dance shows, albeit not much: a fifteen-minute segment of the Opry cost an advertiser a mere $100 in 1936. This allowed them to pay musicians at least a token amount for their radio work, but rates were alarmingly low, even for the Depression. The Delmore Brothers started at WSM in 1933 at $5 a week between them, for duties that included appearances on the Opry as well as regular morning shows. Smaller stations were even worse. The Callahan Brothers, who soon became major recording stars, worked at their home base, WWNC in Asheville, North Carolina, for $4 between them. Most musicians quickly learned that the real money was to be found in personal appearances (a fact that remains true today), and that the importance of their radio jobs was as a means to this end. Radio gave them a showcase, and most stations allowed them to advertise their

Diminutive DeFord Bailey, dubbed the "Harmonica Wizard" by Judge Hay, was perhaps the Opry's single most popular performer prior to 1930. He was an elevator operator at the National Life Building in 1926, when he was first invited to play a number on the air. Two years later he made twice as many appearances (forty-nine times in fifty-two weeks) as any other act. He was mysteriously dropped from the Opry around 1941.

Dr. Pepper could hardly have done better than the Callahan Brothers for plugging their product among the good people of Wichita Falls, Texas, during the 1940s. Bill (born Homer) and Joe (Walter) trekked across the South and Midwest, working one radio station after another, building a following wherever they went. According to Bill, "We drew over 1700 letters a day for Dr. Pepper."

The Pickard Family (ca. 1933) —Obed "Dad" Pickard with his daughters—joined the Opry in 1926 and became its first star singers. "I am mighty glad of the opportunity to play and sing these old ballads and folk songs," Pickard once told a Radio Digest reporter. "I feel that we are doing something worthwhile, for we are helping to preserve something very sweet and fine, which otherwise would be lost."

Raised on a played-out farm in the red clay hills of northern Alabama, Alton Delmore (right) secretly aspired to be a novelist. Instead, he and younger brother Rabon molded blues and country gospel into a lithe, driving sound that influenced hundreds of country musicians who heard them on the Opry (1933–38) and on record. Ultimately, Alton wrote more than a thousand songs, including such classics as "Brown's Ferry Blues" and "Blues Stay Away from Me."

upcoming concerts free of charge. Thus, musicians would work an area within a radius of a hundred miles around their station, doing weeknight concerts in schoolhouses, lodge halls, and movie theaters. With luck, they would make two or three dollars a night and could put together a living wage. And in a larger sense, the music itself benefited: by working at their music full-time, these performers became technically more proficient, and they were forced to find new and original material.

Through the 1930s the barn dance fad grew, spreading like kudzu throughout the South and into other parts of the country. At the beginning of the decade, in 1932, there were 137 stations in the South and Southwest, most of them broadcasting at less than 1,000 watts; only nine stations were broadcasting with more

70

Like most of the Opry's first acts, Paul Warmack & the Gully Jumpers were talented amateur musicians who held down other jobs to make a living. A Nashville auto mechanic, Warmack led the group for nearly twenty years. Pictured here (ca. 1930) are carpenter Burt Hutcherson on guitar, mechanic Roy Hardison on banjo, farmer Charlie Arrington on fiddle, and Warmack on guitar.

Early Opry string bands like the Fruit Jar Drinkers (left) felt they ought to dress in their finest when they performed. Not Judge Hay, who constantly admonished them to "keep it down to earth." Soon all the Opry string bands had overalls and floppy hats to go with the rural names he'd given them.

71

In the 1930s, almost a decade before Minnie Pearl's first How-deee!, *Sarie & Sallie (Edna Wilson and Margaret Waters) brought small-town, gossipy humor to the Opry. Their routines usually consisted of the elder Sarie making wisecracks about the townsfolk to good-natured Sallie.*

than 20,000 watts: Atlanta, Birmingham, Louisville, Charlotte, Cincinnati, Tulsa, Nashville, San Antonio, and Dallas. Only 45 of the 137 stations had made affiliations with the national broadcasting networks, which meant that most were still originating most of their programming live—a good thing for local country music and barn dances. (Even stations that had network affiliations, like Nashville's WSM, worked compromises between canned network feeds and local shows: for years every Saturday night the Grand Ole Opry stopped for thirty minutes so WSM could take the NBC show "Amos 'n' Andy.") Station signals, too, carried much farther in those days of uncluttered airways; WSM's original signal was heard easily throughout the eastern United States, and even 100-watt stations could be heard for a hundred miles across the flatlands of the deep South or Southwest. Some stations had directional signals that beamed their shows toward a specific area. WWVA in Wheeling, West Virginia, for instance, tended toward the Northeast, creating country fans in Pennsylvania and Maryland; KVOO's signal from Tulsa carried westward well into California, but a motorist driving into town from the east could pick up the signal only a few miles from the city limits.

A list of even the major barn dance shows that emerged in the thirties would be impressive. It would have to include

"They could hardly be called 'country boys,' " Judge Hay wrote of the crooning Vagabonds, "but they loved folk music." After starring in St. Louis, Herald Goodman, Dean Upson, and guitarist Curt Poulton took their barber-shop harmonies to WSM (in 1931) where they became, next to Uncle Dave Macon, the Opry's most popular act.

The Binkley Brothers' Dixie Clodhoppers possessed a delicate, restrained sound for an old-time string band—a reflection perhaps of the band's leaders, banjoist Gale and fiddler Amos Binkley, watch repairmen by trade. The Clodhoppers were the first act to record in Nashville, in 1928 sessions conducted by Ralph Peer.

ANATOMY OF A BARN DANCE

The following script from the "Dixie Jamboree" radio show, broadcast over a CBS southern regional network during the mid-1940s, reveals some of the formulas that performers and executives used to reach rural and small-town audiences during radio's golden era. Claude Casey, the show's emcee and headline act, wrote the scripts for this weekly program, originated for CBS by station WBT, Charlotte, North Carolina.

Many shows in this series were staged in WBT's auditorium studio, located in the Wilder Building on South Tryon Street. Here audiences of a hundred people or more could watch the performers as they gathered around the microphone, scripts in hand. The audience also joined in the applause at the end of each number. Vernon Hyles, a member of the Rangers Quartet, usually gave cast members their cues with hand signals. His directions, however, did not stop onstage horseplay, and musicians sometimes looked down in the middle of a number to find lighted matches in the soles of their shoes—much to the audience's delight.

1 Theme song played and sung by cast.

2 Radio engineer turns volume up for instrumental continuation of the theme, then brings the volume down so music continues "under" the announcer's introduction.

3 Casey sets the program's informal, family tone. Note deliberate use of folksy patter, re-creation of old-time square dance, and the choice of a traditional fiddle tune.

4 Introduction romanticizes the Old West, setting up the rendition of a standard western number. Western songs were then key elements of most country broadcasts.

WBT
THE COLUMBIA BROADCASTING SYSTEM, INC.
CHARLOTTE, 2, N. C.

Program: DIXIE JAMBOREE Date: Thursday, October 5, 1944
Talent: Time: 8:30 To: 8:55 PM
Continuity: Agency:
Announcer: Client:

ANNCR: THE DIXIE JAMBOREE

(1) THEME: WE'LL HAVE A LITTLE DANCE TONIGHT, BOYS DOWN SOUTH

INSTRU: WE'LL HAVE A LITTLE DANCE TONIGHT, BOYS — UP AND UNDER

(2) ANNCR: 8:30 Thursday night, and time for another Dixie Jamboree, your program of music and songs. Now meet your Master of Ceremonies... Claude Casey.

(3) CASEY: From the Queen City of The South in the Heart of the Carolinas it's 8:30 Thursday night....time for all the boys and firls at the Dixie Jamboree to gather round the microphone and sneak into your hearts with a song or two/ Now the first little ditty comin' atcha is one the fiddlers kinda shine on...and the rest of the fellers twang their guiters and slap the bass fiddle while Ma and Pa and all the younguns join hands and circle round for an ole square dance...
PRETTY LITTLE PINK

MUSIC: PRETTY LITTLE PINK

(4) CASEY: The slow lazy rhythm of the West....the carefree life of the old cowhands...Folks it's all here in this number the Rangers are going to sing. It's a favorite of theirs.. and maybe that's why they sing it so pretty...Tumblin Tumble Weeds"

The cast of Charlotte's "Dixie Jamboree," 1942. Debonair emcee Claude Casey, script in hand, stands at the mike.

5 **ANNCR:** Neighbors....right here we're going to take the words right of Claude Casey's mouth....and tell you about this song he's going to do for you now. Several weeks ago, Claude sang this number – one of his own compositions – and asked you folks to tell him how you liked it. Well....you wrote so many nice letters and cards to Claude telling him just how much you did like his new song – that he's singing it again tonight......IT DOESN't MATTER.

VOCAL: IT DOESN'T MATTER

CASEY: HERE THEY ARE FOLKS....those two fellers from the hills of Gastonia... with a number that's brand-new to the Jamboree...and I know you're going to like it. Come on, Whitey and Hogan....we're waiting for you to sing "EACH MINUTE SEEMS A MILLION YEARS"

VOCAL: EACH MINUTE SEEMS A MILLION YEARS

6 **MUSIC (COLD) KITTY CLYDE**

7 **CASEY:** NEIGHBORS, here's that general handy-man around the Old Jamboree.... Arthur Smith....And when I say handy-man, I mean just that. One week Arthur plays his fiddle...and the next the guitar....and he's even done a little singing, too. Seems like whatever you folks ask for...fiddle...guitar....it don't matter which, Arthur's always ready with a bang-up good tune like the one he's going to play now.... AFTER YOU'VE GONE.

MUSIC: AFTER YOU'VE GONE

CASEY: And now, neighbors it's time to turn away for a minute from these sorta hot tunes....to some real old-fashioned gospel music....the kind that comes so near to the hearts of every one of us. The Johnson Family are ready to sing now....

8 *To MORROW MAY MEAN GooD By*

5 Announcer introduces the next number, a song written by Casey and "tested" on earlier programs.

6 The next piece, an instrumental by the ensemble, starts "cold," i.e., without introduction.

7 Casey brings on Arthur Smith, who eventually has his own radio and TV shows, based in Charlotte. Smith's instrumentals, often jazzy versions of pop songs like "After You've Gone," add further variety to the Jamboree.

8 Late substitution of one song for another.

9 *Introduction cut to keep the show within its half-hour limit. Timing of the program during rehearsal often led to such changes.*

10 *Kirby's patriotic song heralds the enemy's impending defeat during World War II.*

11 *Introduction of the Tennessee Ramblers plugs this group's next show date. Casey was then a member of the band.*

12 *Another song begun cold.*

13 *Casey emphasizes family themes again, invites listener response, and closes with familiar tag line: "Thanks heaps and oodles for dialing our way . . ."*

14 *The announcer concludes with a run-down of the show's cast, followed by station and network identification.*

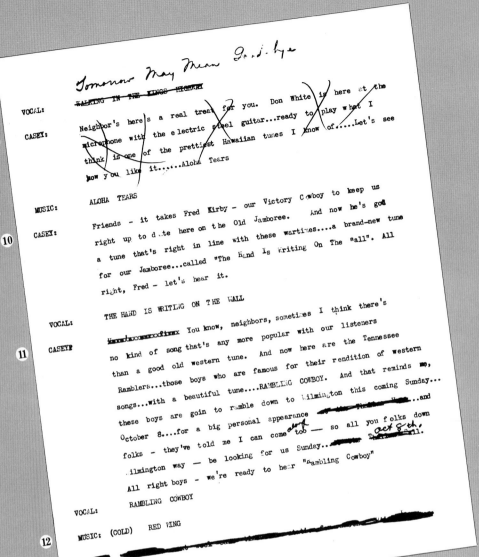

Tomorrow May Mean Good-bye

VOCAL: ~~WALKING IN THE KINGS HIGHWAY~~

CASEY: Neighbor's here's a real treat for you. Don White is here at the microphone with the electric steel guitar...ready to play what I think is one of the prettiest Hawaiian tunes I know of.....Let's see how you like it......Aloha Tears

MUSIC: ALOHA TEARS

CASEY: Friends - it takes Fred Kirby - our Victory Cowboy to keep us right up to date here on the Old Jamboree. And now he's got a tune that's right in line with these wartimes.....a brand-new tune for our Jamboree...called "The Hand Is Writing On The Wall". All right, Fred - let's hear it.

VOCAL: THE HAND IS WRITING ON THE WALL

CASEY: ~~Introduction~~ You know, neighbors, sometimes I think there's no kind of song that's any more popular with our listeners than a good old western tune. And now here are the Tennessee Ramblers...those boys who are famous for their rendition of western songs...with a beautiful tune....RAMBLING COWBOY. And that reminds me, these boys are goin to ramble down to Wilmington this coming Sunday... October 8....for a big personal appearance ~~there~~...and folks - they've told me I can come *along* too — so all you folks down Wilmington way — be looking for us Sunday... *Oct 8th.* All right boys - we're ready to hear "Rambling Cowboy"

VOCAL: RAMBLING COWBOY

MUSIC: (COLD) RED WING

CASEY: Well neighbors, that kinda winds up the little ball of yarn... here at the old Dixie Jamboree tonight....We think it's been mighty nice of you to open up your doors and let us come in. Don't forget - keep your carsd and letters coming into us - so we'll know what you'd like to hear best. So until next week- the whole gang here joins ~~xxxxxxxxxx~~ in with me in saying' thanks heaps and oodles for dialing our way again and we jist love you to pieces fer listenin in.

ANNCR: Tune in next week - same time and same station - for ~~xxxxx~~ another Dixie Jamboree when your Master of Ceremonies, Claude Casey will be back again with the Tennessee Ramblers, the Rangers Quartet, Arthur Smith, Ma Johnson's Family and The Briarhoppers. This program originated in ths studios of WBT Charlotte. J. B. Clark speaking. This is CBS, The Columbia Broadcasting System.

the "Wheeling Jamboree" (WWVA, 1933), the "Crazy Barn Dance" (WBT, Charlotte, 1934), the "Old Fashioned Barn Dance" (KMOX, St. Louis, ca. 1930), the "Boone County Jamboree" (WLW, Cincinnati, 1936), the "Renfro Valley Barn Dance" (WHAS, Louisville, 1937), "Saddle Mountain Round-Up" (KVOO, Tulsa), the "Old Dominion Barn Dance" (WRVA, Richmond, Virginia, 1938), the "WSB Barn Dance" (Atlanta, 1940), and "KWKH Roundup" (Shreveport, 1939). The fad even spread to the North and Midwest: the three-hour "Iowa Barn Dance Frolic," from WHO in Des Moines, was airing as early as 1932, and by 1935 WHN in New York had a barn dance show hosted for a time by young Tex Ritter.

Most stations sponsored tours and concerts featuring their program casts, often in open-air venues during the summer. In 1937 the Grand Ole Opry tour group attracted some 30,000 to an all-day shindig in the small town of Backusburg, Kentucky; four

Vito Pellettieri, one-time dance band leader, became the Opry's stage manager in 1934, allowing Judge Hay to devote himself to his roles as announcer and master of ceremonies. Here Vito checks song lists with the Gully Jumpers, while Sarie & Sallie and others wait their turn. It was a scene that Vito would repeat nearly every Saturday for the next forty years.

Few radio acts tugged harder— or more successfully—on the heartstrings than Asher Sizemore and his son, Little Jimmie. On the Opry during the thirties they specialized in sad, sentimental numbers and sold thousands of their own songbooks over the air. During good weeks, they drew 40,000 pieces of mail.

Chicago's WLS and Nashville's WSM weren't the only radio stations to feed country shows to the major networks. Here the Duke of Paducah guest stars on "Pappy Cheshire's National Champion Hillbillies" show over St. Louis's KMOX and the CBS network, ca. 1940.

years later promoter Foreman Phillips attracted 22,000 at the Venice Pier for a staging of the "Los Angeles County Barn Dance"; about the same time "Renfro Valley Barn Dance" tour groups played to 10,000 over three nights while working from tent shows in rural Ohio. By the time of World War II, the Opry was touring in 15 states and 2,500 towns annually.

In 1944, during the high-water mark of live radio, *Billboard* magazine estimated that there were some six hundred regular country radio shows in the United States and that they played to a combined audience of around forty million people. All, of course, were not barn dances; country singers were quick to develop other formats. One was the solo show sponsored by one particular company; in fact, some artists, such as Bill and Charlie Monroe, worked out their contracts directly with sponsors and then the sponsors found them radio slots. By the end of the 1930s there were about 250 single-artist shows under such sponsorship. The makers of patent medicines sponsored many programs, maintaining an ages-old link between the music and old-time touring medicine show barkers. One of the most popular of the patent medicines was Crazy Water Crystals, sponsors of the Monroes, the Callahan Brothers, Lew Childre, the Tennessee Ramblers, and others. It was never quite clear just what Crazy Water Crystals did for you, but the shows were full of references

78

to "regaining pep" and "regularity." And there were many others, with such exotic, potent names as the Retonga Medicine Company, Herbolac, Man-O-Ree, Black Draught, and Peruna. There were flour mills (like the Light Crust Doughboys' sponsor, Burrus Mill), coffee companies (JFG Coffee), farm machinery companies (AllisChalmers), and lesser-known patrons like the American Snuff Company, Carter's Chickery, and Old Sam Cola. Some artists, like Asher Sizemore and his precocious six-year-old son Little Jimmie, were clever enough to sponsor themselves, hawking song books on the air and handling the mail orders.

NEW PE-RU-NA

The famous tonic that helps to WIN FIGHTS WITH COLDS by helping to build up resistance, such resistance often preventing and relieving colds.

AT ALL DRUG STORES

Peruna, the All-Purpose Tonic: Whitey & Hogan, stars of Charlotte's WBT during the 1940s, recalled that "if you sent a Peruna box top, you could get a picture of Whitey & Hogan with the Briarhoppers, and a song. We got as many as ten thousand in one week."

The Crazy Water Crystals Company was the top radio sponsor of hillbilly programs in the 1930s. During the thirties, the firm sold an estimated boxcar load of the mineral laxative a day, largely because of promotion through hillbilly radio shows.

From Mineral Wells, and Thorndale, Texas
TO MILLIONS EVERYWHERE

Crazy Water Crystals Are Shipped in Car
Lots to Distributors in U. S. and Canada

What is Crazy Water?

More than 56 years ago, the original Crazy Well was discovered. A pioneer family, James Alvis Lynch, and his wife, Amandy, dug a well for drinking water. Mrs. Lynch, who had been in poor health, was the first to discover its unusual powers.

The fame of this mineral water spread; soon a little tent city sprang up around the well. Now, more than 56 years later, a thriving health resort has grown up around the Crazy Water Hotel, built at the site of the original Crazy Well. Year after year, thousands of the sick and near sick from all over America, suffering from many disorders brought on or made worse by faulty elimination, make the journey to the Crazy Wells.

What Are Crazy Water Crystals?

Crazy Water Crystals are the minerals which are taken from natural Crazy Mineral Water from our wells at Mineral Wells and Thorndale, Texas, by simply evaporating the water away. Nothing is added. You simply dissolve them in ordinary drinking water, and make your drinking water contribute to your physical well-being. At home, at work, wherever you are, you can drink Crazy Water—at just a few cents a gallon.

From the beginning of the practice of medicine doctors have recognized the importance of cleansing the bowels as the first step in treating almost every ailment. If you suffer from rheumatism, neuritis, arthritis, biliousness, constipation, acid and upset stomach, extreme nervousness, kidney trouble, or any other disorder brought on or made worse by sluggish, clogged up bowels, drink Crazy Water frequently, made from Crazy Water Crystals.

Try Crazy Water Crystals — See What Nature Can Do!

39 orth Tryon
HARLOTTE, N. C.

Crazy Water Crystals Co.

21 Arcade Building
ATLANTA, GA.

OF THE CAROLINAS AND GEORGIA

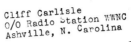
Weslaco, Texas
May 12, 1939

Cliff Carlisle
C/O Radio Station WWNC
Ashville, N. Carolina

Dear Cliff & Sunnyboy Tommy:

Well, I am in the radio business again, and I notice in our record library that we have a few of the Carlisle records including Cliff & Sunnyboy Tommy and a few of Carlisle Brothers.

I played one of yours and Sunnyboy Tommy's records the other morning and received a letter from a Baptist preacher in Santa Rosa, Texas expressing his appreciateion of it and he wanted to know where he could find a copy of the song. I gave him your name and address and suppose he will write you.

Cliff, I am in such a rush I don't have time to write a letter, but I have thought of you and the other boys quite often; especially Sunnyboy Tommy.

I am managing the station at Reynosa, Mexico, which is located just across the border from McAllen and about twenty-six miles from where I live here in Weslaco, and it is about to run me to death going back and forth to my work. This is the station that Dr. Brinkley used to own, but we took it over the 23 of March. Please write me, Cliff, and tell me what became of all of the old gangs. I understand J. E. has his old group, but Charley and Bill have separated, Dick Hartman and his gang has split up, the Tobacco Tags seem to be lost, Byron Parker took J. E. Mayners group away from him so I have been told, and I am wondering what has become of Pop Ekler who was down in Atlanta when I left there. Please give my very best regards to Sunnyboy Tommy and remember me to the rest of the boys.

Yours very truly *Jim Fincher*

Jim Fincher

In 1934, as a sales representative for Crazy Water Crystals, Jim Fincher hired hillbilly musicians and founded the "Crazy Barn Dance" to promote the patent medicine over WBT, Charlotte, North Carolina. By 1939, Fincher had moved on to a Mexican border radio station, as he explains in this letter to his former WBT employee, Cliff Carlisle. ("Charley and Bill have separated" refers to the Monroe Brothers; "J. E." is J. E. Mainer.)

Few country fans today have ever heard of Nolen "Cowboy Slim" Rinehart; he never released a commercial record. But in his day (roughly 1935–45), no other Mexican border station performer had a larger following. Through live appearances and transcription recordings, he was heard on nearly every border station, until his death in an automobile accident in the late 1940s.

A second staple of country radio programming was an informal system of syndication made possible by a form of recording known as the "electrical transcription." Typically, a transcription was a twelve- or sixteen-inch disc that contained fifteen minutes of programming; in the days before tape, it was the logical way to record a program and mail it around to different stations. Transcriptions were in use as early as 1931, but the earliest country use of them seems to have been a set of 1933 shows for Crazy Water Crystals by an Alabama string band called Colonel Jack and Shorty's Hillbillies. Such transcriptions as have survived—and countless thousands did not, going instead to roof chicken coops and stock shooting ranges—give us our only lasting traces of what these early radio shows actually sounded like, and thus our only glimpse into the most important era of country music and mass media.

Gene Autry, then the nation's number-one cowboy star, paid a visit to Pee Wee King and the WSM gang around 1938. On hand are (standing, from left) Nashville music promoter J. L. Frank, Milton Estes, Sarie, Autry, Sallie, Cowboy Jack Skaggs, Pee Wee King, Asher Sizemore, and (kneeling) Abner Sims, Buddy Sizemore, Texas Daisy, Jimmie Sizemore, and Curly Rhodes.

WSM musicians record a transcription show called "Uncle Jim's Crossroads Store" (1939). Pictured are guitarist Jack Shook, fiddler Mac McGar, accordionist Elbert McEwen, Nap Bastien, guitarist Dee Simmons, and WSM dramatic director Lark Taylor.

'GRAND OLE OPRY'

WEAVER BROTHERS
and ELVIRY
LOIS RANSON
ALLAN LANE
HENRY KOLKER
And Radio's Popular Artists
UNCLE DAVE MACON and his SON, DORRIS
ROY ACUFF and his SMOKY MOUNTAIN BOYS
with RACHEL
GEORGE DEWEY HAY, The Solemn Ole Judge
FRANK McDONALD Director

A REPUBLIC PICTURE

Less than a year after the NBC network picked up the Grand Ole Opry broadcasts, Republic Pictures released The Grand Ole Opry. *A box-office success in its day, the 1940 film is now an invaluable resource for archivists. It includes Roy Acuff's earliest film appearance and the only extant footage of Uncle Dave Macon. Featured in this lobby card shot are Acuff on fiddle and Judge Hay at the far right.*

Another arrangement—one that worked especially well on smaller or mid-size stations—was the "P.I.," or "per inquiry," system. P.I. advertisers paid a station not at a flat rate, but by a commission for each unit of product sold by the station. The more bottles of Hamlin's Wizard Oil sold, the more the station made. It was a good system in the Depression, when sponsors were nervous about committing good flat-rate money to an unproven act or singer or product. The Monroe Brothers, Buddy Starcher, Lew Childre, Clayton McMichen, the Bailes Brothers, Blue Grass Roy, and Little Jimmy Dickens are only a few stars who at one point worked with this system; indeed, it still exists today in different forms at independent television stations and cable systems like the Nashville Network and has helped singers like Slim Whitman sell thousands of their own records. It was a system that forced entertainers and announcers to become personalities and pitchmen, and it helped define country performing style.

Some singers who liked regular radio work and who had repertoires large enough to support it, but did not care for constant touring, found a home at the so-called border stations just across the Texas-Mexico line. These stations were in fact operated by Americans (like Dr. John Brinkley, with his "goat-gland" cure for flagging sexual potency) and aimed at the American South and Southwest; they broadcasted at signal strengths two or three times the legal limit in the U.S. and drowned out any smaller stations near their wavelength. Advertisers contracted with a number of major established country groups and sent them to fly-specked towns like Del Rio, Texas, where they would go into a studio to perform and watch their signal sent across the border to the station's transmitting tower. The Carter Family tried border radio for a couple of years; June Carter later recalled that in 1938 you could hang a tin can on any barbed wire fence in Texas and hear the Carter Family. Record sales back home soared, and five thousand letters piled up at their home base in Virginia. Mainer's Mountaineers, the Pickard Family, the Delmore Brothers, and Jimmie Rodgers's cousin Jesse were other favorites of these early superstations.

For years, radio dominated country music's other mass medium, records. Many performers saw little real connection between their radio work and their record making. Radio was a livelihood; record making was an exotic novelty. Bluegrass great Bill Monroe recalls that he and his brother Charlie were well

One of the first country disc jockeys: Randy Blake of WJJD, Chicago, 1940s. His "Suppertime Frolic" show was heard in more than half of the forty-eight states, and his smooth, dignified style set a standard for country disc jockeys who followed.

The John Daniel Quartet, early 1940s. Leader John Daniel is second from left; behind him is Wally Fowler, who would go on to found the Oak Ridge Quartet, forerunner of the Oak Ridge Boys. (The youngster up front is the quartet's piano accompanist, Boyce Hawkins.) Such gospel harmony groups were considered an essential element of country radio shows.

83

Robert Lunn's claim to fame was his "Talking Blues," a comic musical monologue that had so many verses he used different parts of it on different Opry shows during the thirties and forties.

established in radio before they got around to recording: "We had two programs a day on radio, one in Greenville, South Carolina, and one on WBT, Charlotte, really early in the morning. We drove about one hundred miles from one place to another, and then we played schools at night. They kept after us to make these records, but we threw away the first several letters they wrote us. We finally went up to their studio in Charlotte, but we told 'em we didn't have much time, that we had to get back in time to play a school that night."

Record royalties were small or nonexistent: the Crowder Brothers, a well-known group earning $15 a week on radio in North Carolina, were offered a 1934 record date for the flat rate of $10 a side, with no royalties. Small wonder that there were numerous major figures in country radio who left us few or no commercial records, including Sarie and Sallie, the Opry comediennes; Robert Lunn, popularizer of the talking blues; singer and entertainer Lew Childre; duet singers Lonnie and Roy; Cowboy Slim Rinehart; banjoist Cousin Emmy; and many others. On the other hand, with the sole exceptions of Jimmie Rodgers and Vernon Dalhart, virtually no country figure of any magnitude sold records without relying on radio performances to spread the word. Records were simply not played much on radio in the early days; until a Supreme Court ruling in 1940, many broadcasters

thought commercial records were "not licensed for radio airplay," and some record companies actually fought to keep their product off the airways. Pioneer country music disc jockeys (apparently the term was coined in 1941) like Randy Blake over WJJD, Chicago, Hugh Cherry in Nashville, Nelson King at WCKY, Cincinnati, and Lee Moore at WWVA were changing all this by the late 1940s. By then record companies had even started issuing special "DJ copies" of their records, mailing them out to radio stations free of charge. The modern era of country radio and records was dawning.

Radio did far more than merely spread country music to a wider audience; it affected the very nature of the music. The new, sensitive carbon microphones of the mid-1930s changed singing styles, moving them away from the older, piercing singing of Vernon Dalhart to the quiet, modulated, intricate harmonies of the Blue Sky Boys. Subtlety and dynamics were now possible, more so even than on the cabin porches where so much of the folk music was born. The personality of the singer became important, as he had to read his mail and answer requests and fill air time with jokes, character impersonations, and poetry recitations; the classic country humor of Minnie Pearl, Rod Brasfield, Whitey Ford (The Duke of Paducah), and Hank Penny was, and is, primarily verbal humor, a legacy of its radio origins.

85

In the twilight of radio's golden years, groups like Happy Wilson's Alabama Hayloft Gang kept live country on the airwaves, even as televisions were replacing radio sets in living rooms across the country.

By 1944, when Paramount Pictures released The National Barn Dance *movie, it was not much of an exaggeration to call the WLS program "America's favorite radio show."*

Not least, the radio singer developed a closeness to his audience that also remains a hallmark of country music today; those cards and letters did come in, and those requests were answered, and dedications were made to the sick and shut-in. Bradley Kincaid spoke for a generation when he wrote in one of his little mail-order songbooks: "When I sing for you on the air, I always visualize you, a family group, sitting around the radio, listening and commenting on my program. If I did not feel your presence, though you be a thousand miles away, the radio would be cold and unresponsive to me, and I in turn would sound the same way to you."

3

NEW, IMPROVED, HOMOGENIZED: COUNTRY RADIO SINCE 1950

Edward Morris

The supposedly sedate 1950s were anything but that for American radio. The medium was taking a battering from that glamorous upstart, television, in a bid for the affections of a common audience. Radio's traditionally successful mixture of local daytime programming (including live music segments) and nighttime network shows was no match for the moving images—however tiny and indistinct—that appeared on the flickering tube.

That radio did not die but flourished is due in large part to such technological advances as improved audio fidelity and, ultimately, the development of portable, low-priced radios. But the credit for getting radio through the grim interim must be given to the pioneering programmers who were able to find something alluring to fill the broadcast hours.

Early in the history of radio, programmers had discovered the virtues of phonograph records—though live talent dominated the airwaves until the 1940s. Unlike live musicians, records were always there when one needed them, and they made no demands. Moreover, as postwar recording technology got better at capturing the real sound of professional performers, good records became more pleasing to hear than often unrehearsed or indifferently talented musicians. Still, the programmers concluded, there had to be a more effective way to select and make use of records.

Like many would-be country stars, journeyman recording artist Texas Bill Strength kept bread on the table by putting platters on turntables during the 1950s and 1960s.

Starting out as the Country Music Association's only employee (and little more than a glorified secretary at that), Jo Walker (now Jo Walker-Meador) helped to develop the Country Music Association into the music industry's most successful trade organization. Walker-Meador is now its executive director.

Broadcasting magnate Gordon McLendon is generally credited with developing the concept of Top Forty radio—that is, a pattern of repeatedly playing throughout the broadcast day the forty or so most popular records in the country, as determined by surveys of record retailers, selected radio stations, or both. But broadcaster Bill Stewart maintained that he and fellow programmer Todd Storz may have "invented" the format "about 1955" as they sat in a bar across the street from their Omaha, Nebraska, radio station: "We were sitting there and the jukebox was playing. And it kept coming up on the same song. And I can't even remember what the song was, but it was a rock 'n' roll type song. . . . The waitress went over and put a quarter in the jukebox, and . . . played the same record three times in a row—the same record we'd heard all night long. . . . I don't know whether you could say that Todd literally discovered Top Forty or whether I did or whether someone in the company did. I don't know. I know it was not Gordon McLendon, . . . because Gordon's experience with that kind of radio came after Todd's."

Stewart and Storz had learned that some people actually enjoy hearing the same songs over and over. It was a programming epiphany.

90

Regardless of who made the discovery, the something-familiar-every-time-you-tune-in concept helped save radio from the ravages of television; and it became a model of programming that country radio—indeed, popular music in general—still follows.

But if radio generally was suffering in the 1950s, country radio was in particularly bad shape. Around the middle of the decade, rock 'n' roll was becoming the big musical news, and that bustling young sound was nudging country music out of the radio crevices it had long occupied. In 1958, the Country Music Association was chartered, built on the skeletal remains and treasury of the Country Music Disc Jockey Association, which had gone defunct a few months earlier after only four years of existence.

Gaining a place for country music on radio was one of the first aims of the CMA—and it remains one of the organization's prime concerns. Harry Stone, a veteran of WSM in Nashville, was the CMA's first executive director, but there were so few resources for the fledgling organization that Stone soon relinquished the post to Jo Walker (now Jo Walker-Meador).

The task of spreading country music into radio was a Herculean one. To convince radio stations to give country music a try, the CMA undertook some basic, but systematic, studies of the

To convince advertisers that country radio could sell their products, the CMA staged lavish dinner presentations. It worked: the number of country stations rose dramatically, from 81 in 1961 to 606 in 1969.

CMA board, November 1960. Seated: Steve Sholes, Wesley Rose, Connie B. Gay, W. D. Kilpatrick, Cindy Walker, Pee Wee King, Cracker Jim Brooker. Standing: Len Ellis, Joe Lucus, Paul Ackerman, Ken Nelson, Don Pierce, Jim Denny, Mac Wiseman, Harold Moon.

In the days when disc jockeys actually chose what records they would play, some folks would stop at nothing to get their attention. In November 1955, Opry star Hank Snow welcomed DJs to their annual Nashville convention with this unforgettable promotion.

market potential. As Walker-Meador explains it: "We subscribed to *Broadcasting* magazine and got their yearbook and *Standard Rate & Data* and began to contact stations. . . . We looked at their ratings and everything else we could come up with and began going after certain stations. In order to help these stations sell their time, we did major sales presentations—two in New York, one in Chicago, one in Detroit, one in Toronto, and one in L.A. We started [in New York] in May of '63. Joe Allison wrote and produced the first show, and Tex Ritter hosted it. We had live entertainment. RCA recorded the show, CBS pressed it, and Capitol packaged it. And we sent one of these albums to each person who had attended the show."

The CMA's aim throughout the series of sales presentations was to convince advertisers and their representatives that country music radio could sell products. To a great degree, the history of the CMA has been the fleshing out of this theme, whether applying it to radio and television, concert halls, or record stores.

According to Walker-Meador, the presentations and follow-ups worked so well that the CMA was finally able to abandon them: "Every once in a while, stations would call us and say that this client or this person or this agency was opposed to country, and we would send a team in with a presentation. These teams did some really good jobs of turning around broadcasters. It sort of mushroomed, and then we just kind of pulled out of doing much of anything like that, because there was really not that much need for it. Particularly, there was no need to try to influence more stations to go country. Sometimes there'd be two or three country stations in the same market, and we'd have the original guys [we helped] saying, 'Hey, you've overkilled. We don't want all this competition.' "

The CMA made its first tabulation of country music radio stations in 1961 and found that there were 81 playing the music full-time. By 1969, this number had risen to 606. It was an impressive and hard-earned gain, but it was only a small fraction of the expansion yet to come.

It is difficult to gauge the importance of disc jockeys in the perseverance and triumph of country radio, especially since DJs long ago lost the right to select the records they play. Those decisions are now left to staff program or music directors or to outside consultants. Radio no longer relies on DJ hunches and preferences. The movie *Coal Miner's Daughter* depicts a youthful and earnest Loretta Lynn taking her records from one disc jockey to another until she had cultivated enough airplay to have a national hit. That was true—but that was 1960. Were she to try that approach in today's play-it-safe radio scene, she would

The Voice of the Opry: Grant Turner came to Nashville's WSM in 1944 after several other radio jobs. His easy-going manner helped convey the Opry's folksy atmosphere.

"Smilin' " Eddie Hill: one of many disc jockeys from country radio's Golden Era who doubled as country singers. Hill worked at stations in Knoxville, Chattanooga, and Memphis before becoming a well-known figure on Nashville television and radio.

Trucker's best friend: Charlie Douglas of WWL, New Orleans, was one of several disc jockeys specializing in late-night programs for truckers. His long-running "Road Gang" show established a bond of such strength between him and the gentlemen of the road that he served as a truckers' liaison during a strike in 1972. Since 1983 he has headed Opryland's Music Country Radio Network.

Charlie Walker worked with Bill Boyd's Cowboy Ramblers in the 1940s before becoming a well-known San Antonio disc jockey. His fortunes as a performer revived when his friend Ray Price passed along a honky-tonk song Harlan Howard had written for him. "Pick Me Up On Your Way Down" became a #2 hit for Walker in 1958.

Cliffie Stone, 1950s: Capitol recording artist and producer, TV producer, and popular air personality in Southern California.

be an old woman by the time she got past her first receptionist, and when she did, she would encounter a helpless disc jockey, working from a playlist harder to amend than the Constitution.

For years, beginning in the 1950s, the Nashville record industry toasted disc jockeys in a yearly autumn bacchanal that came to be known as "DJ Week." As the programming significance of the DJ declined, the direction of the record companies' affections changed. Now the focus is on courting radio station general managers, program directors, and music directors. The vehicle for this courtship nowadays—and for the past several years—is the Country Radio Seminar held in Nashville in late February or early March.

DJs were undeniably influential in the early days of country radio. Some, such as Cracker Jim Brooker and Smokey Smith, worked both as disc jockeys and as country music show promoters, in addition to lending their counsel and weight to the young CMA. Wayne Raney, Bob Jennings, Lee Moore, and Sleepy Jeffers—to cite four among dozens—doubled as performers and recording artists. Other jocks, including Lowell Blanchard and Ralph Emery, were noted discoverers of major country music talents. Top country stations were able to attract and hold legendary DJs. In 1964, for example, KFOX, in Long Beach, California, boasted a staff of such luminaries as Biff Collie, folk music scholar Hugh Cherry, musician and producer Cliffie Stone, Joe Allison, Dick Haynes, Lee Ross, and Squeakin' Deacon Moore—all at one time.

There were only a few women DJs in country music during the late fifties and early sixties, but CMA pioneer and broadcasting mogul Connie B. Gay managed to stock an entire station with them. His deliberately named station, WYFE, in New Orleans, had an "all-girl" DJ staff in 1959, consisting of Jeanne Reynard, Roberta Mould, and Sylvia Holmes, all of whom had had radio experience by the time they gave themselves over to this quirky promotion.

In spite of the erosion of DJ programming power, there are a number of hardy influentials still around, among them WSM's gentle-voiced Grant Turner, now enshrined in the Country Music Hall of Fame; Charlie Douglas, once the truck driver's delight and now the presiding spirit of the satellite-carried nightly show, "Music Country Radio Network"; singer Billy Parker of KVOO, Tulsa; the much-syndicated Lee Arnold, of "On a Country Road"; and Bob Kingsley, "American Country Countdown."

Stations that agreed to "go country" (at a time when precious few had) often complained that they couldn't get enough records to play. In 1964, Chris Lane, program director of KAYO, Seattle, charged in an open letter to the CMA's *Close Up* magazine that record company promotion was practically "non-existent." This drew a response from Tommy Wiggins, publisher of the *DJ's Digest*, that low country record sales made supplying records to all country stations impossible. The following year, the CMA announced its willingness to intervene with labels on behalf of the stations in an attempt to get better service. It also offered to act as a public relations conduit between radio stations and the major music and trade publications.

During the late sixties and early seventies, many stations announced their preference for "modern country" or "countrypolitan" programming. KBBQ, Los Angeles, described its "Sizzlin' Sixty" playlist as "the best of the modern-country music by top name performers, many from the pop field . . . augmented by a supplementary list of more of the best country sounds." WZIP, Cincinnati, WTCR, Ashland, Kentucky, WSLR, Akron, WCJW, Cleveland, and KSON, San Diego, all reported to the CMA their preference for modern country—as did KRAM, Las Vegas, WROL, Knoxville, and WVOJ, Jacksonville, Florida.

WWVA, home of the fabled "Wheeling Jamboree" barn dance, took pains to correct a profile *Close Up* had published by stressing that the "Jamboree" did *not* program any "mountain and hillbilly music." In 1970, Nashville's WKDA proclaimed that it was switching to a modern country format, presumably one with a minimum of fiddles and steel and a maximum of strings and lush background vocals.

Not every station, of course, was limiting itself to the mellow voices of Sonny James, Eddy Arnold, Ray Price, and Charley Pride. During the 1960s and 1970s the earthier Buck Owens, Merle Haggard, Tammy Wynette, and Conway Twitty were also

Biff Collie was an up-and-coming DJ and promoter in Houston when this photo was taken in the 1950s. He later worked in Los Angeles and more recently has hosted a syndicated country radio show out of Nashville.

Carl "Squeakin' Deacon" Moore, DJ at KXLA, Pasadena, and recording artist for 4-Star, 1950s.

95

WHAT HAPPENED TO THE BARN DANCE RADIO SHOWS?

Not all barn dances withered with the emergence of television. Springfield, Missouri's "Ozark Jubilee" began on the ABC radio network in 1954 and became a television show the following year. Here host Red Foley hits a high, hard one for the folks at home.

During the prosperous decade following World War II, radio barn dance shows flourished as never before. In 1955, weekly barn dance broadcasts were thriving in many major cities and in locations as far-flung as Minneapolis, Dallas, Los Angeles, and Knoxville. Within ten years, however, most of these country variety shows were gone, and with them hundreds of daily early morning country programs. The heyday of live country radio was over.

It's tempting to blame rock 'n' roll for the demise of the radio barn dance, but this explanation is too simple. Much more than rock 'n' roll, urbanization, and the rise of television sealed the fate of the barn dance. As Americans increasingly migrated from country to city, broadcasting and advertising executives became more and more uncomfortable with the hayseed images most barn dances projected.

Meanwhile, television undercut live country radio by capturing an ever larger share of the nation's nighttime entertainment audience. In response, radio stations dropped variety programming and adopted specialized formats such as Top 40 pop, Easy Listening, and AOR (album-oriented rock); country music sometimes got lost in the shuffle. In addition, an increasingly competitive environment forced many sta-

tions to rely on disc jockey programs instead of expensive live talent. Advertisers soon shifted their sights from rural radio listeners to urban TV viewers, and one by one, network radio barn dances folded.

For a time, some radio barn dances adapted well to television. For example, Cincinnati's "Midwestern Hayride" began local TV broadcasting in 1948 and became a network summer replacement show in the 1950s. Syndications of this program ran until 1972. ABC-TV aired Springfield, Missouri's "Ozark Jubilee" for most of the 1955–60 period. Syndications such as Connie B. Gay's "Town and Country Time" and Al Gannaway's "Stars of the Grand Ole Opry" both used traditional barn dance sets and featured plenty of old-time music and rube comedy.

Overall, though, country television broadcasting largely abandoned barn dance formats in favor of approaches similar to those used on contemporary pop variety shows. The most successful country TV shows of the fifties and sixties were hosted by broadly popular stars such as Eddy Arnold, Jimmy Dean, Glen Campbell, and Johnny Cash, whose programs included both country and non-country performers. Since then, most country TV programming has consisted of specials and award shows that bear little, if any, relationship to the barn dance of yesteryear.

Nevertheless, the barn dance tradition has not completely disappeared. As a stage show, the Grand Ole Opry now draws more fans than at any time in its history, and cable TV's Nashville Network has carried a half-hour of the program since 1985. Smaller barn dances also survive at Renfro Valley, Kentucky, and Wheeling, West Virginia. "Hee Haw," which began as a network TV show in 1969 and now continues in syndication, relies heavily on barn dance formulas, even though it is less a barn dance than a countrified version of the late-1960s "Rowan & Martin's Laugh-In" series. There's no denying that the barn dance's glory days have long since passed, but country music will probably feel the barn dance's influence for a long time to come.

During the thirties and forties, radio barn dances thrived in many of America's larger cities. The "Hayride" (seen here during a 1945 broadcast) made the transition to television, but most barn dances didn't.

97

recording hits. In a headlong plunge into eclecticism, KCMO, Kansas City, jumped from a "soft" middle-of-the-road format in 1970 to one that embraced folk-rock and country and combined James Taylor, the Nitty Gritty Dirt Band, Carly Simon, Johnny Cash, Merle Haggard, and Lynn Anderson on the same playlist.

Playlists, by the way, were still relatively long throughout this stretch of broadcast history, with lists of fifty or sixty titles or more being fairly common. Overall, though, the trend was toward programming pop-sounding countrypolitan music, and in spite of the fairly long playlists, many of the older, more traditional artists found themselves shut out.

As country music found a home at more and more radio stations, increasing numbers of young disc jockeys and (more importantly) young program directors found themselves having to play country music records—when they had grown up on rock 'n' roll! Little wonder, then, that they let old twangers like Ernest

The Big Apple's first hillbilly disc jockey was singing cowgirl Rosalie Allen, who recorded for RCA Victor, solo, and with Elton Britt, from 1946 to 1953.

Tubb and Hank Snow fall by the wayside, while embracing art-ists who gave country a pop sheen.

Entertainment trade magazines—*Billboard*, at first, and later *Cashbox*, *Record World*, and *Radio & Records*—had an inordi-nate influence on what country radio played and how much. Basically, then as now, the smaller stations used the trades' popularity charts to determine which records to add to their playlists. The trades, in turn, compiled their charts by polling a cross-section of their designated "reporting stations" to see what songs they were playing and which ones were being played most often.

Billboard is the veteran chart maker and still one of the most influential. Beginning in 1944, the magazine compiled its first weekly country record chart, which listed records that were played the most on jukeboxes. In 1948, the magazine published for the first time a Top Fifteen "Best Selling Retail Folk Rec-ords" chart. The following year, *Billboard* began a separate

Nelson King of WCKY, Cincinnati, consistently topped Billboard's "Favorite Disc Jockey" polls during the late 1940s and early 1950s. Many acts like young Eddy Arnold here stopped by King's show for a live interview when they came to town.

99

chart to keep track of country radio airplay as well, and the magazine replaced the term *folk* with *country & western*. The current designation of "Hot Country Singles" came into play in 1962, and for the next twenty-five years the chart reflected the combined influence of radio airplay and retail sales more or less equally. Since January 1987, however, the "Hot Country Singles" chart has been based on radio airplay only: its list of one hundred songs is, to quote *Billboard*, "compiled from a national sample of radio playlists."

While the charts have been a commercial blessing to radio stations, record companies, record promoters and—not the least —to the trade magazines themselves, they have had a homogenizing effect on the music they purport to monitor. There are several reasons for this.

By offering a list of records that are said to be the most popular in the nation at a given time, the trades relieve programmers of having to listen to *all* the records that come to them and thus making their playlist choices with their own ears. Naturally enough, this leads to a sameness of sound from one station to another; regional distinctions are erased. Worse still, by pro-

Ralph Emery began at Nashville's WSM doing live interviews with artists before their Opry performances. Emery's guest for WSM's "Opry Star Spotlight" on November 7, 1960, was up-and-comer Buck Owens, who made an Opry appearance the following night.

Nashville broadcasting personality Ralph Emery carried on the tradition of transcription radio and of personality interviews with his syndicated "Ralph Emery Show," which aired from 1971 to 1985; Rodney Crowell and his wife Rosanne Cash chat with Emery.

gramming according to national standards, radio stations stifle the growth of local talent. It is almost impossible these days to get a record on the radio unless it comes from a major label, i.e., one of the international corporate entertainment conglomerates —CBS, RCA, MCA, Warner Brothers, Capitol-EMI, PolyGram.

The trades undermine the charts' potential validity by revealing to record labels, promoters—indeed, to almost anyone who wants to know—the identity of the reporting stations. Moreover, the trades take the reporting stations' word that they are actually playing what they say they're playing. This method of sampling and reporting lends itself to all manner of chicanery. In knowing which stations to target, the record labels can persuade and pressure the programmers to play a particular record (or, at least, report that they are playing it), even if it has no musical merit or local listener support. What the record labels gain from this immediately is a valuable publicity device—one that enables them to boast, "We're Top Ten" or "We're #1." And, of course, the labels save themselves an enormous amount of money by having to provide free records only to reporting stations instead of giving discs to every country station that might use them. For their part, the stations clamor to be reporters, knowing that such status will assure them of free record service from the labels, as well as other kinds of psychological and material tribute that supplicants pay to the mighty.

The charts have given rise to that most egregious of creatures, the professional record promoter. Stripped to its essentials, a promoter's job is to telephone station programmers and try to convince them to add particular records to their playlists. Why

HOW THE RECORD CHARTS WORK

A country record's success is measured by how high it climbs on charts compiled by music industry trade magazines like *Billboard, Radio & Records, The Gavin Report,* and *Cashbox. Billboard*'s "Hot Country Singles" chart derives its rankings from a complex process that involves polling 148 country radio stations, called "reporting stations," regarding the records on their weekly playlists. Like the rest of the trades, *Billboard* chooses its reporting stations according to market size (the number of listeners reached by a station's signal), ratings of the station in the market, length of the playlist, and how the playlist is prepared.

On Wednesday and Thursday of each week, *Billboard* checks in with reporting stations for an update on playlist activity. Sales reports from retail outlets do not figure in the "Hot Country Singles" chart, since *Billboard* assumes—rightly or wrongly—that local radio playlists reflect local sales activity. After polling all of its reporting stations, *Billboard* compiles the information in a national chart made available each Monday through the Billboard Information Network, an online computer service. The chart is also published in the next issue of the magazine.

Billboard arrives at a record's position on its national chart by using a formula that multiplies "weight" times "points." Weight is assigned according to the market size of reporting stations. Major market stations (more than 250,000 potential listeners) carry a weight of 2.0, medium markets (100,000 to 249,999) carry 1.5, small markets (50,000 to 99,999) get a 1.0, and the smallest markets (under 50,000) get a .5 weight.

A record's position on the playlist at a reporting station determines its point total for that reporting station. At any position below #40, the record gets *5 points x weight* of the reporting station. At #40, 35, 30, 25, and 20 the record receives an additional *1 point x weight*. From #20 to #1, a point is added at every even number, with a #1 record earning *20 points x weight*.

To take an example: if hypothetical radio station WWWW, in Big Metropolis, New York (market over 250,000), reports that the new George Jones single is at #17 on their playlist, the record's point tally would be:

2.0 (market weight) x (5 + 1 [#40] + 1 [#35] + 1 [#30] + 1 [#25] + 1 [#20] + 1 [#18]) = 2 x 11 = 22 points.

As the record moves up the reporting stations' playlists from week to week, it will accumulate more points. To appear on *Billboard*'s charts, a record must register a minimum total of 75 points from any combined tally of reporting stations. An average of seven or eight new records are added to the chart each week.

If a record's point total increases significantly each week, the record earns a "bullet," representing fast upward movement. As the record climbs higher, larger point total increases are required to retain the bullet. For example, a record at #40 must increase its point total by 120 over the previous week to earn or keep a bullet. A record at #9 needs a 200 point jump to retain a bullet. Once a record loses its bullet, it usually begins to descend on the charts.

Record companies do all they can to help a record up the charts. The major labels have their own in-house promotion teams and a network of regional representatives, but as a record climbs higher and the competition grows more intense, the majors frequently hire the services of independent promoters who bombard station program directors with phone calls clamoring for lofty positions for their clients' latest records. The irony in all this scrambling for position on the "Hot Country Singles" chart is that the rankings do not translate directly into record sales. The country single does not generate profits. However, a #1 ranking—the brass ring on this chart-watching merry-go-round—does draw attention to an artist, and the attention encourages album sales, the primary source of record company income.

Billboard® HOT COUNTRY SINGLES™

Compiled from a national sample of radio playlists.

THIS WEEK	LAST WEEK	2 WKS AGO	WKS. ON CHART	TITLE PRODUCER (SONGWRITER)	ARTIST LABEL & NUMBER/DISTRIBUTING LABEL
				★★ **No. 1** ★★ 1 week at No. One	
(1)	2	3	14	**TENNESSEE FLAT TOP BOX** R.CROWELL (J.CASH)	◆ ROSANNE CASH COLUMBIA 38-07624
2	3	4	16	**ONE STEP FORWARD** P.WORLEY (C.HILLMAN, B.WILDES)	THE DESERT ROSE BAND MCA/CURB 53201/MCA
(3)	4	9	13	**TWINKLE, TWINKLE LUCKY STAR** K.SUESOV,M.HAGGARD (M.HAGGARD)	MERLE HAGGARD EPIC 34-07631
(4)	6	11	13	**I WON'T TAKE LESS THAN YOUR LOVE** J.CRUTCHFIELD (P.OVERSTREET, D.SCHLITZ)	TANYA TUCKER WITH P. DAVIS & P. OVERSTREET CAPITOL 44100
(5)	8	14	11	**FACE TO FACE** H.SHEDD,ALABAMA (R.OWEN)	ALABAMA RCA 5328-7
6	7	12	14	**PLEASE PLEASE BABY** P.ANDERSON (D.YOAKAM)	DWIGHT YOAKAM REPRISE 7-28174/WARNER BROS.
(7)	10	17	10	**TOO GONE TOO LONG** K.LEHNING (G.PISTILLI)	RANDY TRAVIS WARNER BROS. 7-28286
8	9	13	15	**SURE THING** B.LLOYD,R.FOSTER (R.FOSTER, B.LLOYD)	FOSTER AND LLOYD RCA 5281-7
(9)	12	16	14	**OH WHAT A LOVE** M.MORGAN,P.WORLEY (J.IBBOTSON)	NITTY GRITTY DIRT BAND WARNER BROS. 7-28173
(10)	11	15	15	**DO YOU BELIEVE ME NOW** B.MONTGOMERY (V.GOSDIN, M.D.BARNES)	VERN GOSDIN COLUMBIA 38-07627
(11)	13	20	14	**THAT'S MY JOB** J.BOWEN (G.BURR)	CONWAY TWITTY MCA 53200
(12)	15	21	14	**TELL ME TRUE** R.LANDIS (B.MAHER, P.KENNERLEY)	JUICE NEWTON RCA 5283-7
(13)	16	22	13	**I'M GONNA MISS YOU, GIRL** S.GIBSON,J.E.NORMAN (J.WINCHESTER)	MICHAEL MARTIN MURPHEY WARNER BROS. 7-28168
(14)	17	23	11	**THIS MISSIN' YOU HEART OF MINE** R.CHANCEY (W.MULLIS, M.GEIGER)	SAWYER BROWN CAPITOL/CURB 44108/CAPITOL
15	5	8	16	**LYIN' IN HIS ARMS AGAIN** J.L.WALLACE,T.SKINNER (T.SKINNER, J.L.WALLACE)	THE FORESTER SISTERS WARNER BROS. 7-28208
16	18	24	14	**SOME OLD SIDE ROAD** B.MEVIS (R.FERRIS)	KEITH WHITLEY RCA 5326-7
17	1	2	16	**WHEELS** T.DUBOIS,S.HENDRICKS,RESTLESS HEART (D.LOGGINS)	RESTLESS HEART RCA 5280-7
(18)	21	27	6	**LIFE TURNED HER THAT WAY** S.BUCKINGHAM (H.HOWARD)	◆ RICKY VAN SHELTON COLUMBIA 38-07672
(19)	25	34	5	**TURN IT LOOSE** B.MAHER (D.SCHLITZ, C.BICKHARDT, B.MAHER)	THE JUDDS RCA/CURB 5329-7/RCA
(20)	23	28	10	**SHOULDN'T IT BE EASIER THAN THIS** J.BRADLEY (J.JARRARD, R.GILES)	CHARLEY PRIDE 16TH AVENUE 70408/CAPITOL
(21)	26	32	8	**TOUCH AND GO CRAZY** J.BOWEN,L.GREENWOOD (M.GARVIN, T.SHAPIRO, B.JONES)	LEE GREENWOOD MCA 53234
(22)	27	29	11	**TALKIN' TO MYSELF AGAIN** S.BUCKINGHAM (J.O'HARA)	TAMMY WYNETTE EPIC 34-07635
23	29	30	11	**SOMEWHERE BETWEEN RAGGED AND RIGHT** J.BOWEN,J.ANDERSON (W.JENNINGS, R.MURRAH)	JOHN ANDERSON MCA 53226
24	24	26	12	**THIS OLD HOUSE** J.STROUD (T.SCHUYLER, C.BICKHARDT)	◆ S-K-B MTM 72100/CAPITOL
(25)	35	38	4	**LOVE WILL FIND ITS WAY TO YOU** J.BOWEN,R.MCENTIRE (D.LOGGINS, J.D.MARTIN)	REBA MCENTIRE MCA 53244
26	28	31	9	**THE BIRD** B.SHERRILL (A.L.OWENS, D.KNUTSON)	GEORGE JONES EPIC 34-07655
(27)	31	35	9	**WILDER DAYS** K.LEHNING,P.DAVIS (C.BICKHARDT, M.BONAGURA)	BAILLIE AND THE BOYS RCA 5327-7
(28)	32	33	11	**LOUISIANA RAIN** B.BECKETT (R.ALVES, R.MURRAH)	JOHN WESLEY RYLES WARNER BROS. 7-28228
(29)	34	37	5	**I WANNA DANCE WITH YOU** R.LANDIS (E.RABBITT, B.J.WALKER,JR.)	EDDIE RABBITT RCA 5238-7
(30)	33	36	10	**I DIDN'T (EVERY CHANCE I HAD)** T.COLLINS (B.P.BARKER, K.PALMER)	JOHNNY RODRIGUEZ CAPITOL 44071
(31)	37	40	6	**SANTA FE** E.GORDY,JR. (D.BELLAMY, R.TAYLOR)	◆ THE BELLAMY BROTHERS MCA/CURB 53222/MCA
(32)	38	42	8	**IT'S ONLY MAKE BELIEVE** R.MCDOWELL (C.TWITTY, J.NANCE)	RONNIE MCDOWELL CURB 10501/MCA
				★★★ **POWER PICK/AIRPLAY** ★★★	
(33)	46	—	2	**FAMOUS LAST WORDS OF A FOOL** J.BOWEN,G.STRAIT (D.DILLON, R.HUSTON)	GEORGE STRAIT MCA 53248
(34)	42	47	5	**TIMELESS AND TRUE LOVE** P.WORLEY (C.BLACK, A.ROBERTS, B.CASON)	THE MCCARTERS WARNER BROS. 7-28125
35	19	5	18	**I'LL PIN A NOTE ON YOUR PILLOW** N.LARKIN (C.BERZAS, D.GOODMAN, N.LARKIN)	◆ BILLY JOE ROYAL ATLANTIC AMERICA 7-99404/ATLANTIC
(36)	40	41	10	**STOP THE RAIN** R.HALL,R.BYRNE (W.HOLYFIELD, R.LEIGH)	SHENANDOAH COLUMBIA 38-07654
37	14	1	18	**GOIN' GONE** A.REYNOLDS (P.ALGER, B.DALE, F.KOLLER)	KATHY MATTEA MERCURY 888 874-7/POLYGRAM
38	39	43	6	**SIX DAYS ON THE ROAD** S.EARLE,T.BROWN (E.GREEN, C.MONTGOMERY)	◆ STEVE EARLE & THE DUKES MCA/HUGHES 53249/MCA
39	20	10	17	**I WOULDN'T BE A MAN** D.WILLIAMS,G.FUNDIS (R.M.BOURKE, M.REID)	DON WILLIAMS CAPITOL 44066
(40)	45	49	6	**A LITTLE BIT CLOSER** J.CRUTCHFIELD (KENNEDY, ROSE, SCHUYLER)	◆ TOM WOPAT EMI-MANHATTAN 50112
(41)	49	54	4	**IT'S SUCH A SMALL WORLD** T.BROWN (R.CROWELL)	RODNEY CROWELL AND ROSANNE CASH COLUMBIA 38-07693
(42)	48	51	5	**STRANGERS AGAIN** T.WEST (H.DUNN, C.WATERS)	◆ HOLLY DUNN MTM 72093/CAPITOL
(43)	52	81	3	**I'LL ALWAYS COME BACK** H.SHEDD (K.T.OSLIN)	◆ K.T. OSLIN RCA 5330-7
44	44	48	9	**ROSES IN DECEMBER** R.BAKER (L.BOONE, P.NELSON)	LARRY BOONE MERCURY 870 086-7/POLYGRAM
(45)	47	52	4	**THE LAST RESORT** B.LOGAN (BROWN, BOUTON, BURCH)	T. GRAHAM BROWN CAPITOL 44125
46	30	7	18	**JUST LOVIN' YOU** K.KANE,J.O'HARA (J.O'HARA, K.KANE)	THE O'KANES COLUMBIA 38-07611
(47)	51	53	4	**IF OLE HANK COULD ONLY SEE US NOW** J.BOWEN,W.JENNINGS (W.JENNINGS, R.MURRAH)	WAYLON JENNINGS MCA 53243
(48)	53	59	3	**EVERYBODY'S SWEETHEART** R.LANDIS (V.GILL)	VINCE GILL RCA 5331-7
				★★★ **HOT SHOT DEBUT** ★★★	
(49)	NEW▶		1	**CRY, CRY, CRY** P.WORLEY (J.S.SHERRILL, D.DEVANEY)	◆ HIGHWAY 101 WARNER BROS. 7-28105
50	36	18	16	**I WANT A LOVE LIKE THAT** T.WEST (T.SCHUYLER, J.IAN)	JUDY RODMAN MTM 72092/CAPITOL
51	22	6	18	**CRYING SHAME** B.MAHER (M.JOHNSON, D.SCHLITZ, B.MAHER)	MICHAEL JOHNSON RCA 5279-7
(52)	56	58	5	**YOU JUST WATCH ME** H.SHEDD (R.GILES, B.REGAN)	LIBBY HURLEY EPIC 34-07650
(53)	57	78	3	**AMERICANA** J.KENNEDY (L.ALDERMAN, R.FAGAN, P.RYAN)	MOE BANDY CURB 10504/MCA
(54)	60	72	3	**SHE'S NO LADY** T.BROWN,L.LOVETT,B.WILLIAMS (L.LOVETT)	◆ LYLE LOVETT MCA/CURB 53246/MCA
(55)	59	68	3	**I TAUGHT HER EVERYTHING SHE KNOWS ABOUT LOVE** W.ALDRIDGE (W.ALDRIDGE, T.GENTRY, G.FOWLER, J.JARRARD)	THE SHOOTERS EPIC 34-07684
(56)	61	67	3	**IT GOES WITHOUT SAYING** J.RUTENSCHROER,T.MALCHAK (L.PALAS, J.JARRARD, M.SANDERS)	TIM MALCHAK ALPINE 008
(57)	NEW▶		1	**I'M GONNA GET YOU** B.BECKETT (D.LINDE)	EDDY RAVEN RCA 6831
58	58	64	4	**UNATTENDED FIRE** R.WILKERSON (R.BAILEY, R.FRENCH)	RAZZY BAILEY SOA 002
59	41	19	17	**WHERE DO THE NIGHTS GO** R.MILSAP,R.GALBRAITH,K.LEHNING (M.REID, R.M.BOURKE)	RONNIE MILSAP RCA 5259-7
60	43	25	18	**ONE FRIEND** K.LEHNING (D.SEALS)	DAN SEALS CAPITOL 44077
(61)	69	—	2	**IF MY HEART HAD WINDOWS** E.GORDY,JR.,T.BROWN (D.FRAZIER)	PATTY LOVELESS MCA 53270
62	55	45	19	**I CAN'T GET CLOSE ENOUGH** E.SCHEINER (S.LEMAIRE, J.P.PENNINGTON)	◆ EXILE EPIC 34-07597
(63)	71	—	2	**OVERDUE** T.BRASFIELD (T.BRASFIELD, R.BYRNE, R.BOWLES)	CANYON 16TH AVENUE 70410/CAPITOL
64	54	39	20	**STILL WITHIN THE SOUND OF MY VOICE** J.BOWEN,G.CAMPBELL (J.WEBB)	GLEN CAMPBELL MCA 53172
(65)	73	—	2	**STILL I STAY** D.MORGAN,S.DAVIS (M.P.HEENEY, P.MCMANUS)	CHARLY MCCLAIN EPIC 34-07670
(66)	74	—	2	**AFTER LAST NIGHT'S STORM** M.LLOYD (J.C.KELLY)	RIDE THE RIVER ADVANTAGE 189
(67)	NEW▶		1	**RIDE THIS TRAIN** J.KENNEDY (T.WALKER)	MEL MCDANIEL CAPITOL 44127
68	63	56	23	**DO YA'** H.SHEDD (K.T.OSLIN)	K.T. OSLIN RCA 5239-7
(69)	80	—	2	**THANKS FOR LEAVIN' HIM (FOR ME)** M.DANIELS (P.MCCULLA, J.GOODWIN)	PAULA MCCULLA RIVERMARK 1001/NORTHPORT GROUP
(70)	NEW▶		1	**ALL OF THIS & MORE** J.E.NORMAN (B.FOSTER, J.KIMBALL, G.PRESTOPINO)	CRYSTAL GAYLE WARNER BROS. 7-28106
71	70	74	4	**SAD CLICHES** D.JOHNSON (B.BUIE, R.HAMMOND)	ATLANTA SOUTHERN TRACKS 1091
72	72	86	3	**I OWE, I OWE (IT'S OFF TO WORK I GO)** J.FORD,B.FISHER,D.CHAMBERLAIN (D.CHAMBERLAIN, M.SHERRILL)	DAVID CHAMBERLAIN COUNTRY INTERNATIONAL 214
73	68	55	11	**CRYING (FROM THE "HIDING OUT" SOUNDTRACK)** P.ANDERSON,D.WAS,D.WAS (R.ORBISON, J.MELSON)	◆ ROY ORBISON & K.D. LANG VIRGIN 7-99388
74	62	50	19	**HEAVEN CAN'T BE FOUND** B.BECKETT,H.WILLIAMS,JR.,J.E.NORMAN (H.WILLIAMS,JR.)	HANK WILLIAMS, JR. WARNER/CURB 7-28227/WARNER BROS.
75	81	—	2	**DON'T FORGET YOUR WAY HOME** P.WAGONER (E.HUNNICUTT, J.R.BRANNEN)	MELISSA KAY REED 115
76	50	46	10	**BAD DAY FOR A BREAK UP** F.KELLY (F.KELLY, R.BARLOW)	CALI MCCORD GAZELLE 011/ARTS
77	65	44	17	**ONLY LOVE CAN SAVE ME NOW** J.E.NORMAN (B.JONES, C.WATERS, T.SHAPIRO)	CRYSTAL GAYLE WARNER BROS. 7-28209
(78)	NEW▶		1	**YOU ARE MY ANGEL** B.BARTON (D.BYRAM)	BILLY PARKER CANYON CREEK 1208
79	66	57	21	**SOMEWHERE TONIGHT** P.WORLEY (H.HOWARD, R.CROWELL)	HIGHWAY 101 WARNER BROS. 7-28223
80	78	76	12	**COME ON JOE** R.BENNETT,B.HALVERSON (T.ROMEO)	JO-EL SONNIER RCA 5282-7
(81)	NEW▶		1	**YOUNGER MAN, OLDER WOMAN** R.ROSE,G.ROSE (R.ROSE, G.ROSE)	RICHARD AND GARY ROSE CAPITOL 44118
82	67	63	6	**BE SERIOUS** B.KILLEN (C.CURRY, R.LAYNE)	DONNA MEADE MERCURY 888 993-7/POLYGRAM
83	77	60	6	**WHEN WE'RE TOGETHER (LOVE'S SO STRONG)** G.CHAPMAN,B.BANNISTER,M.WRIGHT (M.WRIGHT, A.SKY, G.CHAPMAN)	◆ GARY CHAPMAN RCA 5285-7
84	79	73	21	**THOSE MEMORIES OF YOU** G.MASSENBURG (A.O'BRYANT)	◆ DOLLY PARTON, LINDA RONSTADT, EMMYLOU HARRIS WARNER BROS. 7-28248
(85)	NEW▶		1	**HERE COMES THE NIGHT** A.KITCHEN,B.VAUGHN (V.GOSSETT, R.GOSSETT)	DOLLY HARTT KASS 1015
86	86	84	10	**BACK IN BABY'S ARMS** J.BOWEN,E.HARRIS (B.MONTGOMERY)	EMMYLOU HARRIS MCA/HUGHES 53236/MCA
87	84	61	19	**I PREFER THE MOONLIGHT** B.BANNISTER (G.CHAPMAN, M.WRIGHT)	KENNY ROGERS RCA 5258-7
88	76	80	3	**RICHER NOW WITH YOU** C.FIELDS (R.J.CANNON)	NINA WYATT CHARTA 207
89	87	70	18	**I'M TIRED** R.SKAGGS (M.TILLIS, A.R.PEDDY, R.PRICE)	RICKY SKAGGS EPIC 34-07416
90	89	83	10	**CATCH 22** N.LARKIN (D.HOLT, N.GELIN)	DARRELL HOLT ANOKA 222
91	83	71	24	**ONE FOR THE MONEY** R.HALL (B.MOORE, M.WILLIAMS)	T.G. SHEPPARD COLUMBIA 38-07312
92	91	79	6	**BLOWIN' LIKE A BANDIT** R.BENSON (G.CLARK)	ASLEEP AT THE WHEEL EPIC 34-07659
93	90	69	22	**THE LAST ONE TO KNOW** J.BOWEN,R.MCENTIRE (M.BERG, J.MARIASH)	◆ REBA MCENTIRE MCA 53159
94	92	90	11	**SURE FEELS GOOD** T.COLLINS (C.WHITSETT, F.KNIGHT)	BARBARA MANDRELL EMI-AMERICA 50102/CAPITOL
95	88	62	8	**DON'T START THE FIRE** J.MORRIS (T.ROCCO, T.SKINNER, J.L.WALLACE)	MARCIA LYNN EVERGREEN 1063
96	95	93	25	**ONLY WHEN I LOVE** T.WEST (H.DUNN, C.WATERS, T.SHAPIRO)	HOLLY DUNN MTM 72091/CAPITOL
97	82	85	3	**MACON GEORGIA LOVE** B.GREEN (R.SUMMERVILLE)	BILLY MATA BGM 92087
98	98	96	21	**GOOD GOD, I HAD IT GOOD** M.WRIGHT (M.WRIGHT, R.NIELSEN)	PAKE MCENTIRE RCA 5256-7
99	75	77	4	**DANCE FOR ME** J.CARROLL (D.HENSON, B.JOHNSON)	DON MALENA MAXIMA 1311
100	64	65	5	**I WISH WE WERE STRANGERS** E.WINFREY (B.RICE, S.RICE)	OGDEN HARLESS DOOR KNOB 293

○ Products with the greatest airplay this week. ◆ Videoclip availability. • Recording Industry Assn. Of America (RIAA) certification for sales of 1 million units. ▲ RIAA certification for sales of 2 million units.

this function should be necessary (or tolerated) when staff programmers are being paid by their stations to make playlist choices, and when they have the services of trade charts and consultants to guide them, is a question that has no common-sense answer. Most labels have promoters on staff, and many labels hire additional, independent promoters, paying them by the week or for the life of the record, which is until it begins to fall off the charts.

When programmers become used to the flattery and blandishments of record promoters, accepting such behavior as a normal part of business life, then records that have no promoters behind them are ignored, no matter how good they may be. Consequently, new acts, just to stay in the game, must pay promoters money that might better be spent on upgrading their music. To no one's surprise—but to virtually everyone's denial—promoters find themselves periodically accused of practicing "pay-

Marty Robbins belts one out for fans jamming Ernest Tubb's Record Shop in downtown Nashville—and for listeners of WSM. The "Midnite Jamboree" had already become a post-Opry, Saturday-night ritual by the time of this early fifties photo. Begun in 1947, when Tubb opened his Record Shop, and hosted by Tubb until his death in 1984, the weekly live broadcast continues to this day.

ola," that is, paying programmers in one form or another for playing the records they are promoting.

Another consequence of this chart mania is that nowadays records are run through the playlists—from bottom to top and quickly back again—like so much musical sausage. This action is independent of the fact that some records may be better or more popular than others and thus deserve to be played over a longer period of time. Some examples: In 1957, Bobby Helms's "Fraulein" stayed on the *Billboard* charts for fifty-two weeks. Today, a song that has gone #1 will hardly stay on half that long. In 1972, Freddie Hart's "My Hang-Up Is You" stayed at #1 for six weeks in *Billboard*. In 1986, there were fifty-one #1 country songs in *Billboard*, one for each week of publication that year. One reason, according to *Billboard*'s chart manager Marie Ratliff: "The radio stations have shortened their playlists—sometimes playing thirty to thirty-five current records—so when they

In the 1950s, disc jockeys and country performers often got together on the air. Here Smokey Smith, guitar on his lap, interviews Cowboy Copas (in the white hat), Hank Snow, and Rusty Gabbard (black hat) in the studios of KRNT, Des Moines, Iowa.

do move a record to #1, they often take the previous week's #1 off the chart completely to make room for the other product moving up."

The point of all this chart talk is to demonstrate that there is a whole area of radio/record/trade magazine activity that has little, if any, connection to the talents of the acts and the desires of the listeners. This has to be considered in any comprehensive treatment of country radio. Radio remains the chief promotional vehicle for the sale of records, and that singularity will continue to foster abuses that will dismay those who simply want to create or listen to the music. Perhaps the saddest testimony to this occurred in 1985 when a group of Nashville songwriters invited radio programmers to meet with them to tell them the kind of songs radio wanted.

For all its faults, though, country radio has continued to grow. The number of full-time country stations reached 1,116 by 1975 and increased to 1,534 by 1980, the year that the movie *Urban Cowboy* convinced millions of Americans that they were country music fans. For a time, it seemed that any station having trouble in its ratings could overcome the deficiency by switching to a country format.

By 1982, there were 2,114 full-time country stations. The numbers seemed to peak in 1985 at 2,289. The following year, the total had dropped slightly, to 2,275.

Country radio has become an army in straitjackets—powerful in its total impact on the listening public and the recording industry, but limited by caution, tradition, and market conditions in the kind and amount of music it can expose. As a commercial vehicle, country music is thriving, but as an artistic one, it is almost uniformly bland and predictable. One can drive from one end of the United States to the other, listening to country radio, and barely detect a difference in the stations. Playlists are short; the same songs are played over and over again, often "back-to-back" and with no identification of artist or title; DJs are allowed to say little or nothing about the music and those performing it; and only rarely do stations play records that aren't on the trade charts.

Realizing the power of radio (if not its vision), country acts and songwriters have periodically demonstrated their fealty to the medium in song. There is an almost childlike belief and hope that putting the word *radio* in the song title will get it played on the radio. And true to radio's megalomania, the ploy has worked. Thus, in a five-year period, listeners were treated to such major and minor hits as "Somethin' on the Radio" (Jacky Ward, 1981), "Nothing But the Radio On" (the Younger Brothers, 1982), "Listen to the Radio" (Don Williams, 1982), "All the Love Is on the Radio" (Tom Jones, 1984), "Thank God for the Radio" (The Kendalls, 1984), "You Turn Me On (Like a Radio)" (Ed Bruce, 1984), "Radio Heart" (Charly McClain, 1985), and "I'm Gonna Hurt Her on the Radio" (David Allan Coe, 1985).

Country radio has become very good at giving fans steady and reliably pleasant background music. But that is a shamefully tepid legacy for a vehicle that once provided the rough-edged excitement of barn dances, the polyglot programming of bluegrass, country, and gospel (in happy indifference to playlists), and the delightfully suspenseful prospect that any day a new Loretta Lynn might walk into the station with her record and we would be there, listening, at the magical moment.

4

TUMBLING TUMBLEWEEDS: GENE AUTRY, BOB WILLS, AND THE DREAM OF THE WEST

Douglas B. Green

The spirit of the early American pioneers didn't disappear with the last wagon train west. In fact, it lived on well into our century. Nowhere was this more vividly demonstrated than in the 1930s, when, in the face of dust storms and a depressed economy, Southwesterners responded with some of the most lively, moving, and enduring music in our history. It was a rich, creative, fertile explosion, little to be expected in the midst of an economic depression. It was a time of rising unemployment and falling prices, worldwide depression and local bankruptcy, more mouths to feed and less to feed them with—and throughout the Great Plains, dust rolling, blowing over once-fertile land.

And yet this hardship produced two of country music's most important styles: western swing and the western songs of the singing cowboys. Since those days, historians and fans alike have tended to lump the two together when assessing the sounds and styles of the 1930s and 1940s: after all, the two forms often spoke of the same themes of land, livestock, agriculture, and, of course, love. The musicians of both styles often clothed themselves in the striking regalia of screen actor Tom Mix (rather

Gene Autry, the template for the singing cowboy, bashfully strums his custom guitar, ca. 1939. By then the singing cowboy was making about $600,000 annually through radio, records, films, tours, and canny product marketing.

109

than in the style of an authentic cowboy like William S. Hart). The musicians and leading figures also moved comfortably in each other's milieu: western swing stars Bob Wills, Spade Cooley, Bill Boyd, and Tex Williams appearing on film; singing cowboys Ray Whitley and Jimmy Wakely both leading dance bands; all competing for the same places on the "hillbilly" (later country & western) popularity charts. And repertoire also, at least at the start, sprang from the same sources: the cowboy folk songs of the preceeding decades, hoary fiddle tunes, the influence of the jazz and pop music only recently available to all via radio, and the seemingly ubiquitous presence of Jimmie Rodgers, that first great fusion artist, who forged such memorable music from such disparate sources, charging it simultaneously with humor and pathos.

So this is, in a way, an easy and convenient linking of styles, handy though not fully accurate, for the differences are profound, and to seek them out, open them up and understand them, is not merely musicological nit-picking. Despite the similarities in chronology, origin, and visual appearance, the two styles spoke in different languages to different (though overlap-

Bob Wills, 1940: country fiddler, big band leader, hep cat—fanfare supplied by Texas Playboys Jamie McIntosh, Tubby Lewis, and Everett Stover.

ping) audiences. While they both offered escape, a relief from the crises at hand, each did so in a profoundly different way. One offered romance, the other commonality, and this is the heart of the difference.

When Bob Wills and his fellow musicians forged what has come to be called western swing out of a curious mixture of jazz, blues, fiddle tunes, hillbilly songs, German polkas, Mexican *canciones*, and cowboy songs, they started with one boot firmly planted in the rural soil and the past, and the other striding purposefully toward the urban asphalt and the future. They were consciously testing and adapting a new style appropriate to the era, building on several traditions.

The dance tradition in Texas is a strong and time-honored one, which served an important community function, as it does to this day in many places. I recall not long ago seeing Asleep at the Wheel play at an outdoor concrete pavillion in Sabinal, Texas, on a steamy south Texas night, as bankers and lawyers mixed with tradespeople and farmers—the same sort of venue Bob Wills & His Texas Playboys played fifty, forty, and thirty years ago. To be sure, they provided the same sort of escape. A muggy night of dancing, socializing, and gaity, underlaid with that irresistible, joyful beat that so often belied the sorrow of the lyric.

Mac's Haywire Orchestry, 1930s. Knoxville-born Harry "Haywire Mac" McClintock, at the far right, spent his youth traveling as a merchant seaman, soldier, and hobo. During the twenties, he wrote and recorded a pair of songs that became hobo anthems— "Hallelujah, I'm a Bum" and "Big Rock Candy Mountain." Beginning in 1925, he sang cowboy songs over West Coast radio.

Asleep at the Wheel, 1987: The latest aggregation of a group that updated western swing during the seventies, when the country industry had all but forgotten it. The lineup has changed many times since the band began in the late sixties, but founding member Ray Benson (the tall fellow in the middle) is still the leader.

Take Me Back to Oklahoma (1940) paired fiddlin' Bob Wills and two-fisted Tex Ritter. At the time, Ritter (a former law student and a veteran of several Broadway musicals) had been starring in westerns for four years; it was Wills's film debut. Ritter went on to do some sixty westerns as well as to record such Capitol hits as "Jingle, Jangle, Jingle" and the theme to High Noon. 36

Tomorrow the strains of the workaday world would again be felt, but an evening spent dancing to a western swing band is an evening that puts off tomorrow and, in a sweet incandescent glow, imparts the heady feeling that tomorrow will never come. It is truly living in the here and now.

The escape offered by the singing cowboys was of a quite different texture. It was remote, idealized, purely in the realm of fantasy. It spoke in grand themes of courage, love of nature, and of an idyllic fantasy cowboy life that had already been codified by the close of the previous century: a life free and unfettered, in which a man lived or died by his own skill and resources, in harmony with the glory and majesty of nature around him, answering to nothing but the innate goodness of nature's own code. Reduced from the realm of feeling to mere words, it seems implausible, but who among us cannot recall being caught up in this delightful and exciting suspension of disbelief?

It is easy enough to see why children have always been so taken with the cowboy fantasy, but precisely the same romantic notion has had a profound effect on adults as well; the image is that powerful. Who wouldn't, for an hour, like to right wrongs with quick fists and sure guns, then ride off into the sunset, without the endless nagging questions of mortgages, bills,

In 1946, Detroit businessman Tom Saffady hit upon the idea of manufacturing "picture discs" of pop, country, and cowboy acts, such as the Down Homers, Patsy Montana, and Lulu Belle & Scotty. High production costs and fierce competition quickly put Vogue Records out of business.

113

The Girls of the Golden West, 1930s: The Good sisters, Dorothy and Mildred, were Illinois farm girls who, on the advice of their agent, dressed like cowgirls and claimed to be from Muleshoe, Texas. Their western harmonies and duet yodels were featured on midwestern stations during the thirties and forties, including Chicago's WLS from 1933 to 1937.

Like most western singers, Patsy Montana wasn't a real cowpoke, but the western image fit her well. After starting out on the West Coast and then fiddling on a few recordings for Jimmie Davis, the WLS singer wrote "I Wanna Be a Cowboy's Sweetheart." Her 1935 recording became the first legitimate hit for a woman in country music.

bosses, marital aggravation, unpleasant neighbors, and moral ambiguities? And who wouldn't like to win the admiration of men and the interest of women with a pearly smile and a lilting voice? (I do not wish to make this fantasy quite so gender-specific. Women can be every bit as moved to escape or dream of long rides in the great outdoors.)

At any rate, the difference is clear. Whereas the dancers at a ballroom or pavillion physically worked (and, yes, sometimes drank) their daily concerns away, the moviegoers (or radio or record listeners) dreamed theirs away in mental isolation.

Of course, the argument can be made that *all* music is inherently escapist, but rarely have two musical styles that so admirably serve this function been so closely linked yet so inherently disparate. A look at history, with the benefit of hindsight, may help explain why the image of the Westerner, the cowboy, so strongly overpowered the genuine and fundamental musical and cultural differences in these two vivid and memorable styles.

The creaking wagons of the Pioneers, the Gold Rush, the Battle of the Alamo were all far closer than a century from the time Bob Wills and Gene Autry—the dominant figures in western swing and cowboy singing, respectively—began their careers, no further from them than the Gay Nineties are from us. The closing of the western frontier, the novels of Zane Grey, Buffalo

Louise Massey & the Westerners, 1930s. After getting their start on the Chautauqua circuit in their native New Mexico, the family group (consisting of Louise, her husband, her two brothers, and another musician) came to the "National Barn Dance," where they popularized the western look and western songs.

Bill's Wild West Show, the first western film—*The Great Train Robbery*—and the cowboy songs collected in books by N. Howard "Jack" Thorp and John Lomax were recent history. The West, its lore and legend, were still very fresh; much of its most vivid drama was not much further removed than we are from World War II, and it was still very much a part of the memories of their fathers and grandfathers.

This may account, partially, for the romance with western dress, for the clothing marked them as men of the West, and men of the West were dusted with the aura of glamor and heroism. The musical tradition was, of course, quite another thing, mingling the sometimes ironic, sometimes sentimental songs and poems of real-life cowboys with the strains of Broadway, the hot jazz from Chicago, the deep blues, dashes and dollops of Mexi-

115

can, Czech, and German ethnic strains, southern ballads and fiddle tunes, and the stately, sentimental songs of the Gay Nineties. Clearly, the real-life songs of the working cowboy played only a relatively small part in the formation of either musical style, other than image, the same image the cowboy and the Westerner gave to popular literature and art. Still, all these elements, whatever the catalyst, created something new and of great unconscious psychological power, right for the times and forged by the times, as the highly charged, turbulent 1930s opened.

Dale Evans, cowgirl deluxe, 1940s. Today, her name is inseparable from that of husband, Roy Rogers.

Wilf Carter ("Montana Slim") was a genuine cowboy—from Nova Scotia. Inspired by Jimmie Rodgers, the yodeling singer began recording in 1933 and carved out a long radio career in Canada and the northeastern United States.

Balding, cigar-chomping, sometimes semi-stout Bob Wills was unquestionably the central figure in the growth of western swing; his stamp remains on the style, indelible to this day. A fiddler and singer of modest abilities, he excelled in showmanship, determination, ambition, and eagerness to experiment musically. Born in east Texas but firmly associated with Turkey, Texas (to which he moved in 1913, at the age of eight), James Robert Wills grew up in a thoroughly musical family: his father was a fiddler, as were both his grandfathers, and nine uncles, and five aunts. Young Bob started off learning the guitar and the mandolin to accompany his father's fiddling at dances in and around Hall County, Texas. His first chance to play fiddle at one of these dances, at age ten, came when his father got drunk one night and failed to show up. Bob filled in, and a career was launched. Almost.

By 1944 Hank Snow, here on guitar, rivaled Wilf Carter as Canada's most popular western singer. But at the time Hank the Singing Ranger was still small potatoes compared to the "King of the Cowboys," Roy Rogers, when the six-gun-toting movie star, backed by the Cactus Cowboys, visited Montreal on a rodeo tour.

As far as piano player Roy Newman was concerned, his elegant Texas string band played hot jazz, not country. He organized his boys in 1933, and they made their Vocalion recording debut less than six months after Milton Brown's first western swing discs. Based in Dallas, Newman shared the WRR mike (and, often, musicians) with fellow western swinger Bill Boyd.

From the moment eighteen-year-old Hank Penny first heard the records of Milton Brown and Bob Wills in 1936, he was inspired. This 1939 photo finds the Alabama coal miner's son with his eastern swing band during their stint at WSB, Atlanta. Pictured are Radio Cowboys Louis Dumont on banjo, fiddler Sheldon Bennett, Noel Boggs on steel, Carl Stewart on bass, fiddler (and future tunesmith) Boudleaux Bryant, and Penny.

118

Bill Boyd, who played guitar on a Dallas session for Jimmie Rodgers in 1932, had his own western swing outfit two years later. For the next sixteen years, the recordings of Bill Boyd's Cowboy Ramblers featured top-flight musicianship, exemplified by their classic instrumental "Under the Double Eagle" (1934).

The Hi Flyers, 1941: One of many hot string bands that sprang up around Fort Worth during the early thirties. The Flyers—fiddler Sheldon Bennett, guitarist Buster Ferguson, leader Elmer Scarborough at the mike, accordionist Darrell Kirkpatrick, and bass player Andrew Schroder—broke up the year the picture was taken.

Music wasn't an easy way to make a living in the Depression, so Wills did what he could to get by, working by turns as a preacher, a life insurance salesman, a telephone company employee, a carpenter, a farmer, and a barber. The year 1929 found him in Dallas-Fort Worth, unable to find a barber job. So he fell back on music, joining a newly formed medicine show as fiddler and black-face comic. This job ended, too, though, when the medicine show folded. Luckily, one of the guitarists with the show, Herman Arnspiger, stayed with Wills; together they called themselves a band—the Wills Fiddle Band. Though the duo played only house dances and made occasional early morning radio appearances, the experience helped give Wills confidence as a professional musician.

One night at a gig in Fort Worth, an amiable cigar salesman who fancied himself a singer joined the duo as a guest vocalist in a rendition of "St. Louis Blues." Wills was impressed. Weeks later, when Milton Brown was no longer selling cigars, Wills hired him. Brown's younger brother, Durwood, soon joined the group on second rhythm guitar, and a genuine band was born.

The next three years were rocky but filled with promise. In the fall of 1930 they began regular appearances on WBAP in Fort Worth, on a show sponsored by the Aladdin Lamp Company. They were known then as the Aladdin Laddies. When Aladdin pulled their sponsorship, the Burrus Mill and Elevator Company was there to keep the boys on the air. Burrus Mill manufactured Light Crust Flour, so the Aladdin Laddies quickly became the Light Crust Doughboys.

Beginning to swing, 1933: the Light Crust Doughboys, sponsored by the Burrus Mill and Elevator Company. Ready to deliver entertainment are Burrus Mill manager and radio emcee W. Lee O'Daniel, and Mill employees Bob Wills (fiddle), Herman Arnspiger (guitar), Tommy Duncan (guitar), Clifton "Sleepy" Johnson (banjo), and the driver.

During World War II, western swing even penetrated the wilds of York, Pennsylvania, where the 101 Ranch Boys held forth at WSPA.

For a while the situation was cozy: the band worked by day at the mill, appeared live on the radio, pushed the product, played dances (where the real money was), all the while synthesizing what would become known as "hot string band music" in its time and, eventually, western swing. It could have gone on this way for a long, long time, but Burrus Mill's sales manager W. Lee "Pappy" O'Daniel got greedy; he wanted the Doughboys to perform exclusively for the radio, which meant no dances, which meant a lot less dough for the boys. Milton and Durwood Brown left and formed the Musical Brownies. Wills stayed on. When he finally did quit a year later in a dispute over salary and his proposal to add his brother Johnnie Lee to the band, Bob took most of the band with him to Waco, Texas. Another move to Oklahoma soon followed, and it was at KVOO in Tulsa that the Texas Playboys found a home and a devoted following for eight years, until World War II temporarily broke up the band.

At each step, Wills proved unafraid to experiment: in time, he added drums, electric string instruments (first and most notably the steel guitar), and brasses and reeds, anything and everything necessary to support his vision of a solid and lively dance band on the one hand, and to accompany adequately his increasingly eclectic big band material on the other. This seemingly awkward mating of styles (a cowboy big band?) was not an immediate success, but once the ball got rolling it rolled ferociously, until Wills's music became the musical trademark of the Southwest.

*Crystal Springs flyer,
ca. 1932–36.*

ORIGINS OF WESTERN SWING

When Bob Wills asked Milton Brown in 1930 to become the third member of his fledgling Wills Fiddle Band, neither one of them realized that they were taking the first steps toward a new style of music. They were just trying to make a living.

As Bob Wills's biographer Charles Townsend has noted, what began as old-time fiddle and string-band music evolved into western swing almost out of necessity. Although plenty of folks in the Fort Worth area loved to hear an old-time fiddle tune done by a smart fiddler, the real money to be had was at dances. Naturally, folks in a big, modern city like Fort Worth liked to dance to modern music, which in 1930 meant hot jazz. It was an easy order for Bob Wills to fill, for although he was raised in an old-time fiddling family, he loved jazz and blues. So the Wills Fiddle Band learned some modern numbers.

Beginning in the summer or fall of 1930, rhythm guitarist Herman Arnspiger, Wills, and Brown began performing old-time fiddle tunes and dance numbers regularly over WBAP, first as the Aladdin Laddies and later as the Light Crust Doughboys. Musically, they were a fairly daring young group, and they enjoyed a large local following. When the trio played dances at a local dance pavillion known as Crystal Springs, they mixed musical styles even more freely. Furthermore, their lineup often swelled, with Clifton "Sleepy" Johnson and Milton's younger brother Durwood regularly coming aboard on tenor banjo and guitar. As these musicians and others joined in to jam on various numbers, bringing their own styles and preferences, the seeds of western swing were sown.

When the ultimatum came down from WBAP manager W. Lee O'Daniel that the Doughboys had to stop playing for dances, a funny thing happened: Milton Brown, the former policeman and cigar salesman, quit. After two years as the singer in Wills's band, Brown figured he knew a thing or two about being a bandleader. Immediately after resigning in September 1932, he formed his own band, Milton Brown & His Musical Brownies, negotiated a radio slot with Fort Worth's KTAT, and kept right on playing at Crystal Springs.

Like Wills, Brown encouraged musical experimentation; he, too, attracted musicians with eclectic tastes. His younger brother Durwood left the Doughboys and became the Brownies' rhythm guitarist. Country fiddler Jesse Ashlock, who also happened to be a jazz fan, became a charter member, as did Ocie Stockard on tenor banjo and Wanna Coffman on bass fiddle. Cecil Brower, with a music degree from Texas Christian University, soon joined on second fiddle, and, late in 1933, an Earl Hines devotee, Fred "Papa" Calhoun, joined as pianist.

This Brownies' nucleus, sans Ashlock, recorded eight sides in San Antonio on April 4, 1934, for the Bluebird label—the first recordings of what would later come to be known as western swing. Although today Bob Wills is universally acknowledged as the Father of Western Swing, clearly in 1934 he and

Milton Brown were still neck-and-neck for that title. Brown played a different brand of country jazz from Bob Wills, but one that became just as influential. Whereas Wills generally jazzed up older tunes, Brown covered the popular hits of the day string-band style. In words, the distinction might seem a mere matter of semantics, but the difference in Brown's sound was noticeable. And it was widely copied: Milton Brown's crooning style (sort of a country Crosby) became popular with country singers; fiddlers like Cecil Brower and Cliff Bruner (who would go on to lead his own successful western swing outfit) paved the way for jazzy improvisation; and Bob Dunn, perhaps the most influential of all, brought the first amplified steel guitar to the group—and to country music. Not only did Dunn have state-of-the-art gear (which in 1934 consisted of an old Mexican guitar with a home-made pickup attached), he also had a style that was far ahead of his time. As Nick Tosches has pointed out, he played steel the way Django Reinhardt played jazz guitar—three years before the Frenchman began to record! Dunn's hornlike style was a distinctive feature on all of the Brownies' Decca recordings from January 1935 sessions in Chicago and March 1936 sessions in New Orleans.

Unfortunately, Milton Brown did not have the chance to drive his band further. On the night of April 13, 1936, Milton was returning from Crystal Springs in his new auto. A rear tire blew and the car careened out of control, overturning several times before coming to rest on its wheels against a telephone pole. The speedometer was jammed at ninety-three miles per hour. A companion, Katherine Prehoditch, who had been trying out as a vocalist with the band, was killed instantly. Brown was rushed to the hospital and was expected to recover; but complications followed, including pneumonia. He died at the age of thirty-two, on April 18. In two years his band had recorded more than a hundred selections, and five decades later that music still stands as one of the great achievements of western swing.

Milton Brown & His Musical Brownies in the studio of KTAT Fort Worth, ca. 1935: Wanna Coffman (bass), Cecil Brower and Cliff Bruner (fiddles), Bob Dunn (steel guitar), Fred Calhoun (piano), Milton Brown (at the mike), Ocie Stockard (banjo), and Durwood Brown (guitar).

123

A third-generation descendant of Czech immigrants, Adolf Hofner freely mixed Bohemian waltzes and polkas with western swing. In this 1940s photo, the Texas band leader, hands upraised, pilots a parade float for his sponsor, Pearl Beer, and conducts his band, the Texans.

When Milton Brown left the Light Crust Doughboys in 1932, Bob Wills auditioned sixty-seven singers before finding Tommy Duncan singing for tips at a Fort Worth root-beer stand. Duncan's smooth baritone became an essential ingredient in Wills's best recordings. He formed his own band in 1948.

In the meantime, former bandmate Milton Brown, that other great pioneer of western swing, carried on with his own band all too briefly. His potential success will always remain a subject for speculation, for he died in the first flower of his career from injuries sustained in an April 1936 automobile accident.

At the same moment, Wills was adding the men who shaped his style and sound: Leon McAuliffe on electric steel guitar, Tommy Duncan with his warm, yet often bluesy vocals, and a succession of excellent fiddlers who aggressively pursued swing, not traditional styles. Like many a successful bandleader, Wills was eager to feature these musically adventurous young men, who all contributed in various ways and degrees to develop the style that became known as western swing, and the sound took the dust-and-poverty-wracked Southwest by storm in the mid-1930s.

As the decade progressed the style lost its fertile, raw, experimental sound, and much as jazz evolved from Dixieland to big band, so western swing evolved into a more orchestrated, but still fundamentally danceable, sound. Wills's Texas Playboys reflected this, of course, but the trend was brought to its acme by Spade Cooley, whose orchestra (yes, that's what he called it) featured complicated charts, full string sections, and even a harp. Cooley himself was a dynamic and charismatic bandleader

—like Wills, a fiddle player—and his records frequently featured the baritone vocals (they would become contrabass on many of his own recordings) of Tex Williams, who later led his own swing band, the Western Caravan.

Though its musical roots were firmly in the 1930s, western swing reached the height of its popularity just prior to, during, and after World War II, and many of the songs so closely associated with the style came out of this period: "San Antonio Rose," "Shame on You," "Time Changes Everything," "Take Me Back to Tulsa," among many. By the time "Faded Love" became a hit in the late 1940s, western swing was being supplanted (at least on the record charts) by newer sounds and stars, most of whom, in that curious and inevitable musical cycle, achieved success with raw, fresh styles far less imaginative and sophisticated than the music they supplanted. Many western swing bands continued to tour and perform well into the rock 'n' roll era (though increasingly pruning personnel), and the occa-

The cowboy big band hit the big time in 1943, when Bob Wills moved his outfit to the West Coast. "They say, 'That guy made $340,000 last year and don't know what he's doin','" Wills told Time *magazine three years later. "Hell. I know what I'm doin' all right—I'm just playin' the kind of music my kind of folks like to hear."*

When Bob Wills was discharged from the army in 1943, he took up residence in Los Angeles and got a weekday noontime show over KMTR. Here are Wills, vocalists Laura Lee Owens (his first female singer) and Tommy Duncan at the mike, and the Texas Playboys behind them, in the KMTR studio, ca. 1944.

In 1946–47, Bob Wills & His Texas Playboys recorded a radio transcription series for Oakland, California-based Tiffany Music, Inc. During the two-year period, the band cut more than two hundred selections, which were distributed to stations nationally. Here Wills, holding his fiddle, gathers the Playboys together for a transcription recording session.

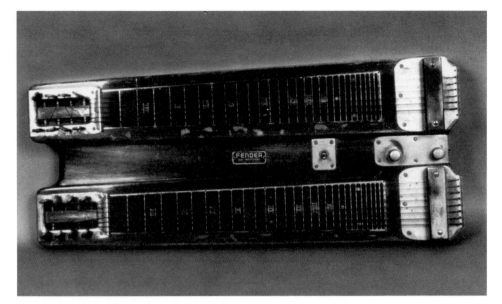

Leon McAuliffe owned this steel guitar, the first electric made by Fender, 1930s.

Having previously turned down a lucrative opportunity to play in Gene Autry's band, nineteen-year-old Leon McAuliffe jumped at the chance to join Bob Wills for the princely sum of $30 a week in 1935. During his seven years with Wills and a long career as band leader, McAuliffe brought a lively and influential steel guitar sound to country music with such hits as "Steel Guitar Rag" (1936). This publicity shot dates from the 1950s.

Spade Cooley, the self-proclaimed "King of Western Swing": His "orchestra" (as he liked to call it) sometimes employed as many as twenty-two musicians—including a harpist. A star of California radio, TV, and movies during the forties and fifties, Spade scored his biggest hit with "Shame on You" (1945). He went to prison for the murder of his wife in 1961 and died of a heart attack while on furlough in 1969.

When Gene Autry went to Hollywood in 1934, he left his band behind in Louisville. The groups five-foot-seven accordionist, Pee Wee King (who got his nickname from Autry), soon formed the Golden West Cowboys and moved on to the Opry in 1937, bringing a sharp western look and a smooth swing sound to the show. Here's the band at their first WSM broadcast, June 1, 1937, when King was just twenty-three.

sional western swing song found its way into the record charts, not infrequently a lighthearted novelty tune like "Slow-Poke" or "Smoke, Smoke, Smoke." In the land of its birth, it continued to serve its crucial social function, and it lingered—especially in the recordings of Hank Thompson and the early Ray Price—well into the 1960s, before it became ripe for revival by Asleep at the Wheel, with the occasional foray by Merle Haggard and, more recently, George Strait.

This entire process may have mostly to do with the natural entropy of any musical style, which goes through creation, discovery, explosive growth, maturity, and eventual decline before limited rediscovery and revival. The parallel with the popular swing bands of the same era is uniform.

If the insistent beat of the western swing bands provided the here and now side of the western musical experience, the songs of the singing cowboys furnished the dreamy, romantic, faraway side, the obverse of the same coin. Gene Autry, two years younger than Wills, began recording in the late 1920s, in slavish imitation of the then phenomenally popular Jimmie Rodgers, whose yodeling and low-down blues gave early impetus and inspiration to most singers in both these styles. Within a very few years Autry developed his own, very western style, and relying on his own songs ("There's an Empty Cot in the Bunkhouse") and those of Billy Hill ("The Last Roundup") and Bob Nolan

Tex Williams onstage at the Riverside Rancho, Hollywood, late 1940s. The former singer in Spade Cooley's band went solo in 1946 and scored a national hit the following year with Merle Travis's "Smoke, Smoke, Smoke (That Cigarette)." The Riverside Rancho was Williams's base in the late forties and early fifties; there he played host to top country and western talent.

Hank Thompson, part honky-tonker, part western swinger, 100 percent Texan. Hank's modus operandi was to write clever songs about beer-drinking and honky-tonkin'; his band then made the songs swing—to the tune of twenty-one Top Twenty country hits between 1949 and 1958.

("Tumbling Tumbleweeds"), launched a recording career of astonishing proportions, and a film career that lasted more than twenty years.

The basics of Gene Autry's career are well documented. Born to a rancher in Tioga, Texas, on September 29, 1907, Orvon Gene Autry learned the elements of guitar from his mother. The family moved to Ravia, Oklahoma, when Gene was in his teens, and there he showed enough interest in music and show business to spend part of a summer with the Fields Brothers Marvelous Medicine Show, in which he sang, acted, did black-face comedy, and even played the saxophone.

As Autry said in his 1978 autobiography, *Back in the Saddle Again*, "When the Fields Brothers Marvelous Medicine Show came to town one summer, looking for a local boy to sing with them, I was recommended to Professor Fields. I traveled with them for three months, softening up audiences with mournful ballads before the professor began pitching his wares: liniment and pills, and his own product, a patent medicine called Fields' Pain Annihilator. . . . I earned fifteen dollars a week. For a teenaged boy, in the 1920s, this was more than money: it was the riches of Arabia."

After graduation from high school in 1925 he was hired by the St. Louis & Frisco Railroad; he worked in a variety of positions before rising to the rank of relief telegrapher. Sometime in 1928

129

THE REAL SINGING COWBOYS

Jules Verne Allen was a genuine Texas bronco buster, who later made a living singing cowboy songs on record and radio during the twenties and thirties. He's pictured here on the cover of the sheet music of a popular American folk song.

Before Gene Autry, Roy Rogers, and other singing cowboys of the silver screen became major stars of western music and country, a number of much more authentic cowboys (and cowgirls) had already blazed a trail, recording traditional cowboy songs as early as 1925. Many of these singers actually grew up on ranches or were working cowboys, and they performed and recorded traditional folk songs that reflected the real life of the working cowboy—herding cattle, breaking wild horses, fighting bad hombres and Indians, and living the hard life on the cattle trails. These work songs were a far cry from the slick, sophisticated music of the movie cowboys, whose Tin Pan Alley and pop-styled compositions depicted a romantic and unrealistic image of western life, extolling the pleasures of riding a pastoral, carefree prairie.

Genuine cowboy folk songs first became widely known in the early 1900s with the appearance of two books that collected many of the songs—N. Howard "Jack" Thorp's *Songs of the Cowboys* (1908) and folklorist John Lomax's *Cowboy Songs and Other Frontier Ballads* (1910). Although some of the best-known cowboy songs published in these books, like "Bury Me Not on the Lone Prairie," were actually reworked versions of older traditional verses, many of them were original poetry made up by the cowboys themselves. Out on the range, cowboys often entertained one another by putting their original verses to the tune of a familiar melody and then singing them unaccompanied; sometimes they merely recited the verses.

The movie cowboys had fancy guitars, but—in the beginning—the real ones usually didn't. Instead, they passed the time on cattle drives with harmonicas, Jew's harps, and an occasional fiddle—all small, easily portable instruments. Not until the turn of the century, as inexpensive, mass-produced models (like Sears Roebuck's) became available, did the guitar eventually become more popular with working cowboys —and even then it was still probably left at the bunkhouse more often than not.

Carl T. Sprague, who grew up on a ranch in Texas, was one of the first real cowboys to make a record. His 1925 recording of Montana cowboy poet D. J. O'Malley's classic "When the Work's All Done This Fall" sold a remarkable 900,000 copies and was largely responsible for the booming interest in cowboy material that was to follow. Another important early cowboy singer was Jules Verne Allen, also from Texas, who began ranch work at the age of ten and went on to become an experienced veteran of the long trail drives. Allen made a series of important recordings for Victor during 1928 and 1929, including such traditional cowboy songs as "Little Joe, the Wrangler," "The Cowtrail to Mexico," and "The Cowboy's Dream." Among the other important authentic cowboy singers were Harry "Haywire Mac" McClintock, Charles Nabell, Billie Maxwell (a cowgirl singer from the White Mountain region of New Mexico), and rodeo rider Ken Maynard, who became the first motion picture singing cowboy with his 1929 appearance in *The Wagon Master*.

While traditional cowboy folk songs had little direct influence, either musically or lyrically, on Hollywood western music, country songwriters and performers certainly appropriated the western theme and cowboy image. The close ties between the cowboy image and country music continue, in songs like Ed Bruce's "Mamas Don't Let Your Babies Grow Up to Be Cowboys," the *Urban Cowboy* craze of the early 1980s, and the popularity of groups like Riders in the Sky, who are revitalizing the old Sons of the Pioneers-style sound. But there are still strong ties as well to real cowboys and ranch life of the present. Reba and Pake McEntire and George Strait all come from rodeo and ranching backgrounds, as do a

number of other contemporary artists, like Red Steagall, bronc-riding champion Chris LeDoux, and Canadian Ian Tyson. Real cowboys inspired the western legend with songs about their lives, and real cowboys are still singing about ranch and rodeo life, and providing the image that inspires their more urban imitators.

Raised on a south Texas ranch, Carl T. Sprague was a college student at the time he took a genuine cowboy song, "When the Work's All Done This Fall," to Victor in 1925; the record became the first cowboy hit, selling nearly a million copies. But Sprague never took singing very seriously, preferring instead to complete his degree at Texas A&M.

131

So enamored was Merle Haggard of Bob Wills's music that he taught himself the fiddle—in three months. The 1970 album he subsequently recorded—A Tribute to the Best Damn Fiddle Player in the World (Or My Salute to Bob Wills)—*helped rekindle a revival of interest in western swing.*

When rancher Otto Gray became a western band leader, he did it in style. During the twenties and thirties, Gray's band toured vaudeville, rode in his $20,000 car, and were one of the few country groups to advertise regularly in Billboard. *Their records for Vocalion and Gennett were forgettable—but the group did inspire other country bands to dress like cowboys.*

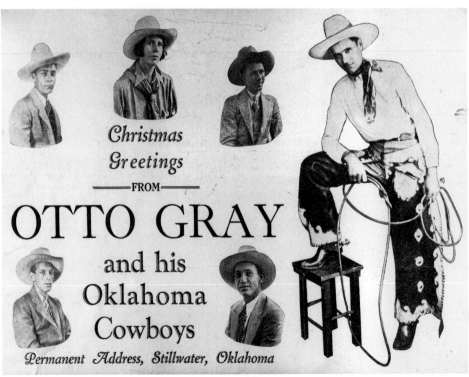

132

he fell under the spell of Jimmie Rodgers and became devoted to that sound. That year also saw his fateful meeting with Will Rogers in Chelsea, Oklahoma. Rogers, in the railroad office to send a telegram, heard Autry singing and playing, whiling away the empty hours. Words of encouragement from Rogers—surely they could not have been much more than a simple offhand compliment—stoked the fires of Autry's naive ambition, and, taking advantage of the free railway pass available to all Frisco employees, he headed for New York, the entertainment capital of the world, where he knew absolutely no one.

Inexperienced but optimistic, he immediately set about looking up Johnny and Frankie Marvin, two of the most popular entertainers in the city. Johnny, in fact, was a toast of the town, a performer on record, on Broadway, in vaudeville (he toured with Nat Shilkret's orchestra), and on radio as "The Lonesome Singer of the Air." Frank, seven years John's junior, was not only a comedian and musician in his brother's act, but recorded on his own as well. Most important for Autry, the Marvins were from Oklahoma, and he had met their parents.

If he had nothing else, Autry did have innocent confidence. He walked up to the Marvins and introduced himself with a big smile, saying that he was Gene Autry, a fellow Oklahomian, and that he, too, wanted to make records. Legends are made of this kind of youthful optimism, this blissful naiveté, and a legend (as well as a fortune) was indeed in the making, though it hardly happened overnight. He auditioned a couple of tunes for Nat Shilkret, then A&R for Victor, who didn't think Autry was ready to record but did see some promise in the young man. The Marvins suggested that Autry learn some "yodel songs" and practice singing in general. So Autry returned to Oklahoma and his telegraph job, but he also worked on his singing career—performing over the radio at KVOO in Tulsa (which would be Bob Wills's station in another five years), making appearances at schools, private parties, and civic clubs. Then, persistent fellow that he was, he went back to New York and Victor Records. This time it worked. With the help of the Marvins, he cut his first sides, "My Dreaming of You" and "My Alabama Home," on October 9, 1929—just twenty days before the wildly careening Jazz Age collided head on with the Depression, which cut quickly and deeply into the recording business. It would be a full sixteen months before Autry returned to the Victor microphones.

In the meantime, he made use of another free pass and took a sixty-day leave of absence from the St. Louis & Frisco Railroad —to which he never returned—and ventured once again to New York. He soon was recording for a host of labels, exclusive con-

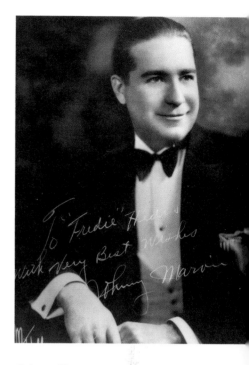

Johnny Marvin had performed on Broadway, in vaudeville, and on radio in New York when he and brother Frankie helped fellow Oklahomian Gene Autry land his first recording deal in the fall of 1929. Frankie and Johnny then backed Autry on his first two sides for Victor, "My Dreaming of You" and "My Alabama Home."

133

tracts being rare then, including the American Record Company and its affiliate labels—Banner, Melotone, Oriole, Perfect, and Romeo—and Columbia, Grey Gull, and Gennett as well.

As he became more and more familiar with recording, his shaky guitar playing improved noticeably, and his voice, particularly his yodeling, gained authority. In the interim he had also fallen even more deeply under the influence of Jimmie Rodgers, whom he idolized and imitated, his voice at times virtually indistinguishable from Rodgers's. He began to develop his talents as a songwriter as well, although the early efforts were basically Rodgers-style blue yodels that would have fit unobtrusively into the repertoire of the Singing Brakeman. (In fact, Autry recorded two of Rodgers's most intensely personal songs, "Jimmie the Kid" and "T.B. Blues," on Victor's budget label Timely Tunes, in the spring of 1931. Autry's rendition of "Jimmie the Kid" was so similar to Rodgers's that, years later, in the 1970s, when RCA rereleased a number of Rodgers recordings for the *Legendary Performers* series, the record company accidentally included Autry's version instead of the original!)

Nevertheless, by the end of 1931, as his recordings clearly reveal, Autry was becoming a seasoned professional who was well aware that he needed to forge an identity of his own. While the Rodgers influence remained quite evident, there were songs other than blue yodels, sung in a voice recognizable as a young version of the singing cowboy who would fill thousands of movie screens for three decades.

Jimmie Rodgers exerted the single biggest influence on the early singing style of Gene Autry. When the Blue Yodeler died in May 1933, several tribute records appeared, Autry's among them. Though this 1933 ad for "The Death of Jimmie Rodgers" suggests that Autry knew Rodgers well, they had, in fact, met only once, during New York recording sessions.

134

It was during this same time—October 1931—that Autry and Jimmy Long (a guitarist and singer who not only had been his boss on the St. Louis & Frisco, but was also his uncle-in-law) recorded a sentimental mountain tune for the American Record Corporation called "That Silver Haired Daddy of Mine." It was the first of many hit records for Autry, and it radically changed his life. It turned him into an up-and-coming national star and initiated a whole series of sentimental mountain ballads firmly in its tradition.

Somewhere along the line came yet another change in the musical emphasis of his career, which in its early years displayed a remarkably chameleonlike ability to shift styles. From the Jimmie Rodgers blue yodels he moved smoothly to mountain ballads, and from mountain ballads shifted once again, this time to western songs, and ultimately to the development of a sound and style quite his own—a warmer, mellower, more nasal singing tone, brimming with sincerity. In 1931, he joined the National Barn Dance in Chicago as "Oklahoma's Singing Cowboy."

In addition, he obtained a radio show of his own, "Conqueror Record Time," in which he was portrayed as a cowboy fresh off the range, ready to sing a few western songs for the folks. This format, by Autry's own admission, was the brainchild of his producer at the American Record Corporation, Art Satherley, and Ann Williams of the WLS production staff. Autry wanted to sing love songs in the manner of Rudy Vallee, but Satherley insisted on cowboy songs, and it quickly paid off.

Soon Sears Roebuck, which then owned WLS, was boosting this cowboy singer's image and popularity with a host of song books (one of which shows Autry doing a series of rope tricks) and through mail-order sales of their Gene Autry Roundup guitar, retailing for $9.98. And then came the movies.

There is considerably more confusion concerning the how of Autry's movie career than the when. As always seems to happen in the case of unexpected success, there are quite a few who step forward to take credit for it: in this case they were Art Satherley, film producer Nat Levine, and Herbert G. Yates, head of American Record Corporation and soon-to-be head of Republic Studios. Regardless of who arranged for the opportunity, Autry stole his first picture—*In Old Santa Fe* (1934)—from reigning singing cowboy star Ken Maynard, and an astonishing career began to mushroom. He made his first feature film, *Tumbling Tumbleweeds*, in 1935; two years later he was voted the nation's number one western star. With records aiding the success of his films and vice versa, Autry suddenly became one of the most popular film stars of the era, his movies always landing

Frankie Marvin was well established in New York (as a recording artist, and in his brother Johnny's act) when he first met Gene Autry in 1928. He had even been the first to cover a Jimmie Rodgers song on record. But as Autry's star ascended, Frankie hitched his wagon to it and became Autry's longtime sidekick and dobro player on record and in the movies.

135

The Jimmy Wakely Trio—Johnny Bond, Jimmy Wakely, and Dick Reinhart—ca. 1940. Within six months of moving from their native Oklahoma to Hollywood in 1940, each had landed a recording contract. All three appeared in movies. Wakely eventually made thirty westerns and some big hits for Capitol Records in the late forties. Bond played guitar for Autry, took supporting roles in the shoot-em-ups, and had hits on the charts right up to 1971.

near the top of the box office lists, much as Elvis Presley's would a generation later.

He was everywhere: his records ("Tumbling Tumbleweeds," "South of the Border," "Mexicali Rose") sold in the millions; in 1939 he began the CBS radio show "Melody Ranch," which ran for seventeen years; in the meantime he had a traveling stage show that would often play in theaters in conjunction with the latest Autry film release.

World War II erupted at the height of Autry's career, and the three years he put in as a pilot in the Army Air Corps had serious consequences for his performing career. In 1941 he reported having made $600,000 from his various enterprises; the Army reduced him to $125 a month. As Autry himself has said, "If it hadn't been for royalties from things such as sweatshirts, pistols, boots and hats and records, I would have been in a mess. I knew I could make good money as long as I could work. But suppose I was incapacitated? Where would I get my income?"

Autry found a way: he invested in oil, real estate, radio and television stations, recording companies (Republic and Challenge), and hotels. Eventually he even became owner of the California Angels baseball team. It had been quite a ride.

Autry was our idea of the singing cowboy, a prototype for the genre, though others (Ken Maynard and even John Wayne, with dubbed singing voice) had come before him. He was quickly followed into films by a strange variety of other singing cowboys, boosted by studios that hoped to enjoy some of the financial reward Republic was reaping: country singer Ray Whitley, big band singer and leader Smith Ballew, ex-opera and light opera

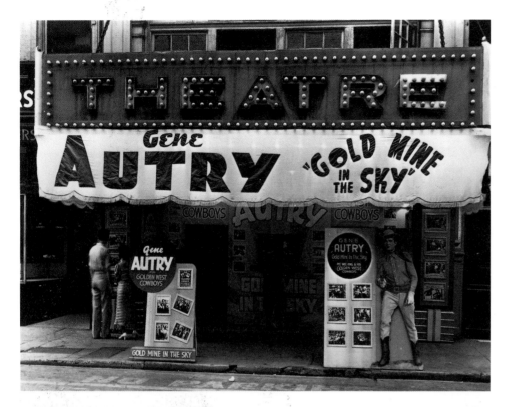

By 1938, when Gold Mine in the Sky *was released, Gene Autry was so popular that it hardly mattered what the name of the picture was or who appeared with him (in this case, it was Pee Wee King & His Golden West Cowboys).*

Although he had four years' head start on Gene Autry as a singing cowboy onscreen, former stuntman Ken Maynard was upstaged by the newcomer in their first film together, In Old Santa Fe *(1934). Pictured here with a banjo (and actress Cecilia Paker) in this still from* The Trail Drive *(1933), Maynard could also play fiddle and guitar.*

137

Gene Autry AND HIS FAMOUS ROUND UP GUITAR

$9.98 LESS CASE

—Genuine Mahogany back and sides.
—Selected clear Spruce top.
—Genuine Mahogany neck.
—Top and back edge and soundhole inlaid with black and white and bound with white celluloid.
—Top decorated with striking Western Ranch Scene and reproduction of Gene Autry's own signature.
—Standard size.
—Patent heads.
—Ebonized fingerboard.
—Rayon covered neck cord.
—EXTRA! Gene Autry's own Guitar Instruction Book, and his Book of Cowboy Songs (many his own) his photograph and a pick like his are also included with this instrument only.
—12 Lesson Scholarship Certificate (See Page 512).

Gene Autry endorsed this guitar for those who like the guitar and cowboy songs as he sings them. Unknown a very few years ago, his ability to play a guitar and sing naturally and well, gave him his chance for fame and popularity over the radio that many would like to imitate. This "Gene Autry" model is your opportunity. We include Autry's own books to start you and our regular lesson offer besides. The instrument itself is well made, worth hearing and easy to play. "Round-up" real quality here for few dollars. Not Prepaid.

12 E 216—Without case. Shpg. wt., 9 lbs. **$9.98**
12 E 2216—With canvas case. Shpg. wt., 10 lbs. **$11.50**

Sears Roebuck owned Chicago's WLS during 1931–34, when Gene Autry ("Oklahoma's Yodeling Cowboy") was one of the station's biggest stars. Shrewdly capitalizing on his appeal, the company mass produced this Gene Autry "Round Up" guitar and sold thousands through its catalog—along with Gene Autry records and songbooks. The guitar with Gene's name on the fretboard is the real thing—Autry's own 1926 Martin.

Gene Autry onscreen, 1930s.
The singing cowboy starred in
more than ninety pictures
between 1934 and 1953. With
him are longtime sidekicks
Smiley Burnette on accordion
(who appeared in eighty-one
pictures with him) and Frankie
Marvin on string bass.

Gene Autry owed his good
fortune in part to farsighted
A&R man Art Satherley, who
prodded Autry into singing
cowboy songs on Chicago's WLS
when the young singer was more
interested in crooning like
Rudy Vallee. Satherley
remained his record producer
for many years. This shot dates
from the early forties after both
men had moved to California.

vocalists Fred Scott and George Houston, Hollywood actor-singers Bob Allen and Jack Randall, and even two fellows with authentic western backgrounds, Bob Baker and Tex Ritter, the only one of the bunch to begin to approach Autry's record sales. Later came Jimmy Wakely, Eddie Dean, Rex Allen, and of course Roy Rogers, who eventually rivaled and may have eclipsed Autry's popularity on film. There was even a black singing cowboy, Herb Jeffries, and a singing cowgirl, Dorothy Page. All were variations on the familiar theme of the peaceable cowboy hero who was quick to right wrongs with fist and guns and gallant steed, but who also broke into song at the drop of a Stetson, often a love song but more often than not a hymn of praise to the great outdoors and the lonely but independent life of the cowboy.

In 1937, Ray Whitley collaborated with the Gibson Guitar Company to design this J-200 prototype. The model proved immediately popular with cowboy singers, thanks in part to its strong bass sound.

Bar Buckaroos (1940) was one of Ray Whitley's few star roles in the movies. Seen here with his trusty Gibson guitar, Whitley is better remembered as the writer of "Back in the Saddle Again" and other western classics.

Perhaps because the haunting, ghostly images of Bob Nolan's "Cool Water" comprise my own first memory of music, I've long felt escapist lyricism was the primary, profound appeal of the music of the singing cowboys, transcending the more obvious appeal of, say, Autry's charming boy-next-door quality on screen and on record, Tex Ritter's quirky, distinctive, and thoroughly believable voice, or Roy Rogers's boyish, athletic screen presence. Somehow the appeal of western music was greater than any individual, touching the mystery of nature, the heart of the myth of the West that lies deep within all of us.

Songwriters like Tim Spencer, Billy Hill, Ray Whitley, Stan Jones, Johnny Bond, and even Autry and Rogers themselves touched on these powerful feelings, but primarily it was Bob Nolan who took the western mythic themes (evident in the works of Zane Grey and many other writers of western novels) and wedded them to lyrics and music. Nolan, who with Spencer and Rogers formed the Sons of the Pioneers in 1933, was clearly the figure who time after time made these images of the West and of western life come to life in vivid, memorable song. Although, with the exception of "Cool Water" and "Tumbling Tumbleweeds," few of his compositions are known to the general public, he composed hundreds of western classics for the Sons of the Pioneers over the years, many of which graced the films of Charles Starrett and Roy Rogers (who left the group in 1937 to

Farley's "Gold Star Rangers"
K.F.S.D. 5:30 to 6 P.M. Daily
Sunday 12:30 to 1 P.M.

pursue his solo career), and he was composing elaborate and moving poetry about nature up until his death in 1980. The music of Bob Nolan and these other western writers was profoundly different from the songs and poems of the cowboys it was intended to evoke onscreen, though it came from their tradition. Both lyrically and musically, this "new" western music conveyed a sophisticated poetic romanticism, far removed from the sentimental or faintly ironic vignettes of ranch and trail life typical of the cowboy songs of the previous decades.

Whether sung in the Pioneers' forceful, outdoorsy style, thick with harmony and counterpoint, or as a solo by any of the singing cowboys, these songs speak of an ethereal, almost spiritual West, in vivid contrast to the happy, sweat-soaked atmosphere of the dance halls in which western swing flourished. A few song titles tell the tale: "Blue Prairie," "Moonlight on the Trail," "Blue Shadows on the Trail," "The Everlasting Hills of Okla-

Unlike so many singing cowboys, the Sons of the Pioneers are better remembered for their influential recordings than for their many films. This 1935 photo features the harmony group's most famous lineup: ace guitarist Karl Farr, brother Hugh on fiddle, Tim Spencer, guitarist Len Slye (who would later become Roy Rogers), and bass player Bob Nolan, with Gus Mack.

143

Texas Jim Robertson (born in Batesville, Texas) sang cowboy songs over New York radio and for the NBC network during the forties and fifties. His records for Bluebird and RCA Victor include "Rainbow at Midnight" (1947).

Ken Hackley's Oklahoma Cowboys toured the vaudeville circuit during the early thirties and performed on radio well before singing cowboys were in vogue.

homa," "The West Is in My Soul," "Rainbow over the Range" —the list could go on and on and on.

Western song's inevitable decline was more rapid than western swing's, for the western song lacked the powerful social convention of the dance to sustain and support it. To maintain their careers when the popularity of singing cowboy films waned in the late 1940s and early 1950s, the stars turned to touring and to records (in what was then commonly called country-*western* music because of the involvement and the glamor of these movie stars). Only Tex Ritter and Rex Allen continued to have any significant recording success into the 1960s, and despite the Outlaw and Urban Cowboy vogues in country music and popular culture, the style of the singing cowboys has not been successfully revived on a national basis, although the cult success of Riders in the Sky suggests that something in the appeal of the singing cowboys endures.

If the primary function of the singing cowboys and the western swing bands was escape, the crucial difference in methods of escape was borne out in the lyrics and music. Western swing is, obviously, a dance music first and foremost, and to call the tempos fast or slow is fairly relative, musically speaking. The two-step was the dance, and the tempo of many of the songs reflected this, although, of course, every dance engagement featured waltzes, schottisches, polkas, cotton-eyed joes, and even the bunny hop. The songs of the singing cowboys tended to be dreamy, giving plenty of room for the lazy harmonies to weave and meander like campfire smoke. Films and live performances dictated a need for uptempo tunes as well, of course, but for every "Skyball Paint" and "A Cowboy Has to Sing" there were two or three songs like "Wagon Wheels," "Trail Dreaming," and "Song of the Prairie," and these are the tunes that tend to haunt our memory.

The physical release of the dance and the mental release of the film or record also played a part in separating (though not polarizing) these styles in a purely musical sense. Faced with night after night of playing the same or similar songs for a similar purpose, the musicians in western swing bands prized the ability to improvise, to stay on one's toes, to challenge each other, just as in jazz, ever that great influencer of western swing. Musicians played frequently not only for the dancers, but for the cognoscenti in the audience and for each other, stretching their musical limits and providing the spark to ignite themselves and each other in the endless grind of dance halls and one-nighters.

The songs of the singing cowboys were in general more arranged and deliberate. It is dangerous to generalize too broadly, but while western swing stuck to more conservative chord and rhythm structure, it punctuated these conventions with frequently sparkling, dazzling solos. The cowboy song, on the other hand, was often musically adventurous (in the context of its era and its folk roots), exercising freedom with time signature, melody, and especially harmony, which in western swing bands tended to be spontaneous rather than premeditatedly bold. Some of this adventurousness can be traced to the influence of Tin Pan Alley and the film score (always more flexible with time signature than a dance band can be) and partly to the experimental orientation of Nolan and some of his fellow songwriters, who expressed their musical creativity not in improvised solos but in the fundaments of song structure and, of course, lyrics. Consequently, the names of many western swing musicians—Leon McAuliffe, Joe Holley, Al Stricklin, Joaquin Murphy, Noel Boggs, Eldon Shamblin, Tiny Moore, and others—are well known to fans, and are highly regarded for their individual contributions. While the musicians among the singing cowboys, except for Hugh and Karl Farr of the Sons of the Pioneers, are virtually unrecognized, so great is the importance of the lyrics and the voices. For example, who played those dazzling jazz fiddle licks with Foy Willing and the Riders of the Purple Sage? Only passionate fans can tell you it was Johnny Paul.

Beginning in the thirties, Red River Dave McEnery wrote and sang cowboy songs over New York's WOR and WMCA, San Antonio's WOAI, and other radio stations. His fame is founded on his event songs, like "Amelia Earhart's Last Flight" (1939), which capitalized on tragic news stories. Still performing and writing today, his more recent efforts include "The Ballad of Gary Powers" and "The Ballad of Patty Hearst."

Riders in the Sky: fiddler "Woody" Paul Chrisman, guitarist "Ranger" Doug Green, and bassist Fred "Too Slim" LaBour. Formed in Nashville in 1979, the trio has been harmonizing (and mildly satirizing) the old trail songs with such success that in 1987 they signed with major-label MCA Records after several recordings for Rounder.

By the time Rex Allen appeared in Hills of Oklahoma *(1950), the public's infatuation with singing cowboy movies had run its course, and the newcomer had little choice but to take his fine voice and acting skills to a forgettable television series ("Frontier Doctor") and to Walt Disney Studios as a narrator. He did have an occasional hit record over the next twenty years, though.*

146

Formed in 1933 as the Pioneer Trio, the Sons of the Pioneers made their first film appearance two years later. Over the next twenty-five years, various incarnations of the group appeared in nearly a hundred films. In this 1940s photo, the Sons assemble on a movie set.

Tex Owens, who starred for many years on Kansas City's "Brush Creek Follies" on KMBC, assured himself a place in country history when he wrote and recorded the western classic "Cattle Call" for Decca in 1935. He was also the brother of Opry star Texas Ruby and the father of Texas Playboys vocalist Laura Lee Owens McBride.

This is simply to reiterate that western swing is an instrumental music; whatever is being sung is secondary to the dance feel. The music of the singing cowboys is lyrical music, involving the mind and imagination in active imagery, with scant thought to how well it keeps the toes tapping.

It is interesting to note, however, that if we leave lyrical content aside and consider the human voice as an instrument for a moment, the styles come closer together: Tommy Duncan, Leon Huff, Tex Williams, and most of the other western swing vocalists, despite their individual differences, shared a smooth, relaxed, masculine, sun-warmed vocal character, which contrasts vividly with the nasal southeastern music of the same period. The singing cowboys (with the exception of ex-opera singers George Houston and Fred Scott, and the irrepressibly individualistic Tex Ritter) may have tended to a slightly more tenor range, but they nevertheless shared that same friendly, easygoing vocal style; they all made you feel right at home, as if you were with a friend. Even the Sons of the Pioneers, who as the most precise singers of the lot had the least "swing," usually caught the listener up in the lazy rhythm of the West. It is precisely this vocal quality that most quickly catches the ear and identifies western music in either style, especially as distinct from contemporaneous country music.

Elton Britt, billed as "the highest yodeler in the world," was a member of the Beverly Hill Billies before going solo. He struck paydirt when he recorded Bob Miller's "There's a Star Spangled Banner Waving Somewhere" in 1942: country's first gold record.

Zeke Clements was one of the first western singers to appear on the Opry. Although perhaps best known to country fans for writing the World War II hit "Smoke on the Water," Clements has been heard by millions more as the voice of Bashful in Walt Disney's Snow White and the Seven Dwarfs.

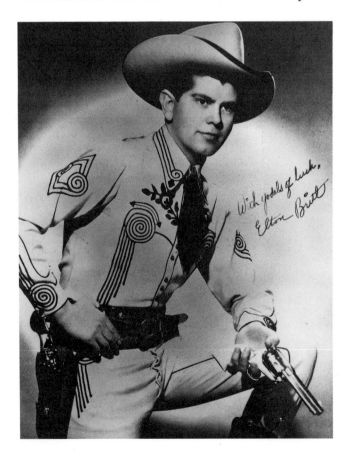

The eclectic Oklahoma Wranglers: guitarist Guy Willis, fiddler Skeeter Willis, accordionist Vic Willis, and bass player "Cherokee" Chuck Wright, 1950s. After joining the Opry in 1946, this western band backed Hank Williams on his first Sterling Records session (1946). They scored their biggest hit in 1964 with a trucker's song, "Give Me 40 Acres (To Turn This Rig Around)."

Although T. Texas Tyler's most memorable impact on country consisted of sentimental hits like "Deck of Cards" (1948) and "Remember Me" (1945), he made his living in Hollywood honky-tonks during the forties leading a western swing band. He left country to sing gospel.

Both styles died as the need for them died. We needed our escapes—and these were but two of many—through the grim depths of the Depression, and then through the threat and actuality of war. But the GIs returning to a new life saw little relevance in this dated music. Both musical styles hung on, of course, thanks to the inertia of show business and the loyalty of fans, but by the mid-1950s there were no more films and few hit records in either style, only an endless string of personal appearances, on which some thrived and others decayed.

The current small-scale revival of both western swing and western song may well reflect not only some aspects of our society that parallel the political and economic climate of the 1930s, but also the enduring appeal of the image, the romance (idealized or real) of the cowboy and the West. They have embodied powerful icons and ideals for well over a century and doubtless will long remain an indelible part of the American psyche, ever touching our communal heart.

149

5

COUNTRY ACROSS THE COUNTRY

Ronnie Pugh

In the public mind and perhaps to an even greater extent in the collective consciousness of the country music industry, Nashville is the locus of country music, the nexus, the place where country music happens. Nashville is "Music City, U.S.A.," the country music capital of the world. And this is more than merely a widely held perception. Most country music in the 1980s *is* written, recorded, and published in Nashville. The writers and performers either live there or make frequent trips to town. Aspiring musicians migrate to Nashville, knowing that is where one makes the grade—or doesn't. Recording studios, dozens of them, dot the city's business districts. Music Row, the area of greatest concentration, is home to numerous publishing companies, record labels, and even the Country Music Hall of Fame. Nashville can boast the Grand Ole Opry, an American institution, the oldest continuous radio broadcast in the world (weekly since 1925), a show still seen by thousands and heard by millions each weekend, home base for country music legends and for some of the best of the newcomers.

That the country music industry is now centered in Nashville, and has been for some three decades and more, is beyond dispute. What is not so widely recognized or acknowledged is the historical unimportance of Nashville to country music, relatively speaking, for that period of time up to and just beyond World War II. Little that occurred during the 1920s, 1930s, and early 1940s presaged Nashville's emergence as a country music center. If anything, Nashville during those years was a centrally

The Sleepy Hollow Ranch Gang with Jimmy Wakely and Ray Whitley. See page 165.

151

located backwater, around which in all directions currents of musical activity were swirling. To the southeast was Atlanta, the single most popular field-recording site for executives in search of hillbilly talent. Due east lay several important country music centers, especially Knoxville and Charlotte. To the west was Memphis, and out in the Far West, California, a world all its own, of vital significance to the music before and after the war. To the southwest, in that vast expanse known as Texas, were several cities whose prewar country music scene matched or exceeded Nashville's in scope and significance—Dallas, Fort Worth, San Antonio, and Houston.

After the war, even as Nashville forged ahead toward its current predominance, other cities emerged, playing key roles in the development of country music—Washington, D.C., in the East, Cincinnati and Springfield, Missouri, in the Midwest, Shreveport in the South, Los Angeles and Bakersfield in the West. Even a brief account of the country recording and broadcasting activity in a few key cities serves to remind us that country music has always been a national (not simply a Nashville) resource.

THE SOUTH: FIELD RECORDINGS, BARN DANCES, AND HOT STRING MUSIC

Given the southern origin and upbringing of just about all of country music's early performers, it is not surprising that many of them migrated to the major southern cities for experience, exposure, and, if possible, a livelihood. Cities offered such tempting opportunities as fiddle contests and fledgling radio stations in need of talent, and, of course (if all else failed), busy street corners. Once convinced of the commercial viability of the music, record company executives discovered that searching out and recording the talent in its native territory made sense. Many times a field-recording trip was cheaper than paying travel and lodging costs for groups of musicians to come to New York or Chicago, and it generally kept the musicians close to their radio jobs or touring dates.

Writer Wayne Daniel has called Atlanta "the cradle of country music," and in many ways this is an apt description. Radio station WSB began broadcasting in 1922, and almost from the be-

Owned by the Atlanta Journal, *radio station WSB began broadcasting on March 16, 1922; it was the first radio station in the South. Among the many hillbilly acts aired were Red & Little Raymond, seen here in a shot from the 1930s.*

Fiddlin' John Carson and his daughter, "Moonshine Kate" (Rosa Lee), onstage in LaGrange, Georgia, 1925. Six months after Atlanta's WSB began broadcasting, Carson became the first country act to perform on the station (September 9, 1922). The following June, the fifty-five-year-old fiddling champion recorded for Okeh record scout Ralph Peer in Atlanta and, within weeks, became Okeh's first "old time" artist.

ginning it programmed fiddlers and string bands for rural listeners across the United States. It was in Atlanta that the best-known of these fiddlers, Georgia native Fiddlin' John Carson, first proved country music's marketability on disc. Polk Brock-man, a furniture dealer who also distributed phonograph records in the Atlanta area, knew of Fiddlin' John's appeal and per-suaded Okeh Records executive Ralph Peer, then based in New York, to come to Atlanta and record Carson in June 1923. The initial pressing—five hundred discs—of Carson's two recorded tunes sold out within a month, much to the surprise of Peer, who immediately signed Carson to an exclusive contract. Ultimately, Fiddlin' John recorded some two hundred songs, and Atlanta had its start as a recording center.

In addition to Carson, such early country music notables as Gid Tanner, Riley Puckett, Clayton McMichen, and Roba Stan-ley (the first female country soloist to record) came from Georgia and the Atlanta area. Atlanta soon became the site of regular field recording sessions held by all of the major record compa-nies. Columbia Records held regular sessions throughout the late 1920s and early 1930s, waxing acts like Puckett, Tanner, Dock Walsh, Uncle Jimmy Thompson, Smith's Sacred Singers, the Allen Brothers, Hugh Cross, McMichen, Darby & Tarleton, and Chris Bouchillon. So, too, did Victor Records, under the intrepid supervision of former Okeh employee Ralph Peer. In Atlanta, Peer found the Georgia Yellow Hammers and the Caro-

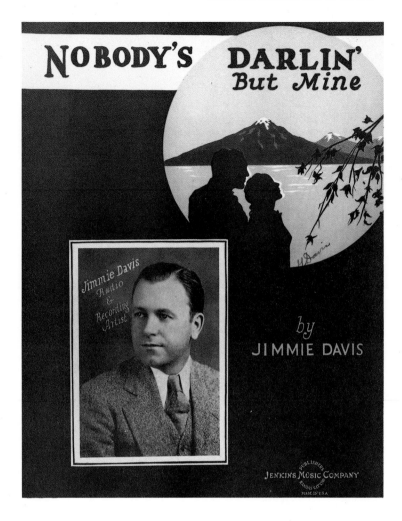

Up until this 1935 Decca release, Davis had recorded raunchy blues songs in the style of Jimmie Rodgers for Columbia and Victor with middling success. This million-seller brought the Shreveport court clerk immediate national attention, which ultimately helped catapult him to the Louisiana governor's mansion in 1944 and 1960. As one of his opponents said: "You can't fight Davis—how in the devil can you fight a song?"

lina Tar Heels, as well as a host of blues and gospel artists, black and white. Even his greatest find, Jimmie Rodgers, recorded on occasion in Atlanta. After Peer parted company with Victor, successor Eli Oberstein continued to record country musicians in temporary studios set up at various locations around Atlanta. During 1940 and 1941, Bill Monroe and his Blue Grass Boys made all of their RCA Victor recordings in the city.

For some years, Atlanta's WSB remained an important radio base for new country talent. The daytime "Cross Roads Follies" featured performers such as the Rice Brothers and Pop Eckler in the 1930s, and in 1940 the station launched the "WSB Barn Dance," which eventually featured Hank Penny, Boudleaux Bryant, James and Martha Carson, and Pete Cassell. But by the early 1950s, the "WSB Barn Dance" had folded, and live radio entertainment was largely a thing of the past. Though Atlanta would re-emerge in the 1960s as a hotbed of musical activity on the club scene, spawning such talents as Ray Stevens, Jerry Reed, Joe South, and Billy Joe Royal, it never became the center for studio recording and music publishing that it might have been, and that Nashville did become.

To the northeast of Atlanta lay the important Piedmont city of Charlotte, North Carolina. In quest of local talent Ralph Peer first supervised Charlotte sessions for Victor on August 9, 1927, just days after his famous stop in Bristol and the first recordings of Jimmie Rodgers and the Carter Family. While Peer found no comparable talent in Charlotte on that trip, he did record Kelly Harrell, the Carolina Tar Heels, the Georgia Yellow Hammers, and others there. Four years later he came back and made a hundred recordings over a two-week period. The Carter Family was among the groups he recorded, plus an aspiring Louisiana singer named Jimmie Davis. When the worst of the Depression was past, Eli Oberstein brought Victor equipment into Charlotte and nearby Rock Hill, South Carolina, on numerous occasions during 1936–38. Bill and Charlie Monroe first recorded in Charlotte, as did other popular brother duets of that era—the Blue Sky Boys (Bill and Earl Bolick) and the Dixon Brothers. Several Grand Ole Opry acts made the trek to Charlotte to record, among them Fiddling Arthur Smith, the Delmore Brothers, and Uncle Dave Macon. And of course much of local station WBT's talent—Fred Kirby, Claude Casey, the Tennessee Ramblers,

"Carolina Hayride" cast, late forties. This CBS network barn dance—originating from WBT, Charlotte, North Carolina—was one of many live regional radio shows that aired nationally before the advent of television.

ON LOCATION WITH ART SATHERLEY

When the country recording industry began in 1922, there were no record producers as we know them today, and the few recording studios were located in the big city—New York, Chicago, Los Angeles—far away from country talent. To find and record new hillbilly acts, the record companies employed artist & repertoire (A&R) men, who functioned as a combination of traveling talent scout and record producer. In order to record country artists on their own turf, enterprising A&R men lugged portable recording equipment down south and adapted warehouses, hotel rooms, and vacant buildings into makeshift recording studios.

Along with Ralph Peer, Arthur "Uncle Art" Satherley is widely recognized as one of country's pioneer A&R men. Born in Bristol, England (not Tennessee), Satherley boarded a steamship for America at the age of twenty-three. Settling in Wisconsin, he found a job with the Wisconsin Chair Company in Port Washington, but was transferred to the company's Grafton plant around 1917 when the firm branched out and began manufacturing the Paramount line of phonograph records— which is where his life's work commenced.

By 1923 he had worked his way from Paramount's research division to the marketing staff, and on to an A&R position based in New York. In the late twenties, he joined Plaza Music, which later became the American Record Corporation. For ARC he scouted and recorded blues

and country artists, and gradually helped to establish ARC as a leading firm dealing in country music. When Columbia absorbed ARC in 1938, Satherley took charge of country and blues recording, remaining with the company until his retirement in 1952.

Few were better acquainted with the process of field recording than Uncle Art. Although he often worked in Chicago and Hollywood studios, he also logged thousands of miles annually, recording musicians in radio stations, hotel rooms, and even in mountain cabins.

Until the advent of magnetic recording tape shortly after World War II, A&R men like Satherley recorded country artists on delicate wax master discs. Refrigerated until needed, a blank disc was first scraped with a razor to make the recording surface smooth; then it was placed in a warming cabinet to bring the wax to the required consistency. During the recording session, the disc rotated on a turntable as a diamond or sapphire stylus cut recording grooves into the surface. Bad masters could be reshaved and used again, much as modern magnetic tape can be erased. After a session, A&R men sent the masters to New York or Chicago for processing. What follows is Satherley's reminiscences of a typical field recording job:

I'd make a date, then have about eight or nine aggregations come in around that time, say, in Memphis,

Chicago, or New York. When Roy Acuff came in one particular time, we went down to the Gayoso Hotel in Memphis. We brought our machinery down from New York, portable, and the only reason I took the Gayoso Hotel in Memphis was that they had the large old-fashioned rooms whereby we could take two rooms big enough [for a temporary studio and control room]. So we used the bathroom for putting the recording machine in.

On this particular date, the recording machine was standing in the bathtub. We'd got a deal from the [hotel] manager to cut a window [in the bathroom wall]. Later, we would replace the wall as we had found it. Anyway, to show you what a wonderful job Roy does and what a sincere fellow he is, he recorded for me eight numbers in one hour and three quarters. Bang, bang, bang, bang. One master at a time but three of everything to make sure we'd get it back [intact] to New York because of the heat.

The man that was carving the waxes . . . sat on the toilet with this little machine and a turntable, a steel turntable with a wax disc on top of it. [If mistakes occurred,] he was the one that shaved off the recorded music and got ready for the next recording. These waxes were kept in a cupboard up here with an electric light to keep them at a temperature so that the wax wouldn't break on the cutting machine, and the sapphire [disc cutter] wouldn't crack the disc.

In those days, if it was cold in New York and I was on a weekend, I would take a plane and I would jump to New Orleans. There I could work Saturday and Sunday nights down in the old French district, listening to the bands and their songs. Then on Monday I would be down on the bayous of Louisiana, on a raft, going across the water to some bayou singers and Cajuns. See, always on the go to find something to sell. The object of the recording man is twofold: number one is buying, and number two is selling. You have to buy the artists, you have to buy the songs, but the objective must always be to sell records. Of course, I made quite a few that didn't sell, but I made a lot that did.

(Transcribed and edited from a taped interview in the Oral History Collection of the Country Music Foundation.)

157

Brother duets were so common when Bill (mandolin) and Earl Bolick first recorded in 1936 that producer Eli Oberstein suggested they find a new name, which they did: the Blue Sky Boys, a nod to their native Blue Ridge Mountains, "the Land of the Sky." By the early fifties, country music's increasing sophistication had left their melancholy treatments of traditional songs behind, and they retired from regular performing while still young men.

During the thirties and forties, country radio performers often became regional stars without the benefit of records. Doc Williams & His Border Riders, for instance, joined Wheeling, West Virginia's "World's Original Jamboree" (WWVA) in 1937 and were well established in the Northeast before finally getting the opportunity to record in 1947.

Bill and Cliff Carlisle, J. E. and Wade Mainer—recorded in Charlotte whenever RCA or Decca came to town. Nevertheless, World War II largely marked the end of major label recording activity in Charlotte, even though WBT continued to be home base for a number of popular and significant country performers.

If we look now to Nashville's own state, we find at least three other cities whose prewar roles in country music's development outstripped its own. Chief among these was Memphis. As with Atlanta, the major record companies found sufficient talent in the Memphis area to prompt them to come back again and again. Much of the music recorded in Memphis was well outside the hillbilly or country field—only to be expected in a city so laden with blues, jazz, and gospel talent. As early as 1927, Victor began its Memphis sessions, and the next year recorded Floyd Ming & His Pep Steppers and McLaughlin's Old-Time Melody Makers. Peg Moreland, the Carter Family, David McCarn, and Jimmie Davis were among the more prominent country performers to record in Memphis between 1929 and 1931.

In the meantime, mountainous Bristol, situated on the Tennessee-Virginia border, was the site of the legendary sessions of July and August 1927, which included Ernest V. "Pop" Stoneman, Charles and Paul Johnson, Blind Alfred Reed, Alfred Karnes, Henry Whitter, and the Tenneva Ramblers. These were the same sessions that yielded the famous first recordings by the Carter Family and Jimmie Rodgers. Encouraged by the success

158

Cast of the WWVA "World's Original Jamboree," late forties. Founded in 1933, Wheeling's barn dance beamed unadulterated hillbilly music into the Northeast and featured many fine country acts, including Wilma Lee (seated, fourth from left) & Stoney Cooper (seated, seventh from right); the Lilly Brothers, Everett (standing, second from left) and Mitchell (standing, fourth from left); and Doc Williams (standing, eighth from left).

of the sessions, Peer came back to Bristol once more, in October and November 1928, recording a few of the same artists again (the Stoneman Family and Uncle Eck Dunford), but looking for more Rodgerses and Carters in acts like the Carolina Twins and Shortbuckle Roark. Such Bristol-area musicians as Fiddlin' Dudley Vance, G. B. Grayson, and Clarence Tom Ashley also made their mark on record during this era. It was not without reason that Peer could tell the Bristol newspaper editor upon his first visit, "In no section of the South have the prewar melodies and old mountaineer songs been better preserved than in the mountains of east Tennessee and southwest Virginia." Peer's observation held true for years to come: during the late 1940s, Bristol became a bluegrass stronghold, with radio station WCYB in the late 1940s featuring the Stanley Brothers and Flatt & Scruggs.

Just as Bristol was a lively meeting place for musicians from North Carolina, Virginia, and Tennessee, Knoxville drew upon talents in nearby Georgia and Kentucky. Long a center for fiddling contests and old harp-singing schools, Knoxville attracted ex-farmers into its coal mines and factories, many of them bringing their musical interests and aspirations. The city produced numerous local favorites who won acclaim in the country music

Frankie More's Log Cabin Boys & Girls, Louisville, 1934. This popular WHAS act made few records but proved to be a great training ground for several performers. Pictured, from left, are Pee Wee King, Shorty Hobbs, Johnny Hagerty, Cousin Emmy (Cynthia May Carver) flanked by the Hoosier Maids, Frankie More, Jerry Wallace, Bill and Joe Callahan.

field—George Reneau, Charlie Oaks, and Hugh Cross among them. Never the site of much field recording, Knoxville nevertheless became the radio home of a great many country performers. Lester McFarland and Robert Gardner, a team of blind musicians best known as Mac & Bob, performed on WNAV in Knoxville as early as 1924. This duet team became well known in later years through Brunswick Records and WLS, the powerful Chicago station. Roy Acuff began his professional career in the Knoxville area, leading a band dubbed the Crazy Tennesseans by a WROL announcer. He first recorded for the American Record Corporation (ARC) in 1936; two years later he made the jump to Nashville and the Grand Ole Opry. During the mid-1930s, WNOX began its long-running "Mid-Day-Merry-Go-Round" program, and many are the legends who worked on the show—the Carlisle Brothers, Lost John Miller, Molly O'Day, Smilin' Eddie Hill, "Grandpappy" Archie Campbell, Johnnie &

Wilma Lee & Stoney Cooper with their daughter Carol Lee, ca. 1944. The native West Virginians performed on a number of radio stations from Nebraska to North Carolina before finding a home at Wheeling's WWVA in December 1947. There, Wilma's old timey voice and Stoney's fiddling earned them a devoted following for a decade. In 1957 they moved to the Grand Ole Opry and an even larger audience.

Jack and the Tennessee Hillbillies, guitarist Chester "Chet" Atkins, and many others. Lowell Blanchard, director of the "Merry-Go-Round," launched the "Tennessee Barn Dance" as a Saturday night feature over WNOX in 1942; later it became a CBS network broadcast with many of the "Merry-Go-Round" veterans, along with newer talent like Carl Smith, Carl Story, the Webster Brothers, Carl Butler, Mac Wiseman, and Don Gibson.

In the 1930s, the music of Texas emerged as country's cutting edge. Station WBAP in Fort Worth had aired what appears to be the first country radio barn dance in January 1923 when Captain M. J. Bonner fiddled square-dance tunes for an hour and a half. During the 1930s Dallas was second only to Atlanta as a regional recording site for the major record labels. Jimmie Rodgers, who spent his last several years in Texas, recorded in both Dallas and San Antonio. As the 1930s progressed, Texas became the hotbed for popular new styles. Every major city could boast hot string bands on its radio stations, whose music was soon dubbed "western swing." Dallas had Roy Newman & His Boys and Bill Boyd & His Cowboy Ramblers; Fort Worth had Burrus Mill's Light Crust Doughboys, Milton Brown's Musical Brownies, the Hi Flyers, and—later—the Crystal Springs Ramblers; Houston was home to the Blue Ridge Playboys, Shelly Lee Alley's Alley Cats, the Bar-X Cowboys, and Cliff Bruner's Texas Wanderers;

161

Bob Miller: New York's country song manufacturer. Born in Memphis, Miller played piano on a Mississippi riverboat before moving to New York, where he joined the Irving Berlin Company as an arranger. He made his fortune in country music during the thirties and forties, writing hundreds of hillbilly tunes ("Twenty-One Years," "Rocking Alone in an Old Rocking Chair"), many of which he published through his own company.

Probably the most popular country gospel act of all time, this family group derived their name—the Chuck Wagon Gang —from the cowboy songs that made up their earliest material. Based in Fort Worth, they recorded for ARC-Columbia for forty years. Pictured here in 1936, the year of their first recordings, are D. P. "Dad" Carter, Effie Juanita "Anna" Carter, Rose Carter, and Ernest "Jim" Carter.

San Antonio could claim Jimmie Revard's Oklahoma Playboys and the Tune Wranglers; Austin even had W. Lee O'Daniel's Hillbilly Boys after O'Daniel was elected governor in 1938. Recording executives regularly set up makeshift studios in Dallas, Fort Worth, Houston, and San Antonio hotels to record these bands and countless other acts in the years just before World War II. Among the other acts were Ted Daffan, Al Dexter, and Ernest Tubb, who constituted the first generation of a new style called honky-tonk, named for the rowdy bars in which the music was forged and performed. Texas was the formative home of all these men. Not surprisingly, cowboy music of the type popularized in the movies of Gene Autry and Tex Ritter (Texans both) found a ready audience in the Lone Star State as well.

COUNTRY MUSIC IN THE BIG CITY

The nation's three largest cities, New York, Chicago, and Los Angeles, *did* bid to become country music centers. In fact, as entertainment, recording, and publishing centers, all three cities were vital to country music in the years just before World War II.

Most of the major record companies had their home offices and best studios in New York. So, naturally, some country music

162

performers migrated there, even from faraway Texas and Oklahoma, to make it in the business. Eck Robertson and Henry Gilliland were simply the first of many who came for the sole purpose of recording; when they persuaded Victor to record their fiddle tunes in 1922, commercial country music had its beginning. Gene Autry lived there for a while, rooming with the Marvin Brothers (Frankie and Johnny) and making his first recordings. Tex Ritter came in 1928, lured first by the Broadway stage. Within a few years, though, Ritter found regular work on New York City radio, WINS's "Cowboy Tom's Roundup," WOR's "Lone Star Rangers," and even as co-host (with Ray Whitley) of "WHN Barn Dance."

Despite the trend toward field recordings in the pre-World War II years, more country discs were recorded in New York than anywhere else. The prolific Vernon Dalhart alone—some five thousand releases of nearly one thousand different songs—could account for the city's predominance!

New York also was the capital of the nation's music publishing business, and of the few publishers that would handle country music in its early years most were based in and around the famous Tin Pan Alley. The venerable Shapiro Bernstein, Inc., acquired a few lucrative hillbilly copyrights; Leeds Music and Robbins Music did likewise. Biggest, though, of the New York hillbilly publishers early on was Bob Miller, Inc., founded by its namesake, a writer from Memphis who penned such country classics as "Twenty One Years" and "There's a Star Spangled Banner Waving Somewhere." Miller made New York City his base throughout his professional life. Record producer turned publisher Ralph Peer founded the giant Southern Music in New York in 1928, and an empire was born with his country and blues copyrights. Carson Robison, Kansas-born guitarist/whistler/singer/writer and veteran of hundreds of New York recording sessions, also published his large catalog out of New York.

Even with the emergence of areas closer to home as country music centers, the lure of New York still drew some country performers in later years. Jim Robertson came from Texas, Wilf Carter from Canada, yodeler Elton Britt from Arkansas via California, his duet partner (and New York disc jockey) Rosalie Allen from Alabama, and of course many others spent large parts of their careers in the Big Apple. As late as the 1950s, major labels were still holding some country recording sessions in New York, though of course much less frequently—Hank Snow, for example, cut "I Don't Hurt Anymore" there for RCA in 1954, and Marty Robbins "A White Sport Coat" there for Columbia in 1957.

Hoyt "Slim" Bryant, KDKA, 1930s. In addition to his work over the Pittsburgh station, Bryant is best remembered for the hot guitar playing he brought to recordings by Jimmie Rodgers and, for several years in Louisville, to Clayton McMichen's Georgia Wildcats.

One of the earliest stars of Chicago's WLS was Claud Moye from southern Illinois, who went by the name of Pie Plant Pete, "The Ozark Mountain Boy." Nearly forty years before Bob Dylan and the folk revival, he entertained by alternately singing and loudly blowing his harmonica—all the while accompanying himself on a rapidly strummed guitar.

Los Angeles's KMPC organized southern California's most popular traditional country group, the Beverly Hill Billies, in the spring of 1930. That same year they made their first records for Brunswick. Pictured in this 1934 photo are Hank Skillit (Henry Blaeholder), Maranda (Marjorie Bauersfield), Cyprian "Ezra" Paulette, Gus Mack, Elton Britt (James Britt Baker), Lem Giles (Aleth Hansen), and Jad Dees (Ashley Dees).

Chicago became important in the country music world because of radio station WLS and its "National Barn Dance." Founded in 1924 and featured on NBC radio from 1933 to 1946, this was country music's most popular barn dance until the end of World War II. Its stable of stars was considerable—the Hoosier Hot Shots, Lulu Belle & Scotty, Arkie the Arkansas Woodchopper, Mac & Bob, Doc Hopkins, Gene Autry (early on), and Red Foley (later). Small wonder that major labels held frequent Chicago sessions, the American Record Corporation in particular. During the war years, World Transcription Service used Chicago as one of its major centers for hillbilly recording (the other was Hollywood), putting Foley, Jenny Lou Carson, the Hoosier Hot Shots, and others onto their sixteen-inch long-playing discs for later radio broadcast. One music publisher there, M. M. Cole, was especially receptive to rural music, and during the 1930s and 1940s Cole's songbooks found ready markets across the nation.

Los Angeles was primarily important as the nation's film capital. Some country acts made a good living from radio shows and personal appearances, of course, such as Charlie Marshall & His Mavericks, the Beverly Hill Billies (not to be confused with the television series of the same name), and the Sons of the Pioneers, but it was mainly the lure of the movie industry that drew country talent to the Golden West. Gene Autry left Chicago to make his first films in 1934, Tex Ritter came from New York

in 1936, and soon Hollywood studios were turning out dozens of singing westerns each year. Dick Foran, Monte Hale, Bob Baker, Ray Whitley, Roy Rogers, and the whole host of singing cowboys of the 1930s and 1940s called Hollywood their home. And even if you weren't a cowboy but had achieved some measure of hillbilly stardom, chances are that you came to Hollywood to make at least some movie appearances. Ernest Tubb, Jimmie Davis, Red Foley, Bill Boyd, Roy Acuff, Lulu Belle & Scotty, the Hoosier Hot Shots, Pee Wee King & His Golden West Cowboys, and many more rural entertainers secured starring or supporting roles in B westerns or musicals. Tubb, for example, even considered staying in Hollywood only weeks before opting for Nashville and the Grand Ole Opry in January 1943—a propitious decision, maybe even a turning point for Nashville's postwar fortunes.

The migration of the Okies and other impoverished southwesterners to California in the 1930s, followed by countless others looking for war work in the 1940s, created a vast new market for hillbilly entertainment, which artists and entrepreneurs were quick to tap. During World War II, Bob Wills moved his operations from Tulsa to California, where fiddler Spade Cooley was already forming one of the biggest bands and bidding to become "King of Western Swing." Bert "Foreman" Phillips booked the biggest-name country talent into shows at Venice Pier and other California venues.

Not surprisingly, Los Angeles became a busy recording center. Autry, Rogers, the Sons of the Pioneers, and all the singing cowboys signed to major labels recorded there. Pioneer A&R

East meets West: the Sleepy Hollow Ranch Gang with Jimmy Wakely and Ray Whitley. Wakely (standing, center) and Whitley (crouching, center) were popular Hollywood cowboys; the Ranch Gang sang western music back East (Pennsburg, Pennsylvania), during the forties. They also recorded for Majestic and RCA Victor.

Bob Atcher cried all the way to the bank in 1939 when he recorded a weepy novelty version of the Carter Family's "I'm Thinking Tonight of My Blue Eyes." The Kentuckian remained a favorite performer in the Chicago area through the forties and fifties, eventually becoming mayor of suburban Schaumburg, Illinois.

165

Promoter Bert "Foreman" Phillips and cowboy star Ray Whitley, 1942. During World War II, ballroom dances became big business on the West Coast. In 1942, Phillips opened the Venice Pier, the top western dance spot in L.A. Whitley, Spade Cooley, Hank Penny, T. Texas Tyler, and other musicians provided the entertainment.

Freddie Hart was a regular on L.A.'s "Town Hall Party"— and still nearly twenty years away from his first #1 hit, "Easy Loving."

man Uncle Art Satherley devoted much of his time to southern California, establishing his base for Okeh-Columbia Records in Hollywood after the war. In 1942, Johnny Mercer started the Capitol label, signing Tex Ritter as his first country act, but many more were soon to follow. Smaller independent labels abounded on the West Coast, particularly after the war.

POSTWAR PROSPERITY

The West Coast remained a country music center throughout the prosperous early postwar years. The first weekly *Billboard* charts to track the popularity of country discs (beginning with a jukebox chart in 1944) were largely dominated by West Coast artists—Ritter, Cooley, Merle Travis, Jack Guthrie, Bob Wills, Tex Williams, Jimmy Wakely, and Gene Autry. Magazines like *Tophand* were devoted solely to the thriving California scene. Large venues like the Riverside Rancho and the ballrooms at Santa Monica booked big country dance bands, and honky-tonks from L.A. to Bakersfield throbbed with the sounds of country music. During these years, Hollywood's movie industry lost much of its usefulness for country artists, as the B western bit the dust after the war. Only a few newcomers such as Eddie Dean and Rex Allen made names for themselves in singing westerns after 1945. Sensing the signs of the times, Gene Autry turned businessman once he returned from the service, buying his old Republic westerns, TV stations to air them, and his own studio to make new ones. Autry even entered the publishing business, tapping his orchestra leader Carl Cotner to head up Golden West Publishing. Heretofore, Sylvester Cross's American Music, which published much of the Bob Nolan and Tim Spencer catalogs, had been the premier West Coast music publisher. Many others were soon to follow.

Postwar prosperity, coupled with massive wartime population shifts, made country music a truly national industry in these years. East Coast as well as West pulsated with new activity. Even staid New England sported a radio barn dance of its own in the postwar decade, Boston's "WCOP Hayloft Jamboree." Further down the coast, Philadelphia station WFIL hosted the "Hayloft Hoedown," a show that for a time had Clarence "Hank" Snow in its cast. The Northeast gave birth to the new entertainment medium of television, and stations in New York City, Philadelphia, Cincinnati, Louisville, and elsewhere were quick to fill some of their air time with country programs.

The nation's capital, growing by leaps and bounds under New Deal and Fair Deal spending binges, first boasted an active country music scene in this era. No less a celebrity than Jimmie Rodgers had worked out of Washington in 1928, but he moved to Kerrville, Texas, the following year. After World War II and the arrival of one Connie B. Gay, the city began buzzing with country music. Gay, a government bureaucrat turned radio personality and promoter, made a fortune for himself and created opportunities for many aspiring musicians with shows like his "Gay Time" staged at Constitution Hall. For these shows Gay employed veteran area performers like the Stoneman Family, big names brought in from the Grand Ole Opry and other top radio shows, and local talent yearning to make it big. Exposure through Gay's stage, radio, and TV venues helped make stars of Texan Jimmy Dean, Virginians Patsy Cline and Roy Clark, and

Just before the age of television, even New England had its own radio barn dance: Boston's "WCOP Hayloft Jamboree." In this early fifties cast photo, three noteworthy faces are clustered just to the left of the mike—bluegrasser Buzz Busby (in vest and bow tie), star singer Elton Britt (in the fringed shirt), and future Outlaw guru Jack Clement (bow tie).

Stuart Hamblen's long career first took him from his native Texas to New York, where he made his recording debut as "Cowboy Joe." In 1930 he joined the Beverly Hill Billies on the West Coast and soon afterward assembled his own Covered Wagon Jubilee, pictured here (Hamblen's holding the trophy). Decca's first country artist (1934), he went on to radio and songwriting success.

As a teenager in western Kentucky, Merle Travis took up the guitar with coaching from two young coal miners, Mose Rager and Ike Everly. Travis learned his lessons so well that today their distinctive finger-picking style bears his name. Everly (father of the Everly Brothers), Travis, and Rager posed for this photo in 1956, taken at a hometown celebration honoring Travis.

The Drifting Pioneers,
performers on Cincinnati's
"Boone County Jamboree" as
well as the "Renfro Valley Barn
Dance," included among their
number a young guitarist named
Merle Travis in 1938. The rest of
the lineup consists of fiddler
Morris "Sleepy" Marlin,
mandolinist Walter Brown, and
bass player Bill Brown.

Nancy Lee & the Hilltoppers,
stars of WOWO, Fort Wayne,
Indiana. Nancy was known as
the "Bubble Gum Queen,"
because one of her favorite
gimmicks was blowing big
bubbles with her gum.

Illinois native Billy Grammer. Nightclubs such as the Dixie Pig, showcasing local talent, flourished. During the 1950s, Washington became a center for bluegrass music, since so many of the style's best performers hailed from the nearby states of Virginia and North Carolina.

In the Midwest, Chicago declined in importance on the country music scene. After the war, the Grand Ole Opry rapidly eclipsed the "National Barn Dance," which lost its network sponsor in 1946. The major labels continued to do some recording in Chicago, and at least one important independent, Mercury, arose in the late 1940s, signing Rex Allen, the Hoosier Hot Shots, even Flatt & Scruggs to contracts. Detroit, home since the war to thousands of newly arrived Southerners working in defense and auto plants, witnessed an influx of country music talent as well. Detroit's Fortune Records became the first label to record a Kentucky duo who went on to fame with RCA—the Davis Sisters.

The busiest midwestern country music center after the war was Cincinnati, which built on the base John Lair had established in the late 1930s between his stint with Chicago's WLS and his eventual return home to Renfro Valley, Kentucky. WCKY employed probably the number-one country disc jockey, Nelson King, whose influence extended far and wide. WLW's "Midwestern Hayride," formerly the "Boone County Jamboree," soon graduated to television. As a recording center, Cincinnati made great strides in the postwar decade. Entrepreneur Syd Nathan started King Records in 1943, making and marketing black and country music very successfully for the next twenty years. Grandpa Jones, the Delmore Brothers, Moon Mullican, and Cowboy Copas were his biggest country stars, who did practically all their recording at Herzog's Studios in downtown Cin-

"Renfro Valley Barn Dance" cast, ca. 1937. Irritated by the way western music was displacing the old-time tunes of the Southeast, WLS's John Lair (seated, center) organized a new barn dance to preserve the music of his youth. After starting it at Cincinnati's WLW in 1937, Lair brought the radio show two years later to his native Renfro Valley, Kentucky —where it continues as a stage show to this day.

cinnati. Talented Nashville sidemen Jerry Byrd, brothers Zeke and Zeb Turner, and fiddler Tommy Jackson moved up to Cincinnati for a while in the late 1940s, so busy was the studio there. Though a little of Cincinnati's luster tarnished as Nashville became home to most country recording, its country music scene proved remarkably durable: both King Records and the "Midwestern Hayride" lasted well into the 1960s.

In the South, Nashville was not the only city to foster country artists and businessmen. Dallas continued to support popular radio shows like KRLD's "Big D Jamboree" and WFAA's "Saturday Night Shindig," the former mixing the veteran talents of the Shelton Brothers and the Callahan Brothers with those of newcomers like Billy Walker, Sonny James, and Lefty Frizzell. In 1950, Jim Beck opened a recording studio at 1101 Ross Avenue, and soon Frizzell, Ray Price, and several other Columbia artists were regularly recording there, supervised by Columbia's Don Law. Other labels also used Beck's facility, and Decca's Paul Cohen even considered bringing his business to Dallas and Jim Beck. When Beck died in 1956 of carbon tetrachloride poisoning—he accidentally inhaled the vapors when he was cleaning recording heads in his studio—Dallas's glory as a recording center faded fast. Live radio shows in the area soon succumbed in great measure to the onslaught of recorded music, TV, and rock 'n' roll.

Less than two hundred miles due east of Dallas lay Shreveport. This north Louisiana city was home to the single most successful radio and stage show after World War II, aside from the Grand Ole Opry. April 3, 1948, marked the premiere of

Columbia's Don Law and Jim Beck flank singer Sonny James in the control room of Beck's Dallas studio. Law, an A&R man for Columbia, was planning to transfer all his recording projects from Los Angeles and Nashville to Dallas when Beck died suddenly in May 1956. The city's hopes of becoming a country recording center died with him.

Marty Robbins records at the Jim Beck Studios, ca. 1953. Robbins was one of several Columbia artists (Lefty Frizzell, Carl Smith, Ray Price) who cut a great deal of material at the Dallas studios between 1950 and 1956. Here Johnny Gimble plays the fiddle, Joe Knight is on rhythm guitar, and Jimmy Rollins handles the lead guitar.

171

CAJUN SPICE

The Hackberry Ramblers, ca. 1935. Named after a south Louisiana town, the group combined Cajun string-band music with western swing and began recording for Bluebird in New Orleans (1935). Here is one of the group's earliest lineups: Floyd Rainwater on resonator guitar, leader Luderin Darbone on fiddle, Lonnie Rainwater on steel guitar, and Lennis Sonnier on resonator guitar.

A particularly robust form of regional country music is the Cajun music of southwest Louisiana and east Texas. The Cajuns are descendants of the Acadians, French colonists from the Canadian province of Acadia. Many Acadians immigrated to French Louisiana in the mid-1700s after being expelled from Canada by the British during the struggle between the French and English for control of North America. In the Louisiana bayous, the exiles adapted quickly to the familiar French culture and mixed easily with the local inhabitants descended from French and Spanish colonists, African slaves, and Native Americans.

The Acadians brought to Louisiana their folk music, which in turn changed and evolved as it reacted to influences in the new environment. Before the turn of the nineteenth century, the Cajuns had a well-established tradition of instrumental fiddle music, played mostly for dancing. Around the middle of the 1800s, German settlers from Texas introduced the accordion to Louisiana, and it wasn't long before Cajun musicians were playing it along with the fiddle. By the early 1900s, typical Cajun dance bands included a fiddle, accordion, and triangle, and soon the guitar was also common. By the time accordionist Joe Falcon and his wife, guitarist Cleoma

Breaux Falcon, made the first commercial recording of Cajun music ("Allons à LaFayette") in 1928, the basic Cajun style was fairly well established.

With the spread of the radio and phonograph in the 1930s, Cajun musicians began listening to various forms of pop music, including country. They listened avidly to the blue yodels of Jimmie Rodgers and the western swing of Bob Wills, and they began to incorporate these sounds into their own music.

Even though popular Cajun music was moving toward becoming a hybrid of traditional Cajun sounds and commercial country music, it was still basically regional, sung in French for a French-speaking audience. Although many important Cajun performers made fine recordings on small local labels for this limited regional market, it was not until 1946 that Cajun music had any real national impact. That year fiddler and singer Harry Choates had a hit with his recording of the now-classic and much-copied "Jole

Blon" ("Pretty Blonde"). Mainstream country performers were soon attracted by the good-time sounds of this powerful, happy music, and singers like Hank Williams, who wrote and recorded "Jambalaya," and Jimmie Davis, who recorded Cajun favorites like "Colinda," helped bring Cajun music to a much wider country music audience. By the 1950s Cajun artists like Jimmy C. Newman and Rusty & Doug Kershaw had become important mainstream country music stars.

Today there is a strong revival of traditional music, language, and culture among the Cajun people. It's still possible to hear the old-time fiddle, triangle, and accordion bands of musicians like Dewey Balfa and Marc Savoy alongside the more modern Cajun honky-tonk music of D. L. Menard. Like the people who play it, Cajun music has remained faithful to its traditions while absorbing new influences, and it stands as one of country's liveliest strains.

Cajun singer Jimmy C. Newman made his first recordings in 1946 in the patois of his native southwestern Louisiana, but scored his biggest hits in English with "Cry, Cry Darling" (1954) and a "A Fallen Star" (1957). A member of the Opry since then, he now performs both mainstream country and Cajun music.

Leo Soileau & His Rhythm Boys, 1940s. Soileau made his first fiddle recordings at sessions in Atlanta in 1928, during which he met Jimmie Rodgers. He later formed this Cajun dance band, which at one time included Harry Choates ("Jole Blon") among its members. Soileau stands at left, bowing the fiddle.

173

The Bailes Brothers, ca. 1947: steel player Shot Jackson, mandolinist Ernest Ferguson, guitarist Walter Bailes, fiddler Homer Bailes, guitarist Johnnie Bailes, and bassist Kyle Bailes. The group left Nashville's WSM in 1946 to join Shreveport's KWKH and became charter members of the station's "Louisiana Hayride" in 1948. They sang sentimental and gospel tunes ("Dust on the Bible") with religious intensity; Walter and Homer eventually became preachers.

Bonnie Lou Carson and Texas Bill Strength get the star treatment on a promotional tour, 1950s. Bonnie sang on the "Midwestern Hayride," broadcast from WLW, Cincinnati. Texas Bill, who had a knack for turning up in photos next to real stars, spent more time as a disc jockey than as a singer in his various stints across the Southeast. 11

Arleigh Duff was teaching and coaching sports in 1953, when his song "Y'all Come" became a hit record. He never had another hit to match it, but he did become a regular cast member of ABC TV's "Ozark Jubilee" before eventually settling into DJ work.

KWKH's "Louisiana Hayride" at Shreveport's Municipal Auditorium, and for the next ten years or so this Saturday night program hosted an outstanding array of stars. Horace Logan, manager of the show, displayed an unmatched star-building talent, and the list of "Hayride" alumni is impressive—Hank Williams, Slim Whitman, Webb Pierce, Jim Reeves, Floyd Cramer,

Faron Young, Elvis Presley, Johnny Cash, Johnny Horton, and David Houston, to name only the best known. Unfortunately, a full-fledged music industry never grew up around the "Hayride," so that Shreveport failed to develop into the center that Nashville became. KWKH did maintain an artists' service bureau for booking road shows, but very little recording was ever done in Shreveport. Logan and Webb Pierce started Pacemaker Records, and the West Coast independent label Imperial cut its biggest Slim Whitman hits there, but that was about all. Song publishing was almost nonexistent, and Shreveport TV did not make effective use of the radio talent. WSM and the Opry began siphoning off KWKH's top names once they had achieved stardom, and though the "Hayride" survived the rock 'n' roll crunch longer than most barn dances by adapting an if-you-can't-beat-'em-join-'em attitude, the loss of its last big star—Johnny Horton, in a 1960 car accident—hastened the end.

Giving Shreveport, Dallas, and Cincinnati their due, the one city that most closely rivaled Nashville as a country talent center during the late 1950s was Springfield, Missouri, all on account of one radio show that switched to television—"Ozark Jubilee." Springfield's KWTO radio launched the show in July 1954 and soon lined up ABC radio affiliates to carry it on a network basis. By early 1955, ABC-TV began weekly coverage, and for the next six years former Opry star Red Foley hosted "Ozark Jubilee" and its later versions, "Country Music Jubilee" and "Jubilee USA." This consistently well-rated show provided country music with its first long-term exposure on national TV, and it showcased the talents of Brenda Lee, Porter Wagoner, Leroy Van Dyke, Bobby Lord, and numerous special guests. Growing up alongside the Springfield program were booking agencies and a music publishing company in addition to radio and TV production companies. When ABC cancelled the show in 1961, NBC briefly produced "Five Star Jubilee" out of the same Springfield site, featuring five guest hosts on a rotating basis—Snooky Lanson, Jimmy Wakely, Tex Ritter, Carl Smith, and Rex Allen. But Springfield's zenith as a music center had passed; even before cancellation of the "Ozark Jubilee," Nashville had clearly cornered the market in every area except TV production.

In California country music hadn't cooled off completely from the heady days of the late 1940s, when California-based acts filled the *Billboard* charts. Barn dances flourished on the West Coast. KNX had the "Hollywood Barn Dance," hosted by Cottonseed Clark, first broadcast from the CBS studios and, later, from the Western Palisades Ballroom in Santa Monica. Cliffie Stone started his "Hometown Jamboree" on KXLA in 1949.

Clyde Moody, "the Hillbilly Waltz King." Born in North Carolina, Moody apprenticed in string bands with Wade Mainer (1937–40) and Bill Monroe (1940–45) before going solo. On his own he made an about-face from old-time music to love songs like "Carolina Waltz" and the million-selling "Shenandoah Waltz" (1947) for Cincinnati-based King Records.

Cast of "Town Hall Party," late fifties. Broadcast from the old town hall of suburban Compton, California, Los Angeles's leading radio barn dance of the fifties successfully made the transition to local and syndicated television in the late fifties. The star-studded cast featured Tex Ritter, Merle Travis, Rose & Joe Maphis, and Johnny Bond (all standing, back row).

Then, in 1952, William Wagnon, Jr., bought Compton's Town Hall from Foreman Phillips and began his "Town Hall Party," broadcast over KFI Radio and KTTV-TV and later carried by a network of NBC radio stations. Shows were added on Friday nights, even on Sunday afternoons up in the Santa Monica Mountains at Sierra Creek Park. Movie cowboy and Capitol hit-maker Tex Ritter hosted the shows, whose cast came to include Joe and Rose Lee Maphis, Johnny Bond, Freddie Hart, Jenks "Tex" Carman, Les "Carrot Top" Anderson, Skeets McDonald, Wesley Tuttle, and the Collins Kids. Late in the 1950s, Screen Gems filmed some thirty-nine episodes for syndicated TV as "Ranch Party."

With the occasional exception of a record like Tex Ritter's "High Noon" (hit theme of the 1952 Gary Cooper western) or the early discs of young Tommy Collins, California-based recording artists did not command the attention they once had. Ritter, Tex Williams, Merle Travis, Jimmy Wakely, Wesley Tuttle, and

Eddie Kirk no longer regularly made the charts. California had everything it needed to stay on top as a country music center—radio and TV shows, great studios, publishing companies, Hollywood glamor—but most country hits of the 1950s came out of Nashville.

California recaptured some of its luster in the 1960s; this time, however, the center of activity was not in the Los Angeles area, but in Bakersfield, some hundred miles to the northwest. During the 1930s and 1940s, a great many of the migrants to California had settled in Bakersfield, an oil and farming community that then began to support a lively country music scene. One of the popular local night spots was Bill Woods's Corral, where Joe Maphis was inspired to write the classic "Dim Lights, Thick Smoke (And Loud, Loud Music)." At that time, the early 1950s, the Corral's house band, the Orange Blossom Playboys, featured a lead guitarist from Sherman, Texas, named Alvis Edgar "Buck" Owens. Buck later got the job playing guitar for Capitol artist Tommy Collins—Buck picks the lead on those Collins hits "You Better Not Do That," "It Tickles," and "You Gotta Have a License." After making a few records of his own on the Pep label, Buck signed as a solo act with Capitol in 1957. For the next five years, his hits were steady and his star was rising, but in 1963 his career really took off. Buck Owens and the Buckaroos had seventeen #1 hits over the next six years, including such well-remembered tunes as "Act Naturally," "My Heart Skips a Beat," "Together Again," "Waitin' in Your Welfare Line," and "Sam's Place." By the late 1960s, Buck led a huge organization

In 1954, eighteen-year-old Semie Moseley built this custom Mosrite guitar for ace picker Joe Maphis. The bottom neck is standard; the other is tuned an octave higher. Maphis played the instrument for eighteen years before donating it to the Country Music Hall of Fame in 1973. Mosrite Guitars became popular with California rock 'n' roll groups like the Ventures.

Joe & Rose Lee Maphis met and married while working at Chicago's WLS in the forties. In 1951, they moved to the West Coast, where they recorded together ("Dim Lights, Thick Smoke") and appeared on local radio and TV. In between, Joe contributed lightning-fast guitar licks to countless record sessions (Johnny Bond, Ricky Nelson, Wanda Jackson) as well as movie soundtracks (Thunder Road).

A popular singer in Bakersfield beginning in the fifties, Wynn Stewart finally found a #1 hit in 1967 with "It's Such a Pretty World Today."

Bakersfield favorite Tommy Collins employed Buck Owens as lead guitarist on many of his Capitol hits of the fifties, like "You Gotta Have a License" and "It Tickles." Tommy's friend Merle Haggard later immortalized him in the song "Leonard" (his real name is Leonard Sipes).

based in Bakersfield, with a booking agency, a publishing company, his own recording studio, a management company, and a TV production company. Other artists came into the Owens orbit there in Bakersfield; Tony Douglas, Buck's son Buddy Alan, and Buck's duet partner Susan Raye all achieved at least a modicum of success. Owens became co-host of "Hee Haw" in the summer of 1969; the TV exposure kept him before a national audience even after his hits came with less frequency. The death of Owens's guitarist Don Rich in 1974 was a considerable blow to Owens personally and professionally, but by that time he was a wealthy mogul with no need of further hits. In 1986 Owens left his "Hee Haw" role and has since been musically inactive.

From Bakersfield's heyday as a country music hotspot in the 1960s, two other artists deserve mention. Missouri native Wynn Stewart was based there in the 1950s, struggling on Capitol Records and later moving on to Challenge. He returned to Capitol in the mid-1960s and finally scored a #1 hit with "It's Such a Pretty World Today" in 1967. One of the singers he influenced was Bakersfield native Merle Ronald Haggard, who blended Stewart's style with strains of Jimmie Rodgers, Bob Wills, and Lefty Frizzell in forging a sound all his own. One of country music's most talented songwriters, Haggard penned and recorded "Workin' Man Blues," "Swinging Doors," "The Bottle Let Me Down," "Okie from Muskogee," and "Mama Tried." Though he has switched labels in recent years (Capitol to MCA to CBS), he remains a top-flight country star and still lives in the Bakersfield area.

Just as Bakersfield produced a successful hard-country reaction to the overproduced blandness of the Nashville Sound in the early 1960s, the so-called Outlaw movement represented a similar response in the 1970s. Many of its early figures worked in and around Austin—Willie Nelson, Michael Martin Murphey, Doug Sahm, Guy Clark, Gary P. Nunn, Asleep at the Wheel, Alvin Crow & the Pleasant Valley Boys. The last two groups moved to the forefront of a western swing revival out of Austin, which witnessed the reactivation for a decade of Bob Wills's original Texas Playboys. The popular PBS "Austin City Limits" TV program (first aired in 1976), though it has since branched out to include nearly every significant country performer, began as a showcase primarily for Austin-based acts. Except for the continuing excellence of this show, the 1980s have witnessed a decline in Austin's musical prominence. Nelson himself is now a national media celebrity, and the major country music trends of the decade—the *Urban Cowboy* craze, the rise of the pop-coun-

Buck Owens and Buckaroo Don Rich recording, 1960s.

Alvis Edgar "Buck" Owens, the pride of Bakersfield (by way of Sherman, Texas), late 1950s.

*Merle Ronald Haggard:
Bakersfield native, son of Okies
(from near Muskogee), reformed
convict, disciple of Rodgers and
Wills, poet of the common man,
keeper of the flame.*

try singers, then the coming of the neotraditionalists—passed
Austin right by.

ALL ROADS LEAD TO NASHVILLE

The story of Nashville's rise as Music City, U.S.A., is well
chronicled in books, articles, and travelogues describing the city
to prospective tourists. The Country Music Association has done
its work well. And from the standpoint of one who has lived in
Nashville for almost a decade and made a livelihood from the
industry centered here, I can certainly appreciate that story.

But of course there was nothing inevitable about Nashville's
climb to pre-eminence. In 1928 when Victor Records held their
sole prewar Nashville sessions, there simply was not enough
talent in the area to justify further trips. But the growth of
WSM's Grand Ole Opry into a star showcase by the end of World

War II changed that. WSM's Studio B was the site of Eddy Arnold's first RCA session in December 1944, and soon Opry announcer Jim Bulleit had started Bullet Records and was regularly recording country, pop, and blues artists there. The Brown Brothers set up a transcription service in Nashville about this time, and WSM engineers Aaron Shelton and Carl Jenkins started Castle Studios in their spare time, first at WSM's studios but later at the Tulane Hotel. Paul Cohen, Decca's country A&R man, made the decision by 1947 to make most of his country records there, and the other major labels slowly followed suit. The location of permanent studios in Nashville was almost dictated by the presence of not just the vocalists but the wealth of talented sidemen like Chet Atkins, Grady Martin, Bob Moore, Farris Coursey, Harold Bradley, and others, some of whom would soon assume A&R duties themselves. Publishing companies to copyright songs and market them to the A&R men increased in number—Acuff-Rose, Wallace Fowler, Tree, Cedarwood, and the many since. The presence of the publishers attracted talented writers from across the nation. Soon there was more business in town than a single booking office (WSM's Artist Service) could handle, and new ones came to meet the need. Disc jockey conventions evolved into annual extravaganzas, with awards ceremonies and all the rest. All these factors, in simultaneous operation, built Nashville's foundations as country music capital so firmly that it may no longer have any serious rivals.

No city or region has been intentionally slighted in this brief essay. Of course there were barn dances in Wheeling, Des Moines, St. Louis, Minneapolis; even my hometown of Marshall, Texas, had a barn dance for a while in the 1950s. Many major cities since World War II have had recording studios, independently owned and operated, and every community of any size at all is home to local nightclub talent and aspiring songwriters. America is a large, proud, diverse land, and no section, let alone city, has a monopoly on talent, luck, and determination. Just as cities like Memphis, Atlanta, Charlotte, Dallas, Shreveport, Cincinnati, Springfield, and Washington, D.C., had important roles to play in the past, these same cities or others like them will contribute to the future of country music. When the product gets too bland or too formulaic, new sounds will be heard, new styles will arise—or old ones will come back. Nashville may or may not continue to assimilate the trends successfully, but periodic challenges from other areas will come. However the map of business topography may be altered, country music's here to stay.

COUNTRY
CLUBS

One of the most vital aspects of the country music scene involves neither records nor radio. Laboring in obscurity from coast to coast are thousands of working musicians whose only venue is the "club scene." Almost every successful country singer pays his or her dues in these establishments, variously known as dives, beer joints, night clubs, country clubs, or honky-tonks. The customers come from all walks of life and congregate in these establishments for different reasons —some to eat, most to drink, many to dance, a lot just to stay away from home for a while. Common to all these spots, though, is country music, whether provided by the juke box, aspiring musicians, or (in the bigger, nicer places) big-name talent passing through town.

No state of the union is now without examples of the country music night club, proof positive of the broadened geographic base of the music's appeal. Of course a great many of the clubs are short-lived, ephemeral in the extreme: these either go out of business entirely, or go the way of many radio stations and change musical formats. For these reasons, the compilation of any sort of comprehensive listing of country music clubs is next to impossible and, if ever completed, would be outdated by the following week!

Consensus picks for the top clubs today would include the following few, with no slight intended for those omitted:

New York City can boast at least two prominent clubs, the Lone Star Cafe and O'Lunney's. Both came to prominence during the *Urban Cowboy* craze of the early 1980s. The Lone Star Cafe, a bit of Texas in the Big Apple (complete with chili on the menu), was host for a time to a syndicated radio series, "Live from the Lone Star Cafe."

Washington, D. C., has long been renowned for its club scene. Sadly, such local fixtures as the Cellar Door and the Childe Harold (both places where Emmylou Harris once worked) are no more, but the Birchmere continues, transplanted from Arlington, Virginia, to suburban Alexandria. Though not exclusively devoted to country music, it has long been the primary venue for the many great bluegrass acts in the area, such as the Seldom Scene; the Johnson Mountain Boys even recorded a live album there.

Ironically, Music City has never been noted for a vibrant club scene. The many stars who live in Nashville prefer resting to performing locally, since they spend so much time on the road. However, newcomers who may one day be famous jump at the chance to play the clubs while waiting for their big break on records. Two or three years back, one could have seen Randy Travis singing at the Nashville Palace out near Opryland—when he wasn't back in the kitchen cooking the hamburgers. Songwriters are often easier to find performing in Nashville's clubs than the stars. At present, Amy Kurland's Bluebird Cafe is the city's premiere showcase for songwriters. Elsewhere, publishing magnate Buddy Killen occasionally brings big names to the Stock Yard Restaurant, Boots Randolph still plays in his own club in downtown Printers Alley, and J. T. Gray consistently books top bluegrass acts at his Station Inn on 12th Avenue South.

Texas, traditional home and spawning ground of so much country music, sports its own dynamic club scene. The state's capital, Austin, birthplace of the 1970s Outlaw movement, can still boast of the Broken Spoke. Just outside of San Antonio, New Braunfels regularly draws acts like Asleep at the Wheel and Steve Earle to its Gruene Hall. Houston (suburban Pasadena, actually) has Gilley's, the club that inspired an *Esquire* article and the movie *Urban Cowboy* (largely filmed there); the film's aura still clings to the club.

Finally, heir and successor to Venice Pier or Compton's Town Hall as California's top country music venue is the Palomino Club on Lankershim Boulevard in North Hollywood. Every top performer has played the Palomino.

Urban Cowboys: cousins Jerry Lee Lewis and Mickey Gilley play the world's most famous nightclub. Mickey is no longer a part owner of Gilley's, but the club and the famous name remain.

The Golden Age of
Hillbilly Music

6

BLUE MOON OF KENTUCKY: BILL MONROE, FLATT & SCRUGGS, AND THE BIRTH OF BLUEGRASS

Neil Rosenberg

In October 1939, twenty-eight-year-old Bill Monroe joined the cast of the Grand Ole Opry. He brought with him his band, the Blue Grass Boys (named after the Bluegrass State, Kentucky, his home), and his own ideas on how to play old-time hillbilly music.

Raised on a farm near Rosine in western Kentucky, Monroe was the youngest of eight children. His mother died when he was eight, his father when he was fifteen. Shy and bashful, with poor eyesight, he was drawn to the music of his uncles, mother, and siblings. When he wanted to take up a musical instrument, his brothers Birch and Charlie already played fiddle and guitar, so they pressured young Bill into playing a less desirable stringed instrument—the mandolin. In response, the willful youngster mastered the instrument, creating his own style along the way. Nevertheless, through his youth he continued to assimilate various musical influences. As a teenager he played at dances with locally renowned black musician Arnold Schultz, and learned from the older musician. After his father's death, Bill "batched it" with his mother's brother Pendleton Vandiver—an old-time

William Smith Monroe, architect of bluegrass, in a photo taken when he was finally becoming recognized as such, ca. 1962.

Though their recording career together lasted just two years, the Monroe Brothers, Charlie and Bill (with the mandolin), influenced countless musicians across the Southeast with their hard-driving rhythm and sky-high harmonies. When they split in 1938, each formed a new band: Charlie's Kentucky Pardners (originally Monroe's Boys) and Bill's Blue Grass Boys.

The band Bill Monroe brought to the Opry, 1939: fiddler Art Wooten, Monroe, guitarist Cleo Davis, and bass player Amos Garen. Davis and Garen had left by the time of the band's first Bluebird recording session in October 1940, replaced by Clyde Moody and Bill "Cousin Wilbur" Wesbrooks, respectively.

fiddler he would later immortalize in song as "Uncle Pen," who played the fiddle so well "you could hear it talk, you could hear it sing." When Uncle Pen died in 1930, Bill, then eighteen, moved north to the Chicago area, lived with his brothers and sister, and went to work in an oil refinery. In his spare time he played music with Charlie and Birch on small northern Indiana radio stations and with them joined a square dance team associated with the "National Barn Dance" at WLS in Chicago.

In 1934, Bill and Charlie, under the sponsorship of a laxative called Texas Crystals, became full-time professional radio hillbillies. After starting at stations in Iowa and Nebraska, they moved in 1935 to South Carolina, where they quickly became popular. In April 1936, they recorded for the first time, in Charlotte, North Carolina; over the next two years the Monroe Brothers would go on to cut sixty songs for RCA Victor's Bluebird label. With gospel songs like "What Would You Give in Exchange for Your Soul?" and old-time songs like "Nine Pound Hammer Is Too Heavy" they combined high-pitched vocal duets with hot instrumental breaks, featuring Bill's prominent mandolin. Their radio broadcasts, recordings, and well-attended personal appearances made them widely influential in the Southeast within a remarkably short time.

In 1938 the Monroe Brothers split to form separate bands. By early 1939 Bill and his Blue Grass Boys were playing at small stations in Appalachia. The band he took to WSM in the fall of 1939 consisted of a string bass, a guitar, a fiddle, and his mandolin. In 1940, when they made their first recordings for RCA Victor, Bill and his guitarist Clyde Moody sang duets in the "brother style," as he'd done with Charlie. The band became a gospel quartet for numbers like "Crying Holy to the Lord." Fiddler Tommy Magness played old-time tunes like "Katie Hill" in a hot, undanceably fast way while Monroe helped lay down a solid rhythm with his mandolin. Bill, who had always sung a high tenor part with his brother, began singing solos. His first was a hit with Opry audiences and record buyers—a high-pitched up-tempo version of Jimmie Rodgers's "Blue Yodel Number 8," also known as "Mule Skinner Blues."

In "Mule Skinner Blues" was the essence of what would later be called bluegrass music. Rodgers had originally composed the song from fragments of black blues. Monroe then set this blues patchwork to an up-tempo rhythm suitable for a fiddle version of "John Henry." From the fiddle, the heart of old-time southern music, Monroe always expected not just the old tunes done correctly but innovations in technique. In the early forties Monroe worked with his fiddlers to develop a new hard-driving, bluesy sound. In "Mule Skinner" he got just that: the fiddle echoed Monroe's sharp tenor voice and also played a riff on the lower strings, which, in turn, was echoed by the guitar.

Bill Monroe & His Blue Grass Boys, ca. 1942: bassist Bill Wesbrooks, fiddler Tommy Magness, Monroe, and guitarist Clyde Moody. Note the riding-boots and jodphurs, typical costume for the group at the time: Monroe used this attire to convey an image of the band as landed southern gentry (which they weren't).

189

During these formative years of bluegrass (1939–46), Bill Monroe articulated his ideas about music only through his performances. Even then, he often stood back, letting his guitarist do much of the lead singing and his fiddler much of the lead instrumental work. Off-stage he was a man of few words who seemed aloof. His personal life was turbulent: though he was married, there were other women in his life; though he never drank, he had a reputation as a fighter. If the Nashville country music scene of the forties had gotten the kind of media scrutiny it does today, he might have been labeled a rebel. But his energy was focused on his band members, loyal young men who regarded him as teacher, pal, older brother, and boss. During the war years, when it was hard to keep a band together, the Blue Grass Boys got better and better. Southeasterners were listening

The band that first brought folks around to bluegrass, late forties: Bill Monroe with Chubby Wise, Lester Flatt, Earl Scruggs, and Birch Monroe in their stretch limousine.

closely to Bill Monroe & the Blue Grass Boys. Ambitious young musicians worked hard to imitate his sound. Whenever word got out that a Blue Grass Boy had left the band, young hopefuls took the bus to Nashville for an audition, confident that they could play the same music better.

By 1945 Bill Monroe & the Blue Grass Boys were one of the Grand Ole Opry's biggest draws. In February 1945 Monroe signed with Columbia Records, and by the following year his recordings of "Kentucky Waltz" and "Footprints in the Snow" were hits. During the next five years he was at the pinnacle of his career, riding the crest of country music's postwar popularity. Indeed, Monroe was so popular that he traveled with a circus tent, because most towns he played in did not have halls large enough to accommodate the audiences he drew. With his Blue Grass Boys and a few additional performers, Monroe's traveling show presented a gospel quartet, a comedian, a buck dancer, an old-time fiddler, a second singer who did the hits of other stars, and often a gal singer. As if that wasn't entertainment enough, Monroe's road show included the added attraction of the Blue Grass Boys and other members of the troupe dressing out as a baseball team to play the local sluggers!

At the heart of Monroe's show, of course, was his band—the hottest group of Blue Grass Boys to date. Fiddler Robert "Chubby" Wise, who had helped compose "Orange Blossom Special," and bassist-comedian Cedric Rainwater joined guitarist Lester Flatt and banjoist Earl Scruggs to create a sound that logically extended the music Monroe had been making since 1939 while including some striking new features. Part of the sound came from Flatt, whose mellow voice blended with and softened Monroe's piercing tenor. Flatt's subtle rhythm-guitar work enabled the band to stay together while playing incredibly fast, with the result sounding relaxed and smooth. Flatt was also a gifted songwriter whose collaborations with Monroe produced songs now considered bluegrass standards, such as "Will You Be Loving Another Man?"

Earl Scruggs's banjo style, built on musical traditions he encountered growing up in southwestern North Carolina, made the banjo an integral part of Monroe's sound. Today, when people think of bluegrass, this banjo sound often comes to mind first, even though it was, in Monroe's words, "the fifth child"—the last instrument added to his band. With Scruggs's banjo Monroe's basic sound was at last complete. Future refinements Monroe made would explore the various arrangement and harmonic possibilities that the instrumentation implied. But Scruggs's banjo—with that distinctive sound Pete Welding later described

Bill Monroe's classic band, on the Opry, ca. 1947: Chubby Wise on fiddle, Monroe, Lester Flatt on guitar, Earl Scruggs on banjo (with Lonzo of Lonzo & Oscar watching on the left).

as "corruscating arpeggios"—was the element that set bluegrass on the road to mass popularity. Monroe, however, viewed Scruggs's playing simply as a refinement, not a key element. His idea of bluegrass was not defined by the banjo. Thus, when Monroe made his influential second recording of "Blue Moon of Kentucky" in 1954, he omitted the banjo in favor of a third harmony fiddle. And in the formative years, the banjo was not used when the Blue Grass Boys sang gospel numbers.

In the 1940s Bill Monroe was not consciously developing "bluegrass music." The use of that term, and the idea of the musical genre that it now represents, didn't begin to emerge until after Lester Flatt and Earl Scruggs had left him. What then *was* Bill Monroe doing? From his retrospective statements in recent years it is clear that he was most interested in making a lasting personal statement about the essence of old-time music. In doing this he was fashioning, as Robert Cantwell has argued,

192

a powerful musical fiction about his cultural experience. Like any good fiction, it dealt with ultimate truths.

Not all those who heard Monroe agreed with him. Sam McGee, the middle Tennessee guitarist who had helped shape old-time country music on the Grand Ole Opry, told Charles Wolfe he liked Monroe but didn't really care that much for bluegrass: "Just plain old country music played too fast; bluegrass, crabgrass, it's all the same to me." The record critics who reviewed Monroe's records for *Billboard* called his music "backwoods" and "for the old folks."

Monroe's fellow country stars on the Opry didn't always quite know what to make of this intense, laconic man and his music. But he had a core of loyal and enthusiastic followers, musicians who copied his every move, tried to be more like Bill Monroe than Monroe himself, imitating not just his voice and his picking but details of his behavior onstage. For example, to hide bad teeth (before he got dentures), Monroe sang out of the side of his mouth. Consequently a generation of bluegrass mandolin pickers and tenor singers sang out of the sides of their mouths. One such Monroe follower was Darrell "Pee Wee" Lambert, a young Virginian who helped the Stanley Brothers start their band in 1947. With Lambert's impetus, this group began to sound more and more like Bill Monroe's Blue Grass Boys. Playing on WCYB at Bristol in the heart of Appalachia, they were a solid hit with rural mountain listeners.

Bill Monroe & His Blue Grass Boys (and Girl), ca. 1944: fiddler Chubby Wise, bassist Curly Bradshaw (on harmonica here), Monroe, singer and accordionist Wilene "Sally Ann" Forrester, guitarist Clyde Moody, and Dave "Stringbean" Akeman on banjo. Akeman left Monroe in 1945 and eventually became a well-known comic star of the Opry. Forrester was married to sometime Monroe fiddler Howdy Forrester.

FESTIVALS FOR THE FAITHFUL

The love affair between country fans and mainstream country artists is a special one, but it doesn't begin to approach the fervor of bluegrass fans. Within the bluegrass cult—and in many ways the phenomenon does resemble a religion—musicians are virtual high priests, standard songs comprise a sacred canon, and fans are the faithful flock. Most important of all is the bluegrass festival, a kind of camp meeting that has become the fullest expression of the bluegrass world, uniting performers and fans through the music they love so zealously.

Bluegrass festivals began early in the 1960s, when the slick, country-pop Nashville Sound all but eclipsed such tradition-based sounds. In a sense, early festivals were a form of protest against modernizing trends in country music. Performer Bill Clifton organized a one-day affair in Luray, Virginia, in 1961, but the bluegrass festival as we know it didn't come into being until promoter Carlton Haney staged the First Annual Roanoke Bluegrass Festival, held September 3–5, 1965, at Cantrell's Horse Farm in Fincastle, Virginia. The three-day event was based, in part, on the famous Newport Folk Festival. But whereas Newport featured traditional folk, blues, and bluegrass artists under the general heading of "folk music," the Roanoke festival showcased bluegrass exclusively. That first festival lineup included many top bluegrass acts, including Bill Monroe & His Blue Grass Boys, the Stanley Brothers, Jimmy Martin, and Don Reno. For bluegrass fans, it was Hillbilly Heaven.

Far from preserving a dying art form—as some who attended thought they might be doing—the first Roanoke festival heralded an explosion in the popularity of bluegrass and set standards for hundreds of festivals that followed, including those at Berryville, Virginia; Cosby, Tennessee; Lavonia, Georgia; Kerrville, Texas; and Bean Blossom, Indiana. Of the four hundred or so bluegrass festivals now held annually, the Bean Blossom Festival is the largest and the most prestigious. Begun by Bill Monroe in 1967 on his own property in southern Indiana, the event lasts for several days each June, drawing the top bands and thousands of fans.

194

Stages and seating arrangements vary widely from festival to festival. Some events are held at outdoor amphitheaters. Others take place at baseball fields or race tracks, where promoters build stages in the infield and listeners sit in the grandstands. Other, smaller gatherings are held in open fields, using simple plywood stages; at these events festival-goers simply bring lawn chairs and find themselves a vacant patch of ground. Whatever the degree of comfort, most festival grounds have camping facilities and fans can often enjoy several days of entertainment at prices ranging from no cost to about twenty dollars a day per person.

A typical bluegrass festival is a beehive of activity, on and off the stage. The stage, of course, is the focal point of the event, where local and nationally known bands perform —and expert musicians give free lessons. Bands usually begin playing by mid-morning and frequently continue late into the night. Many festivals also include a Sunday-morning gospel sing involving all the festival performers.

Off-stage, music is just as prevalent. Many of those who attend festivals are musicians themselves, and there is plenty of entertainment to be found in the parking lots and camping areas. Impromptu jam sessions often mingle professionals and amateurs, or professionals from different bands. Many festival-goers take cassette tape recorders and search the grounds for "dream" jam sessions that might include Sam Bush on mandolin, John Hartford on banjo, Norman Blake on guitar, or Kenny Baker on fiddle. In fact, the prospect of witnessing these spur-of-the-moment sessions probably draws as many fans as the headline artists do.

While festivals are great fun for everyone involved, they are also the lifeblood of professional bluegrass musicians. Most full-time bands depend heavily on festival bookings, not only to earn concert fees but also to sell albums. These bands record for small, independent companies whose releases are often ignored by record stores. Since bluegrass has very little radio exposure, festivals are absolutely essential to an artist's marketing efforts. Almost every festival has a row of booths offering band recordings, T-shirts, and souvenirs. Meanwhile, other vendors hawk instruments, parts for instruments, strings, food and drinks, camping supplies, and every kind of art and craft imaginable.

Because bluegrass festivals draw fans young and old, they have become the means by which musical traditions, instrumental techniques, and stagecraft are passed lovingly from one generation to the next. Despite the ebb and flow of mainstream trends, bluegrass stubbornly persists, a stylistic stream that meanders its own way.

Ticket to Bill Monroe's annual festival, before it was officially called Bean Blossom.

The bluegrass festival, where disciples gather for the gospel according to Lester, Earl, Bill, and Ralph.

Program for Bill Monroe's annual festival.

Bill Monroe's 15th Annual Bean Blossom Bluegrass Festival June 12 — 21, 1981

FRIDAY, June 12
Bill Monroe
James Monroe
Birch Monroe
Dry Branch Fire Squad
Raymond Fairchild

SATURDAY, June 13
Bill Monroe
James Monroe
Birch Monroe
Don Reno & The Tennessee Cut-ups
Jimmy Martin & The Sunny Mountain Boys
Blue Grass Cardinals
Dry Branch Fire Squad
Raymond Fairchild

SUNDAY, June 14
Bill Monroe
Don Reno
Del McCoury & The Dixie Pals
Dry Branch Fire Squad
Lillimae & The Dixie Gospel Aires
Birch Monroe

MONDAY, June 15
Bill Monroe
Birch Monroe
Wildwood Pickers
Blue Grass Boys

TUESDAY, June 16
Bill Monroe
Birch Monroe
A. L. Wood
New Horizon

WEDNESDAY, June 17
Bill Monroe
Birch Monroe
A. L. Wood
New Horizon

SPECIAL EVENTS

Mon, 15th - Bean Day
        (Beans, slaw & cornbread)
Tues, 16th - Banjo Contest
Wed, 17th - Little Miss Bluegrass contest
Thurs, 18th - Band contest

THURSDAY, June 18
Bill Monroe
Birch Monroe
Mac Wiseman
Lost Kentuckians
Goins Brothers

FRIDAY, June 19
Bill Monroe
Wilma Lee Cooper & The Clinch Mtn. Clan
Lost Kentuckians
James Monroe
Boys from Indiana
Goins Brothers

SATURDAY, June 20
Bill Monroe
James Monroe
Birch Monroe
Wilma Lee Cooper
Jim & Jesse & The Virginia Boys
Ralph Stanley & The Clinch Mtn. Boys
Carl Story & The Ramblin' Mtn.
Doyle Lawson & Quicksilver

SUNDAY, June 21
Bill Monroe
Jim & Jesse
Ralph Stanley
Carl Story
Sullivan Family

Carter and Ralph Stanley, 1949. At the time of this Columbia promotional photo, the brothers had emulated Bill Monroe's sound so successfully that Monroe quit the label in protest and moved to Decca. In mid 1951, Carter briefly joined Monroe's Blue Grass Boys; when the Stanleys regrouped later that year, Monroe had become one of their biggest supporters.

Early in 1948, Monroe's crack band suddenly came apart. Fiddler Chubby Wise headed to Washington to work with former Blue Grass Boy Clyde Moody. Flatt, Scruggs, and Rainwater left a few weeks later and were soon playing together with guitarist and vocalist Mac Wiseman and fiddler Jim Shumate as Lester Flatt, Earl Scruggs & the Foggy Mountain Boys at WCYB in Bristol, alternating shows with the Stanley Brothers. It was hardly coincidental, then, that Ralph Stanley's five-string banjo soon began to sound more like Earl Scruggs's than it had before. The Stanleys fired Leslie Keith, the old-time fiddler who had been with them from the start, and hired Art Wooten, a former Monroe fiddler. Soon they recorded their version of "Molly and Tenbrooks," an obscure Kentucky blues ballad Bill Monroe had arranged and was performing on the Opry to showcase his singing and Earl Scruggs's banjo. Monroe had already recorded it but Columbia had not yet issued his original when the Stanley Brothers' copy was released on a small local label. In their version, Pee Wee Lambert's voice was pitched higher than Bill's and Ralph Stanley's banjo was picked faster than Earl's. In 1949 their success with this and other recordings, along with their radio fame, helped the Stanleys secure a recording contract with Columbia—the same label Monroe recorded for. Monroe, angered that Columbia had signed someone who sounded so much like him, moved to Decca in protest. On the Decca records, a new crop of Blue Grass Boys—including singer-guitarist Jimmy Martin, fiddler Vassar Clements, and banjo picker Rudy Lyle— embellished but did not substantially alter the sound Monroe had established with his ace unit of 1946–48.

When Flatt and Scruggs left Monroe, the distinctive sound of his 1946–48 band ceased to be Monroe's private possession: the word was spreading; there was a new sound to emulate. By 1949 the term *bluegrass* was being used by a few close followers of the music to describe that sound. The usage spread steadily in the early fifties as more and more bands began performing and recording in the style of the famed Blue Grass Boys.

The workings of this fast-paced music—the tight vocal harmonies and intricate instrumental techniques—were not easy to learn. But as the fifties wore on, young musicians, many of them from the Appalachian regions of Tennessee, Kentucky, Virginia, and the Carolinas, fell in love with the new sound and eagerly delved into it. Tearing it apart, they put it back together in their own way. For example, the banjo pickers took Flatt & Scruggs 78s and played them at 45 rpm, playing along at half speed to figure out how one of Earl Scruggs's fingers followed another.

Flatt & Scruggs's popularity blossomed in the fifties. After leaving Monroe and Nashville, they gradually built a reputation at small radio stations across the Southeast. By 1951 the group was recording for Columbia. Scruggs's banjo instrumentals "Earl's Breakdown" (1951) and "Flint Hill Special" (1952) were widely used as theme songs on country radio stations. In 1953 Martha White Flour, a Tennessee company that had been using country music to promote its product, began to sponsor Flatt & Scruggs and moved them back to Nashville to do a daily live early morning radio show on WSM. Martha White wanted them to join the cast of the Opry, but Monroe used his influence with manager Jim Denny to keep them off. So from 1953 they remained on the fringe in Nashville, biding their time while they appeared on a radio barn dance in Richmond, Virginia, on Saturday nights. While Flatt & Scruggs were not yet as well known as Monroe, their records and broadcasts were being followed

Most bluegrassers are known for their picking, but Mac Wiseman's bread-and-butter has been his robust tenor voice. After working as a sideman and singer for Molly O'Day, Flatt & Scruggs, and Bill Monroe, Wiseman led his own bluegrass band, the Country Boys, from 1950 to 1956—until it proved more profitable to go solo.

Flatt & Scruggs on the Martha White TV show, 1950s. The Martha White Flour Company began sponsoring the band on radio in 1953, and the partnership continued for the next sixteen years. "Flatt & Scruggs and the Grand Ole Opry built the Martha White Mills," maintained company president Cohen T. Williams.

closely by hundreds of young musicians all over the Southeast, just as they had followed Monroe closely a decade before. At the same time, bluegrass had another, less direct, impact. In west Tennessee and northern Mississippi, young men like Carl Perkins and Elvis Presley had grown up listening to Monroe and heard the blues connection in his music. Perkins began doing bluesman John Lee Hooker's songs "Monroe style, blues with a country beat." Presley turned the trick the other way when, cutting his first record in the summer of 1954, he transformed Monroe's country waltz "Blue Moon of Kentucky" into an up-tempo blues.

Monroe reacted by rerecording the song on the afternoon of September 4, 1954, with a band that included three fiddles (but no banjo). He did the first part of the song in the original waltz time, then he shifted into his up-tempo version of Presley's treatment. A month later, on October 2, Elvis Presley was a guest

198

The Bluegrass Cardinals, 1980s: bassist Dale Perry, mandolinist Larry Stephenson, fiddler Mike Hartgrove, banjoist Don Parmley, and guitarist David Parmley. Kentuckian Don Parmley played background banjo for the "Beverly Hillbillies" TV show before forming this outfit in the mid seventies; at the time, their lead singer, Parmley's son David, was just fifteen.

performer on the Opry—the only time in his career. Backstage, he drew Monroe aside and apologized for the changes he'd made in the song. Monroe encouraged him, saying that if he could make a hit with it, he was welcome to it. According to Sun Records owner Sam Phillips, "Elvis was thrilled. Jim Denny saw us backstage before and after the show, and let us know he was pleased with Elvis's show. But as always, he was concerned about keeping Opry performances country." Legend has it that Denny advised Elvis to return to his old job of driving a truck.

In the opinion of many music moguls in Nashville, Presley, Perkins, and the other rockabillies endangered country music. Though these youngsters got their start in country music and were musically indebted to bluegrass, they became part of the rock 'n' roll revolution that not only cut into country music sales but also created what was perceived in Nashville as a threatening ideological stance. Like rock 'n' roll, bluegrass was a new form. It, too, was a response to the forces of modernity, but bluegrass projected a different worldview. Rock 'n' roll was for youth; bluegrass for the whole family. Rock 'n' roll celebrated contemporary urban life, while bluegrass idealized the rural life of the past and dwelt on harsh realities of contemporary urban adulthood. Whereas Flatt & Scruggs lamented about "Crying My Heart Out over You" and recalled "The Cabin on the Hill" (their first two country chart hits, in 1959), Elvis sang "I Wanna Play House with You" and Perkins advised everyone to get

199

Kentucky Colonels poster, ca. 1964, when the group's lineup consisted of mandolinist Roland White, bassist Roger Bush, guitarist Clarence White, fiddler Bobby Sloane, and banjoist Billy Ray Lathum.

BLUEGRASS'S WESTERN FRONT

Although bluegrass music started in the Southeast with Bill Monroe, Flatt & Scruggs, and the Stanley Brothers, it was by no means confined to that area. A vital strain of bluegrass—related but distinct—surfaced in Southern California in the late 1950s and early 1960s, just as the style was becoming well known to the followers of folk music. The Southern California bluegrass community was small, but what it lacked in size it made up in energy and innovation, as a handful of musicians added new dimensions to the style, laying groundwork for

what was later to become known as country-rock.

The three most successful bluegrass bands performing in the Los Angeles area during this fruitful period were the Kentucky Colonels, the Dillards, and the Golden State Boys. All three had at their core groups of brothers—much like many pioneering bands that helped define country music forty years earlier.

The Kentucky Colonels (a.k.a. the Country Boys) were brothers Roland (mandolin), Clarence (guitar), and Eric White (bass), who began performing in and around Los Angeles as teenagers in 1954. In the late 1950s, the Whites added Billy Ray Lathum and LeRoy Mack on banjo and dobro, and the group worked steadily in the area, making regular TV appearances on "Town Hall Party" and "Hometown Jamboree." By 1961, the Colonels were generally recognized as the best working bluegrass band in Southern California, and they parlayed their command of bluegrass into an audition for "The Andy Griffith Show," which led to two appearances on the top-rated CBS program. Subsequently, they cut four sides with Griffith on his Capitol Records LP released that same year.

In the early sixties, the Colonels added a fiddler to the band, first Bobby Sloan and later Scotty Stoneman, a fiddle contest champion and the son of string-band pioneer Ernest V. "Pop" Stoneman. In 1964, the group made an extensive East Coast tour, including a well-received appearance at the Newport Folk Festival (in a lineup that included Bob Dylan and the Stanley Brothers). Despite glowing reviews, the group disbanded a few years later. Roland continued performing, first with Bill Monroe's Bluegrass Boys and later Lester Flatt's Nashville Grass, eventually settling into

the L.A.-based Country Gazette, which included banjoist Alan Munde and L.A. session fiddler Byron Berline. Today, the Gazette, featuring Roland and Munde, plays a host of bluegrass festivals and workshops.

For his part, Clarence developed into a very influential electric guitarist. His distinctive style led to session work for Ricky Nelson, Linda Ronstadt, and the Byrds, whom he joined in 1968 after playing on their landmark country-rock LP *Sweetheart of the Rodeo*. With fellow Byrd Gene Parsons he developed the Parsons-White String Bender, a guitar mechanism that simulates the sound of a pedal steel guitar, now standard-issue equipment for many country guitarists. Clarence died in 1973 just as his star was ascending, the victim of a hit-and-run driver in a club parking lot in Palmdale, California.

In response to an ad in *Variety* placed by Elektra Records, the Dillards picked up where the Colonels left off, making several appearances on Griffith's show as the moonshining string band, the Darling Family. Missouri-born Rodney and Doug Dillard were the sons of an old-time fiddler and played in the St. Louis area with mandolinist Dean Webb and bassist Mitch Jayne. Looking for a more lucrative career, the band set out for Los Angeles, landing at the Ash Grove—the city's top folk club and a haven for bluegrassers— on their first night in town. Some backstage jamming after the show caught the attention of free-lance producer Jim Dickson. Although primarily a jazz fan, Dickson appreciated bluegrass's improvisational turn and got the Dillards their deal with Elektra, putting the group on the same label with folk-based acts such as Judy Collins and Phil Ochs.

The Country Boys, later known as the Kentucky Colonels, from a 1961 appearance on "The Andy Griffith Show."

After some successful LPs for the label, the group disbanded. Doug Dillard went on to join former Byrd Gene Clark, future Eagle Bernie Leadon, and, later, Herb Pedersen in the Dillard and Clark Expedition, an experimental bluegrass/folk-rock group. The original Dillards band regrouped briefly in 1987 for the made-for-TV movie "Return to Mayberry" and a single appearance on the Nashville Network's "Nashville Now" show. Today, Doug heads the Nashville-based Doug Dillard Band.

Jim Dickson also served as a promoter for Chris Hillman of the Golden State Boys, a group that included Vern and Rex Gosdin and Don Parmley. Unfortunately, the group lasted all too briefly, making only one recording around 1963–64, which was not released until long after they had disbanded.

Vern Gosdin has since achieved some renown as a solo performer singing hard-country songs. Don Parmley teamed up with son David and mandolin player Larry Stevenson to head one of today's premiere bluegrass bands, the Bluegrass Cardinals.

Chris Hillman helped shape the history of rock 'n' roll as a founding member of the Byrds, then later teamed up with erstwhile Byrd Gram Parsons in the Flying Burrito Brothers during the formative years of the genre now known as country-rock. Today Hillman heads up the Desert Rose Band, a popular country group that synthesizes the various styles he helped to develop.

Brothers Rex, Vern, and Ray Gosdin with Chuck Reeves, ca. 1965. Mandolinist Vern (here clowning with Reeves's fiddle) and bassist Rex (with Ray's guitar) had previously worked as the Golden State Boys with Chris Hillman and Don Parmley.

Formed in 1972 as part of a Flying Burrito Brothers tour package, Country Gazette gained the respect of the bluegrass establishment while also appealing to younger fans. The group's original lineup: Alan Munde on banjo, Byron Berline on fiddle, Roger Bush on bass, and Kenny Wertz on guitar.

"Dixie Fried." The up-tempo beat of bluegrass was not very different from that of the rockabillies, but it was frequently the backdrop for lyrics that in other forms of country music would have been sung slowly and mournfully. In this combination of fast music and sad or sentimental words, bluegrass frequently projected an ambivalence about meaning. If the story is so sad, why not sing it at a mournful pace? A feeling of mixed motives is apparent too in Monroe's remake of "Blue Moon of Kentucky," where he used three fiddles, the symbol of old-fashioned country music. Was this a statement about tradition, or a simple move to cash in on Elvis's makeover of his waltz?

In the next few years the forces represented by Jim Denny, Presley, and Monroe would mix, collide, and remix in events that shaped bluegrass as it began to move from being a subspecies of country music to a more independent status.

Denny was a key figure in the Nashville music establishment that came to power in the fifties. As the record business boomed in the postwar years, Nashville became the country music recording center. With that came professional songwriters, publishing companies, and talent agencies. Denny had, as manager of the Opry, made WSM's barn dance prosper when many others were suffering because of competition from television. He did this in part by capably promoting and booking Opry artists like Monroe. He also developed his own successful publishing business. In September 1956, WSM fired Denny following accusations of conflict of interest—some felt that, as Opry booking manager, Denny discriminated against artists who didn't publish

203

Passing the torch: Jimmy Martin apprenticed as singer and lead guitarist in Bill Monroe's Blue Grass Boys before forming his own group, the Sunny Mountain Boys, with Bobby Osborne in mid 1951. Like Monroe, he employed a succession of talented young sidemen; two of the finest (flanking Martin in this ca. 1956 photo) were banjoist J. D. Crowe and mandolinist Paul Williams. Crowe, in turn, went on to form his own band.

their songs through his private company. Beneficiaries of this business feud were Flatt & Scruggs, who finally became Opry cast members in 1956, after Denny left. This gave added impetus to an already growing career. In addition to their radio show they had a series of live weekly television programs in Tennessee, West Virginia, South Carolina, and Georgia. They were heard regularly by thousands of country fans who responded enthusiastically to what was increasingly seen as a conservative country style.

The Nashville establishment was hustling in 1956–57 to make the sound of country music competitive with the forces unleashed by Elvis and his followers. In order to compete, they had to make records that would appeal to a wide variety of radio listeners and thereby attract advertising revenue. They had to sound more urban, less rural. Hence the Nashville Sound, an idea more than a style, which strove to bring recorded country music uptown by utilizing the best studio musicians to give the music the polished trappings of popular sounds. They used drums, pianos, string sections, and electric guitars, but fiddles and banjos didn't fit this idea. Many bluegrass acts, along with other rough-edged country performers, disappeared from major

*Jim & Jesse McReynolds had
considerable success in taking
bluegrass and traditional
brother-duet harmonies toward
the mainstream. They joined
the Opry in 1964 and two years
later began a syndicated TV
show, on which they substituted
drums and electric guitars for
banjos and fiddles. Despite
these heresies—and having
recorded a hit trucker's song
and an album of Chuck Berry
songs—they remained favorites
of the festival scene.*

*A prodigy who won his first
fiddle contest at age ten
(besting his father), Byron
Berline joined the Dillards for
their classic* Pickin' and
Fiddlin' *album (1964) while
still a student at the University
of Oklahoma. A cofounder of
Country Gazette, he has also
played with Bill Monroe's Blue
Grass Boys and in L.A. sessions
for the Rolling Stones and other
rock groups.*

record labels at this time; the country music businessmen just
didn't think the sound was commercial. A new word, *bluegrass*,
became the country music businessman's term for the old-fashioned stuff many were trying to distance themselves from. Ironically, this perception of non-commerciality started bluegrass on
the road to revival.

At almost the same time the word *bluegrass* became part of
the vocabulary of the country music business, it also appeared
in the folk-song revival. *Bluegrass* first appeared in print in September 1956 when a disc jockey loyal to the material stated
proudly he was "programming practically all blue grass and true
hillbilly material." A few months later, New York-based Folk-
ways Records released the first LP of bluegrass music, *American
Banjo Scruggs Style*; the brochure that accompanied it included
young Ralph Rinzler's brief description and history of bluegrass
music, stressing its relationship to folk music.

Folk was becoming a kind of popular music in the late fifties,
and as it grew in this direction the need for authentic new folk
sounds drove young revivalists into discovering artists in genres
that young urban middle-class people had not previously patron-
ized. For example, from the rough black working-class bars of
Houston came Sam "Lightnin' " Hopkins, a prolific bluesman
who was persuaded to swap his electric guitar for an acoustic
model, so as to sound more "authentic" when playing folk festivals. Similarly, the five-string banjo of Earl Scruggs attracted

Born in rural West Virginia, Everett and Mitchell B. ("Bea") Lilly grew up on the music of the Monroe Brothers and the Blue Sky Boys, and began performing as the Lilly Brothers in the early forties. In 1952, following Everett's brief stint as mandolinist and tenor singer for Flatt & Scruggs, the brothers brought the bluegrass sound to Boston, where they remained local favorites on radio and in the clubs for eighteen years.

Gospel songs are central to the bluegrass canon. After playing fiddle briefly for Bill Monroe (1942–43), Carl Story (on guitar) led his own group, the Rambling Mountaineers, and became noted for his gospel material at Atlanta's WSB, Knoxville's WNOX, and, later, on the bluegrass festival circuit.

the attention of the folk-song revivalists because they saw it as a folk instrument. Popularized by Pete Seeger, the banjo was being taken up by young, urban middle-class youth for whom rock 'n' roll was ideologically unacceptable because of (1) its "mindless" lyrics and (2) the electric guitar, which they saw as a symbol of everything artificial and decadent in contemporary society. Among the invited performers at the first Newport Folk Festival in 1959 was Earl Scruggs.

Scruggs, but not Flatt! The revivalists were not really very interested in the vocal sounds of bluegrass—and many also found the fiddle hard to listen to. Bluegrass was to them squeaky, whiny, nasal, hillbilly music punctuated by brilliant folk banjo sounds. So the organizers of Newport invited Scruggs, and Flatt stayed in Nashville. For his backup band, Earl used Martha White's number-two bluegrass outfit, Hylo Brown & the Timberliners, who were playing in nearby Providence that week. Pictures of Scruggs and Brown taken at this festival still show up labeled as "Flatt & Scruggs."

Lester and Earl's sponsors, Martha White Flour, attached little importance to Earl's breakthrough to a new audience—after all, you couldn't buy Martha White Flour in Rhode Island or anywhere else north of the Mason-Dixon line. Nevertheless, the next year Earl returned to Newport with Lester and the entire band. That this happened was typical of this band, which, though in some ways musically conservative, was independent and adventurous in developing its business.

206

By 1960 Flatt & Scruggs were big-time in Nashville. Their Columbia singles were hitting the country charts regularly. They were heard every Saturday night on the Opry's prime-time slot, 8:00 (Central), 9:00 (Eastern). Their Martha White television shows were now syndicated rather than live, which freed them to play personal appearances. One of the busiest acts in country music, they were on the road almost continually, traveling by bus to play in packed auditoriums all over the South and Midwest. Yet in several respects they were unlike contemporary country stars. They maintained an unusual degree of control over their sound. They weren't using the Nashville Sound in their recordings to the same extent as others did. When you bought a Flatt & Scruggs record, you heard basically the same musicians you saw when you went out to one of their shows, saw them on television, or heard them on the radio.

Flatt & Scruggs also maintained an unusual degree of control over their bookings. Unlike most other country acts, they were managed not by an agency (such as that established by Jim Denny after he left the Opry) but by Earl Scruggs's wife, Louise. She'd begun handling bookings in the mid-fifties, and by the time Newport called she had become deeply involved in the management of the band. Not only did she handle tour arrangements, she wrote the copy for the songbooks the band sold over the radio, and she orchestrated their publicity. Louise Scruggs recognized that while Kingston Trio fans and other young middle-class urban Yankees at Newport might never buy Martha White Flour, they would buy Flatt & Scruggs. In the early sixties, a series of concept LPs, aimed at this market, proved her right: the first one, *Foggy Mountain Banjo*, focused on Earl's banjo and got a rave review in the jazz monthly *down beat*. An album of Carter Family songs exploited the band's connection with that old-time country music group so popular with folk music fans. An album of folk songs, along with live concert LPs from Carnegie Hall and Vanderbilt University, dramatized the changes in repertoire and venue that marked Flatt & Scruggs's metamorphosis from favorite of the Martha White circuit to all-American act. When they played at the Ash Grove, a Los Angeles folk music coffee house, TV producer Paul Henning saw Flatt & Scruggs for the first time and chose them to perform the theme music for his new television series, "The Beverly Hillbillies." With "The Ballad of Jed Clampett" in 1963, bluegrass had its first #1 country chart single.

What of the other bluegrass acts? Since the late forties, the Stanley Brothers had been playing at radio stations, mainly in the southern mountain region and later in north Florida. They

Frank "Hylo" Brown, 1950s. Nicknamed for his wide vocal range, Hylo played bass for Flatt & Scruggs's Foggy Mountain Boys during the late fifties. In 1959, Hylo and his band, the Timberliners, backed Earl Scruggs during his first Newport Folk Festival appearance. Pictures of Scruggs and Brown taken there still show up labeled "Flatt & Scruggs."

Flatt & Scruggs, 1960s.

Don Reno, who replaced Earl Scruggs as Bill Monroe's banjo player in 1948, organized his own band a year later. Guitarist Red Smiley joined Reno's Tennessee Cutups soon after; by the late fifties, Reno & Smiley's popularity matched that of Flatt & Scruggs in the Southeast, and Reno's jazzy picking proved nearly as influential as Scruggs's. Their classic lineup: fiddler Mack McGaha, Reno, Smiley, and bass player John Palmer.

The Osborne Brothers, 1980s. During the late sixties, purists criticized Sonny and Bobby Osborne for mixing drums, electric basses, and steel guitars with bluegrass, but the results were impressive.

LEAVES OF GRASS

When Lester Flatt and Earl Scruggs parted ways in 1969, ending a partnership that stretched back more than twenty years, few bluegrass fans or musicians were surprised. After all, the disputes Flatt & Scruggs had over musical direction —Flatt wanting to return to the style he and Scruggs had pioneered in the late forties, and Scruggs looking to extend his experiments with pop and rock music—simply reflected the dilemma that many bluegrass fans and musicians faced in the seventies: to cleave to tradition or venture into experimentation? While the purists (who tended to be older and more conservative politically) held fast to the acoustic, string-band standards established by Bill Monroe, Flatt & Scruggs, and the Stanley Brothers, a countercultural element in bluegrass—bolstered by the recent influx of young rock fans— asked what was wrong with amplifying banjos, fiddle, and mandolins, and playing on them anything they wanted. Nothing, replied the old guard, but it ain't bluegrass— and don't come to our festivals until you get your hair cut.

Historian Bill Malone cites the Country Gentlemen as one of the earliest of the so-called "newgrass" groups, who freely mixed electric instruments and rock songs with more traditional acoustic bluegrass as early as the mid-1960s and were occasionally snubbed by older bluegrassers because of it. Nevertheless, the creative possibilities of newgrass enticed many young musicians, and in time the Country Gentlemen were joined by such progressive bands as J. D. Crowe & the New South, the Second Generation

New Grass Revival, then and now. Then (late seventies): Curtis Burch, John Cowan, Sam Bush, and Courtney Johnson. Now (pictured opposite): John Cowan, Pat Flynn, Bela Fleck, Sam Bush.

(founded by banjoist Eddie Adcock, a former Country Gentleman), and the Seldom Scene (organized by mandolinist John Duffey, also a Country Gentlemen alumnus), Poor Richard's Almanac, Country Gazette, Spectrum, Hot Rize, and the Bluegrass Alliance.

The most successful of these progressive groups, at least in terms of longevity and exposure, was formed in 1972 by four members of the Bluegrass Alliance. Dubbed the New Grass Revival by fiddler-mandolinist Sam Bush, the group didn't hesitate to combine bluegrass picking with folk songs and rock-style jams, and, by the 1980s, Motown covers and reggae rhythms. Although the group experienced personnel changes (Bush is the only remaining original member), New Grass Revival endured and devel-

oped a loyal following for their concert appearances and LP releases on the Flying Fish, Rounder, and Sugar Hill labels. By 1986, they were the only bluegrass act—with the exception of Bill Monroe and Earl Scruggs—to hold a major-label recording contract (Capitol).

Meanwhile, traditional bluegrass continued to have its share of performers. Among the more successful of these groups were the Bluegrass Cardinals (led by virtuoso banjoist Don Parmley) and Lester Flatt's Nashville Grass, headed by Curly Seckler, following Flatt's death in 1979. Of course, Bill Monroe, Ralph Stanley, the Osborne Brothers, and Jim & Jesse continued to travel the country, carrying on the bluegrass tradition that they had helped to establish.

Of all the traditional acts, though,

Founded in 1978, the Johnson Mountain Boys sounded (and looked) like the classic bluegrass bands of the 1950s. Pictured in this 1987 photo are fiddler Eddie Stubbs, banjoist David McLaughlin, singer-guitarist Dudley Connell, banjoist Tom Adams, and bass player Marshall Wilborn.

the one that seemed to hold the most promise for eventually breaking through to a wider audience was the Johnson Mountain Boys, a quintet of young musicians from the Washington, D. C., area, who began playing together in 1978. Their strict, but spirited adherence to the traditional singing and picking styles endeared them to fans of old bluegrass everywhere. Their seven Rounder albums (one of them featuring gospel numbers only) sold in modest numbers, but always consistently. To the regret of many oldgrassers, the group disbanded in February 1988, citing the difficulty of earning a living as a working bluegrass band.

Though there still remain dogmatic traditionalists in bluegrass today, by the early 1980s the battle seemed hardly important anymore. As the breakup of the Johnson Mountain Boys suggests, the audience for bluegrass—which during the euphoric, eclectic sixties seemed to be ever-expanding—was shrinking. The baby boom was over and so was the folk revival that had contrib-

uted so much to the national prominence of bluegrass. The problem was no longer adulteration, but extinction.

One musician who appeared to have reconciled the purist vs. newgrass argument quite successfully—and who appealed to young and old alike—was Ricky Skaggs. With a background that encompassed traditional bluegrass (Ralph Stanley's Clinch Mountain Boys), newgrass (the New South), and contemporary country (Emmylou Harris's Hot Band), Skaggs naturally brought musical styles and people together. Like the newgrassers, Skaggs confidently mixed bluegrass instruments (mandolin, fiddle) and bluegrass standards ("Don't Get Above Your Raisin'," "Uncle Pen") with other types of music—in his case, honky-tonk and contemporary country. Though the product wasn't really bluegrass, it still appealed to many traditional fans if only because when Skaggs did play bluegrass, he did the classics of Monroe and Flatt & Scruggs energetically and faithfully. Skaggs's breakthrough success has since made room for others from the festival circuit, like the Whites (featuring Ricky's wife, Sharon) and Keith Whitley (who played in Stanley's band with Ricky), who have made their mark on contemporary country.

Bluegrass may never again attain the prominence and popularity it enjoyed in the early sixties, but its influence is being felt in the wider country market through artists like Skaggs and top session players like dobroist Jerry Douglas and fiddler-mandolinist-guitarist Mark O'Connor. Meanwhile, bluegrass is still heard on more than eight hundred radio programs across the country, and bluegrass bands continue to play the festivals and the clubs, mostly for the sheer fun of it.

appealed mostly to listeners in the mountains, where they cultivated a following of diehard fans. Their popularity was greatest
in their home state of Virginia, and they were particularly influential in the Washington-Baltimore area where groups of young
musicians like the Country Gentlemen drew heavily from the
Stanleys' repertoire. Hardcore cult favorites, they never attained
the level of popularity of Flatt & Scruggs. But they did find favor
with folk audiences in the early sixties. In this respect, the Stanleys were unlike another regional band, Don Reno and Red
Smiley, whose popularity with country music audiences in the
Southeast during the late fifties and early sixties rivaled that of
Flatt & Scruggs. Reno & Smiley were typical of the many bluegrass outfits that simply never made it into the folk arena. Yet in
the early sixties bluegrass did become an important part of the

*Although not a bluegrass
musician, Arthel "Doc" Watson
has been a favorite at bluegrass
and folk festivals since the
early sixties, when, in his
middle age, he was
"discovered" by the folk
revival. Blind almost from
birth, weaned on country radio
and records from the twenties
and thirties, Watson taught
himself the guitar, eventually
developing a high-speed flat-
picking style reminiscent of old-
time fiddling.*

*Stalwarts of bluegrass gospel,
the Lewis Family, 1950s.
Among the first bluegrass bands
to feature female vocalists, the
Lewis Family got their big
break appearing on an all-
night gospel program booked by
the Grand Ole Opry's Wally
Fowler. Later they became
popular on the festival circuit.
Here they are at WJBF,
Augusta, Georgia, where they
had a TV show in the mid
fifties.*

Jimmy Martin—sometimes billed as "The King of Bluegrass"—dressing the part, 1970s. During the sixties and seventies, Monroe's one-time vocalist was a powerful voice for traditional bluegrass and a mainstay on the festival circuit.

Ralph Stanley & His Clinch Mountain Boys, 1968: fiddler Curley Ray Cline, bassist Melvin Goins (here on guitar), guitarist Larry Sparks, Stanley. After the death of his brother Carter in 1966, Ralph Stanley took command of the band and headed them back toward the old-time sound. Tapped to fill Carter's shoes, Sparks later became an influential bluegrass songwriter and bandleader in his own right.

folk revival. Flatt & Scruggs, the Stanley Brothers, and the Country Gentlemen were the most popular of the many bluegrass bands that played at folk festivals, gave college concerts, and appeared at coffee houses. It is not surprising that some of the young people in their audiences began playing this music. Ironically, these young urban imitators of the bluegrass sound, who typically began their bluegrass education with Flatt & Scruggs and the Stanley Brothers, ultimately were the cause of a renewed interest in Bill Monroe.

In the late fifties, as Flatt & Scruggs's star rose, Monroe's was in decline. Managers came and went; bookings dropped off. Invitations to play at folk venues did not initially bear fruit. Monroe watched in anger as Flatt & Scruggs's profile rose at the Opry. Like Flatt & Scruggs, he maintained independence in the studio, but Decca released his singles infrequently, and his transition to LPs was not marked with the same degree of success. As Monroe's drawing power waned, personnel turnover in his bands increased, and the sound of his music suffered. Moreover, Monroe had ambivalent feelings at this time about the word *bluegrass*, for it seemed to him that other bands, like Flatt & Scruggs, were making money using his word and his music.

But until 1962 these were for Monroe private feelings. In that year Ralph Rinzler, mandolin player of the New York City blue-

The Country Gentlemen, early 1960s: mandolinist John Duffey, banjoist Eddie Adcock, guitarist Charlie Waller, and bassist Tom Gray. Throughout the sixties and seventies, the Washington, D. C.-based group served as a bridge between bluegrass and urban folk music, with authentic treatments of old country standards and bluegrass versions of contemporary folk and pop material.

Flatt & Scruggs with the "Beverly Hillbillies" cast and Perry Botkin, the show's music director, 1963. When first approached about performing the program's theme song, the duo balked; after all, they were sophisticated musicians who didn't like the connotations implicit in the word hillbilly. *After viewing the program's pilot episode, they agreed to participate; it paid off in a #1 country single and invaluable national exposure.*

Formed in 1971 by ex-Country Gentleman John Duffey, the Seldom Scene were—indeed—seldom seen at first except for their weekly gigs at Washington-area clubs. By the time of this 1985 photo, taken in Nashville, they had stepped up their touring pace. From left: Ben Eldridge (banjo), Duffey (mandolin), Mike Auldridge (dobro), guest singer Jonathan Edwards (guitar), Phil Rosenthal (guitar), and Tom Gray (partially hidden, on bass).

A gifted guitarist and singer, Tony Rice is well respected among bluegrass musicians and cognoscenti, but, as with most bluegrassers, stardom has eluded him. His resume includes stints with the Bluegrass Alliance, J. D. Crowe's New South, and jazz mandolinist David Grisman; in 1980, he and Ricky Skaggs recorded a critically acclaimed acoustic album in the traditional brother duet style.

grass band the Greenbriar Boys, read an article on Earl Scruggs in the folk-song magazine *Sing Out!* that angered him because it implied that Scruggs, along with Flatt, was essentially responsible for the development of bluegrass. Rinzler, who had always liked Monroe's music and had seen Monroe perform at country music parks in the Washington, D.C., area, told the magazine's editor that Monroe ought to receive credit. The editor urged him to submit an article on Monroe. Monroe was not easy to approach: he associated bluegrass folk enthusiasts like Rinzler with Louise Scruggs and was too angry to talk. Finally, through the intercession of Carter Stanley of the Stanley Brothers, Rinzler was able to interview Monroe for the article.

It was as if a dam burst. For the first time, Monroe put into words what he had previously communicated only through music. As he explained himself to Rinzler, a bond of trust was created, which led early in 1963 to Rinzler becoming Monroe's manager. He helped Monroe assemble a hot new band, including innovative banjoist Bill Keith and Del McCoury, a powerful singer and guitarist from North Carolina. Rinzler initiated a series of concept albums at Decca in which Bill's strongest recordings from the early fifties were reissued along with liner notes identifying for the first time the musicians on the records and quoting Monroe extensively about his musical philosophy and personal history. Rinzler encouraged Monroe to develop his role as the father of bluegrass music and booked him at festivals like Newport. He also helped to attach to Monroe's singing the term "high lonesome sound" (coined by filmmaker and old-time re-

In a nod to Flatt & Scruggs, Hot Rize took their name from an advertised ingredient in Martha White Flour. Like many young progressive bluegrass bands, this Colorado group freely mixed the sounds of traditional bluegrass and country with jazz and other pop music styles. Pictured are guitarist Charlie Sawtelle, bassist Nick Forster, fiddler Tim O'Brien, and banjo player Peter Wernick.

The Nashville Bluegrass Band, 1986: Stuart Duncan (fiddle), Alan O'Bryant (banjo), Mike Compton (mandolin), Pat Enright (guitar), Mark Hembree (bass). Organized in Nashville in 1984, this traditionalist group has developed an unusual specialty —vintage songs from black gospel quartets, sung a capella.

vival musician John Cohen to describe the mountain music of Kentucky). In 1963, then, Bill Monroe acquired an image and a voice.

It was a crucial year for bluegrass: Bill Monroe was successfully introduced to folk music fans as the originator of the high lonesome sound, the father of bluegrass music; and Flatt & Scruggs were being heard in millions of homes performing "The Ballad of Jed Clampett," their theme to one of the 1962–63 season's most successful TV situation comedies.

For Flatt & Scruggs, this was the pinnacle of success. Their records, particularly the albums, would continue to sell well.

Husband-and-wife team Norman and Nancy Blake, ca. 1978. Comfortably straddling old-time and bluegrass music, Norman and Nancy Blake are each adept at several instruments: Nancy on cello, violin, and mandolin; Norman on guitar, fiddle, dobro, and mandolin. Norman has played many Nashville sessions, including those for Bob Dylan's Nashville Skyline *and Johnny Cash's TV series.*

Bluegrass's first generation consisted of blue-collar musicians like Bill Monroe and Ralph Stanley. Bill Clifton epitomized the next generation: college-educated, drawn to bluegrass by a love of folk and old-time music, and eager to spread the word. In 1961 Clifton organized the first bluegrass festival; two years later, he moved to England, where he converted a whole new audience.

The Earl Scruggs Revue, the band Earl formed so he could join the young whippersnappers who were electrifying bluegrass —his sons Randy (on guitar) and Gary (on bass) among them.

Lester Flatt with his post-Scruggs group, the Nashville Grass, 1970s. The band based its sound on the music Flatt & Scruggs had pioneered in the late forties; it got its name through a write-in contest sponsored by Nashville's WSM. The lad holding Roland White's guitar is the group's youngest member, teenager Marty Stuart.

They were to bring bluegrass to markets never before tapped by the form—they played to the counterculture in San Francisco's Avalon Ballroom in 1967 and toured Japan in 1968. But the very popularity of the band introduced tensions between Scruggs, who was eager to explore new repertoire of the kind that went over well with younger listeners, and Flatt, who remained loyal to and more comfortable with the tastes of the duo's original fans. In the short run, Columbia Records supported Scruggs's preferences, installed rock producer Bob Johnston in Nashville, and put him in charge of Flatt & Scruggs's recording sessions. From then on, Johnston played a key part in the choice of songs the band recorded. But Flatt just couldn't sing "Where Have All the Flowers Gone" with the same kind of feeling that he put into "You Are My Flower" or "Give Me the Flowers While I'm Living." His dissatisfaction and Earl's desire to perform with his sons led to the splitting of Flatt & Scruggs early in 1969. During the seventies, Scruggs performed with his sons as the Earl Scruggs Revue, and Flatt reorganized a band based on the early Foggy Mountain Boys, calling it the Nashville Grass. In May 1979, a decade after the split with Scruggs, Flatt died. In 1985 Flatt & Scruggs became members of the Country Music Hall of Fame.

Meanwhile, Bill Monroe had become the focus of a movement that was to revitalize his career. As young musicians began to

Pickin', grinnin': Lester Flatt and thirteen-year-old Marty Stuart in 1972. Flatt had recently hired the kid mandolinist to be the newest member of his band, the Nashville Grass. Stuart stayed in the band right up until Flatt's death in 1979; today Stuart is a solo country artist.

learn more of his ideas through his statements in personal appearances and also from Ralph Rinzler's writings, Monroe's role in shaping bluegrass music became better understood. The first bluegrass festival—organized by Carlton Haney (with the help of Ralph Rinzler) and based in large part on the Newport Folk Festival—was held at Cantrell's Horse Farm in Fincastle, near Roanoke, Virginia, in 1965. This festival and those that were to follow honored Monroe as the father of bluegrass music, and by the early seventies there were hundreds of such festivals, with Monroe at the center of a movement that strove to revive, preserve, and spread bluegrass music. Monroe was inducted into the Country Music Hall of Fame in 1970, and as this is written, in his seventy-sixth year, continues to tour with his Blue Grass Boys.

Bill Monroe leans into a tune with a 1970s edition of his Blue Grass Boys. At left is Kenny Baker, the best fiddler in bluegrass, according to Monroe. A fan of swing and jazz, Baker maintained that "bluegrass music is nothing but a hillbilly version of jazz."

7

HONKY-TONKIN': ERNEST TUBB, HANK WILLIAMS, AND THE BARTENDER'S MUSE

Nick Tosches

The town of Ardmore was and is the county seat of Carter County, Oklahoma, about twenty miles north of the Red River, which separates Oklahoma from Texas. On Saturday, February 24, 1894, Ardmore's little newspaper, *The Daily Ardmorite*, reported on page one that "the honk-a-tonk last night was well attended by ball-heads, bachelors and leading citizens."

It was, as far as is known, the earliest recorded appearance, and the earliest form, of the term *honky-tonk*. Exactly how did that phrase come into being, and exactly what did it originally denote? Well, when we figure out what "ball-heads" were, perhaps we'll have a clue about "honk-a-tonk." It suffices to say that it signified an occasion of merriment—probably more genteel than vulgar; otherwise the "leading citizens" likely would not have attended. It might even have been an all-male affair, judging by the item in the paper. One thing is certain: Everyone in Ardmore, and probably everyone for miles and miles around, knew what a "honk-a-tonk" meant and had been using the term for quite a while. By the time any colloquialism appears in a newspaper, it has long grown familiar to the ears and voices of its readers.

Unlike the baffling *ball-head*, *honky-tonk* eventually became a living part of the American language. In April 1916, Charles

"The Hillbilly Shakespeare," Hank Williams, 1951. As he explained to Nation's Business *magazine in a posthumously published interview: "You got to have smelt a lot of mule manure before you can sing like a hillbilly."*

223

Ernest Tubb, late 1940s: though he still had his idol's guitar, by this time he had developed a sound all his own.

McCarron and Chris Smith copyrighted a piece of one-step dance music titled "Honky Tonky." It was recorded by both the Victor Military Band and Prince's Band. In 1918, the Tin Pan Alley musical *Everything* (staged at the New York Hippodrome with a cast that included Houdini) featured the song "Everything Is Hunky Dory Down in Honky Tonk Town." Fletcher Henderson & His Club Alabam Orchestra recorded "Those Broken Busted, Can't Be Trusted Blues (A Honky-Tonk Blues)" for Vocalion in 1924. The following year, Bennie Moten's Kansas City

Orchestra cut "Sister Honky-Tonk" for Okeh. Meade Lux Lewis spread the boogie-woogie gospel with his Paramount recording "Honky Tonk Train Blues" in 1927. That was the year Carl Sandburg used the term "honky tonks" in his *Songbag*. In thirty-three years, that odd word had traveled in print from bleak little Ardmore to Pulitzer Prize territory in the big city. Later, Faulkner, Steinbeck, and then countless more would also work the word into the national literature.

It entered country music nearly a decade after it entered Pulitzer country, when, on November 28, 1936, Vocalion released Al Dexter's recording of "Honky Tonk Blues."

Dexter (1902–84), an east Texan who grew up not too far from ball-head country and who later wrote and recorded what was one of the biggest honky-tonk hits of all time ("Pistol Packin' Mama"—it hit #1 on both the pop and country charts in the spring of 1943), claimed that he had never heard the term *honky-tonk* until 1936.

"One day I went to see Paris," he told me in the summer of 1975, referring to his friend James B. Paris, the songwriter, not the world-renowned seat of Lamar County, Texas; "and he said, 'I thought of a title last night that'll set the woods on fire.' I asked him what it was, and he said, 'Honky Tonk Blues.' I asked him where he got that idea. I never heard the word, so I said, 'What is a honky-tonk?' So he said, 'These beer joints up and down the road where the girls jump in cars and so on.' I said, 'I never thought about it like that.' He said, 'Use your thinker-upper and let's write a song like that.' "

Dexter himself had owned and operated a honky-tonk, the Round-Up Club in Turnertown, Texas, since the early 1930s. He had always called it a tavern. As for Paris's brainstorm, it came a year after Pat Shelton copyrighted "Honky Tonk Blues," seven years after Hunkie Smith came up with "Hunkie Tunkie Blues." But, then again, those weren't country songs. In any event, it was Al Dexter's Vocalion recording of "Honky Tonk Blues" that brought country music and honky-tonk fever together, then and forevermore. By 1938, even Roy Acuff was singing about "Honky Tonk Mamas."

The first country honky-tonk songs, like the earlier songs that grabbed onto the label, were, for the most part, upbeat and trifling. But, before long, that was to change. Instead of being just a genre of nugatory songs tacked onto a catch-phrase, honky-tonk music was to become a state of mind. Eventually, it was to recast the nature of country music. But first country music was to recast it. No longer would honky-tonk music be the music solely of beer-drinking and dancing on a good-time Friday

Albert Poindexter not only had the good sense to shorten his name—Al Dexter—he also wrote and recorded "Honky Tonk Blues" (1936), the first hillbilly song to cash in on the hot slang for bar. He followed it in 1943 with "Pistol Packin' Mama," a pop crossover smash that proved so infectious Life magazine called it the "national earache."

HONKY-TONK PIONEERS

Floyd Tillman's songwriting career began inauspiciously when a number he sold to Jimmie Davis for $300 in 1938 —"It Makes No Difference Now"—turned into a national hit for Davis, Gene Autry, Bing Crosby, and others. Before long, Tillman had hits of his own—"Each Night at Nine" (1944), "I Love You So Much It Hurts" (1948), and "Slipping Around" (1949)— that set standards for honky-tonk songwriting and singing.

Dressed a cut above your average radio repair shop owner, Ted Daffan—honky-tonk tunesmith, dance band leader, and 1940s Columbia record star—poses here with an acoustic guitar (he usually played steel).

Influential as Al Dexter, Ernest Tubb, and Hank Williams surely were in shaping the honky-tonk style, they did not define it entirely. At least five other performers— Floyd Tillman, Ted Daffan, Lefty Frizzell, Hank Thompson, and Ray Price—have also been important honky-tonk role models.

Floyd Tillman, born just outside of the Lone Star State in Ryan, Oklahoma, grew up in the cotton mill town of Post, Texas, the youngest of eleven children born into a sharecropper's household. He began his career playing guitar and mandolin in a trio with two of his brothers and later worked with two western swing bandleaders, Adolph Hofner in San Antonio and Leon "Pappy" Selph's Blue Ridge Playboys in Houston. But it was primarily as singer and songwriter that Tillman helped shape the development of honky-tonk. "It Makes No Difference Now," written by Tillman in 1938, became a classic of the new style. Two of the favorite subjects of honky-tonk music, drink and infidelity, were important themes in Tillman's own subsequent recordings. With his distinctive half-spoken vocal style, he cut the definitive version of Jerry Irby's "Drivin' Nails in My Coffin" (". . . everytime I drink a bottle of booze"), and in 1949 he wrote and recorded the granddaddy of all country cheating songs, "Slipping Around."

Theron Eugene "Ted" Daffan, born in Louisiana, was raised in Houston and was a cohort of Tillman's in the Blue Ridge Playboys, joining them in 1934. A steel guitarist, Daffan demonstrated songwrit-

ing ability about the same time Tillman did, writing "Truck Driver's Blues," a hit for Cliff Bruner in 1939. On the strength of that Decca record, Okeh producer Art Satherley offered Daffan a contract, and with his newly formed group, the Texans, Daffan cut three numbers in the early 1940s that have since become honky-tonk standards— "Worried Mind," "No Letter Today," and "Born to Lose." Among his other well-known tunes are "Heading Down the Wrong Highway," which expressed the hopelessness of the honky-tonk wastrel, and "I've Got Five Dollars and It's Saturday Night," a devil-may-care celebration of nightlife.

Another Texan of enormous influence in the development of honky-tonk was William Orville "Lefty"

Frizzell. Nicknamed for his south-paw punch (according to legend), Frizzell honed his singing skills while still a teenager in rough oil-town nightspots where the punch would have come in handy. At Jim Bulleit's suggestion, Don Law of Columbia Records signed Frizzell to a contract in 1950, and almost immediately a succession of classic honky-tonk hits began: "I Love You a Thousand Ways," "If You've Got the Money, I've Got the Time," "I Want to Be with You Always," and others. Frizzell's early 1950s hits, cut in the Dallas studios of Jim Beck, featured a heavy sock rhythm that stressed the offbeats, electric guitars, the rinky-tink piano of Madge Bowlan, and—most distinctive of all—the note-bending, almost note-searching voice of Lefty.

Hank Thompson & His Brazos Valley Boys (with Wanda Jackson), 1950s. Named the trade magazines' top country band every year from 1953 to 1966, the Brazos Valley Boys were a western swing outfit that could sound as smooth as a pop dance orchestra—and often did. It was Hank's clever songwriting and singing that made them honky-tonk.

Lefty Frizzell's custom-made Gibson SJ-200 guitar with special Bigsby neck.

Lefty Frizzell, ca. 1951. A member of the Opry cast for eight months (1951–52), the young Texan slugged four hits simultaneously into the Top Ten in a single month (October 1951)—"Always Late" (#1), "Mom and Dad's Waltz" (#2), "I Want to Be with You Always" (#7), and "Travellin' Blues" (#8).

Though Frizzell's career saw occasional hits in later years ("Long Black Veil," "Saginaw, Michigan"), the songs from his 1950–53 heyday doubtless influenced a variety of vocal stylists in years to come, including George Jones, Merle Haggard, Johnny Rodriguez, John Anderson, and Randy Travis.

Hank Thompson's style might best be described as Ernest Tubb put to swing accompaniment. Associated with both western swing and honky-tonk today, Thompson and his Brazos Valley Boys did much to merge the two, beginning with his first hit, "Whoa, Sailor," in 1946. Even when his band played its smoothest, Thompson usually wrote lyrics that were standard, hard-hitting honky-tonk. "The Wild Side of Life," a William Warren composition that was a #1 for Thompson in 1952, is probably his best-known hit. It evoked the barroom atmosphere that Thompson would return to over and over again in songs like "Honky Tonk Girl," "Hangover Tavern," "Smoky the Bar," "On Tap, in the Can, or in the Bottle," and many others.

Perhaps the most influential of all

PHOTO-BY
WALDEN S. FABRY

228

as a honky-tonk hitmaker—though often overlooked in discussions of the genre's giants—is the Cherokee Cowboy, Ray Price. Clearly influenced at first by his friend and one-time roommate Hank Williams, Price developed his own sound by the mid-1950s, after a brief flirtation with Thompson-esque western swing. A long succession of honky-tonk hits began, coming at the very moment when rockabilly threatened to obliterate country music. Price introduced a distinctive shuffle-beat to honky-tonk music, tailor-made for jukebox patrons. "Crazy Arms," "City Lights," "I've Got a New Heartache," and many other Price hits showcased pedal steel guitar and fiddle leads, a shuffling drum beat, a walking electric bass, and duet harmonies on the choruses—all later employed by many honky-tonk singers. Almost every major songwriter has supplied hits for Price; Cherokee Cowboy alumni include Roger Miller, Willie Nelson, Johnny Paycheck, and Buddy Emmons; and such popular honky-tonkers as Johnny Bush, Darrell McCall, and Tony Booth exhibit an obvious Ray Price influence.

A former veterinary student from Texas, Ray Price was a honky-tonker going places when he joined the Opry in 1952. "He can sing when he wants to," scrawled Opry stage manager Vito Pellettieri on this early publicity photo.

229

During the rise of honky-tonk music, country's hottest record-seller was, in fact, a crooner. A bonafide "Tennessee Plowboy," Eddy Arnold got his big break in 1940 with Pee Wee King's Golden West Cowboys. Signed to a solo contract with RCA Victor in 1943, he soon dominated Billboard's *newly created "Folk Record" charts with such hits as "It's a Sin" (1947) and "Bouquet of Roses" (1948)—which also reached #13 on the pop charts.*

night. Country music would take honky-tonk to the dark obverse of that carousing spirit as well: remorse and guilt and world-weariness. Honky-tonk music would come to be a howl of abandon followed by a lament of anguish.

Which brings us to Ernest Tubb.

He was born Ernest Dale Tubb, on a farm near Crisp, Texas, about forty miles south of Dallas, on February 9, 1914, the youngest of five children. When he was twelve, his parents separated. In the years that followed, work took precedence over schooling. "When I realized what I had missed," he once said, "I began educating myself." Later in life, it was not uncommon for him to read a dozen or more books a month. But, back then, it was all labor: "I had a lot of jobs and I hated them all." After the farm, after traveling from relative to relative to live, he ended up on a road crew near Benjamin in 1933. The W.P.A. put him to work on construction jobs around San Antonio. Then he worked for beer distributors, in San Angelo and in Corpus Christi. He was still working for the outfit in Corpus Christi—Southern Brewing, owned by Howard Hughes—when it went out of business in 1939. By then, he had a wife named Lois Elaine, a son named Justin (a second son, Rodger Dale, had been killed in a car accident at the age of seven weeks, in 1938), and, though few outside and not many more within Texas seemed to know it, a recording career.

His idol had always been Jimmie Rodgers, who had passed on in the spring of 1933, when Tubb was nineteen. Four years before that, Tubb's sister had brought home one of Rodgers's recordings —"In the Jail House Now," Tubb remembered it to be —and the world had seemed to change.

Rodgers, of course, was no ordinary country singer. He certainly was no hillbilly. Cool, sagacious, urbane, more comfortable in a tuxedo than in fustian britches, he was the man who established that not everyone who sang with a southern accent was necessarily a clay-eating hick who believed that the Holy Ghost was Casper's uncle. Infused with jazz and black blues, pop and tent-circuit sleaze, the sacred and the profane, the music of Jimmie Rodgers was the first great music of America— a music that rarely has been equaled since. Today, more than half a century after his death from tuberculosis at the age of thirty-five, the music he made still stands as better, harder, more strikingly original, and more powerful than most of what is to be heard. In a recording career that lasted barely six years, Jimmie Rodgers transformed the course of the music that he had inherited. His first record, "Sleep, Baby, Sleep," had moved from the country market to become a pop hit at the end of 1927. A few months later, his "Blue Yodel"—the first of many, the one in which he wanted to "shoot poor Thelma, just to see her jump and fall"—became an even bigger pop hit. By the time young Ernest Tubb first heard him, in 1929, Rodgers was as big in his way, and as good in his way, as Al Jolson.

In 1935, in addition to his W.P.A. work, Tubb had a fifteen-minute, early-morning radio show at 250-watt KONO in San Antonio. That summer, he was sitting at home one Sunday playing Jimmie Rodgers records when it occurred to him that Rodgers had been living in San Antonio at the time of his death. Opening the city directory, he found the telephone number of Jimmie's widow, Carrie. He dialed. She answered, and he began to speak awkwardly. In the end, she invited him to visit her the following Sunday. After that visit, Carrie Rodgers began listening to Tubb's radio show. Two months passed, and Mrs. Rodgers phoned. "Ernest," he remembered her saying, "I like your show. I've listened for a while, and I think you can go places, so I'd like to help you."

"And that's how I got started," Tubb recalled.

Carrie Rodgers arranged Tubb's first recording session, with her late husband's company, Victor. That session took place at the Texas Hotel in San Antonio, on the afternoon of October 27, 1936. At that session, Tubb recorded two maudlin tributes, "The Passing of Jimmie Rodgers" and "The Last Thought of Jimmie Rodgers" (both written by Carrie's sister, Mrs. Elsie Mc-Williams), and four songs written and sung by Tubb in the manner of his idol—two sacred ("My Mother Is Lonely" and "The Right Train to Heaven"), two profane ("Married Man Blues" and "Mean Old Bed Bug Blues"). At his next Victor session, in March 1937, also arranged by Carrie Rodgers, Tubb once again sang of his idol, in the manner of his idol, in a song he wrote called "The T.B. Is Whipping Me."

Tubb was dwelling in the shadow of Jimmie Rodgers. Carrie had loaned him Jimmie's custom-made Martin guitar, and the labels of Tubb's first records bore, beneath Tubb's name, the words "Singing and yodeling with accomp. played on Jimmie Rodgers' own guitar." For his first photo session, he wore one of his dead idol's tuxedos. The pants did not fit. Later, Mrs. Rodgers bought him a new pair. The whole matter has about it a whiff of the macabre: the widow trying to breathe life into the ghost of her husband, and the ghost's protégé seeking to inhale that spectral life.

But the ghost music, fine as it was, did not sell. Victor lost interest, and it took three years for Carrie and Tubb to get another deal. He began recording for Decca in April 1940, in Houston. His first Decca release, from that session, "Blue-Eyed Elaine" with "I'll Get Along Somehow" on the B side (both orig-

Without Carrie Rodgers's unflagging support during the lean years, Ernest Tubb might never have made it in country music. This testament appeared as a foreword to Ernest Tubb's Folio of Sensational Success, *the young singer's first songbook, published by American Music in 1941.*

A PERSONAL FOREWORD BY MRS. JIMMIE RODGERS

Of all the artists I've auditioned since the passing of my husband, Ernest Tubb is my choice.

I think America's Blue Yodeler would have been proud of my having selected Ernest Tubb to sponsor as he has proven worthy in every respect.

He has the voice, personality and ability to put the feeling into his songs that have won him many admirers among Jimmie's fans and Ernest is very grateful, as Jimmie Rodgers has been his inspiration since his youth.

For radio work and personal appearances, as well as recordings, I am proud to extend to Ernest the privilege of using Jimmie's famous guitar, for which privilege he has expressed his gratitude.

MRS. JIMMIE RODGERS.

inal compositions), did what his Victor records had not done—they sold.

Something had happened: Ernest Tubb had begun to discover his own voice. Instead of trying to duplicate the vocal mannerisms and style of his idol, he had begun to express, in his natural way, the sensibilities he had absorbed from Rodgers. At the same time, Tubb had become aware of the new barroom music called honky-tonk. By this time, returned to San Angelo, Tubb had opened a honky-tonk of his own, the E&E Tavern. The honky-tonk music he heard was lively but insubstantial. If Rodgers had taught him anything, it was that music without power —be it the power of meanness, the power of love, the power of sentimentality, the power of sadness or madness, sweetness or venom—was music without worth. Ernest Tubb was on his way to empowering country music and recasting honky-tonk with his own new-found voice, a voice that was the sum of all he had learned from the master, and from himself. And he was on his way to glory.

Decca released his "Walking the Floor over You" in the summer of 1941. He had recorded it in April, in Dallas, backed by electric lead guitar, bass, and his own rhythm guitar. It was the anthem that every honky-tonk had been waiting for—unknowingly. It crossed to the pop market, and eventually sold a million copies. Though he wrote and recorded a song that fall called "I Ain't Goin' Honky Tonkin' Anymore," Tubb continued to be the apotheosis of honky-tonk throughout the decade. The best of his

Ernest Tubb, from his first publicity photo session, ca. 1936. The tuxedo jacket, lent by Carrie Rodgers, once belonged to Tubb's idol. Other shots from the session feature Tubb sporting the Blue Yodeler's bowler hat. All the shots had to be close-ups, since Jimmie's pants didn't fit.

Ernest Tubb and wife Elaine, ca. 1941. Behind them is the Plymouth he traveled in for two years promoting Gold Chain Flour. On the car's roof was a makeshift platform, which became Tubb's stage when he appeared at stores, singing for his supper.

work—such as "Wasting My Life Away" (1941), "Tomorrow Never Comes" (1944), "Drivin' Nails in My Coffin" (1946), his version of Jimmie Rodgers's "Waiting for a Train" (1947), "Warm Red Wine" (1949), and others, commercial hits and stiffs alike—became the classic, nickel-a-play corpus of honky-tonk.

(Interestingly, though, the term *honky-tonk* doesn't appear to have been applied to Tubb-style country music until a generation later, when an academic historian, Bill Malone, used it in his doctoral dissertation, which was published in an expanded form as *Country Music, U.S.A.* by the University of Texas Press in 1968. Of course, by this time, most country music no longer sounded like it belonged in a honky-tonk; the term had become necessary to describe contemporary country music's nearly extinct ancestor.)

Ernest Tubb continued to produce hits through the 1950s and, decreasingly, into the 1960s. His marriage fell apart at the height of his glory; he married again, in 1949. His emphysema got worse, and he quit smoking. Then everything got worse, and, in 1964, he quit drinking. But still he stood there and smiled and sang his songs, as noble and as endearing a figure in his later years as country music has ever been fortunate enough to claim as one of its own. In 1975, after thirty-five years with Decca (by now it was MCA), he was cast aside. He made a few records for small Nashville labels. His last session was held on August 5, 1982. Johnny Walker of Atlas Artists, Tubb's booking agency,

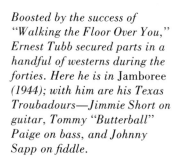

Boosted by the success of "Walking the Floor Over You," Ernest Tubb secured parts in a handful of westerns during the forties. Here he is in Jamboree *(1944); with him are his Texas Troubadours—Jimmie Short on guitar, Tommy "Butterball" Paige on bass, and Johnny Sapp on fiddle.*

234

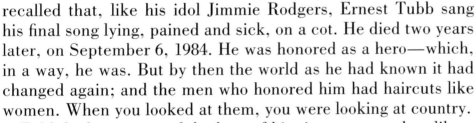

Ernest Tubb in Wichita Falls, Texas, 1948—well-established as a recording star and by then a member of the Opry. Tubb's smiling face had not yet begun to show the toll that the road would exact from him. To his left, guitar in hand, is Tommy "Butterball" Paige, Tubb's lead guitarist of the period.

With the success of "Walking the Floor Over You" in 1941, Ernest Tubb finally found a radio sponsor for his spots on KGKO. It meant an immediate raise in pay from $20 a week to $75, allowing Tubb to devote himself to music full-time.

recalled that, like his idol Jimmie Rodgers, Ernest Tubb sang his final song lying, pained and sick, on a cot. He died two years later, on September 6, 1984. He was honored as a hero—which, in a way, he was. But by then the world as he had known it had changed again; and the men who honored him had haircuts like women. When you looked at them, you were looking at country.

Tubb had seen one of the best of his time come and go like a storm of light and darkness. He had taken over the torch from Rodgers; but, in the end, which came all too fast, the torch burned out with him.

Hank Williams—his true Christian name was Hiram, the sort of name that a father named Elonzo would bestow on a son—was born near the railroad town of Georgiana, Alabama, on September 17, 1923. He grew up several miles north of there, in Greenville. It was there that young Hank met and was influenced by Tee-Tot, an unknown black musician who has figured prominently, although vaguely, in numerous romanticized accounts of Hank's life. All that is known for sure about Tee-Tot is that his real name was Rufe Payne, and he lived in Greenville until his death, about 1950. Farther north, in Montgomery, Hank began performing at radio station WSFA in 1936. He was still working

Ernest Tubb's Nashville record shop and road show, ca. 1958: Texas Troubadours Billy Byrd, Ray "Kemo" Head, Tubb, Jack Drake, and Rusty Gabbard; Kitty Wells, Johnnie & Jack and their Tennessee Mountain Boys: Shot Jackson, Ray Crisp, and Joe Zinkan; and Teddy & Doyle Wilburn.

When Little Jimmy Dickens sang "I'm Little But I'm Loud," he meant it. Standing all of four foot eleven, Jimmy was a compact bundle of energy with a big sound. A radio performer since his teens, he joined the Opry in 1948 and scored his first hit the following year with the novelty song "Take an Old Cold Tater (and Wait)." Novelty tunes, often trading on his diminutive stature, became his trademark.

236

Faron Young was already an Opry star when the army drafted him in 1952; he received special permission to perform on radio during his two-year tour of duty. Known as the "Hillbilly Heartthrob" for frisky hits like "If You Ain't Lovin' (You Ain't Livin')" and "Live Fast, Love Hard, Die Young," he later acquired the nickname "the Young Sheriff" after appearing in the 1955 western Hidden Guns.

Faron Young's custom-made Gay guitar. During the 1950s, several country singers, including Carl Smith and Webb Pierce, tried Canadian Frank Gay's guitars because of their unusual styling. These instruments were more appealing to look at than to play; they never caught on with a wider market.

there ten years later, in the fall of 1946, when he journeyed to Nashville and met Fred Rose.

It was Rose, a Tin Pan Alley veteran, who set up Williams's first session, on December 11 of that year, at WSM Studio D in Nashville. Rose sold the recordings to Sterling, the new subsidiary of Al Middleman's year-old Juke Box Record Company, located in New York.

The Sterling records—there were four of them—did not sell well, though they were good records. (The last of them, "Honky Tonkin'," proclaimed Hank's allegiance to the Ernest Tubb sound that was in the air.) In the early spring of 1947, Williams signed with the newly formed MGM label. His first MGM release, "Move It On Over," was issued in May 1947, and by midsummer it was high on the hillbilly charts. It was a raucous record whose lyrics, sultry rhythms, and electric-guitar break presaged white rock 'n' roll while at the same time sounding irrefragably country. Hank's "Rootie Tootie" (written by Fred Rose) went even further toward establishing a new sound—a sound that, in eight years' time, would be known as rockabilly.

Hank's music—Hank himself, really—was a mixture of whiskey, lamb's blood, and grave dirt. It was for him quite natural to drift, as he did in the studio on April 21, 1947, from "Move It On

BAKERSFIELD'S HONKY-TONKERS

A hundred miles north of Los Angeles (and light-years away from what Nashville was doing at the time), the California oil town of Bakersfield spawned a group of country musicians largely responsible for what historian Bill Malone described as "the reinvigoration of honky-tonk" during the 1960s. An oasis for many

an Okie on his westward trek during the dustbowl days and, later, during the economic boom sparked by World War II, Bakersfield always had its share of nightclubs and honky-tonks catering to a beer-drinking crowd who loved hillbilly music. By the 1950s, this club scene was lively indeed. Bill Woods led the band at his Corral club, when he wasn't directing the musicians on Jean Shepard's Capitol Sessions. Recording artist Billy Mize based his band in Bakersfield as well, and Tommy Collins, a hot newcomer in the mid-1950s, regularly worked in and around the town.

The electric lead guitarist on several of Collins's hits was a talented young man from Texas by the name of Alvis Edgar Owens. A ninth-grade dropout, Buck (as he was called) had worked with several bands by the time he was twenty, learning in the process to play guitar, mandolin, steel guitar, saxophone, piano, and drums. In 1956 Owens got the chance to make few solo records on the Pep label, and by the next year was under contract to Capitol. Together with his band, the Buckaroos, Owens blended hard-edged honky-tonk with the drive of rockabilly, adding a new dimension to the honky-tonk sound at a time when the smooth, cosmopolitan Nashville Sound of Jim Reeves, Patsy Cline, and Eddy Arnold was in its ascendancy. The high-octane honky-tonk/rockabilly mixture fueled a remarkable run of twenty #1 country hits, stretching from "Act Naturally" in 1963 to "Made in Japan" in 1972. Buckaroo Don Rich contributed greatly to Buck's success with a sharp, staccato lead guitar style that was distinctive and immediately recognizable. His high harmony singing with Owens further stretched the honky-tonk sound to new limits, until Rich's untimely death in 1974.

Bakersfield native Merle Haggard apprenticed in numerous area clubs after his celebrated prison stint (two years for second-degree burglary at age twenty) and made the most of his chance with Wynn Stewart's band. Haggard signed with a friend's company, Tally Records, and, after a 1965 hit, "Strangers," moved over to Capitol. Beginning in 1967 he wrote and recorded a string of #1 hits ("Branded Man," "Mama Tried," "Hungry Eyes," "Workin' Man's Blues") distinguished by their simple, direct, heartfelt lyrics. His versatility in treating many themes successfully (night life, prison, work, love, patriotism) propelled him to the forefront of the country field, earning him the nickname "Poet of the Common Man" and a virtual sweep of the Country Music Association Awards in 1970.

Stylistically, Haggard's band, the Strangers, featured at first the same sort of straightforward California honky-tonk as did Owens's Buckaroos—pedal steel guitar work by Norman Hamlet, and the loud, distinct, bluesy "chicken picking" of lead guitarist Roy Nichols. Influenced heavily by Bob Wills, Jimmie Rodgers, and Lefty Frizzell, Haggard branched out in later years, and the Strangers became more of a country-jazz ensemble.

Still, during the 1960s, Bakersfield's two best-known sons, Buck Owens and Merle Haggard, managed jointly to renew the honky-tonk sound and extend its boundaries. Even when Ray Price had defected to bland Nashville Sound ballads (after years of holding out against the trend), the powerful music of Buck Owens and Merle Haggard kept the sound of hard country on the radio and on the charts when the rest were no longer honky-tonkin'.

The band that put Bakersfield on the map: Buck Owens & the Buckaroos, June 1964. The classic lineup comprised (from left) steel guitarist Tom Brumley, bass guitarist Doyle Holly, Owens, drummer Willie Cantu, and lead guitarist Don Rich.

Riding the popularity of "Okie from Muskogee," Merle Haggard dominated the 1970 CMA Awards, winning for Single, Album, Male Vocalist, and Entertainer of the Year.

Opposite
A session musician-turned-star, Buck Owens runs through a song in Capitol's Hollywood studios, early 1960s.

239

Over" to "I Saw the Light" to "Six More Miles (to the Graveyard)."

Hank Williams was a consummate songwriter. This is a statement so obvious that it would not even have to be made, were it not for the mundane fact that paragraphs need beginnings. From the perfect simplicity of "Cold, Cold Heart" and "You Win Again," to the accomplished imagery of "I'm So Lonesome I Could Cry," to the sublime surliness of "Mind Your Own Business," Hank gave country music its most enduring songs. Yet it was a song older than he that brought him two things he could handle no better than liquor: Fame and Fortune, those twin bitches from across the tracks.

"Lovesick Blues" was copyrighted on April 3, 1922. Its music was written by Cliff Friend, a vaudeville pianist born in Cincinnati in 1893; the words were made by Irving Mills (1894–1985), the Russian-born bandleader, singer, and lyricist who later col-

In the fall of 1946, Hank Williams interrupted a lunchtime ping-pong match between music publisher Fred Rose and his son Wesley to ask if he could pitch them his songs. He did, and a deal was soon struck. Here is a letter (October 31, 1946) from Hank to Fred Rose about that burgeoning association, and the manuscript of one of Hank's earliest songs, "Six More Miles to the Graveyard."

laborated with Duke Ellington in writing "Mood Indigo," "It Don't Mean a Thing (If It Ain't Got That Swing)," and other standards. The publisher of "Lovesick Blues" was Jack Mills, Inc., operated by Irving's brother.

Elsie Clark recorded the song for Okeh late in 1922. The mysterious Emmett Miller—the unique jazz singer who almost certainly influenced Jimmie Rodgers—cut a version of the song,

Hank Williams & His Drifting Cowboys, 1951: bass player Howard Watts ("Cedric Rainwater"), fiddler Jerry Rivers, Hank on rhythm guitar, lead guitarist Sammy Pruett, and steel guitarist Don Helms.

241

When honky-tonk and rockabilly were all the rage, the Louvin Brothers stubbornly persisted in harmonizing like the traditional brother duets. Initially typed as a gospel act, Ira (who sang tenor and played mandolin) and Charlie (baritone and guitar) hit the mainstream in 1955, when they first appeared on the Opry and debuted on the charts with "When I Stop Dreaming," a love song.

Emmett Miller, 1920s: a mysterious yodeler and black-face comedian who recorded in New York with Tommy and Jimmy Dorsey (1928) and with Fiddlin' John Carson (1929). Miller's records made a deep impression on Bob Wills, and his rendition of "Lovesick Blues" inspired Rex Griffin and Hank Williams.

with yodeling, in September 1925, in Asheville, North Carolina, for Okeh. Bertha "Chippie" Hill also recorded it for Okeh, in Chicago, in November 1926, accompanied by Richard M. Jones's Jazz Wizards. In June 1928, Emmett Miller cut the song again for Okeh, this time in New York, accompanied by Jimmy Dorsey, Tommy Dorsey, Eddie Lang, and others. (The records bore the name of Emmett Miller and His Georgia Crackers.) Again Miller yodeled. More than a decade later, in 1939, country singer Rex Griffin of Alabama recorded "Lovesick Blues" for Decca, copying Miller's performance in every accessible way, down to the bizarre yodeling that had been Miller's vocal signature. Similar as it was, though, Rex Griffin's "Lovesick Blues" emerged as a country song, pure and simple.

That Hank Williams was acquainted with both Miller's and Griffin's versions is confirmed by a letter written to Hank by Wesley H. Rose, son of Fred Rose and general manager of Acuff-Rose Publications. Dated March 28, 1949—several weeks after Hank's MGM recording of "Lovesick Blues" was released—the letter concerns Rose's attempts to trace the song's publisher, and his hope that the song might be up for grabs. "Just got back from New York," he wrote from Nashville to Hank at KWKH in Shreveport, "and have a hint regarding publisher on LOVESICK BLUES unless we can prove this tune is public domain. You

Hank Williams with his peers from the Opry—Milton Estes (literally in Hank's shadow), Red Foley, Minnie Pearl, Wally Fowler (crouching), WSM general manager Harry Stone, Eddy Arnold, Roy Acuff, Rod Brasfield, and Lew Childre; 1950. The gent with his hand on Stone's shoulder is George Rosen, radio editor for Variety *and an honorary member of the Opry.*

In 1939–40, Williams played several dates with Rex Griffin, who had just recorded "Lovesick Blues"; in 1949, it became Hank's first #1 hit.

mentioned that you had an old Decca record by Rex Griffin and also an old record by Emmett something or other on this tune. Please mail these to me at once."

Hank's "Lovesick Blues" stayed on the country charts for some forty-two weeks, the most successful country record of the year—written by a Jew from Russia, midwived by a jazz singer from parts unknown. After that, the hits just kept coming—twenty-two of them in the less than four years that remained of his life; and the twin bitches raised their skirts higher.

The happiness and pride in Hank's cockeyed quasi-yodeling in "Lovesick Blues" was a part of what made his version blaze. Like Ernest Tubb before him, Hank had grown up listening to Jimmie Rodgers. Now, for one wild, wonderful moment, which was both the end and the beginning of something, they were kindred.

"Hank couldn't yodel," Ernest Tubb recalled, long after he and Hank had become friends, and long after death had ended that friendship. "He could break his voice pretty good like he did on 'Lovesick Blues' and other things, but that wasn't a real yodel. Anyway, he loved Jimmie Rodgers as much as I did, and he could do his songs well, too; not like Jimmie, but like himself. Well, Hank was scared to death to record any of Jimmie's songs, because he was afraid Mrs. Jimmie Rodgers would hear them and make fun of him. He'd call her and sing one of Jimmie's songs to her over the phone, and ask her what she thought, and she'd say, 'Well, it ain't Jimmie, but it's you, Hank. Why don't you record it?' But he never would. That's how much the legend of Jimmie Rodgers meant to him." In the spring and summer of 1950, "Long Gone Lonesome Blues" and "Why Don't You Love Me" were back-to-back #1 country hits for Hank. That autumn, he became a television celebrity as well, performing on WSM-TV. The following summer, Tony Bennett covered his "Cold, Cold Heart" and had a #1 pop hit with it. A year later, Rosemary Clooney hit #2 on the pop charts with a cover of Hank's recording of "Half as Much." (Mitch Miller, who produced both these covers for Columbia, was said to have been eager to sign Hank to that label. To coin a phrase: That would have been something.) In August, Hank's own recording of "Jambalaya" became a minor pop sensation.

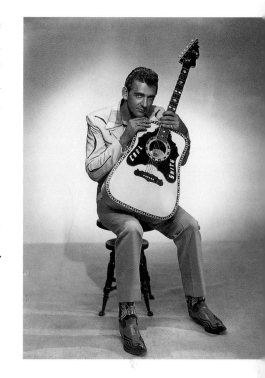

A protégé of both Hank Williams and Ernest Tubb, Carl Smith dabbled in honky-tonk but found his greatest success in romantic ballads that capitalized on his good looks. Though his biggest hits came during his first five years with Columbia (1950–55), he eventually sold some fifteen million records during a quarter-century with the label.

Red Sovine replaced Hank Williams on the "Louisiana Hayride" when Hank moved up to the Opry. Sovine—the tall gent in the middle—went on to record some of the most popular trucking songs of the sixties and seventies, including "Teddy Bear," before a fatal auto accident in 1980.

By the time Ferlin Husky appeared in this 1964 movie, Country Music on Broadway, *he had established a solid career with a pop crossover hit ("Gone," 1957), a hit gospel tune ("On the Wings of a Dove," 1960), and a down-home comedic alter ego, Simon Crum.*

Webb Pierce (fresh from his job in haberdashery at a local Sears Roebuck store) at the studios of Shreveport's KWKH. After joining the station's "Louisiana Hayride" show in 1950 (without pay), he graduated to the Opry in the fall of 1952 and, in effect, took up where Hank Williams had left off—on the show and on the charts. Among his honky-tonk triumphs is "Slowly" (1954), the first hit to feature a pedal steel guitar (played by Bud Isaacs).

246

Hank Williams sings one for the folks tuned in to WSM, ca. 1949. With him are fiddler Jerry Rivers, guitarists Grady Martin and Bill Drake, mandolinist Rollin Sullivan, and bass player Hillous Butrum.

Curley Williams & His Georgia Peach Pickers, late 1940s. Williams's music owed more to western swing than to honky-tonk, but he is probably best remembered as the author of "Half as Much," a 1952 honky-tonk hit for the more famous Williams—Hank. By the time of this photo, Curley (on fiddle) had left the Opry and was working for KTBS in Shreveport.

Carl & Pearl Butler in full voice at the Opry, 1960s. Carl Butler was well established as a honky-tonk singer and songwriter in 1962 when his wife Pearl made her first recording, singing harmony on "Don't Let Me Cross Over." The record's immense popularity inspired a revival of male-female harmonizing that included Ernest Tubb & Loretta Lynn, George Jones & Melba Montgomery, and Porter Wagoner & Norma Jean.

Hank and Audrey, ca. 1948. He was nineteen and working a medicine show when they met; they were married by a justice of the peace at a gas station. In song after song—"Why Don't You Love Me" (1950), "Cold, Cold Heart" (1951), "I Can't Help It If I'm Still in Love with You" (1951), "Your Cheatin' Heart" (1952)—Hank told his side of their tempestuous relationship.

In 1951, Tony Bennett's recording of "Cold, Cold Heart" by Hank Williams became a #1 pop hit; three years later, his cover of Hank's "There'll Be No Teardrops Tonight" went to #11. This supportive backstage visit from Ray Price and Ernest Tubb notwithstanding, Bennett never had another hit with country material.

Hank Snow inspects the fretwork of Perry Como, as Hank's Rainbow Ranch Boys stand by. The Opry star had scored a prodigious hit with "I'm Movin' On" (forty-four weeks on the charts in 1950–51), earning him an appearance on Como's TV show. With Snow are fiddler Tommy Vaden, bassist Cedric Rainwater, steel guitarist (and future music business exec) Joe Talbot, and rhythm guitarist Hillous Butrum.

But less than a month after that, Hank was in the worst shape of his life, living in physical and emotional wretchedness at his mother's boardinghouse in Montgomery. He pined for his faithless wife, Miss Audrey, drank, took chloral hydrate, drank, fell down and cracked his skull, drank some more, and wrote "I'll Never Get Out of This World Alive."

That October, it was reported that Hank "has gained thirty pounds and . . . is in the best of health." On the nineteenth of the month, without truly divorcing his wife Audrey, he married Miss Billie Jones of Bossier City, Louisiana, on the stage of the New Orleans Municipal Auditorium. Tickets to the hallowed event were priced from $1 to $2.80, and an estimated fourteen thousand paid to attend. Little more than ten weeks later, in the first few hours of the new year, 1953—"I'll Never Get Out of This World Alive" was on the charts—Hank Williams was dead in the backseat of a chauffeured Cadillac en route to an engagement in Canton, Ohio. He was twenty-nine years old.

"When Hank was ready to leave," recalled Billie Jean, his bride, "he came and sat down on the edge of the bed. He just looked at me, not saying a word. 'What're you lookin' at Hank?' I asked him. 'I just wanted to look at you one more time,' he said. I stood in front of the mirror, my back to him, and he came over and kissed me on the cheek. Then he said good-by and left."

After crooning for Pee Wee King's ultra-smooth Golden West Cowboys, Lloyd Copas went solo. As "Cowboy" Copas, he had a number of hits, beginning with "Filipino Baby" (1946) right up through "Alabam" (1960). His 1947 weeper "Signed, Sealed, and Delivered" is considered classic honky-tonk. He died with Hawkshaw Hawkins and Patsy Cline in a 1963 airplane crash.

George Jones, honky-tonk's baroque stylist, late 1950s. Heir to the heart-rending vocal tradition of Roy Acuff and Hank Williams, Jones developed his voice into the most expressive of honky-tonk instruments, capable of rumbling and hiccuping a novelty song like "White Lightning" (1959) or mimicking the gliding moan of a steel guitar on a weeper like "She Thinks I Still Care" (1962).

250

About a year before his death, Hank Williams took Ray Price under his wing. Soon the young Texan was using Hank's Drifting Cowboys in the studio and making honky-tonk music like Hank's; after Hank died, Price briefly employed Hank's band. In this early-fifties TV shot, Price leads Hank's former steel player Don Helms and two other musicians who often played Hank's sessions, fiddler Tommy Jackson and bass player Ernie Newton.

Hank Williams and his new bride, nineteen-year-old Billie Jean Jones Eshliman Williams, cut their wedding cake in a ` ceremony at the New Orleans Municipal Auditorium, October 19, 1952. Tickets to the event ranged from $1 to $2.80, and an estimated fourteen thousand attended. Actually, the couple had been married at a private ceremony the previous day.

Gary Stewart, 1970s. With a build like Hank Williams and similar self-destructive tendencies, Stewart gave the sedate Nashville Sound a brief run for its money in the mid seventies with spirited records that fused honky-tonk pathos and rock 'n' roll energy. He made his last record for RCA in 1983; as of mid 1988 he was playing bars in his hometown of Fort Pierce, Florida.

Opposite, left
When Moe Bandy recorded "I Just Started Hating Cheating Songs Today," he and his producer Ray Baker had to pay for the pressing themselves; but GRC Records soon picked it up, and it became a hit in 1974. Having established his salability, Bandy cut against the crossover grain with one honky-tonk record after another for CBS during the seventies and early eighties.

Opposite, right
Gene Watson was working in a Houston body shop in 1974 when Capitol heard his independent recording of "Love in the Hot Afternoon" and signed him. Here he is during his tenure at Capitol in the seventies; during the eighties he acquired a perm and a beard, but his records for MCA and CBS remained unadorned honky-tonk.

(Billie Jean also recalled that, a few years later, another husband, singer Johnny Horton, kissed her on the very same cheek before leaving on a trip. There was a wreck on the highway, and he never returned.)

"They came from everywhere," declared the Montgomery *Advertiser* on January 5, the day after Hank's funeral, "dressed in their Sunday best, babies in their arms, hobbling on crutches and canes, Negroes, Jews, Catholics, Protestants, small children, and wrinkled faced old men and women. Some brought their lunch. . . ."

When Stonewall Jackson drove his logging truck from Georgia to Nashville to audition for the Opry, he didn't have a hit record, an agent, or even an appointment. But Judge Hay and Opry manager W. D. Kilpatrick listened to the twenty-four-year-old, and Jackson made his Opry debut on November 3, 1956. Hits ("Life to Go" in 1958, "Waterloo" in 1959) followed soon after.

253

Carl Belew, late fifties. A star of Shreveport's "Louisiana Hayride," Belew first arrived on the charts with his composition "Am I That Easy to Forget" (1959). His 1965 hit with "Crystal Chandelier" predated Charley Pride's version by several years.

Billy Walker, ca. 1966. A musician for Ted Daffan and then Hank Thompson during the late forties, Walker moved from Dallas's "Big D Jamboree" (1951–52) to Shreveport's "Louisiana Hayride" (1952–55) to the "Ozark Jubilee" (1955–59) before joining the Opry cast in 1960. Combining elements of western swing, Tex-Mex music, and honky-tonk, he scored big hits with "Charlie's Shoes" (1962) and "Cross the Brazos at Waco" (1964).

There was a great legal battle over the estate, with Miss Audrey, Billie Jean, and Hank's mother, Mrs. W. W. Stone, as the disputants. That spring, her mourning apparently done, Miss Audrey advertised in *Billboard*: "THE ONE AND ONLY! AUDREY (Mrs. Hank) WILLIAMS • THE GIRL FOR WHOM THE LATE, GREAT HANK WILLIAMS WROTE HIS FAMOUS SONGS!" She was, announced the ad, "now available as a single or with her own all-star show for auditoriums, parks, fairs, theaters, T.V." So it went, and so it goes.

The passing from glory of Ernest Tubb and the death of Hank Williams were the end of something. To be sure, there have been great country singers since, but country music itself seems to have lost much of its greatness. Long ago, the song "Loveless Love" envisioned a world of "soulless soul." Sometimes, in re-

254

Left
The man who wrote "Lost Highway": Leon Payne at Pappy Daily's Houston record store, 1940s. A blind guitarist who had once worked in Bill Boyd's western swing band, Payne recorded for Bullet and Capitol, crooning in a pleasant tenor; but he made his reputation as the author of such classics as "They'll Never Take Her Love from Me" and "I Love You Because."

Above
An ardent fan of George Jones, Mel Street came to prominence in 1972 with two superb cheating songs—"Borrowed Angel" and "Lovin' on Back Streets." He moved to Nashville from West Virginia to take his place among the stars, but grew restive and unhappy despite several more Top Twenty hits. On his forty-third birthday, during DJ Week in 1978, he took his own life. Jones sang "Amazing Grace" at his funeral.

cent years, hearing the ersatz stuff that passes for honky-tonk music—or for music, period—it seems to have come to that. Who knows? Would Ernest Tubb or Hank Williams even get airplay if they came along today? We have entered an age of Lite Beer and Lite Country Music, an age of all things Lite. Praise the Lord, I saw the Lite.

One thing remains to be said seriously, in the way of tribute and in the way of fact: Were it not for men such as Ernest Tubb and Hank Williams, and others whose names belong with theirs —Jimmie Rodgers and Lefty Frizzell and George Jones and Jerry Lee Lewis and a handful more—country music would have perished beneath a miasma of stagnation a long time ago.

8

HOME IS WHERE THE GIG IS: LIFE ON AND OFF THE ROAD

Alanna Nash

If ole Hank could only see us now
If he could see what we got going down
We got Lear jets and buses
And chauffered limousines
We done moved from the Ryman
And the Opry's on TV
I'd give a hundred dollars
If I could know somehow
What he'd think
If ole Hank could only see us now.

"If Ole Hank Could Only See Us Now" ©
—Waylon Jennings and Roger Murrah

No doubt about it, things have changed a mite in Nashville since Hank rode the Lost Highway to glory in the backseat of a Caddy. Of course, things changed even more so in the sixty-odd years since the Grand Ole Opry first beamed sweet, homey strains into crackly radios, turning the WSM Barn Dance into a regional, and then a national, phenomenon.

From Uncle Jimmy Thompson to Willie, Waylon, and Randy, from radio transcriptions to compact discs, from the humble

Flatt and Scruggs's "Martha White Express." See page 270.

honky-tonk to the outrageous Gilley's, country music has become a half-billion-dollar-a-year business, replete with its own cable TV channels. Ol' Hank, who was country when country wasn't cool, was lucky if he made $100,000 a year. But in 1983, Kenny Rogers, who was never cool, let alone country, toted home some $20 million. Fetch me an Urban Cowboy, son. I'm so lonesome I could cry.

Like the fat lady who loses a hundred pounds and finds a new personality inside her sleek, svelte body, the stars of country music have undergone a metamorphosis of sorts through the years, both individually and as a group.

Roy Acuff's popularity as a traditional mountain singer played an important role in turning the largely instrumental Opry into the most famous radio barn dance. He recalls that when he first arrived in Nashville from his native east Tennessee, "all the bands that were on the Grand Ole Opry had other jobs, or they worked on a farm. . . . They made their living that way. But when I came here I brought a group of boys with me. I *had* to make a living out of country music. After I got to doin' good, other people saw that money could be made out of country music. I had never seen a country music show 'til I put one on. So I built my own show, and I perform it today. I'm not a blueprint; I'm an original."

And as an original, Acuff has been handsomely rewarded. One of the richest of the Nashville luminaries—his wealth has been estimated at $50 million—he was savvy enough to put his money back into the business (establishing the famous Acuff-Rose publishing combine with Fred Rose) as well as in real estate.

Still, in the time-honored country music tradition, Acuff has remained humble. "Are you happy?" I asked Acuff in 1980, before he moved his residence to Opryland and became something of a living museum piece. "Sure, I have no reason to be unhappy," he said. "My home is paid for, my cars are all paid for, and my equipment is paid for. I don't owe one man one cent."

No matter what trappings of wealth fame might bring, this suggests, many of the good ol' boys and gals of country music still cling to the values, habits, and customs of old. Dolly Parton, who commands $350,000 a week in Las Vegas—making her the highest-paid entertainer there, earning more than Frank Sinatra and Diana Ross—says she still prefers shopping at K-mart or Zayre's, where she can get several articles of clothing for the price she'd pay for one at a more upscale establishment.

On the whole, though, of all the changes in country music through the years, the life-style of the stars comes close to top-

ping them all. From Acuff's early days, when none of the hillbilly musicians expected to make a living from their instruments, to the movie and TV show spinoffs of Parton's spectacular singing career, the top country performers have gone from being poor, uneducated farm folk—and often social outcasts, uncomfortable around anyone with a degree from an institution higher than beauty college—to nouveau-riche celebrities whose decorator homes appear in photo layouts for *Architectural Digest* and *Ladies' Home Journal.* Many of them are as astute about business as their parade of managers, accountants, and booking agents. But although the country performers have almost out-Rolls Royced Nashville's old-money constituency, granting many of them membership in the snooty Belle Meade Country Club is another matter—the country music performer has long been a traveling breed, and quick money today could just as easily mean insolvency tomorrow.

Roy Acuff & the Smoky Mountain Boys on the Grand Ole Opry, early forties. During World War II, one G. I. poll placed the Opry's star singer ahead of Frank Sinatra; and legend has it Japanese troops taunted American soldiers with the cry "To hell with Roosevelt, to hell with Babe Ruth, to hell with Roy Acuff!"

259

WSM bigtop, 1942. To accommodate the larger crowds in small towns, WSM equipped its Opry variety shows with tents capable of holding 1,600.

Jamup & Honey, 1940s. This black-face comedy team was so popular that they headlined the Opry's first touring tent show; Roy Acuff, Bill Monroe, and Curly Fox & Texas Ruby headed others.

Opposite, left
Jamup & Honey, in the pink. Honey's real name was Lee Davis Wilds. At the time of this early fifties photo, Bunny Biggs played Jamup.

Opposite, right
During the thirties and forties, even star acts like Uncle Dave and Fiddlin' Sid Harkreader frequently played small-town schoolhouses. This handbill advertises a program at the Barthelia School on June 17, 1930. The price—fifteen cents for children and twenty-five for adults.

While Uncle Dave Macon was helping make the Opry a regional success in the early 1930s, Roy Acuff was cutting his teeth in show business with Dr. Haver's traveling medicine show. Although only a handful of the early commercial performers had had experience in medicine shows or on the vaudeville circuit (Macon had been taking bookings all over the South since 1918), the advent of Chicago's WLS "National Barn Dance" and the Opry legitimized rural southern music, formerly shunned by city theaters, and led to frequent bookings and travel—even if the performers often slept in their cars. Country entertainers entered a new era in the forties, however, when several Opry performers began organizing mammoth tent shows to take across the country.

One of the first such shows was Jamup & Honey's. The popular black-face comedy team carried a caravan comprising ten

trucks, nine of them tractor-trailers, and set up a tent 80 feet wide and 220 feet long, large enough to contain 1,600 people.

"It took twenty-five roughnecks to move it," Honey Wilds recalled years later. "And we moved it every cotton-picking day, feeding the roughnecks three hot meals. With salaries, lot rent, advertising, and licenses, our daily operating expenses fluctuated between $550 and $600. In other words, we had to make $600 a day before Jamup and I would make a nickel. Everybody said we were crazy."

All the same, Roy Acuff and Bill Monroe, who had traveled on the Jamup & Honey show, followed suit, Monroe seating some 3,500 people in the tent, and coupling his shows with exhibition baseball games.

"In the early days, I believe admission was fifteen and twenty-five cents," Monroe recalls. "Then it went on up to twenty-five, forty-five, and sixty, but then we moved on up, and adults would pay ninety cents admission to get in. That was good money back when we had a tent show."

Like Jamup & Honey before him, Monroe fell victim to frequent mechanical breakdowns, struggling to mobilize the ar-

Overleaf
Spreading the word: For years, a little print shop in downtown Nashville, owned and operated by Will T. Hatch, supplied these remarkably stylish posters for dozens of Opry acts. According to Minnie Pearl, "All you needed was a Hatch poster to tell you that the Opry was coming." All the Hatch Show Print advertisements on the next page date from the 1940s, with the exception of the Flatt & Scruggs poster from the late fifties.

261

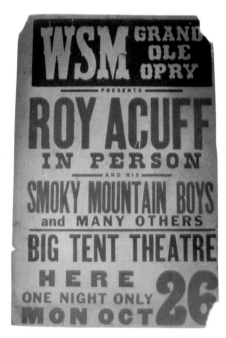

mada of trucks and still make it back to Nashville on Saturdays for the Opry. In 1986, Monroe said that in forty-six years, he'd only been late for the Opry three times—once when he had a flat tire near his Goodlettsville farm just outside Nashville; another time when his stretch limousine caught fire in Monteagle, Tennessee; and finally when his bus got stranded in a cloudburst in eastern Kentucky.

"Benny Martin and I had to get out and hold the old stretched-out bus on the road; it was just floatin' ever'ways," Monroe recalls. "The water went back down in front of us, and we moved on up. And we got on up there and the bridge was washed plumb out. So that stopped us. We never could make it to the Grand Ole Opry."

Despite the inevitability of road mishaps, when Minnie Pearl came to Nashville in 1940 she was shocked to find that "nobody had any insurance.

"For that matter," she says, "nobody owned their home. They lived in trailers or two-room apartments or rooming houses. Very few of them had bank accounts. There was an expression that they used quite frequently when anything came up. They'd say, 'Oh, well, I was looking for a job when I found this one.' There was a transience."

Also prevalent was a peculiar attitude toward money that Minnie Pearl, who had just come off W.P.A. and was "broke deader than four o'clock," couldn't understand. "I had come from people who saved," she says. "My father lost his lumber business in the crash of 1929. I had had money, and I lost it. So I wanted to save my money. And these other people didn't seem to have

In 1949, the Opry organized its first European tour, which appeared at U.S. military bases. On Thanksgiving day in Germany, the road company gathered for this photo. The group includes established stars Red Foley (in the white hat) and Roy Acuff (standing next to him), hot newcomers Hank Williams and Little Jimmy Dickens (in front of Hank), comedians Minnie Pearl and Rod Brasfield (to the immediate left of Minnie), and announcer Grant Turner (between Foley and Williams).

There stands the glass: on an endless stretch of one-night stands, a cold beer or two could smooth the bumps, although for some performers alcoholism proved an occupational hazard. Here Pee Wee King (at left) raises a glass with a group that includes Minnie Pearl.

Cramped dressing rooms and last-minute touch-ups have always been part of country music touring. Here Pee Wee King (on accordion) and Eddy Arnold make do as they prepare for a show along with pop vocalists on the Camel Caravan tour of U. S. military installations, ca. 1942.

that idea at all. They wanted to spend it and have fun, and that was it. Which probably made the Opry sound like it did. They were a fun-loving people. They never talked about capital gain. They never talked about how many dates they could play and not be working for the government.

"Nowadays, the camaraderie is as great as ever, but the performers are business people. Or if they're not, they have agents who are. They figure in thousands, and some in millions. When I came along, most of them carried all the money they had with them. When one of 'em got ready to buy a house, the real estate man would say, 'How do you intend to take care of this?' And they'd say, 'Will cash do?'

"I'll tell you," she adds, shaking her head, "nobody had any idea in the world of how big this thing was going to be."

By the late 1950s, Nashville was fast developing as a music center, but certain aspects of the business still slumbered. Mel Tillis recalls that when he first went to Nashville as a staff writer for Jim Denny's Cedarwood song publishing company, "there were only three publishing companies around [Acuff-Rose, Tree, and Cedarwood], and only about four or five writers that I would call full-time—Boudleaux and Felice Bryant, and Danny Dill and Vic McAlpin. And I think there were only a couple of studios at the time, RCA and Bradley's Quonset Hut. They didn't have the Music Row at that time. The offices of the different artists

During 1941–42, the R. J. Reynolds Tobacco Company, makers of Camel Cigarettes, sponsored the Grand Ole Opry Camel Caravan—a package show that toured U.S. military bases in the States and the Canal Zone. The cast of twenty included bass player Joe Zinkan, fiddler Redd Stewart, pop singer Kay Carlisle, Minnie Pearl, singer-guitarists Eddy Arnold and San Antonio Rose, and accordionist Pee Wee King.

Young Mel Tillis, when he looked like a star but was, in fact, earning his keep by writing hits for others; late fifties.

Brenda Lee, 1960s. Having scored her first hit at age eleven, "Little Miss Dynamite" learned about the rigors of the road early. Huge pop hits like "I'm Sorry" (1960) didn't excuse her from the necessity of touring.

were scattered all over Nashville. Cedarwood was down on Seventh Avenue, right behind the Krystal [hamburger stand]. And they had a little ol' shoe store down there—I believe it was Florsheim's or Bell—and I used to go in there and buy shoes from [songwriter] Curly Putman and [pedal steel guitar player] Lloyd Green."

Before long, with "The Violet and the Rose" and several other singles, Tillis would be recognized as a performer as well as a songwriter. That put him on the big package tours, where entertainers were expected to cover several hundred miles a day by car. Tillis usually drove his own car, and on one such tour, Brenda Lee and her mother rode with him.

"Even up to the middle sixties, we used to travel everywhere by cars," Lee remembers. "And, of course, back in those days, we didn't have interstates. We'd travel those two-lane roads that went through God-knows-how-many little towns. It was great, because you got to see the world. Now you don't get to see those

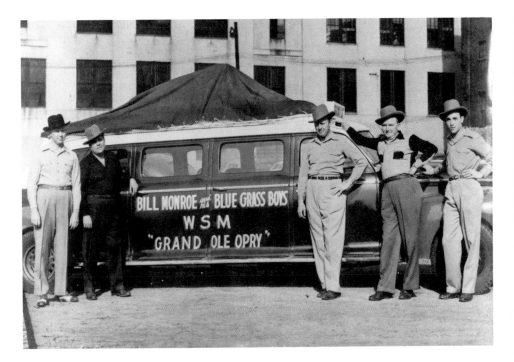

Left
The Blue Grass Special—Bill Monroe's four-seat 1941 Chevrolet airport limousine— heavily laden with instruments and clothes. Pictured (ca. 1947) are the men who lived in it for days at a time: Birch Monroe, Chubby Wise, Bill Monroe, Lester Flatt, and Earl Scruggs.

Above
Roy Acuff's limousine, 1940s. As the Opry's leading singing star of the early forties, Acuff could afford to travel in style; he was among the first country stars to enjoy the comforts of a stretch limo.

Bob Wills & His Texas Playboys assemble in front of one of the best touring buses of the day, 1935.

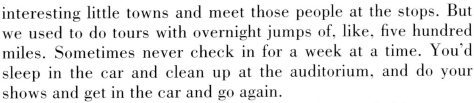

interesting little towns and meet those people at the stops. But we used to do tours with overnight jumps of, like, five hundred miles. Sometimes never check in for a week at a time. You'd sleep in the car and clean up at the auditorium, and do your shows and get in the car and go again.

"Mel would drive all night to get to the date, so he'd want me to tell him stories to keep him awake, because I was a night owl, too. You get to be that way on the road—you can't sleep at night. But then I'd fall asleep five minutes after the show was over. The funny thing was, we'd get to the city limits of the next town,

267

On the road again: before the age of plush tour buses and private jets, country shows hit the road with caravans like this. Johnnie Wright and Kitty Wells stand beside the lead car in this April 1950 photo.

no matter where it was, and I'd wake right up and say, 'Are we there yet?' My manager said it was uncanny. If I ever write a book, I'll call it *Are We There Yet?*, because that's how it becomes after awhile: *Just get me there.*"

Traveling long distances by car was exhausting mentally and physically, and in some cases the road took its toll. In 1965, Ira Louvin died in a head-on car wreck near Jefferson City, Missouri. The year came close to claiming Roy Acuff, as well, who nearly killed himself and a member of his band trying to pass a car on a rain-slicked highway near Sparta, Tennessee. Acuff was left with two pelvic fractures, a crushed rib cage, and a broken collarbone. It was a fear every country performer knew.

"I'm as good a driver as can hit a road," Acuff says. "I'd put 125,000 miles on ever' car I got, ever' year. But I had a premonition it was going to happen. I didn't see how I could go on riding here and there and not have some sort of accident. I'd been traveling thirty years in all sorts of weather. Any game you play, you got to lose sometime."

If one of the mainstays of country song material is the lure and the loneliness of the road, the truth of the matter is that most performers try to soften the bumps as much as possible as they roll along a stretch of endless one-night stands. In achieving that goal, by far the most marvelous invention of the modern-day

268

INSIDE A TOUR BUS

Original floorplan of Dolly Parton's tour bus, 1977.
Model: 1977 MCI 9, built by Motor Coach Industries of Canada.
Specifications: 318 Detroit engine with automatic transmission.
Dimensions: 40 ft. long (bumper to bumper). 7 ft., 9 in. wide. 11 ft., 6 in. high (ground to roof).
Ceiling: 6 ft., 2 in.
Interior length: 37 ft.
Accommodations: Dolly and six band members.
Price: (without customized interior) approx. $125,000; (with customized interior) approx. $215,000.

(Diagram and information courtesy of Klein Brothers Coach Company, Inc., Nashville, Tennessee.)

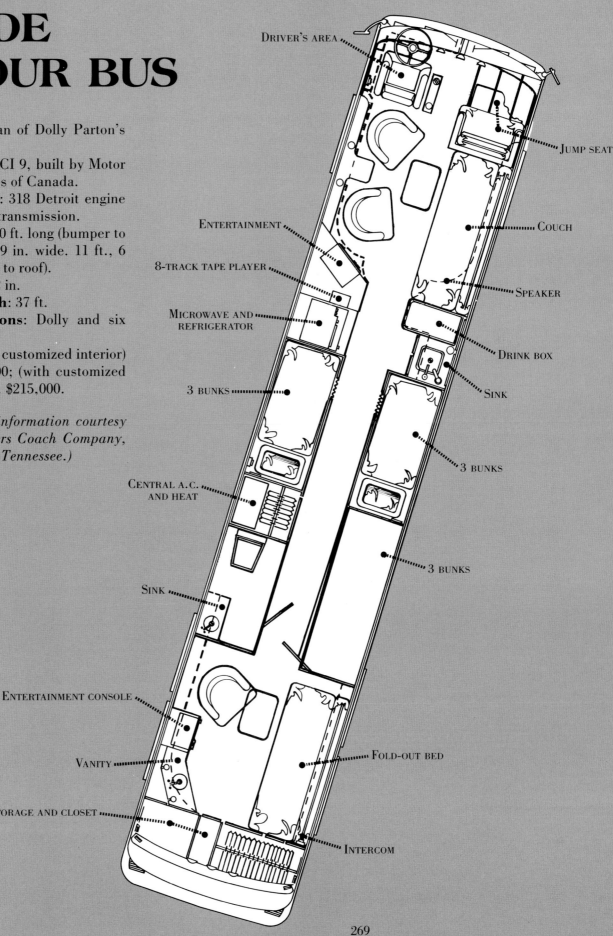

DRIVER'S AREA

JUMP SEAT

ENTERTAINMENT

COUCH

8-TRACK TAPE PLAYER

MICROWAVE AND REFRIGERATOR

SPEAKER

DRINK BOX

3 BUNKS

SINK

3 BUNKS

CENTRAL A.C. AND HEAT

3 BUNKS

SINK

ENTERTAINMENT CONSOLE

VANITY

FOLD-OUT BED

STORAGE AND CLOSET

INTERCOM

Standard transportation for the earliest country acts: Fiddlin' John Carson and his daughter Rosa Lee ("Moonshine Kate"), with their Model A Ford roadster, late 1920s.

Bob Wills & His Texas Playboys had graduated to this streamlined coach by the mid forties.

By 1956, Flatt & Scruggs could afford the latest in touring comfort for the Foggy Mountain Boys. Unfortunately, this bus (their first, nicknamed "The Martha White Express") had a gasoline engine with a maddening tendency to burst into flame. Catching a breath of fresh air with Lester and Earl are Charles Elza, dobroist Josh Graves, mandolinist Curly Seckler, fiddler Paul Warren, and bass player Onie Wheeler.

country music life-style has been the customized touring bus, which virtually all the performers have now—with the exception of Hank Williams, Jr., Charley Pride, and Kenny Rogers, who favor private airplanes.

The reasons are myriad: the buses are enormously convenient ("You finish a concert, the bus is only twelve feet away, so no waiting around," explains Loretta Lynn); with upwards of two hundred gallons of diesel fuel in their tanks, they can handle two-thousand-mile jumps without getting winded; many of the country bookings are in secondary markets, far from major airfields; and the buses easily double as dressing rooms, a distinct advantage when you pull in at the Swingin' Door lounge somewhere and find yourself sharing a unisex bathroom with the club's clientele.

270

Elvis Presley's 1960 custom Cadillac, parked in the Country Music Hall of Fame & Museum since April 1977. When Elvis grew tired of this expensive plaything in the mid sixties, RCA Records used the car as a substitute for the special appearances the reclusive star was no longer making. Known as the "Solid Gold" Cadillac, its paint job includes twenty-four-carat gold dust; the motif is carried on inside with gold records and gold-plated accessories.

Besides, every performer needs someplace to go to escape from overzealous admirers who just *have* to have a lock of their hair. "I like the privacy of the bus," says Tammy Wynette, who has had more than her share of fruitcake fans. "I sleep better on it than I do at home." But Loretta Lynn admits that her bus is both a fortress and a prison: "I've had so many death threats that I don't get out of the bus that much. I just keep my curtains pulled in the back and I read, or I write songs. Never hardly a night goes by on the road when I'm in the back of the bus, and through playin' solitaire, that I don't cry." All the same, Lynn says, she prefers her bus to her house.

Most of the buses are fairly standardized now—they're usually Silver Eagles converted into something resembling a well-to-do ranch house, with a plush bedroom for the star, bunks for the

271

George and Tammy's home away from home—when they were still sharing it—ca. 1970.

backup band, and a lounge or two. (Some of the top headliners carry two buses—one for themselves, and another for their backup musicians.)

Depending on how fancy you want to get, these mobile mansions cost anywhere from $100,000 on up. Even the rather ordinary ones now come equipped with several stereo systems, color TVs, and VCRs, as well as intercoms, microwave ovens, and bars. But the Oak Ridge Boys apparently have the ultimate rolling status symbol—a bus boasting such necessities as a satellite dish, a four-track recording console, 150 first-run films, and a special small ice cream freezer for Duane Allen. That brings the total cost for this comfort coach to a reported one million dollars. And as *Life* magazine once noted, "With a life expectancy of twenty years, the buses will outlast most show-biz careers."

Eventually, of course, the stars do go home, but it's hard to tell which home you mean when you talk about country music personalities, because all country music performers really have three homes—the bus, the motel rooms they check into when bus quarters get too close, and the more permanent brick and stone dwellings they return to occasionally so their families won't forget what they look like.

The homes of the stars are as varied as the personalities of the performers themselves. Brenda Lee, who tries to live as normal an existence as a country star can, resides in a small, charming frame house on the unfashionable east side of Nashville. There she cooks and cans and generally leaves the back door unlocked. At the opposite end of the scale, the ultra-private Donna Fargo lives in a house the size of a K-mart, part of a compound of buildings on remote acreage in Williamson County, Tennessee, where security cameras stare down uninvited guests. Everybody knows about Twitty City, Conway's nine-acre theme park consisting of a multi-media museum, gift shops, botanical gardens, Twitty's business offices, and, incredibly, the Twitty family compound—his private residence and the separate homes of his children! Twitty City might now qualify as the ultimate in fishbowl living and self-exploitation, but it did have its antecedents. In the old days—before neighbors such as Ray Stevens forced him to pull up stakes—Webb Pierce used to do anything short of a strip tease to entice fans to his house and his guitar-shaped swimming pool, where he'd autograph old albums and sell them for new prices. There are stranger life-styles, of course, namely the teepee-dwelling habits of former Oak Ridge Boy William Lee Golden, or the general mind-set of David Allan Coe, who used to live in a cave in Dickson, Tennessee. Or did he? And how many wives *does* he have, anyway?

Who's on first: this group of Opry stars played an exhibition baseball game to raise funds for Nashville's Kiwanis Club Youth Fund, August 1950. Their opponents consisted of WSM announcers, local disc jockeys, and assorted celebrities. Posed for the pre-game publicity shots are (left to right, top to bottom) Ernest Tubb, Hank Williams, Red Foley, Hank Snow, Lloyd "Cowboy" Copas, Bill Monroe, Little Jimmy Dickens, and Dave "Stringbean" Akeman.

Webb Pierce and his luxurious convertible, customized to his standards, early 1960s. Among the accessories were thirteen ornamental pistols and rifles and a set of bull horns attached to the front bumper. As cofounder (with Jim Denny) of the prosperous Cedarwood Publishing Company, Pierce could easily afford such lavish displays of wealth. (He also had his swimming pool built in the shape of a guitar.)

No matter what the stars come home to, there's not much time to enjoy it. Here, as on the road, there are jobs to do, things to attend to: recording a new album, writing for the next one, giving interviews, and calling radio stations to promote their singles; meeting with their managers, record companies, and booking agents; and, of course, seeing to the success of their various sidelines, such as Barbara Mandrell's "Mandrell Country" museum, where for five dollars you can ogle her honeymoon nightgown and first mink coat.

One thing the stars apparently don't do much is visit with each other. Although June Carter Cash occasionally throws "fur parties," inviting wholesale fur dealers down from New York to offer her country cronies fur coats like so much Tupperware, Roy Acuff dismisses the folksy image of the country music entertainers living as one big happy family.

"A lot of people think all of us boys and girls know one another and visit with each other in their homes. That is far from true. We meet here at the Grand Ole Opry, we play it, and we leave. As far as saying to Minnie Pearl, or Hank Snow, 'Come on, go over to the house with me,' I don't do that. And neither do they. They have their little social affairs with whoever they have their friendship with, and I have mine. We don't associate but very little. Now, if there's a party, that's a different thing. But people are misled that think that there is a family of country music people that go around visiting. I'd like to see us be more sociable, but it's just [not] that way."

Part of the reason for that, of course, is most of the performers tour three seasons out of the year. But the number of days each

274

spends on the road differs widely. Conway Twitty, for example, tours 150 days a year, and says he likes being on the road, "although it has its drawbacks." Tammy Wynette, on the other hand, is never away from home more than three weeks at a time. Rosanne Cash, who has small children, tours rarely—and then only when her record company threatens to cut her tongue out.

Perhaps the most insatiable tour junkie is Willie Nelson, who says he could do 365 days if the dates were close enough together. "It's not really that much work to me. I enjoy doing it. If I wasn't allowed to play music, I'd probably get physically sick. It's just something I have to do." Of course, there are trade-offs. Nelson admits he hasn't had a private life in so long that he's about forgotten what one is.

But whereas Don Williams says that "most of all, we try to have a home life" on the road, Nelson has got that down to a science. He doesn't call his group the Family Band for nothing —most of Nelson's musicians have been with him so long that they *have* become his real family, with his wife and children playing secondary roles.

The amazing thing about Nelson's life-style is the way an entire busload of grown men can sit on top of each other nearly three hundred days a year and not slit each other's throats. But Nelson attributes it to an absence of negative thinking—something he insists on. "There's not a negative-thinking person that

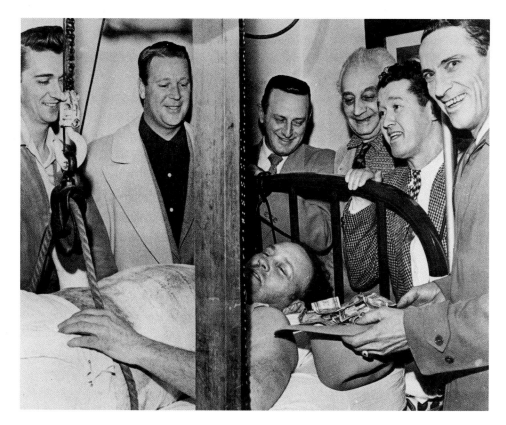

A medicine show of a different sort, 1950s. Well-wishers Carl Smith, Eddie Hill, Opry manager Jim Denny, Vito Pellettieri, Roy Acuff, and Ernest Tubb (passing the hat) visit Bill Monroe, in traction, recuperating from an auto accident.

The best of friends, Red Foley (at left) and Ernest Tubb even recorded hit duets together—"Tennessee Border No. 2" (1949) and "Good Night, Irene" (1950). This humorous letter suggests the difficulty many country performers have had in keeping what they make.

"Red" Foley
Grand Ole Op'ry
Nashville 3, Tennessee

January 5, 1950

Mr. Ernest (Income Tax) Tubb
c/o Ernest Tubb Record Shop
720 Commerce St.
Nashville, Tennessee

Dear Uglier-Than-I-Am:

I more or less hesitate in trying to explain the long delay in re-imbursing you for your most congenial hospitality of your recent loan, and your trust in my honesty.

I think you will be most sympathetic with this particular incident as times are getting tougher all the time; for example: I beg you to consider the drain on my personal billfold, to wit: I have a wife, a home, three children, a brother-in-law, a mother-in-law, and a dog, not to mention the fact that I must pay income tax, personal property tax, social security tax, witholding tax, unemployment tax, union tax, real estate tax, automobile tax, sales tax, royalty tax, gasoline tax, cig-arette tax, dog tax, city tax, county tax, state tax and federal tax, to say nothing of union dues, life insurance, fire insurance, collision insurance, liability insurance, property damage insurance, household goods insurance, accident insurance, tornado insurance, hospital insur-ance, employment insurance and many more expenses that I hesitate to list.

Had it not been for the miracle that happened yesterday, I would still not be able to compensate you for your most gracious hospitality. The proverbial wolf that knocks at everybody's door sooner or later, had a litter of pups on my back porch and I was fortunate enough to be able to sell them for the exact amount of $385.00. Inclosed you will find my check for same.

I trust that you will never have to go through such an embarrassing predicament as I have just recently encountered. After all this I think you will have a more thorough understanding and a broader outlook, and also will be more sympathetic with old age. This is just part of what made me a "Strawberry Roan".

With my head a half mast, I am

Very humbly yours,

"Red" (Wolf) Foley

P.S. In case your bookkeeper, Mr. Mosely, still thinks he has troubles, refer him to this letter. Tell him not to worry about a thing, because nothing is going to be alright!

I know of on the buses," he says. "I don't think he would last long. Because everybody around me knows how I feel, and in keeping those things away from me, consequently they keep them away from themselves. So there are no fights or arguments."

For every one performer who loves the road, there must be two who feel the stress. Every musician reacts to it differently,

276

of course, and some come off the road in a squirrelier state than others. But when you spend more time in the back of a bus than you do with your feet on the ground, your life is bound to have its little eccentricities.

Take, for example, Tom T. Hall. Of all the country performers, Tom and his English-bred wife, Miss Dixie (who changed her name from Iris Buzwell to fit in down south), are said to be the best hosts in Nashville. Accepted by both the country music community and the Nashville social set, Tom T. and his wife throw semi-annual parties at their sixty-acre "plantation" to raise money for causes both animal and political. During Jimmy Carter's term as President, Tom T. and Billy C. got to be spittin' buddies, and Hall headed up a country music campaign to get Carter re-elected.

But even under the best social circumstances, Hall wishes he were elsewhere. Preferably, by himself.

"I enjoy being alone," says the Storyteller, who takes four months off the road each year to concentrate on his prose writing. "I don't like crowds, and I don't go to social functions, except the events that my wife makes me attend. People invite me to go places, and I say no. I genuinely don't want to go, so why trouble myself? A lady came up to me a few days ago, and I thought it was kind of significant. She said, 'You want to dance?' And I said, 'No, I can't dance.' She said, 'Well, I can't either.' I said, 'Well, why bother?' But people will invite you to dance, even though you can't. And they invite me to go out to parties and be sociable when I can't. I'm uncomfortable. I sweat. I get nervous and, therefore, I get drunk. Then I make an ass out of myself, so why go to all that trouble? You can sit home."

In the early days of his career, Hall would go out to a bar, sit around, drink beer, and listen to people talk. He'd be one of them. But those days are over. "Once you become an entertainer, and you get the way I've gotten, you can't really mix into it anymore," he says. "They might not know who I am, but they know I'm somebody, and they start staring at me. So now I go sit out on the boat dock and think about it. But, eventually, I have to get back on the bus and go out on the road and pick and sing."

For Hall, who says he worries what other people are doing to get ahead of him if he happens to sleep late, a normal day at home begins at four or five A.M. After several cups of coffee, he works on his songs, and then tends to his chickens, cows, and vegetable garden. From there, he watches TV, does some reading, and returns to his writing. Then he goes to bed. "I'm like living with a dog," he says. "You just stop and pet me now and then and go about your business. Who couldn't live with a person like that?"

On the road, however, Hall is a different person.

"I spent all my life secluded, writing all of these songs. And it's alien to my nature to go out in front of a thunderous crowd. Entertaining to me is a foolishness, and it depresses me to have

A man and his hobby: Marty Robbins stands beside his 1959 Plymouth with 426-cubic-inch engine, one of several stock cars he owned and raced professionally.

278

The sanctum sanctorum of the Rainbow Ranch: Hank Snow at home with his guitar collection.

Tom T. Hall, 1970s. Inspired by Ernest Hemingway, Hall brought a laconic storyteller's touch to country songwriting and singing with such hits as "Harper Valley PTA" (for Jeannie C. Riley in 1968), "A Week in a Country Jail" (1970), and "The Year That Clayton Delaney Died" (1971). In recent years, he's shown more interest in writing books (a novel and a collection of short stories) than songs.

LACY J. DALTON: THE VIEW FROM THE STAGE

Lacy J. Dalton, early eighties. With a gritty voice she attributes to "singing psychedelic rock for fifteen years," Dalton has scored hits ("Crazy Blue Eyes," "16th Avenue") and impressed critics, but—like most country singers —hasn't made a fortune.

Sometimes I think a performer is a symbol, because performers appear to be successful. You know, you can be a fabulously successful schoolteacher, and it just isn't as visible as being Elvis Presley and having the world know who you are. And I think when people see that visible sign of someone who has creatively actualized success in their life, perhaps it's awesome to them, it's wonderful.

A lot of times, too, I think an audience identifies with a performer's success. But, you know, it's weird, people wanting to get close to you. I'll stand up in front of a big audience, and sometimes it's tough to remember that those are actual people out there, particularly when I can't see a soul. Because the noise that people make at a big concert is like a million insects. You stand up on a concert stage, the bright lights are in your face, and all you hear is weird insect noise.

It's very easy to lose touch with what you're doing and the reasons you're there. I really have to make myself remember that each person is important. It's a discipline. The quality of your contact with them is only what you make it. You can make it just another fan, or you can really try to make it quality contact. And there's a real tendency to just do a lot of people-pleasing and handshaking, because it's so much easier. And you're open to so many weird vibes. I mean, some of the people who come up to you are so damn weird, it's no wonder entertainers close up like clams. Really, you can't believe some of the space cases. Some of them are so desperate! I don't know what they think performers have that they don't, but whatever it is, they're *desperate* for it.

I guess what these people are looking for is a spiritual reality. Maybe they feel that performers have a life that goes on after they die, or beyond the normal life span. They're looking for something spiritual to grab onto. And the closest you can come to satisfying that in those constant contacts with people is to be compassionate toward them, no matter what hideous state they might be in. [*Laughing*] I mean, some of them are in some pretty needy places.

—*from a conversation with Alanna Nash*

280

The Philip Morris Country Music Show, ca. 1957. Shortly after having been ousted from WSM in September 1956, former Opry manager Jim Denny (waving at left) put together one of the largest country package shows yet assembled, for tobacco company Philip Morris. The show ran for sixteen months and featured emcee Biff Collie (first in line), Red Sovine (third), Carl Smith (fifth), and Goldie Hill (fourth, soon to become the second Mrs. Smith).

to do it. The ideal situation is to have success by way of anonymity. Because all the money you make on the road, you spend on the road. And along the way, your health and your mental stability are impaired by it. But if you're running up and down the road entertaining, then you're selling records—and your songs are being played on the air. I'm pretty tough, though. A candyass couldn't do what I do in the fashion that I do it."

When Lacy J. Dalton (a.k.a. Jill Croston) won a CBS record contract in 1980, she quit her job flipping crêpes in a California eatery, thinking her days of financial strain were over. Reality caught up with her.

"Everybody always thinks that if you're on TV, you're fabulously wealthy," says Dalton. "Wrong! That is a myth I have to dispel. I mean, I probably make less money in a week than most secretaries. I think that what people don't understand about show business is that you get maybe—let's take an average price for a gig, say four to six thousand. After the booking agency takes 15 percent, and the manager takes 10 percent or 20 percent, you're left with a little less than half to pay all the traveling expenses, the salaries, and the rooms and meals for yourself and the band. And what you wind up with, unless you're very smart or commanding big fees, is not a great deal.

"The biggest misconception I had about being a *performer*, though, is, 'What's so hard about the road?' Because when you think about the road, you automatically think: There they are traveling in their big, fancy bus, eating at the very best restaurants, having their clothes ready for them. . . . It's not like that. You get there in a thirty-five-foot bus that you share with ten other people, sometimes for six weeks at a time. You have things

happen like somebody throwing clothes that you had cleaned at the Holiday Inn into the equipment truck and they're all wrinkled, and the bass player borrowed your iron at the last place, and you haven't seen it since.

"The road isn't easy. You're in a different bed every night, and the demands on your personal time and space are enormous. Most human beings respond to having some sort of routine in their lives, and on the road there's no routine. One day you get up at 4:30, and the next day you get up at noon. If you don't have your bus, the next day you have to leave right after the show at 11 o'clock and catch a plane, so that at four in the morning you're sitting in Chicago for two hours to save money on plane flights. You fly out again at 6 A.M. and you arrive at 8 A.M., and you spend half an hour waiting for your rent-a-cars with your eyes bleeding all over the airport floor.

282

"Then you get in the rent-a-car, and you go to the hotel, and the air conditioning doesn't work, and it's 110 degrees. And you can't get any sleep, and you have a show to do at 2 o'clock in the afternoon at somebody's fair. You wake up at 12:30, take a bath and get ready, and it's 1:30 and you haven't had time to eat. You jump in the car, you get to the gig, and what do they have as refreshments? Pink meat and American cheese, which is all kind of melted together into a pizza-shaped gob, with nuts glommed in the middle of it, and which has been sitting in the sun for a couple of hours.

"There are people out there who *love* the road, and I wish I were one of them. But most of the time, I *hate* it. Being on the road does funny things to your head.

"When you do finally come off the road, you're dying. Your nerves are shattered. All you want to do is go into a dark room and stay there for about two weeks so that you can become human again. I remember coming home one time after eight months on the road, and my son wanted to go see *Jaws*. Well, seeing *Jaws* after coming off a long hard road tour was probably one of the most traumatic experiences of my life. I got through the part where the shark bit off a few people's legs and ate a couple of kids. But I have this real thing about kids, and it's probably motherly guilt at being gone all the time, and having my son stay with my friend Julie. So during the first scenes, I'd

A typical honky-tonk bandstand, ca. 1949. Rusty Gabbard, future front man for Ernest Tubb's Texas Troubadours, is on guitar.

A family tradition: Hank Sr. serenades Hank Jr. at home, the day after Jr.'s first birthday, May 27, 1950 (right). About three years later, announcer Louie Buck and Lilly Stone (Hank Sr.'s mother) introduced a startled Hank Jr. to a Grand Ole Opry audience (above). By age fourteen he was touring with his mother's "Caravan of Stars" show; he wrote his first hit song, "Standing in the Shadows," two years later.

From the days when Opry stars knew one another just a little bit better: Jimmy Dickens, an unknown soldier, Roy Acuff, Red Foley, and Hank Williams make cocktail conversation as Jimmie Riddle (from Acuff's Smoky Mountain Boys) plays piano during a respite from the Opry's 1949 European tour.

inched my feet up on the seat underneath me. But in the scene where the shark grabbed the little kid off the raft, I pushed my feet up off the chair and landed in the row behind me. If there had been anybody back there, I probably would have killed them. I went out to the lobby where the theater manager walked me around for awhile."

When such episodes occur, Dalton finds it's easy to lose touch with who she is—someone who wants to use her music to heal people, to bring joy into their lives, and to uplift them. "I don't remember that every time I perform," she admits. "But there are lots of times when I do remember, and those are the times when the magic is there."

When it's all said and done, the country music life-style, for all its glamor and reward, is still a risky business, one that often takes more than it gives back. Despite the remarkable changes that turned a front-porch pastime into a multimillion-dollar industry, in the best of cases, the country music game is a cruel gamble, a fleeting fantasy where fame and fortune come and go in the strum of a guitar and the turn of a *Billboard* chart—regardless of talent and good intentions. Even in the best of times, it is enough to make anyone slightly off the wall.

"You mean slightly insane," corrects Tom T. Hall. "Would a sane person do what I do? No way!"

Ol' Hank would understand.

9

GET RHYTHM: ELVIS PRESLEY, JOHNNY CASH, AND THE ROCKABILLIES

Robert Palmer

Even in its mid-fifties glory days, the Sun Records studio at 706 Union Avenue in Memphis was so nondescript that many first-time visitors drove right past it. Sun was just a little downtown storefront, sandwiched between a plate-lunch restaurant and a used-car lot. It was unassuming inside as well, offering few of the amenities of a reputable big-city recording studio.

But Sam Phillips, who originally opened the place in 1950 as the Memphis Recording Service, was neither as ordinary nor as low-rent as the look of his studio suggested. He had turned his back on a solid professional career as a radio announcer and engineer to open the Memphis Recording Service. His calling card—"We record anything–anywhere–anytime"—may have been humble, but Phillips had distinguished himself engineering live radio broadcasts by the top dance bands of the day, broadcasts that fed directly into national network hookups. Some of the bandleaders told him he made their orchestras sound better than the pros who recorded them for major record labels; he was already something of a sonic whiz, experimenting with different balances, using an empty stairwell as an impromptu echo chamber. And once he went into business for himself, Phillips rapidly demonstrated that he could spot raw talent and develop it.

Johnny Cash, early 1960s. Cash never quite fit the rockabilly mold at Sun Records. After signing with Columbia in 1958, he quietly became the most eclectic of all Sam Phillips's discoveries—performing at the Newport Folk Festival, researching and recording ambitious concept albums, appearing at Folsom Prison and San Quentin, starring on TV and in the movies. Despite his broad appeal, he always remained staunchly country.

287

Like W. C. Handy before him, Sam Phillips grew up with blues, gospel, and hillbilly music in Florence, Alabama, moved to Memphis, and found that he had come to the right place at the right time. Young musicians were flocking to Memphis from farms and small towns in nearby Tennessee, Arkansas, Mississippi, and Alabama, and during the early and mid-fifties Sam Phillips's Memphis Recording Service was the major recording studio in town. Phillips didn't have to go out looking for talent, not after word got around that he would listen with a critical but sympathetic ear to aspiring musicians.

The thriving Beale Street scene, with its theaters and bars and gambling dens, brought blues musicians like B. B. King and Little Milton to his doorstep. Howling Wolf and his band had their own radio show originating just across the Mississippi River

Sun Records owner Sam Phillips and Carl Perkins, May 22, 1956. When Phillips let RCA have Elvis for $40,000 in late 1955, he had reason to think Perkins, who played a mean guitar and wrote his own stuff, might be just as sensational. As this plaque attests, Perkins sold a million of his song "Blue Suede Shoes," but though he made wonderful records—"Boppin' the Blues," "Dixie Fried"—he didn't cause women to faint.

in West Memphis. Ike Turner & his Kings of Rhythm drove up from Clarksdale, Mississippi, to audition and recorded "Rocket 88," which became one of 1951's best-selling rhythm-and-blues hits (credited on the label to Jackie Brenston and His Delta Cats) when Phillips leased it to Chess records in Chicago. After recording more rhythm-and-blues hits for other labels, Phillips quite naturally decided to go into business for himself.

Sun's outstanding roster of blues discoveries has tended to overshadow Phillips's substantial accomplishments in the country field. His country recordings failed to achieve a fraction of the commercial success enjoyed by his leading black artists, but not because of any intrinsic lack of worth. Major labels dominated country music in the early and middle fifties, while independent labels were the movers and shakers in r&b. Then, too, the Memphis area, locally referred to as the Mid-South, never developed a single identifiable country music sound or style. In northern Mississippi, country fiddle bands played crisp, biting hoedown music with a bluesy edge and hard rhythmic drive. The Delmore Brothers broadcast over Memphis's WMC in the mid-forties, when they were enjoying their influential string of country-boogie hits. Slim Rhodes, another popular local entertainer, mixed lean, sparse country boogie sounds with sentimental ballads and country gospel tunes. The Swift Jewel Cowboys, who mixed hillbilly inflections, Dixieland jazz, and a sleek swing-band beat, made the last commercial country recordings in Memphis before the coming of Sam Phillips, back in 1939, and

Tennessee Ernie Ford, 1950s. The former disc jockey (and eventual television star) prefigured the coming of rockabilly with rhythmic hits like "Shotgun Boogie" (1950) and "Blackberry Boogie" (1952). In 1955, he scored an enormous pop crossover hit by applying a gently rocking beat and his solid bass voice to Merle Travis's "Sixteen Tons." According to Johnny Cash, Sam Phillips originally intended to give Ford first crack at "Folsom Prison Blues."

Hardrock Gunter & the Thunderbirds, late 1950s. Four years before Sam Phillips ever heard of Elvis, Sidney Louie Gunter growled "We're gonna rock 'n' roll." Unfortunately, that proto-rockabilly record, "Gonna Dance All Night," didn't sell for the Bama label in 1950, and it didn't sell in 1954 when Gunter cut the record again and leased it to Sun. Despite a handful of fine rocking boogie records, Gunter (on guitar) never became a star.

Inspired by black musicians he'd grown up with, Aubrey "Moon" Mullican developed a bluesy boogie woogie piano style, which he polished in the brothels and honky-tonks of Houston. A member of the Opry from 1949 to 1955, he profoundly influenced Jerry Lee Lewis, who eventually covered Mullican's 1949 million-seller "I'll Sail My Ship Alone."

The Maddox Brothers & Rose lived up to their billing as "The Most Colorful Hillbilly Band in the Land" with flashy stage wear from tailor Nathan Turk and a wild, freewheeling style that anticipated the arrival of rock 'n' roll. In this late-forties photo, Cal is on guitar, Henry on mandolin, Don on fiddle, Fred on bass; sister Rose, the singer, is in the middle. They disbanded in 1956, the year they recorded "The Death of Rock and Roll."

Above
*Johnny Horton, late fifties.
Before the million-selling saga
songs "The Battle of New
Orleans" (1959) and "Sink the
Bismark" (1960) that made his
reputation, the "Louisiana
Hayride" star cut hard-edged
records like "Honky Tonk Man"
(1956) that artfully blended the
honky-tonk ethos with the
rockabilly attack. Horton died
in an auto accident after
playing the last club Hank
Williams ever played; he was
married at the time to Hank's
widow.*

Preceding page
*King cowboy: Elvis from the
1968 movie* Stay Away, Joe.
*Elvis made the unthinkable
happen: the sounds of the rural
South became the most popular
music in the world.*

retained their popularity through the forties. Hank Williams also
spent some time broadcasting live from Memphis and helped
popularize the honky-tonk sound there. All these elements influenced the lounge bands that played at night spots like West
Memphis's Cotton Club, bands that often played both popular
and country hits and featured swing-style drumming along with

292

hot solos on pedal steel guitar. And there were still the lone, itinerant songsters, hobos like Harmonica Frank Floyd and wandering evangelists like Howard Seratt, both of whom made memorable recordings for Sun.

Day laborers, salesmen, truck drivers, repairmen—all of them were looking for Sam Phillips, but Sam Phillips was looking for performers with something extra: a sound, a look, something that would enable them to transcend their limited educations and the self-perpetuating cycles of rural poverty and reach out to an audience beyond the local Saturday night honky-tonk crowd. And he found performers like these. In particular, he found Elvis Presley and Johnny Cash. Or did they find him?

Presley and Cash both walked in Sam's front door unannounced. At most other record companies, they would have received a cursory hearing, at best, and been sent right back out the door. Sam Phillips heard something, and took time to bring it out. Perhaps it would be most accurate to say that Phillips and Presley, and then Phillips and Cash, found each other.

Superficially, Presley's and Cash's backgrounds, the records they made for Sam Phillips, and their careers as Sun artists were similar. Both men were born into poor farming families, Presley in north Mississippi, Cash in north Arkansas. Their families moved to Memphis, and they went straight from indifferent public school educations into jobs they probably expected would last a lifetime, Presley as a truck driver for the Crown Electric Company, Cash as a door-to-door appliance salesman. Phillips heard some special qualities in their voices and recorded those voices with minimal instrumental backing, originally just a standup bass and electric guitar with the singer strumming a rhythm guitar, in defiance of the tastes and commercial standards of the time.

Both artists caught the fancy of country music fans first and then broke out into the pop market, with Phillips's encouragement. While at Sun, both established a sound and a direction and did what many people consider their most enduring work. Then they left Sun, for major labels that would never have taken the time and trouble to develop their raw potential, but certainly knew how to market the professionals Sam Phillips had nurtured and molded.

Heard from another angle, the Presley and Cash Sun recordings represent opposite poles of the Sun sound, defining the disparate sources of the music, its possibilities, and, perhaps, its limits. Presley's country and gospel roots ran deep, but he had enriched his music with the rhythmic swagger and sophistication of black rhythm & blues, and adopted the dress codes

Opposite, top right
Guitarist Arthur Smith had long been a local favorite in North Carolina when he cut an instrumental called "Guitar Boogie," in 1946. Eventually selling more than a million copies, it inspired hundreds of young musicians across the Southeast, many of whom would later cite this tune as an early influence on their rockabilly guitar styles. Smith is on the left, with his brothers Ralph (accordion) and Sonny (guitar), at Charlotte's WBT, 1940s.

Opposite, bottom
Bill Haley & His Comets, ca. 1955. At the top of the heap when this publicity photo was taken, Haley labored in country bands before recording "(We're Gonna) Rock Around the Clock," which became the first rock 'n' roll song to top the pop charts in June 1955. After enjoying a brief glimmer of international stardom, he was eclipsed by Elvis and died an alcoholic in 1981.

293

and slang of the black urban hipster as his own—they called him "the Hillbilly Cat." He was a country artist in the tradition of Jimmie Davis and Jimmie Rodgers, men who played and recorded with black musicians and were authentic bluesmen to the core. Cash, who first approached Sam Phillips hoping to record some simple, sturdy gospel songs, belongs to another country tradition, epitomized, perhaps, by the Carter Family. There was some blues coloring in his music, to be sure, but the high lonesome sound of prisoner and murder ballads, mountain laments, plain-spoken narrative songs, and even hoedown music were the dominant influences.

The music Phillips created with Presley, Cash, and his other erstwhile country singers is generally called rockabilly. The term is unavoidable, but problematic; Phillips himself has said he despises it. The image it projects is clear enough: farm boys in garishly colored cat clothes, revved up on black r&b and James Dean movies and ready to rock. And Sun records like Carl Perkins's "Blue Suede Shoes," Billy Lee Riley's "Flying Saucers Rock and Roll," Sonny Burgess's "We Wanna Boogie," and Warren Smith's "Ubangi Stomp" fit the image perfectly. These performers all copied a bit of Presley's style—the moves, the sneer, the sideburns, the vocal slurs and quavers and hiccups. But are records like Presley's "That's All Right"/"Blue Moon of Kentucky" or Cash's "Hey Porter"/"Cry Cry Cry" rockabilly also? These early Sun trio sounds were never really imitated, let alone duplicated. They are so minimal, so *concentrated*, so precariously and yet precisely poised on the knife's edge where country music, old-time blues, bluegrass, gospel, r&b, western swing, pop crooning, and other elements of fifties vernacular music were about to intersect so explosively, they seem to define their own generic niche. Their roots may be rockabilly's roots; their essence is something else. Before we can get at that essence, we're going to have to excavate the roots some more. That means digging into the fertile soil of the Mid-South.

There's an old saying in Memphis that the Mississippi Delta begins in the lobby of the city's Peabody Hotel. And the Delta, a flat alluvial plain that fans out into Mississippi and Arkansas from both sides of the Mississippi River, has traditionally been a region where the population was as much as 75 percent black. This proximity to black culture helps account for the influence of black music, including gospel and jazz as well as blues and r&b, on the Mid-South's country music. The region was an early stronghold of country boogie, as we've seen, but even back-country string bands tended to play with a more emphatic beat and bluesier inflections than in other parts of the South.

Opposite, left
Billy Lee Riley & His Little Green Men, 1958. Handy with a bass, harmonica, guitar, and drums, and with a raspy voice for good measure, Riley had talent to burn but somehow couldn't focus it. His memorable records for Sun include "Red Hot" and "Flying Saucers Rock 'N Roll," from which his band took its name. The lineup here: pianist Jimmy Wilson, saxophonist Martin Willis, Riley on guitar, drummer J. M. Van Eaton, and bass player Pat O'Neill.

Rusty & Doug, late 1950s. One of the Grand Ole Opry's early concessions to the rockabilly craze was to sign the Kershaw brothers in 1958. Ironically, these veterans of the "Louisiana Hayride" were Cajun musicians first, then (perhaps) rockabilly. After hits with Felice & Boudleaux Bryant's "Hey Sheriff" (1958) and their own "Louisiana Man" (1961), the duo split. Fiddler Doug (right) has gone on to a solo career.

294

Above

The Cochran Brothers (ca. 1954) weren't brothers at all. Eddie was a teenage whiz on lead guitar and Hank a budding songwriter, when they met in Los Angeles in 1954. They toured and recorded as a country act for Hollywood's Ekko label until Elvis inspired a fling with rockabilly. After their split in 1956, Hank went on to become a top Nashville songwriter, while Eddie enjoyed two brief years of rock 'n' roll stardom before his death in 1960.

Warren Smith (left) with guitar-toting Faron Young and an unidentified figure in a backstage dressing room, 1961. By the time of this photo, the Memphis rockabilly who had sung "Rock 'n' Roll Ruby" and "Ubangi Stomp" for Sun Records in 1956 had become quite acceptable as a Nashville honky-tonker for Liberty Records.

C'MON EVERYBODY: ROCKABILLY OUTSIDE MEMPHIS

Buddy Holly, ca. 1956. Cedarwood publisher Jim Denny, Decca A&R man Paul Cohen, and his assistant Owen Bradley all had hopes of making a country star of Holly when they brought the young Texan to Nashville for recording sessions in 1956. But two singles failed to dent the charts. A year later, Holly was on his way to pop stardom.

What Sam Phillips achieved in Memphis sounded so deceptively simple that scores of young kids all over the country decided that they too could make rockabilly music. And the fact that Phillips had managed to sell the music on his own record label inspired dozens of little independent record companies to have a go at capturing a share of the youth market. What had begun as a southern phenomenon quickly achieved nationwide currency. Rockabilly records were cut virtually anywhere a young man (and a few young women) could find a guitar and a tape machine.

Some artists, inspired by the example of Phillips and Presley, managed to make a splash of their own. In Norfolk, Virginia, a young ex-sailor, Gene Vincent, attracted the attention of Capitol Records. Producer Ken Nelson brought Vincent to Nashville, where he cut the classic "Be-Bop-A-Lula" in his first recording session, at Owen Bradley's studio in April 1956.

Buddy Holly, a native of Lubbock, Texas, made his first recordings in Nashville, but neither Holly nor his producer, Owen Bradley, felt that the sound they captured in January 1956 represented Holly's musical vision. So the young Texan traveled to Clovis, New Mexico, where he had recorded some early demos with Norman Petty, and cut "That'll Be the Day" and most of his other big hits.

Midwesterner Eddie Cochran (born in Oklahoma, raised in Minnesota and California) also recorded unsuccessfully in Nashville before signing with West Coast-based Liberty Records (run by Mississippian Al Bennett). Cochran recorded most of his classic sides ("C'mon Everybody," "Summertime Blues") at Goldstar Studios in Hollywood.

Like Cochran, television star Ricky Nelson recorded in Hollywood. Although his singing had none of the twangy wildness of the southern rockabillies, Nelson's band did include Louisiana guitarist James Burton, a veteran performer on the country radio show "Louisiana Hayride." Burton's guitar gave some of Nelson's early sides a rockabilly feel.

While some artists enjoyed success, a large part of the rockabilly story was written by regionally popular figures and one-hit wonders, and by country performers who tried to adopt the style at the height of its popularity, only to return to mainstream country when the craze died out. In the thirty years since the heyday of rockabilly in the late fifties, European and American record collectors have elevated to cult hero status many artists whose original efforts failed to make a mark on the national scene. Reissue labels like Bear Family, Ace, Charly, Solid Smoke, Flyright, Rounder, and Rhino have kept in print records by artists who would otherwise have been forgotten. Publications like *New Kommotion*, *Now Dig This*, *Kicks*, *Not Fade Away*, and *Goldmine* have chronicled the careers of famous and obscure alike, in many cases supplying full discographical details. The effect of such recent devotion to rockabilly's brief moment has been that lesser-known, non-Memphis rockabilly acts have assumed an importance beyond any commercial impact they had in the mid-fifties.

Among the most heralded (and highly valued by collectors) of these non-Memphis rockabillies are Ronnie Self (Missouri), Johnny Jano (Louisiana), Glen Glenn (Missouri and California), Ray Campi (Texas and California), Sonny Fisher (Texas), Janis Martin (Virginia), Wanda Jackson (Oklahoma), Ral Donner (Florida), Al Ferrier (Louisiana), Hardrock Gunter (Alabama), Dale Hawkins (Louisiana), Joe Clay (Louisiana), Sleepy LaBeef (Arkansas), Jimmie Logsdon (Kentucky), Rusty & Doug Kershaw (Louisiana) and Sid King (Texas). The list could go on and on. Not all the rockabilly worth hearing was cut in Memphis.

Gene Vincent, ca. 1958. Ex-sailor Vincent Eugene Craddock had performed over WCMS-Norfolk's "Country Time" radio show before being tapped as Capitol Records' early answer to Elvis Presley. His career peaked in 1956 with the release of his first single, "Be-Bop-A-Lula," recorded at Owen Bradley's studio in Nashville.

Ricky Nelson in the studio with the Jordanaires, 1957. The son of Ozzie and Harriet had one thing most teenage rockabilly hopefuls didn't: a TV show to promote his latest record. But he also had good taste, covering records by Fats Domino ("I'm Walkin'") and Carl Perkins ("Boppin' the Blues"), and hiring wunderkind guitarist James Burton.

297

Charlie Rich at the Memphis Rivermont Club, July 1958. "He was just too jazzy for Sun, all thirteenths," according to Sun A&R man Bill Justis (composer of "Raunchy"). "I gave him a bunch of Jerry Lee Lewis records and told him to come back when he got that bad. His voice was fine but his songs and arrangements were too complicated." His biggest hit for Sam Phillips was "Lonely Weekends" in 1959.

Below
Roy Orbison, 1960. Though he had a small hit with "Ooby Dooby" at Sun Records in 1956, Orbison was an indifferent rockabilly singer. He preferred ballads and eventually got the chance to cut them in Nashville. Matched with Music Row's "A Team" of studio musicians, he hit his stride in 1960 with "Only the Lonely," putting together a string of pop hits that continued unabated through 1964's "Oh, Pretty Woman."

298

Above
Charlie Feathers & His Musical Warriors, 1950s. After issuing unnoticed country records at Sun, Feathers went on to make several rockabilly records with a host of labels, including Meteor and King. His alternative to Elvis's vocal mannerisms was a high-pitched muttering; said to be influential in Memphis, his style never caught on nationally.

Top left
Sonny Burgess & the Pacers, ca. 1957. Burgess (on guitar) was one of several talented singers who recorded for Sun Records and somehow failed to catch on nationally. Although he generally leaned more toward rhythm-and-blues styles than country, he did record a raucous version of Hank Williams's "My Bucket's Got a Hole in It" while at Sun.

The Killer, airborne (opposite) and in repose, 1957–58. Of all Sam Phillips's discoveries, Jerry Lee Lewis of Ferriday, Louisiana, had the most potential to unseat Elvis from the throne. But the scandal of his marriage to his thirteen-year-old cousin cast Lewis into darkness for a decade, until he was resurrected as a honky-tonk singer.

The Rock 'n' Roll Trio, 1956: lead guitarist Paul Burlison, and brothers Johnny and Dorsey Burnette (on bass) were part-time musicians from Memphis who landed a contract with Coral Records after appearing on "Ted Mack's Amateur Hour." Though they made only a minor impression in 1956 with the regional hits "Tear It Up" and "Train Kept A-Rollin'," they are now revered by collectors and musicians as one of the wildest of the rockabilly bands.

On April 17, 1960, Eddie Cochran and Gene Vincent were in the midst of a triumphant British tour when this car crashed, killing Cochran and injuring Cochran's fiancée Sharon Sheeley and Vincent. Little more than a year before (February 3, 1959), Buddy Holly, Ritchie Valens, and The Big Bopper (J. P. Richardson) had died in an airplane crash after a show in Clear Lake, Iowa.

During the thirties, the forties, and early fifties, jazz and blues influences permeated country music through the medium of western swing. Memphis is hardly the Wild West, but western swing bands found enthusiastic audiences there. When Art Satherley visited the city with a Vocalion Records mobile unit in 1939, he found that the most popular country performers were the Swift Jewel Cowboys and Gene Steele, who wore western outfits and worked in a western swing vein. When Sam Phillips arrived in Memphis in 1945, one of his first jobs was spinning records over WREC using the pseudonym "Pardner." His show, the station's main country music program, was called "Songs of the West." By then, the hottest country act in town was the Slim Rhodes Band, whose show on WMC lasted from 1944 into the early sixties. Rhodes and his musicians wore Stetsons and other western attire, and recorded for Gilt Edge in a western swing-related style in 1950; the session was engineered by Phillips.

Most of the Memphis musicians who played on Phillips's early country sessions and went on to shape the style subsequently tagged rockabilly had early experience playing the Mid-South's version of western swing. One of the most important of these bands was Clyde Leoppard's Snearly Ranch Boys, whose steel guitarist, Stan Kesler, was later a key Sun session musician. Kesler co-wrote "I'm Left, You're Right, She's Gone" for Presley, and rockabilly tunes recorded by Charlie Feathers, among others. Recordings dating from his tenure with the Snearly Ranch Boys (reissued by Germany's Bear Family label on *The Sun Country Box*) capture a jazz-influenced band driven by

swing-style drumming, hot steel guitar solos, and the boogie-woogie piano of Smokey Joe Baugh, whose gravelly vocals seem to have been a model for many of the Sun rockabillies. Guitarist Scotty Moore and bass player Bill Black were working with a similar band, Doug Poindexter's Starlite Wranglers, when they were first introduced to Elvis Presley. Paul Burlison, a Memphis guitarist who later worked with Johnny Burnette's Rock 'N' Roll Trio, reports that Bill Black began slapping his string bass rockabilly-style after seeing a bass player in Bob Wills's western swing band do it.

Musicians like Kesler, Baugh, Moore, and Black were versatile, flexible stylists because they had to be; a Mid-South lounge band like the Snearly Ranch Boys or the Starlite Wranglers was likely to cover Ernest Tubb, Woody Herman, Dean Martin, Louis Jordan, Count Basie, and Red Foley in the course of a single set. But Sam Phillips realized that any band with a steel guitar would sound like a hillbilly band to the sort of youngsters he wanted his records to reach, and that members of this target audience would find a straight boogie woogie piano sound dated. He was also familiar enough with the rhythm & blues field to realize that artists like Arthur Crudup, Muddy Waters, and Little Walter were getting a big, full sound with nothing but an electric guitar, a bass, and studio echo and reverb.

Good rockin': Ellis Auditorium, Memphis, May 15, 1956. With Elvis is his classic band—Scotty Moore on guitar, Bill Black on bass, and D. J. Fontana on drums. While the fans had their eyes glued to Elvis, young musicians were memorizing what Scotty, Bill, and D. J. were doing.

301

The Hillbilly Cat, Overton Park Shell, Memphis, August 5, 1955. On that night, Elvis was still an aspiring country singer who shared the bill with Webb Pierce, Red Sovine, Sonny James, Wanda Jackson, Texas Bill Strength, and fellow Sun artists Johnny Cash and Charlie Feathers. Memphis photographer Robert Dye caught Presley backstage for this photo.

So Phillips decided to simplify. He may have put Scotty and Bill together with Elvis for rehearsal purposes, but when he heard them in the studio he knew they didn't need additional instrumentation. When Johnny Cash walked into Sun in 1954 and began apologizing for his ragged little trio, which was so minimal it made Elvis, Scotty, and Bill sound almost like an orchestra by comparison, Phillips decided to hang onto that trio and work with it. "Can you imagine 'I Walk the Line' with a steel guitar and a fiddle?" he often asks rhetorically. A country record producer in Nashville or Los Angeles probably wouldn't have been able to hear the song *without* those trimmings.

So, beginning in mid-1953 with Presley, and roughly a year later with Cash, Sam Phillips got down to some serious experimenting. His decision to invest a great deal of time and energy in performers who must have seemed unpromising to most of his associates has generally been attributed to commercial motivations. His secretary, Marion Keisker, has recalled hearing him comment, "If I could find a white man who has the Negro sound and the Negro feel, I could make a million dollars," or something of the sort, and this reported comment has hung over his head ever since. Phillips himself has denied saying it on at least one occasion; he has also been quoted as saying that *if* he made such a comment, it has been quoted out of context and misunderstood.

In particular, Phillips resents the suggestion that he deliberately abandoned the black music, and black artists, who made Sun's initial reputation, in order to cash in with white imitators. Here, certainly, he is on solid ground. As he points out, the black artists abandoned him. B. B. King, Howling Wolf, Ike Turner, Little Milton, all his most promising southern blues artists had left the South by the end of 1954. Some were lured away by established r&b labels like Chess and Modern/RPM, whose expertise at selling records to black consumers across the country far eclipsed anything Sun's limited distribution could accomplish. Other bluesmen seem to have been caught up in the black mass migration from the country to the city, and from southern cities to Chicago, Detroit, and the East and West Coasts. Phillips was faced with a rapidly dwindling talent pool. The question was what to do about it.

As early as mid-1953, when young, outrageously dressed but painfully shy Elvis Presley made his first appearance at 706 Union, substantial numbers of white teenagers were listening to and buying rhythm & blues records. Like most American cities of any size, Memphis had a white disc jockey who held local teens in thrall by spinning the latest r&b releases. Dewey Phil-

lips (no relation to Sam) was already the hottest DJ in Memphis when Sam Phillips presented him with an advance dub of Presley's debut disc, "That's All Right"/"Blue Moon of Kentucky." In general, radio reacted slowly to Presley. The country jocks thought he sounded too black, the r&b jocks thought he sounded like a hillbilly. But Dewey Phillips, and his more devoted listeners, took to the Hillbilly Cat right away. It didn't take a genius to realize that this was something worth developing. And in mid-1954, when that first yellow-label Presley single was released, Sam Phillips didn't have a lot of choice. A million dollars? He would have settled for a good, solid regional success. It wasn't until Presley's second and third Sun releases that that regional success began to materialize.

By the end of 1954, the momentum was building. Elvis had electrified the audience at a July 30 country package show in Memphis with his incendiary version of the Roy Brown r&b anthem "Good Rockin' Tonight," making it abundantly clear that the song should be his second Sun single. By the time the record appeared, in September, the first single had sold close to 20,000 copies and the more "country" side, the Bill Monroe bluegrass tune "Blue Moon of Kentucky," was topping the country charts in Memphis. In October, after being brushed off in no uncertain terms when he auditioned for the Grand Ole Opry in Nashville, Presley landed a weekly slot on the "Louisiana Hayride." Eyewitnesses describe him as heartbroken by the Opry's rejection,

WHOLE LOTTA SHAKIN' GOIN' ON: ROCKABILLY ON THE COUNTRY CHARTS

When Memphis DJ Dewey Phillips played Elvis Presley's "That's All Right" and "Blue Moon of Kentucky" for the first time and then interviewed the nineteen-year-old over the air, station WHBQ received fourteen telegrams and forty-seven phone calls for the local boy. Most were from new fans—but not everyone took an immediate liking to Elvis's sound. And as Presley's records began to gain a foothold on regional country charts in Memphis, New Orleans, and Dallas, the muttering in the country industry began: *It's not country, it's Negro music. It's pop. It's something, but it's not country.*

The protests only became more heated as Elvis and the rockabillies that followed him proved to be the hottest thing going on the country charts. Paul Ackerman, former music editor at *Billboard*, stated in no uncertain terms in a 1958 article for *High Fidelity* that "well-entrenched artists, talent managers and other members of the trade resented him [Elvis] fiercely. One day I had two phone calls from music executives in Nashville, Tennessee. Both demanded that *The Billboard* remove Presley from the best-selling country chart on the ground that—so they said—he was not truly representative of the country field." Nevertheless, he fit right into country package shows: before Elvis

became a national sensation in 1956, he toured for a year and a half with folks like Hank Snow, the Louvin Brothers, Slim Whitman, Faron Young, and Ferlin Husky.

Despite the complaints, many country singers were quick to try the new brand of country on for size, only to find they couldn't fill those blue suede shoes. But there were some successes, artistic and otherwise. Marty Robbins cut "That's All Right" and had a bigger hit with it than Elvis. Webb Pierce covered the Everly Brothers' first single, "Bye Bye Love," and followed the Everlys right up the country charts. George Jones recorded creditable rockabilly under the moniker "Thumper" Jones.

In truth, it was hard for country singers *not* to attempt rockabilly. In the mid and late fifties, Presley, Perkins, Cash, and Lewis looked for all the world like the Four Horsemen of the Apocalypse, laying waste all squares before them. Through all the commotion in the industry, country fans simply bought the records, wrote and called their radio stations, and kept putting nickels in the jukebox. Elvis and the boys were making some of the best country they ever heard.

These *Billboard* "Country & Western" charts from 1956–58 give a good indication of how rockabilly was received in country circles.

FEBRUARY 25, 1956

...NTRY & WESTERN RECORDS

• Best Sellers in Stores

For survey week ending February 15

RECORDS are ranked in order of their current national selling importance at the retail level, as determined by The Billboard's weekly survey of dealers throut the nation with a high volume of sales in country and western records. When significant action is reported on both sides of a record, points are combined to determine position on the chart. In such a case, both sides are listed in bold type, the leading side on top.

This Week		Last Week	Weeks on Chart
1.	I FORGOT TO REMEMBER TO FORGET (BMI)—E. Presley Mystery Train (BMI)—Vic 20-6357-Sun 223	2	24
2.	WHY, BABY, WHY? (BMI)—R. Sovine & W. Pierce Missing You (BMI)—Dec 29755	3	10
3.	LOVE, LOVE, LOVE (BMI)—W. Pierce IF YOU WERE ME (BMI)—Dec 29662	3	23
4.	SIXTEEN TONS (BMI)—Tennessee Ernie You Don't Have to Be a Baby to Cry (ASCAP)—Cap 3262	1	16
5.	EAT, DRINK AND BE MERRY (BMI)—P. Wagoner Let's Squiggle (BMI)—Vic 20-6289	5	13
6.	I DON'T BELIEVE YOU'VE MET MY BABY (BMI)—Louvin Brothers In the Middle of Nowhere (BMI)—Cap 3300	6	5
7.	YOU'RE FREE TO GO (ASCAP)—C. Smith I FEEL LIKE CRYIN' (BMI)—Col 21462	7	11
8.	YOU AND ME (BMI)—R. Foley & K. Wells NO ONE BUT YOU (BMI)—Dec 29740	8	5
9.	FOLSOM PRISON BLUES (BMI)—J. Cash SO DOGGONE LONESOME (BMI)—Sun 232	10	2
10.	BLUE SUEDE SHOES (BMI)—C. Perkins Honey, Don't (BMI)—Sun 234	14	2
11.	I'M MOVIN' IN (BMI)—H. Snow THESE HANDS (BMI)—Vic 20-6379	8	3
12.	ALL RIGHT (BMI)—F. Young Go Back, You Fool (BMI)—Cap 3169	15	29
12.	WHY, BABY, WHY? (BMI)—G. Jones Seasons of My Heart (BMI)—Starday 202	—	10
14.	JUST CALL ME LONESOME (BMI)—E. Arnold That Do Make It Nice (BMI)—Vic 20-6198	12	28
15.	RUN BOY (BMI)—R. Price You Never Will Be True (BMI)—Col 21474	—	1

• Most Played in Juke Boxes

For survey week ending February 15

RECORDS are ranked in order of the greatest number of plays in juke boxes throut the country, as determined by The Billboard's weekly survey of operators using a high proportion of country and western records. When significant action is reported on both sides of a record, points are combined to determine positon on the chart.

This Week		Last Week	Weeks on Chart
1.	WHY, BABY, WHY? (BMI)—R. Sovine & W. Pierce Missing You (BMI)—Dec 29755	3	7
2.	I FORGOT TO REMEMBER TO FORGET (BMI)—E. Presley MYSTERY TRAIN (BMI)—Vic 20-6357-Sun 223	2	15
3.	SIXTEEN TONS (BMI)—Tennessee Ernie You Don't Have to Be a Baby to Cry (ASCAP)—Cap 3262	1	14
4.	EAT, DRINK AND BE MERRY (BMI)—P. Wagoner Let's Squiggle (BMI)—Vic 20-6289	5	11
5.	LOVE, LOVE, LOVE (BMI)—W. Pierce IF YOU WERE ME (BMI)—Dec 29662	4	21
6.	YOU'RE FREE TO GO (ASCAP)—C. Smith I FEEL LIKE CRYIN' (BMI)—Col 21462	6	6
7.	WHY, BABY, WHY? (BMI)—G. Jones Seasons of My Heart (BMI)—Starday 202	7	15
7.	WHAT AM I WORTH? (BMI)—G. Jones Still Hurtin' (BMI)—Starday 216	10	5
9.	THESE HANDS (BMI)—H. Snow I'M MOVIN' IN (BMI)—Vic 20-6379	9	2
9.	I DON'T BELIEVE YOU'VE MET MY BABY (BMI)—Louvin Brothers In the Middle of Nowhere (BMI)—Cap 3300	—	1
9.	YOU AND ME (BMI)—R. & B. Foley NO ONE BUT YOU (BMI)—Dec 29740	—	1

• Most Played by Jockeys

For survey week ending February 15

SIDES are ranked in order of the greatest number of plays on disk jockey radio shows throut the country according to The Billboard's weekly survey of top disk jockey shows in all key markets.

This Week		Last Week	Weeks on Chart
1.	LOVE, LOVE, LOVE—W. Pierce Dec 29662—BMI	2	22
2.	WHY, BABY, WHY?—R. Sovine & W. Pierce Dec 29739—BMI	1	11
3.	I DON'T BELIEVE YOU'VE MET MY BABY—Louvin Brothers Cap 3300—BMI	6	7
4.	I FORGOT TO REMEMBER TO FORGET—E. Presley Vic 20-6357, Sun 223—BMI	4	20
5.	SIXTEEN TONS—Tennessee Ernie Cap 3262—BMI	3	15
6.	WHY, BABY, WHY?—G. Jones Starday 202—BMI	11	12
7.	EAT, DRINK AND BE MERRY—P. Wagoner Vic 20-6289—BMI	5	13
8.	RUN BOY—R. Price Col 21474—ASCAP	8	7
9.	THESE HANDS—H. Snow Vic 20-6379—BMI	7	4
10.	YOU AND ME—R. & B. Foley Dec 29740—BMI	9	2
11.	FOLSOM PRISON BLUES—J. Cash Sun 232—BMI	12	3
12.	YOU'RE FREE TO GO—C. Smith Col 21462—ASCAP	10	12
13.	BLUE SUEDE SHOES—C. Perkins Sun 234—BMI	—	1
14.	SO DOGGONE LONESOME—J. Cash Sun 232—BMI	15	2
15.	IT'S A GREAT LIFE—F. Young Cap 3258—BMI	13	12

WESTERN RECORDS JUNE 17, 1957

• C&W Best Sellers in Stores

For survey week ending June 12

RECORDS are ranked in order of their current national selling importance at the retail level, as determined by The Billboard's weekly survey of dealers throut the nation with a high volume of sales in country and western records. When significant action is reported on both sides of a record, points are combined to determine position on the chart. In such a case, both sides are listed in bold type, the leading side on top.

This Week		Last Week	Weeks on Chart
1.	WHITE SPORT COAT (BMI)—Marty Robbins Grown-Up Tears (BMI)—Col 40864	1	10
2.	FOUR WALLS (BMI)—Jim Reeves I Know and You Know (BMI)—Vic 20-6874	2	8
3.	GONE (BMI)—Ferlin Husky Missing Persons (BMI)—Cap 3628	3	18
4.	GONNA FIND ME A BLUEBIRD (BMI)—Marvin Rainwater So You Think You've Got Troubles (BMI)—M-G-M 12412	4	8
5.	ALL SHOOK UP (BMI)—Elvis Presley That's When Your Heartaches Begin (ASCAP)—Vic 20-6870	5	11
6.	BYE BYE LOVE (BMI)—Everly Brothers I Wonder If I Care as Much (BMI)—Cadence 1315	9	5
7.	HONKY TONK SONG (BMI)—Webb Pierce SOME DAY (BMI)—Dec 30255	6	13
8.	FRAULEIN (BMI)—Bobby Helms Heartsick Feeling (BMI)—Dec 30194	7	12
9.	BYE BYE LOVE (BMI)—Webb Pierce MISSING YOU (BMI)—Dec 30321	8	3
10.	NEXT IN LINE (BMI)—Johnny Cash DON'T MAKE ME GO (BMI)—Sun 266	11	4
11.	WALKIN' AFTER MIDNIGHT (BMI)—Patsy Cline Poor Man's Roses (ASCAP)—Dec 30221	10	17
12.	FALLEN STAR (BMI)—Jimmy Newman I Can't Go On This Way (BMI)—Dot 1289	12	3
13.	TOO MUCH WATER (BMI)—George Jones I've Got to Go Cry (BMI)—Mercury 71096	14	2
13.	I'LL BE THERE (BMI)—Ray Price Please Don't Leave Me (BMI)—Col 40889	—	1
15.	WHOLE LOTTA SHAKIN' GOIN' ON (BMI)—Jerry Lee Lewis It'll Be Mine (BMI)—Sun 267	—	1

• Most Played C&W in Juke Boxes

For survey week ending June 12

RECORDS are ranked in order of the greatest number of plays in juke boxes throut the country, as determined by The Billboard's weekly survey of operators using a high proportion of country and western records. When significant action is reported on both sides of a record, points are combined to determine position on the chart.

This Week		Last Week	Weeks on Chart
1.	WHITE SPORT COAT (BMI)—Marty Robbins Grown-Up Tears (BMI)—Col 40864	1	10
2.	FOUR WALLS (BMI)—Jim Reeves I Know and You Know (BMI)—RCA Victor 20-6874	4	7
3.	GONNA FIND ME A BLUEBIRD (BMI)—Marvin Rainwater So You Think You've Got Troubles (BMI)—M-G-M 12412	5	11
4.	GONE (BMI)—Ferlin Husky Missing Persons (BMI)—Cap 3628	2	16
5.	ALL SHOOK UP (BMI)—Elvis Presley That's When Your Heartaches Begin (ASCAP)—Vic 20-6870	3	10
6.	BYE BYE LOVE (BMI)—Everly Brothers I Wonder If I Care as Much (BMI)—Cadence 1315	—	2
7.	FALLEN STAR (BMI)—Jimmy Newman I Can't Go On This Way (BMI)—Dot 1289	8	2
8.	HONKY TONK SONG (BMI)—Webb Pierce Some Day (BMI)—Dec 30255	6	11
9.	FRAULEIN (BMI)—Bobby Helms Heartsick Feeling (BMI)—Dec 30194	7	5
10.	TOO MUCH WATER (BMI)—George Jones I've Got to Go Cry (BMI)—Mercury 71096	9	3

• Most Played C&W by Jockeys

For survey week ending June 12

SIDES are ranked in order of the greatest number of plays on disk jockey radio shows throut the country according to The Billboard's weekly survey of top disk jockey shows in all key markets.

This Week		Last Week	Weeks on Chart
1.	FOUR WALLS—Jimmy Reeves Vic 20-6174—BMI	1	8
2.	WHITE SPORT COAT—Marty Robbins Col 40864—BMI	2	10
3.	GONE—Ferlin Husky Cap 3628—BMI	3	17
4.	BYE BYE LOVE—Everly Brothers Cadence 1315—BMI	7	6
5.	FALLEN STAR—Jimmy Newman Dot 1289—BMI	9	5
6.	GONNA FIND ME A BLUEBIRD—Marvin Rainwater M-G-M 12412—BMI	4	11
7.	HONKY TONK SONG—Webb Pierce Dec 30255—BMI	6	13
7.	FRAULEIN—Bobby Helms Dec 30194—BMI	8	10
9.	ALL SHOOK UP—Elvis Presley Vic 20-6870—BMI	5	11
9.	BYE BYE LOVE—Webb Pierce Dec 30321—BMI	—	3
11.	NEXT IN LINE—Johnny Cash Sun 266—BMI	10	4
12.	GONNA FIND ME A BLUEBIRD—Eddy Arnold Vic 20-6905—BMI	12	3
13.	FIRST DATE, FIRST KISS, FIRST LOVE—Sonny James Cap 3674—BMI	12	9
14.	I'LL BE THERE—Ray Price Col 40889—BMI	14	2
14.	THREE WAYS—Kitty Wells Dec 30288—BMI	—	2

MARCH 31, 1958 The Billboard's Mu...

• C&W Best Sellers in Stores

FOR SURVEY WEEK ENDING MARCH 22

RECORDS are ranked in order of their current national selling importance at the retail level, as determined by The Billboard's weekly survey of dealers throut the nation with a high volume of sales in country and western records. When significant action is reported on both sides of a record, points are combined to determine position on the chart. In such a case, both sides are listed in bold type, the leading side on top.

This Week		Last Week	Weeks on Chart
1.	BALLAD OF A TEENAGE QUEEN (BMI)—Johnny Cash BIG RIVER (BMI)—Sun 283	1	10
2.	OH, LONESOME ME (BMI)—Don Gibson I CAN'T STOP LOVING YOU (BMI)—Vic 7133	3	6
3.	DON'T (BMI)—Elvis Presley I BEG OF YOU (BMI)—Vic 7150	2	9
4.	BREATHLESS (BMI)—Jerry Lee Lewis Down the Line (BMI)—Sun 288	4	3
5.	OH-OH, I'M FALLING IN LOVE AGAIN (ASCAP)—Jimmie Rodgers The Long Hot Summer (ASCAP)—Roulette 4045	7	5
6.	THIS LITTLE GIRL OF MINE (BMI)—Everly Brothers SHOULD WE TELL HIM (BMI)—Cadence 1342	6	8
7.	THE STORY OF MY LIFE (ASCAP)—Marty Robbins Once-a-Week Date (BMI)—Col 41013	5	19
8.	GEISHA GIRL (BMI)—Hank Locklin Livin Alone (BMI)—Vic 6984	8	32
9.	GREAT BALLS OF FIRE (BMI)—Jerry Lee Lewis You Win Again (BMI)—Sun 281	9	18
10.	JUST A LITTLE LONESOME (BMI)—Bobby Helms Love My Lady (BMI)—Dec 30557	12	4
11.	STOP THE WORLD (BMI)—Johnnie and Jack Camel Walk Stroll (BMI)—Vic 7137	15	4
12.	YOUR NAME IS BEAUTIFUL (ASCAP)—Carl Smith You're So Easy to Love (BMI)—Col 41092	14	3
13.	I CAN'T STOP LOVING YOU (BMI)—Kitty Wells SHE'S NO ANGEL (BMI)—Dec 30551	18	3
14.	STOOD UP (BMI)—Ricky Nelson Waitin' in School (BMI)—Imperial 5483	13	11
15.	ANNA MARIE (BMI)—Jim Reeves Everywhere You Go (BMI)—Vic 7070	11	9
16.	MY SPECIAL ANGEL (BMI)—Bobby Helms Standing at the End of My World (BMI)—Dec 30423	10	25
17.	IS IT WRONG? (BMI)—Warner Mack Baby Squeeze Me (BMI)—Dec 30301	19	33
18.	WHISPERING RAIN (BMI)—Hank Snow I Wish I Was the Moon (BMI)—Vic 7154	—	1
19.	PINK PEDDLE PUSHERS (BMI)—Carl Perkins Jive After Five (BMI)—Col 41131	—	1
20.	MY SHOES KEEP WALKING BACK TO YOU—Ray Price Don't Do This to Me (BMI)—Col 40951	16	34
20.	KISSES SWEETER THAN WINE (BMI)—Jimmie Rodgers Better Loved You'll Never Be (ASCAP)—Roulette 4031	20	16

• Most Played C&W by Jockeys

FOR SURVEY WEEK ENDING MARCH 22

SIDES are ranked in order of the greatest number of plays on disk jockey radio shows throut the country according to The Billboard's weekly survey of top disk jockey shows in all key markets.

This Week		Last Week	Weeks on Chart
1.	BALLAD OF A TEENAGE QUEEN—Johnny Cash Sun 283—BMI	1	11
2.	OH LONESOME ME—Don Gibson Vic 7133—BMI	2	7
3.	CURTAIN IN THE WINDOW—Ray Price Col 41105—BMI	12	5
4.	I CAN'T STOP LOVING YOU—Kitty Wells Dec 30551—BMI	6	5
5.	ANNA MARIE—Jim Reeves Vic 7070—BMI	8	17
6.	BIG RIVER—Johnny Cash Sun 283—BMI	4	8
7.	THIS LITTLE GIRL OF MINE—Everly Brothers Cadence 1342—BMI	5	7
8.	DON'T—Elvis Presley Vic 7150—BMI	3	6
9.	YOUR NAME IS BEAUTIFUL—Carl Smith Col 41092—ASCAP	15	5
10.	SEND ME THE PILLOW YOU DREAM ON—Hank Locklin Vic 7124—BMI	—	1
11.	ONCE MORE—Roy Acuff Hickory 1073—BMI	—	1
12.	I CAN'T STOP LOVING YOU—Don Gibson Vic 7133—BMI	11	3
13.	I BEG OF YOU—Elvis Presley Vic 7150	15	8
14.	STOP THE WORLD—Johnnie and Jack Vic 7137—BMI	—	1
15.	GEISHA GIRL—Hank Locklin Vic 6984—BMI	—	28

The Everly Brothers, Don (right) and Phil, ca. 1957. Originally considered a country act, the Everlys recorded in Nashville with a studio team that included Chet Atkins, had their compositions cut by Kitty Wells and Justin Tubb, and even joined the Opry cast (June 1, 1957). They exceeded all expectations for a country harmony duo when "Bye, Bye Love" hit #2 and "Wake Up, Little Susie" went to #1 on the pop charts in 1957.

but he could console himself with the thought that the "Hayride" had welcomed Hank Williams when Nashville found his rowdy ways unpalatable. A year after his first "Hayride" broadcast, Elvis's new manager, the former carnival huckster Colonel Tom Parker, was negotiating a deal for RCA to buy out Presley's Sun contract. The days of playing honky-tonks and country fairs and opening package shows were over for good.

Can Elvis Presley, or even Sam Phillips, have possibly anticipated the impact they were about to have? Did they intuit, or even idly imagine, that they were about to turn the whole world upside down? Phillips knew exactly what he was doing; he anticipated that through Elvis the rhythmic, blues-rooted music he loved might penetrate the mainstream. But Phillips was betting on a game plan, albeit a brilliant one. If he had understood how singular the impact of Elvis himself was going to be, Phillips would surely have held on to his artist, at least for a while longer. He freely admits that he had high hopes of two of his other artists, Carl Perkins and Johnny Cash, duplicating Elvis's success, bringing the Phillips game plan to fruition. And that expectation suggests that even Sam Phillips misjudged what a unique musical and cultural watershed the coming of the Hillbilly Cat represented. Because Elvis wasn't just a musical flashpoint. Per-

306

kins had effected a similar black-white fusion, but lacked Elvis's James Dean dimension, his Rebel image. Elvis was a hipster for the millions, the fulfillment of every white teenager's fantasy about what it would be like to be black. Perkins was a hillbilly, a rocker, but no Cat. And Johnny Cash was no rebel, although later, in another city, at another time, he would become father figure to a generation of country music rebels. In the fifties, Cash found the very idea of playing the rockabilly star fundamentally inauthentic.

But what did Elvis know, and when did he know it? That's the question, and it's made all the more tantalizing by the impossibility of ever really finding out. There are hints, however, intimations that this walking contradiction—the painfully shy flamboyant dresser, the rebel who yes ma'amed and no ma'amed —did more than passively acquiesce to his date with destiny. One clue can be found on an early live club recording of the trio, just Elvis, Scotty, and Bill playing in Houston. The way the tyro

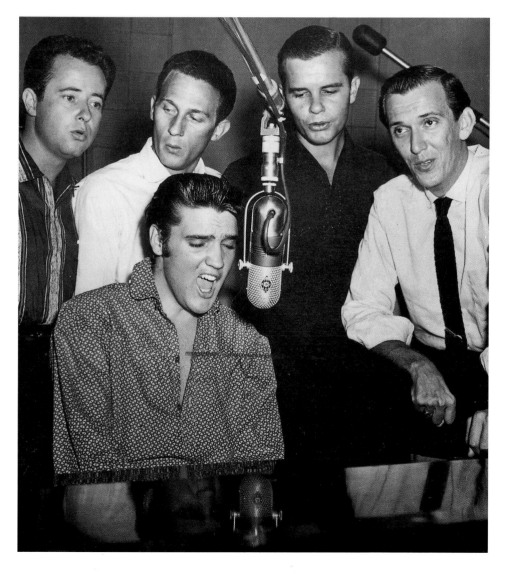

Elvis Presley with the Jordanaires, ca. 1956. Then the Opry's top gospel quartet, the Jordanaires first joined Elvis in the studio for July 1956 sessions in New York and subsequently appeared on many of his biggest hits. From left, they are Gordon Stoker, Hoyt Hawkins, Neal Matthews, and Hugh Jarrett.

performer handles what must have been a tough, skeptical crowd is astonishing. He's modest, even self-deprecating, and yet he's provocative, maybe a little dangerous. You can hear him walking a very thin line, giving nobody anything tangible to take offense at, but at the same time talking right over the heads of the stolid working men and women, right at the young and the nubile: *The men don't know*, he seems to be saying, *but the little girls understand.*

And then, right in the middle of his impossibly jive yet deeply soulful near-desecration of "Blue Moon of Kentucky," he makes a slip, if it is a slip. "Blue-hoo moo-oon of Kintucky just keep on *shakin'*," he sings, and then, stuttering, corrects himself with the perfect timing of a master entertainer, "uh, *shinin'*, *shinin'* . . . " And in that moment, it all falls into place. Because shakin' that jacked-up bluegrass nugget, shakin' it so hard the whole world can feel it, is exactly what this Hillbilly Cat is up to. And whether he's making one of the classic Freudian slips, or pretending to, or, as one is tempted to conclude, doing both at once, no one who hears him do it can doubt that on some deeper level, he *knows*. He knows, among other things, that being a walking contradiction is exactly what it's all about, that however, why ever, he's grabbed the brass ring and is going to get to have his cake and eat it too.

Once that indelible moment comes clear, the rest of the story becomes, if not foreordained, at least comprehensible. The dichotomies between Elvis the rebel rocker and Elvis the model soldier, Elvis the sexually flamboyant and Elvis the meek and shy, Elvis before and after the Army, and later between Elvis the crusading fantasy nark and Elvis the King of the Memphis Pillheads—because he's Elvis—aren't really contradictory at all. When he set that blue moon shakin', Elvis was making a slip of the tongue *and* staking out his turf. He knew. He *knew*.

But he also forgot something Sam Phillips told him, back in the beginning: Simplify. A snippet of studio conversation from a Presley session, preserved in the Sun vaults, finds Sam telling Scotty Moore, definitively, "Don't make it too damn complicated." Phillips probably didn't have to say it to Johnny Cash's guitarist, Luther Perkins, who never played anything that hadn't already been reduced to basic essences. If Scotty Moore's work on the Presley sessions served as a model for rockabilly and rock 'n' roll guitarists to come, Luther Perkins's monolithic economy, that clean, sharp definition and hint of country twang, are the template for later generations of Memphis guitarists, for the soul men, for Steve Cropper, Chips Moman. Simplify, simplify. Play it *country* simple.

Colonel Tom Parker, 1950s. Eddy Arnold's ex-manager (1944–53) was just another hustling country promoter when he took over management of Elvis Presley on August 15, 1955. Swiftly and surely, he guided Elvis from tiny Sun Records to RCA and the big time. Parker's reward: a 1967 agreement giving him 50 percent of Elvis's net income.

But Sam Phillips wasn't so enamored of his own intellect that he allowed cherished principles to cloud sound commercial judgment. When it became apparent that Johnny Cash's Sun releases were striking a responsive chord in the down-home country audience but failing to cross over to the teenage audience the way Presley had, Sam turned his tall, dark, saturnine stranger over to Jack Clement.

Between 1956 and 1958, Jack Clement played a role at Sun that Colin Escott and Martin Hawkins, the company's tireless chroniclers, accurately describe as "songwriter, studio engineer, and musical catalyst." As Sun grew into a real business, Phillips turned more and more of the kind of all-day, all-night studio work he'd put in on Presley and the early Cash over to Clement. And although Jack Clement, a Memphis native, was a devotee of Roy Acuff and Merle Travis and the Louvin Brothers, a country music man to the core, and a gifted string-band musician, he was also an experimenter, and a man with a pop sensibility. He

Johnny Cash sends a jolt of energy into the legs of Roy Acuff, onstage at the Grand Ole Opry, 1963. Lending rhythmic support are the Tennessee Two: Luther Perkins on guitar and Marshall Grant on bass. Initially, Cash's success at Sun Records in Memphis made him suspect in the eyes of some of Nashville's old guard, even though Cash was one of Sun's more modest rockers.

Overleaf
On that fateful Memphis night in July 1954, when Elvis was making his first record, who could have foreseen that twenty years later he would be dazzling crowds in Las Vegas with black-belt karate chops?

309

Johnny Cash, seven o'clock rock, late fifties. Cash came to Sun Records intending to sing gospel, but Sam Phillips was looking for something more commercial. When Cash wrote the required country material, Phillips wisely insisted that Cash stick with the stark, rhythmic sound of his three-piece band. It wasn't quite rock 'n' roll, but it sold like it.

Wanda Jackson & Her Party Timers, early 1960s. Given the green light to rock after a 1955–56 tour with Elvis, Hank Thompson's demure protégée injected numbers like "Fujiyama Mama" (1958) and "Let's Have a Party" (1960) with a primal ferocity to rival Elvis and Jerry Lee.

Conway Twitty, early 1960s. In 1956, when he was still known as Harold Jenkins, he recorded eight sides for Sun Records, but none was ever issued. Two years later, he wrote and recorded a genuine pop smash, "It's Only Make Believe"; at the time his style was so influenced by Elvis that many assumed the record was really Presley's. After a series of dispiriting releases in the early sixties, Conway went country in 1966 and found his niche.

Bob Luman and his Hickory Records producer Wesley Rose, 1960. Like Elvis, Luman played the "Louisiana Hayride," made a rock movie (Carnival), and played Las Vegas. Like Elvis, he was called up for military service shortly after hitting the Top Ten on both the country and pop charts—with Boudleaux Bryant's "Let's Think About Livin'," in 1960. Unlike Elvis, Luman never recovered his rock audience; he joined the Opry in 1965.

tried different guitar sounds, brought in backup singers. Sam Phillips, more truly a maverick than Elvis, heard Johnny Cash's voice sounding stark and alone, with just Marshall Grant's heart-throb bass and Luther Perkins's tolling-bell guitar for company. Jack Clement cast Cash as the rough-hewn, plainspoken romantic lead in a series of rock 'n' roll soap operas, epitomized by "Ballad of a Teenage Queen." The record, and its follow-ups, made Cash one of the era's more unlikely pop stars. Apparently, Cash himself hated them. Reportedly, one of the deciding factors in Cash's 1958 move from Sun to Columbia was the major label's assurances that he could at last record some of the gospel songs so dear to his heart, and that for his secular recordings, he would be allowed to return to his original, sparse sound—the sound Sam Phillips had had to talk him into sticking with and developing to begin with.

The Sun story is chockablock with similar ironies. Intuitive brillance and ambivalent second-guessing, grand vision and parochialism, crowing pride and gnawing self-doubt are inextricably linked. Sam Phillips changed the face of country music almost beyond recognition and was at least as responsible as any other individual for turning American popular music inside-out, and Western culture upside-down. Did he really invent rock 'n' roll, as many would argue, or did he *imagine* it so vividly and magnificently that reality simply had to appropriate his fantasies, ratify his cherished game plan? Phillips himself once said, "My real contribution was showing poor, deprived, downtrodden people that they were as good as anybody; it was enabling them to be free in their expression."

Kitty Wells, husband Johnnie Wright, their son Bobby, and daughter Sue visit Elvis on the set of G.I. Blues, 1960. Some suspect that it was hardly an accident that Elvis was drafted into the army shortly after becoming a teenage idol: Elvis represented teenage unrest and needed to be kept in his place. As it happened, Elvis was a reluctant rebel who dutifully served his full tour from 1958 to 1960.

Carl Perkins tells a story about his days at Sun that makes Phillips's assertion sound less like becoming modesty, and more like the simple truth. "You just forgot about making a record and tried to *show him*," Perkins recalls. "I'd walk out on a limb, I'd try things I knew I couldn't do, and then have to work my way out of it. I'd say, 'Mr. Phillips, that's terrible.' He said, 'That's original.' I said, 'But it's just a big original mistake.' And he said, 'That's what Sun Records is. That's what we are.' " Jerry Lee Lewis, typically, has his own way of looking at it: "Sam's crazy, just like me. It took the two of us to screw up the whole world. We done it."

Sam Phillips and his discoveries dazzled the world, if they didn't screw it up. They brought cotton-patch blues to the rednecks, and country soul to the teenagers. They showed the music establishments, from Nashville and the Opry to New York's Brill Building, that country can be pop, blues can be pop, blues can be country—hey, it's all that American vernacular, the way we walk, the way we talk, the way we move when we get rhythm. The country music audience wasn't fooled for a minute. They bought Elvis's records right along with their Webb Pierce and Bobby Bare, and they bought Minimal Cash, Teen Idol Cash, Cash the Country Outlaw, and finally Cash the Nashville Patriarch. They knew that whatever else it was, wherever else it reached, Sun music was country music all along.

10

HONKY-TONK ANGELS: KITTY WELLS AND PATSY CLINE

Robert K. Oermann

They were more than just two great country stars; they were archetypes for their generation. Kitty Wells and Patsy Cline were country music's first major female figures, and they ruled the hillbilly hit parade during the 1950s and 1960s in a way that no other women had before them.

But they were something else. Each in her own way represented women's changing roles in postwar America. And by extension they represented the entire nation's psychic leap into the modern age. Their lives, personalities, and musical styles can be taken as far more than some simple "angel/devil," "good girl/bad girl" pop music dichotomy. For although these two country music legends do, indeed, seem like the alpha and omega of what it meant to be a woman in show business back then, they are both more complicated than that.

On the one hand there is Wells, the wife and mother who faced modern problems in her songs with tight-lipped intensity. On the other is Cline, the beer-drinking, good-time gal who bared her soul with open-throated fervor. Wells wore gingham, Cline wore lamé. Wells modernized traditional country music and women's place in the country music world. Cline broke with country's musical and cultural traditions, and created new ones.

They were worlds apart musically and socially. But they shared one thing: both spoke eloquently to their generation. America emerged from World War II a profoundly changed society. Country boys had gone to war and had seen the world.

Patsy Cline, 1960s. Now remembered as a pioneer of the elegant Nashville Sound, Patsy was at first reluctant to record pop-country material like "Walking after Midnight," which had been written for pop singer Kay Starr. "It's nothin' but a little old pop song," she declared. "It's awful. I can't stand it."

Kitty Wells, from her days at Shreveport's KWKH, ca. 1950. Within two years, the demure wife and mother would become forever identified with a song of drinking and infidelity—"It Wasn't God Who Made Honky-Tonk Angels."

Country girls had left their homes to work in wartime factories. For the first time, masses of women had tasted social and economic independence. American culture has never been the same since. After the war, romantic relationships became unstable; the rituals of courtship lost their hearts-and-flowers idealism. Likewise, the family dwindled in importance, as the Atomic Age ushered in social forces that made Mom and Pop seem practically obsolete. And the divorce rate soared. America became a mobile society—rootless and restless. Drinking, dancing, sex, and high living no longer seemed so sinful. Women who'd done men's work for years didn't think the neighborhood bar was a den of iniquity anymore.

As people attempted to settle back into "normalcy" in the 1950s, both sexes experienced postwar depression. Men were

316

Curly Fox & Texas Ruby, late 1930s. A deep-voiced belter from the heart of Texas, Ruby Owens first played the Opry (ca. 1934) with cowboy singer Zeke Clements. Later, she teamed up with fiddler Curly Fox, whom she married in 1939. At the height of their popularity in the early forties, they headed one of the Opry's touring tent shows. Ruby died in a 1963 trailer fire as Curly was returning home after playing the Opry.

Bonnie Lou Carson, 1940s. Mary Joan Katt was known as Bonnie Lou to fans of WLW's "Midwestern Hayride." Her biggest hits came in 1953 with "Seven Lonely Days" and "Tennessee Wig Walk," but she starred on the Cincinnati-based radio and TV show for years after that.

emotionally scarred by battle. Women found it difficult to go back to being housewives. War propaganda had stimulated women's aspirations, but once the fighting stopped they were expected to become stay-at-homes in newly created, isolating suburbs.

As always, country singers and songwriters were there to chronicle the frustrations, problems, and insecurities. Country music emerged from World War II as profoundly changed as the lives of its listeners. In the prewar era, family groups and string bands sang of mothers, sweethearts, religion, home, Victorian sentiment, and various tragedies. The sound was soft and rural. In the postwar era, honky-tonk bands addressed such previously taboo topics as infidelity ("cheatin' "), alcohol, and divorce. The sound was histrionic.

Initially, men defined this honky-tonk sound. Ernest Tubb, Al Dexter, Floyd Tillman, and Ted Daffan represent the first of the honky-tonkers who began playing this style of music in the 1930s. Hank Williams and Lefty Frizzell represent the second generation, which brought the style to maturity following the war.

Into this world of smoke-filled taverns, thudding jukeboxes, tear-in-your-beer miseries, and shady romances stepped a gospel-singing woman of the old school, Kitty Wells. She was a thirty-three-year-old mother of three when "It Wasn't God Who

317

Made Honky-Tonk Angels" made her country music's voice of postwar women in 1952.

Indeed, it can be argued that it made her the all-time voice of country music women. To be sure, female stars had preceded her. The Carter Family's Sara and Maybelle, the National Barn Dance's Lulu Belle, the singing cowgirl Patsy Montana, Hollywood's Judy Canova, and numerous vocalists in family gospel music acts were among those who'd become famous in country music prior to Wells's rise to popularity. But none enjoyed the consistency of hits, the concert box-office power, or the unquestioned leadership of Kitty Wells.

When she adopted the honky-tonk style to articulate the woman's point of view, she led country music women into the modern world and gave voice in song to millions of working-class women. Yet Wells was as much a part of the dying, Victorian-influenced old-country culture as she was a pioneer of the emerging postwar style. Publicly she sang of guilt and remorse, of loneliness and illicit romance, of honky-tonks and sin. Privately, she was the ideal shy, soft-spoken wife and mother. She acted out modern women's dramas, but lived her own life according to the old ideals.

It has been said that Kitty Wells was an unlikely choice as the postwar female country standard-bearer. In fact, her deep roots

Jenny Lou Carson, ca. 1946. Lucille Overstake's career began at WLS, Chicago, where she sang with sisters Eva and Evelyn in the Three Little Maids. During the forties, she became a solo act, with a new name and a new western look.

Ann Jones & Her Western Sweethearts, ca. 1950. Popular on the West Coast, Ann (on guitar) was known as "the Kate Smith of the Western Field" as much for her womanly proportions as her voice. She placed at least one record on the Billboard *radio charts— "Give Me a Hundred Reasons," in 1949.*

Opposite
Molly O'Day and Lynn Davis, 1940s. Columbia producer Art Satherley said Molly (born LaVerne Williamson) was the best female country singer he ever heard. The big-voiced girl from Kentucky was also the first artist to record a Hank Williams composition, "When God Comes and Gathers His Jewels," in December 1946.

318

Above

Tex Ann Nation was a pioneer of a different sort. Together, she and husband Buck opened one of America's first country music concert parks in 1934— in Maine! After she and Buck parted ways, she moved to the West Coast, where she performed with Merle Travis, Ray Whitley, and other country stars.

Laura Lee Owens joined Bob Wills's Texas Playboys in 1944, becoming the first female singer to work in a major western swing band. This photo was made when she was starring at KMBC, Kansas City, where her father, western singer Tex Owens, also performed.

WOMEN'S WORK

Although Kitty Wells and Patsy Cline certainly broke new ground for women in country music, they followed in the footsteps of women who had faced even greater obstacles in gaining acceptance as performers.

Southern culture has never been entirely comfortable with the idea of women as professional singers and musicians. In the days before commercial country music, women played an important role in handing down the Anglo-American ballad and singing tradition, but their "performing" was mostly done at home, for family and friends. Instrumental music was largely the man's domain, and public performance of any sort—vocal or instrumental—was almost certainly left to the menfolk. The morals of any woman who dared to pick up an instrument and climb on a stage were considered questionable at best. Even after it became fairly common for women to be included in professional bands, female performers felt it necessary at least to give the appearance that they were married to, or related to, one of the men in the band. A determined, talented group of women eventually broke down the barriers, paving the way for the female stars of today.

Among the very first old-time string-band musicians to record were two women, Samantha Bumgarner and Eva Davis, of North Carolina, who waxed fiddle and banjo duets for Columbia in 1924. The 1920s also saw a few other women emerge as solo performers, including Roba Stanley and cowgirl singer Billie Maxwell. The more

The DeZurik Sisters were star yodelers of the WLS "National Barn Dance" in the late thirties. Later, during their tenure at the Opry in the forties, Carolyn and Mary Jane DeZurik earned the nickname the Cackle Sisters for their melodious chicken imitations rendered during spots sponsored by the Purina company.

common female role, however, was as accompanist or background singer in family bands. Rosa Lee "Moonshine Kate" Carson played guitar for her father, Fiddlin' John Carson. Hattie Stoneman of the Stoneman Family, Alcyone Bate of Dr. Humphrey Bate's Possum Hunters, Irene and Mary Lee Eskew of the Blind Andy Jenkins Family, and Eva Thompson Jones, who played piano for Uncle Jimmy Thompson, were a few of the others who took on supporting roles behind their menfolk.

The first women to break out of this mold—although they had never intended to do so—were Sara and Maybelle Carter, who began recording in 1927. Even though Sara's husband, A. P., was always present and collected most of their song material, Sara and Maybelle did almost all the singing and picking, and became well known in their own right. During the more liberated 1930s, a number of women began to emerge as stars, including Lulu Belle Wiseman, Cousin Emmy, the DeZurik Sisters, the Girls of the Golden West (Dolly and Millie Good), and Patsy Montana. Montana's 1935 recording of "I Wanna Be a Cowboy's Sweetheart" was the first legitimate hit by a country female artist, and in her day she was a national star. Also, the first all-woman string band since Bumgarner and Davis, the Coon Creek Girls, came to prominence in 1937 and became favorites on Kentucky's "Renfro Valley Barn Dance."

The late 1930s and the 1940s saw the emergence of such performers as Louise Massey, Texas Ruby, and Wilma Lee Cooper, as well as the gospel-influenced Molly O'Day, Martha Carson, and Rose Maddox. The precedents set by these women and others made possible the later breakthroughs of Kitty Wells and Patsy Cline, as well as the numerous female performers who have followed them.

Named and organized in 1937 by John Lair, the Coon Creek Girls became national favorites during their two decades at Lair's "Renfro Valley Barn Dance." In 1939, at Eleanor Roosevelt's invitation, they performed their old-time music for the king and queen of England. Pictured are guitarist Rosie Ledford, mandolinist Esther "Violet" Koehler, fiddler Lily May Ledford, and bassist Evelyn "Daisy" Lange.

321

Johnnie Wright & the Harmony Girls, ca. 1936. At seventeen, Kitty Wells (right) began entertaining professionally on Nashville's WSIX with her sisters Jewel and Mae. By the time of this photo, she had joined her future husband Johnnie Wright and his sister Louise (the other Harmony Girl) on the same station. Louise married Jack Anglin, Johnnie's future singing partner.

Kitty Wells, 1943. Encouraged by husband Johnnie Wright, she took her stage name from a folk song and wore outfits that matched her old-timey sound. As it turned out, the real trick was getting the right song.

in older traditions made her the perfect embodiment of the difficulties of adjusting to America's new morality. Her piercing nasality, pent-up intensity, and tearful restraint, so effective in conveying the themes of social dislocation, came largely from a gospel music background. Wells was at once immensely emotional and incredibly reserved as a performer. It is this tension that made her so moving as a stylist. Perhaps not coincidentally, the Grand Ole Opry at first rejected her because she was not exuberant enough, then forbade her to sing "It Wasn't God Who Made Honky-Tonk Angels" on the show because it was too outspoken.

Her demeanor was always prim. She dressed in the prewar "sunbonnet sweetheart" style while singing her honky-tonk laments. She was the spokeswoman for the new independence,

322

Rose Maddox, who began singing professionally with her brothers at age twelve, kept right on after the Maddox Brothers & Rose broke up. During the early sixties, she recorded several Top Twenty hits for Capitol, including the double-sided hit with Buck Owens, "Loose Talk"/"Mental Cruelty" (1961).

Whistle stop: in 1943, Kitty Wells was performing on Knoxville's "Mid-Day Merry-Go-Round" with husband Johnnie Wright (on bass), fiddler Chester Atkins (of guitar fame), Kitty Wells, emcee Smilin' Eddie Hill, and the Johnson Brothers.

yet she spent her whole career being chaperoned by her husband.

Kitty Wells was born Muriel Ellen Deason in Nashville on August 30, 1919. She learned to sing and play guitar from her railroadman father and began as a youngster performing gospel music in church. At age seventeen she began entertaining professionally on WSIX radio in Nashville as one of the Deason Sisters with her sisters Jewel and Mae.

Muriel's husband-to-be, musician, mechanic, and cabinet maker Johnnie Wright, moved to Nashville from nearby Mt. Juliet, Tennessee, in 1933. He went to work in a cabinet-making shop while his singing partner Jack Anglin worked in a hosiery mill. Wright married Muriel in 1937, when she was just eighteen and he was twenty-three.

The family that plays together: Johnnie Wright, wife Kitty Wells, and Wright's brother-in-law Jack Anglin, ca. 1950. RCA signed gal singer Kitty to a record contract primarily because she was part of Johnnie & Jack's act. Within two years, however, her Decca records consistently outsold Johnnie & Jack's RCA releases.

Johnnie initially teamed his new bride with his sister Louise, and the trio performed as Johnnie Wright & the Harmony Girls. When she wasn't singing on the radio, Muriel worked at the Washington Manufacturing Company ironing shirts for nine dollars a week.

From 1937 to 1940 Johnnie & Jack honed their duet sound in their spare time. They decided finally to make music their full-time occupation and set out to seek their fortune on a series of radio barn dance jobs in various southern towns. Muriel dutifully followed along from station to station, filling the role of the "girl singer" who sang the religious numbers during the shows. Johnnie dubbed her "Kitty Wells" in 1943, taking the name from the old Opry song sung by the Pickard Family, "I Could Marry Kitty Wells." Kitty performed in the male duo's shadow, smiling all the while and occasionally adding a third harmony part to their songs.

324

Jean Shepard, in Capitol's Hollywood studio, 1950s. Signed to Capitol right out of high school, this former bass player in an all-girl band scored her first hit singing over a recitation by Ferlin Husky. When "A Dear John Letter" became a #1 smash in 1953, she was not yet twenty-one. She was married to fellow Opry star Hawkshaw Hawkins at the time of his death in 1963.

The war temporarily stalled the group's progress: Jack enlisted, and gasoline rationing forced Johnnie and Kitty to curtail their wanderings from radio show to radio show. For a time, Johnnie went to work at a DuPont plant north of Nashville. When the war ended, the act hit the road with renewed vigor. Johnnie & Jack signed on for a brief stint at the Grand Ole Opry during 1946 and 1947, while Kitty stayed home to raise her newborn son, Bobby.

By the time Johnnie & Jack took up residence at Shreveport's "Louisiana Hayride"—a radio barn dance that at the time served as the de facto "farm team" for the Grand Ole Opry—Kitty was part of the act again. So, when RCA Victor signed Johnnie & Jack to a recording contract in 1949, the company signed Kitty, too. She made her disc debut by recording eight numbers for the label in 1949, all gospel and sentimental old-time tunes. Nevertheless, Johnnie & Jack remained the focus of the family's efforts. It was they who had hits early on, with songs like "Cryin' Heart Blues" and "Poison Love," both of which made *Billboard*'s Top Ten in 1951. In contrast, Kitty's records sold indifferently.

In January 1952, when the troupe finally got an invitation to rejoin the Opry on the strength of Johnnie & Jack's hit records, Wells thought her time to settle down and quietly raise her children had come at last. Johnnie, however, encouraged her to record again. Although she agreed, she didn't think anything of this second chance at record making, for in those days labels promoted only a few female acts, and records by women gen-

ANSWER SONGS: A PRIMER

"One good turn deserves another," the old saying goes. A curious aspect of country music history is described in the paraphrase "One good song deserves another." If a song could capture the public's fancy once, why not try it again, often with the same artist, usually with the same tune, continuing the same story line? This phenomenon of "answer songs"—a later song answering, or responding to, an earlier hit—for years was a hallmark of country music, lending partial credence to the oft-repeated charge of critics, "It all sounds alike." Answer songs abounded in part because of country music's predilection for telling a story; like so many of today's movies, the songs themselves often begged for sequels. In the main, though, the reason for so many answer songs was purely commercial—cash in on the first hit with a similar song and reach the same large market.

Among the earliest examples of the answer song in country music were the sequels by Carson Robison to his own "Barnacle Bill." Bob Miller, Gene Autry, Jimmie Davis, the Mainers, the Monroe Brothers, Karl & Harty, and the Callahan Brothers were the primary exponents of answer songs in the 1930s, a period during which they were very common. Some of country music's biggest hits of the 1940s were also answered on record, usually by the artist who had the first hit. Thus, Ernest Tubb could write the "Answer to Walking the Floor Over You," Red Foley would cut "Smoke on the Water No. 2," and Floyd Tillman, after "Slipping Around," could promise "I'll Never Slip Around Again." The most frequently answered song appeared in the early 1950s, one most fans today have probably never heard: Arkie Shibley's "Hot Rod Race." Within a couple of years, Shibley and various cover artists produced no fewer than four sequels.

When the biggest answer song of all appeared in 1952, Kitty Wells's "It Wasn't God Who Made Honky Tonk Angels" (a bigger hit than the song it answered, Hank Thompson's "The Wild Side of Life"), a whole new chapter in answer song history began. For the next few years, it became popular, almost common, for female singers to answer male artists' hits with the female perspective on the situation. Kitty used the formula repeatedly ("I'm Paying For That Back Street Affair," "My Cold Heart Is Melted Now"), and several female singers broke into the recording industry in this way. Goldie Hill, for example, answered two of Ray Price's hits—"Talk to Your Heart" with "Why Talk to My Heart?" and "Don't Let the Stars Get in My Eyes" with "I Let the Stars Get in My Eyes." When Hank Williams recorded "Jambalaya," Goldie assumed the persona of the Cajun sweetheart in her answer, "I'm Yvonne." June Carter's solo career included "You Flopped When You Got Me Alone," a response to husband Carl Smith's "Just Wait Till I Get You Alone." In the 1960s, the two most successful answer songs were of this type. Jeannie Black for Capitol Records answered Jim Reeves's crossover hit "He'll Have to Go" with her own fairly popular "He'll Have to Stay." And Jody Miller's "Queen of the House" was the domestic answer to rambling Roger Miller's (no relation) "King of the Road."

The heyday of the answer song now appears to be long past. Except for the Homer & Jethro-styled parodies of Pinkard & Bowden or the Geezinslaw Brothers, nothing remains of it today. Although answer songs were at one time all the rage, very few of them were great commercial successes. And thanks to the breakthroughs of Kitty Wells and Patsy Cline, women singers are now so firmly established that they don't need answer songs for material. It's also likely that answer songs are vanishing because the growing complexity of publishing arrangements has made answering a song—and thus cutting in all the publishers, sometimes four or five of them—more trouble than it's worth. Of course, it is also true that answer songs have been replaced by other, less forthright forms of imitation.

Martha Carson, 1950s. When Martha and James Carson, Barn Dance Sweethearts of Atlanta's WSB, divorced in 1951, Martha took her robust voice and country gospel tunes to the Opry the following year. After a promising start with her self-penned "Satisfied," Martha slipped disastrously in popularity in the mid fifties when she flirted with the sort of country pop that later worked so well for Patsy Cline.

erally went unheard on radio. But Kitty's first Decca session, held in Nashville in May 1952, produced a hit that made her a star and launched a whole new phase of her career. The hit was an answer song to Hank Thompson's smash, "The Wild Side of Life," which bemoaned a man's mistreatment at the hands of a faithless woman. In "It Wasn't God Who Made Honky-Tonk Angels," Kitty's answer (written by a man, J. D. Miller) turned the tables and defended the ladies Thompson's record had disparaged. The immense popularity of "Honky-Tonk Angels" transformed the teetotaling, nonsmoking, church-going Wells into a honky-tonk heroine: by July the record made *Billboard*'s Top Ten; eventually it went to #1, and it stayed on the charts for an impressive sixteen weeks. (The irony of Kitty's breakthrough as a honky-tonk singer actually has several layers, for the melody of both Thompson's hit and her ground-breaking answer song is as old as country music itself. It was initially popularized by the Carter Family in "I'm Thinking Tonight of My Blue Eyes" [1929] and later provided the tune for "The Great Speckled Bird," a 1936 hit for Roy Acuff. Indeed, the melody's roots are probably even older still, extending far back to British-American folk tradition.)

Kitty Wells continued to answer male hits with female responses—"Paying for That Back Street Affair" answered Webb Pierce's "Back Street Affair"; "My Cold Cold Heart Is Melted Now" replied to Hank Williams's "Cold Cold Heart"; "Hey Joe" responded to Carl Smith's recording by the same title; and "I'll Always Be Your Fraulein" followed Bobby Helms's "Fraulein." As these titles suggest, her songs expressed a wide range of emotions. Often she adopted the point of view of the victimized woman, as in "Making Believe," "Honky-Tonk Waltz," "After Dark," and "I Don't Claim to Be an Angel." Numbers such as "There's Poison in Your Heart" and "Goodbye Mr. Brown" (the latter a duet with Acuff) showed her staring into the face of carnal temptation and resisting. But whether passing judgment on her weaker sisters ("She's No Angel"), admitting her own moral weakness ("One by One" with Red Foley), or taking a critical glance at the whole honky-tonk life-style ("The Life They Live in Songs"), Wells consistently sang from a woman's point of view.

Even while she was singing of turbulent passions and frankly addressing modern behavior, her publicity consistently played up her virtue. She was heavily promoted as the author of a series of down-home southern cookbooks. Booking agency publicity of the 1960s referred to her as "an active church worker and a true daughter of the South." Even her 1954 testimonial from the gov-

Before and after her spirited fling with rockabilly, Wanda Jackson sang country. Here she is at age eighteen in 1955, on tour with Hank Thompson, who had discovered her two years earlier.

Goldie Hill, ca. 1955. Tagging along with her brother Tommy to a Nashville recording session in 1952, Goldie auditioned for Decca producer Paul Cohen and landed a recording contract at the age of nineteen. Her first session yielded the #4 country hit "I Let the Stars Get in My Eyes," which prompted the Opry to sign her away from the "Louisiana Hayride." Seen briefly as a rival to Kitty Wells, she gave up her career shortly after marrying Carl Smith in 1957.

Always the trouper, Patsy Cline puts her burger aside and smiles for the camera, ca. 1960.

Opposite
Just one of the boys: when Decca artists Rex Allen, Justin Tubb, Patsy Cline, and Arleigh Duff gathered for this contrived promotional shot (ca. 1956), Patsy was still an unknown, probably grateful for any pointers Rex and the others could give her.

Mother Maybelle Carter was, of course, a trailblazer among gal singers. By 1950 she and her daughters, the Carter Sisters, had recently moved from Springfield, Missouri's "Ozark Jubilee" to the Opry. Here June shows off her trademark bloomers, while Mother, Anita, and Helen stand clear.

ernor of Tennessee read: "Kitty Wells, in addition to her artistry, has demonstrated that she is an outstanding wife and mother in keeping with the finest tradition of southern womanhood."

She was, of course, much more. She paved the way for every country female performer who has succeeded her. *Billboard* and *Cashbox* magazines named Wells the top female country performer every year from 1952 to 1965. Her total of seventy charted titles is unmatched by any woman of her era. She was made a member of the Country Music Hall of Fame in 1976. Her enormous popularity earned her the title "the Queen of Country Music."

Only one woman ever seriously challenged her during her heyday—Patsy Cline. Just five years separated Cline's 1957 breakthrough "Walking After Midnight" from Wells's "Honky-Tonk Angels." But the two women were a generation apart in style and content.

Kitty mined the territory of the losers who moaned of "Repenting," "Jealousy," and the "Lonely Side of Town." She sang that "Cheatin's a Sin," recited "I Gave My Wedding Dress Away," wailed "I Heard the Juke Box Playing," and wept of being "Mommy for a Day." Hers was a "Wicked World" where she ruled as "Queen of Honky-Tonk Street."

Patsy was far more familiar with that street in real life, but in song she avoided the beer-and-jukebox sound. Instead, she turned her sizable vocal ability to melodic "heart" material such as "Sweet Dreams," "Crazy," and "I Fall to Pieces." Replacing the whine of the steel guitar were creamy string arrangements and hushed backup singers. In these refined arrangements, orchestrated by producer Owen Bradley, Cline ushered in a contemporary Nashville style. She took the cry in the hillbilly's throat and the soul-wrenching emotion of a honky-tonker's delivery and married them to understated pop instrumentation and sophisticated songwriting. They called it the Nashville Sound, and she was its greatest female exponent—the first great country torch singer.

But her outstanding success with heartache material didn't mean Patsy Cline had a victim's personality. On the contrary,

she was tough, argumentative, assertive, and fearless. There were no ginghams and crinolines for this country diva (she was once forbidden to sing on the Opry when she showed up in a pants suit). She could swear like a sailor and hold her own with any man as a drinker. She fought to get her own way on Music Row, in recording studios, and on the road. During an era when other country music women bickered over their tiny piece of the pie, Cline befriended and supported potential competitors. She was the classic tough-but-tender gal who took no sass but had a heart of gold.

Her voice was a big, astounding thing, capable of yodeling merrily, growling the blues, sobbing with emotion, and vaulting octaves with ease. She could transform even second-rate material into emotional essays. Cline came by her torrid style naturally. While Kitty was singing at radio barn dances in the shelter of her husband's band, Patsy was belting it out alone in rough

Brenda Lee, 1957. One of the biggest female singers on the pop charts from 1957 to 1963 started out in country. Little Miss Dynamite stood less than five feet and had yet to reach puberty when she broke into the big time on Red Foley's "Jubilee, U.S.A." TV series in 1956. She sounded so mature that some foreign record buyers refused to believe that the sexy singer of "One Step at a Time" (1957) and "Dynamite" (1957) wasn't a full-grown woman.

The Davis Sisters, early 1950s. Six days before "I Forgot More Than You'll Ever Know" hit the charts in August 1953, the Davis Sisters were involved in a car crash that took the life of singer-guitarist Betty Jack Davis and critically injured her partner. Skeeter (who was actually a close friend, Mary Frances Penick) recovered, going on to Opry fame and the 1962 crossover hit, "The End of the World."

332

barrooms. Whereas Kitty had a bedrock religious background, Patsy's attitudes were formed by learning to survive on the wrong side of the tracks.

Patsy Cline was born in rural Virginia on September 8, 1932, and christened Virginia Patterson Hensley. When she was in grade school the family moved to Winchester, Virginia. Her father was reportedly a heavy drinker, and her parents split up when she was fifteen. By then the bond between her and her mother, Hilda, was already very strong; the strength of this relationship was to sustain her throughout her subsequent ups and downs in show business.

By all reports she was a fiercely determined little girl who had stars in her eyes from a very young age. Old-time string-band leader Walter Smith said she sang with his troupe in 1939, when she would have been just seven years old. She was a radio regular in her hometown at age fourteen, reportedly having walked

Coal miner's daughter as ingénue: Loretta Lynn, ca. 1962. Married at thirteen, Loretta had four children by the time she was eighteen. At twenty-five, having taught herself guitar, she wrote and recorded her first hit, "Honky Tonk Girl" (1960). An avowed fan of Patsy Cline (who befriended and encouraged her), Lynn has become one of country music's biggest stars— voted the CMA's top female vocalist three times and Entertainer of the Year in 1972.

Around 1960, Jan Howard won several "promising newcomer" awards. Since then, her fine country voice and solo hits ("Evil on Your Mind," 1966) have been somewhat overshadowed by her more successful duets with Wynn Stewart and Bill Anderson and her short-lived marriage to songwriter Harlan Howard.

333

Patsy Cline and George Hamilton IV backstage, late fifties. Both singers received important early exposure in the Washington, D.C., area playing shows promoted by Connie B. Gay.

Melba Montgomery learned the fine points of country harmony from her father, who taught singing in Alabama churches. After a stint with Roy Acuff's traveling show, she went solo in 1961, but duet singing proved to be her forte. She teamed up with George Jones for several records, including the Top Ten hit "We Must Have Been Out of Our Minds" (1963), which she wrote. Later she recorded country hits with pop singer Gene Pitney and Charlie Louvin.

fearlessly into the station alone, asking for an audition. After her father left, her singing became even more important; it became a matter of economic survival. She was performing in clubs by age sixteen, working as a drugstore clerk by day, and singing wherever she could get a job at night. She dropped out of school.

In 1948 Patsy sneaked backstage at a Wally Fowler show in her hometown theater, talked the country gospel singer (and Opry regular) into listening to her, won a spot on his show, and convinced him to get her an Opry audition in Nashville. Despite this minor triumph, nine years of work were ahead of her before she hit the big time. In the interim she met, married, and divorced Gerald Cline (their three-year marriage ended in 1957), and was wooed and won by party-loving rascal Charlie Dick.

334

In 1952 she became the featured vocalist in Bill Peer's Melody Boys of Brunswick, Maryland. Through Peer's influence she gained a recording contract with 4 Star Records in 1954. She began recording in Nashville the following year and soon landed guest-star spots on the Opry and on country TV shows. In late 1955 she became a regular on "Town and Country Time," a Washington, D.C.-area show hosted by Jimmy Dean. Her records were going nowhere, but evidently she remained undaunted. Indeed, it was during this period that she developed her brassy, sassy, sexy reputation.

A nationwide TV success on "Arthur Godfrey's Talent Scouts" show and a Decca Records hit with "Walkin' After Midnight" put Cline in the spotlight in 1957. She was twenty-five

Warming up: Patsy Cline runs through a number before a WSM television appearance, early 1960s. In the background, Ernest Tubb (on guitar) keeps a watchful eye on the proceedings, while mandolinist Rollin Sullivan (Oscar of Lonzo & Oscar) lends an ear.

Tammy Wynette, ca. 1967. She had been raising three daughters on a beautician's salary (and singing professionally off and on) when she auditioned for Columbia producer Billy Sherrill in 1966. He signed her, changed her name, and steered her to material ideally suited to her tearful voice. Between 1967 and 1977, she had twenty-one Top Ten hits in a row, including the #1 "Stand By Your Man," which she co-wrote with Sherrill.

Jeannie C. Riley was working as a secretary for Shelby Singleton when he signed her to his Plantation label. In 1968, "Harper Valley P.T.A." topped both the pop and country charts, giving her the break she needed. Unfortunately, it also typecast her for a few years in the role of the hit song's sassy, miniskirted heroine.

years old at the time and by all accounts was headstrong, opinionated, and ambitious. Nevertheless, she temporarily slowed her hell-bent-for-election pace to bear two children. She and Charlie Dick moved to Nashville in 1959.

The big hits began coming in 1961—"I Fall to Pieces," "Crazy," "She's Got You," "When I Get Through with You," "Imagine That," "So Wrong," and "Leavin' on Your Mind." "Sweet Dreams" was on its way to the top when Cline was killed in an airplane crash with fellow country entertainers Hawkshaw Hawkins and Cowboy Copas on March 5, 1963.

The passage of time and the success of posthumous records such as "Faded Love" (1963) and "He Called Me Baby" (1964) have steadily strengthened her reputation as a stylist. During Patsy's lifetime, Kitty Wells was universally cited as the biggest influence on country female singers. Today, it is Patsy Cline, and it's easy to understand why: she took Music City's songs onto the pop charts. "Walkin' After Midnight" (1957), "I Fall to

Bill Anderson saw Connie Smith win an amateur contest in Columbus, Ohio. He helped her secure an RCA contract and supplied her first single, "Once a Day," a #1 hit in 1964. She is seen here with Anderson (left) and RCA producer Bob Ferguson.

Donna Fargo, born Yvonne Vaughn, was teaching English and struggling as a singer-songwriter when "Happiest Girl in the Whole U.S.A."—a tune she wrote herself—became a #1 hit and the CMA's top single of 1972. Over the next seven years, fifteen more Top Ten hits earned her a roomful of additional awards.

337

Dottie and daughter Shelly West don't perform together, but duets have become something of a family tradition with them. Dottie's duet partners on record include Jim Reeves, Jimmy Dean, Don Gibson, and Kenny Rogers; Shelly's biggest hit was a 1981 duet with David Frizzell, "You're the Reason God Made Oklahoma." In this 1983 shot, Shelly holds the Academy of Country Music award she and Frizzell received for Top Vocal Duet of 1982.

Jack Greene & Jeannie Seely, ca. 1969. Each hit the charts in 1966—Seely with her #2 hit "Don't Touch Me" and Greene with his #1 smash "There Goes My Everything." Three years later, Seely teamed up with the ex-drummer for Ernest Tubb and scored an immediate duet hit with "Wish I Didn't Have to Miss You."

Pieces" (1961), and "She's Got You" (1962) were all Top Twenty pop hits; "Crazy" reached #9 in 1961. In addition to her cross-over chart successes, Patsy left a lasting impression as a personality, and her example taught her contemporaries how to fight for what they wanted.

Kitty's dignity and Patsy's spirit have remained models of behavior for country music's women. In their wake came such stars as Jean Shepard, Jan Howard, Wanda Jackson, Skeeter Davis, Jeannie Seely, Norma Jean, Lynn Anderson, Dottie West, and Connie Smith. Superstar Loretta Lynn cites Wells's singing and Cline's personality as her twin influences. Dolly Parton came to Nashville as a teenager to record a budget LP of Wells's songs. Tammy Wynette, too, felt the influence of the Queen of Country Music. As youngsters, both Reba McEntire and Sylvia were transfixed by the sound of Cline's voice; in fact, Reba included a Cline song on each of her first three LPs, scoring her first Top Twenty hit in 1979 with a remake of "Sweet Dreams." K. D.

The Mandrell Family, ca. 1962. By the time she started high school, Barbara Mandrell had mastered the steel guitar, the banjo, and the saxophone. After her TV appearances on "Town Hall Party" and ABC's "Five Star Jubilee," her father, Irby, formed a family band around the young prodigy. Here she is on steel; on bass is her mother, Mary, on guitar Brian Lonbeck, at the mike Irby, and on drums is her future husband, Ken Dudney.

Dottie West, late 1960s. Though she earned a Grammy for her recording of her song "Here Comes My Baby" (1964), her best-remembered song was an award-winning Coca-Cola jingle. Subsequently released as a single in 1973, "Country Sunshine" logged ten weeks on the pop charts as well as fifteen on the country charts.

*Liz Anderson and daughter
Lynn, 1967. Liz wrote "The
Fugitive" and "(My Friends
Are Gonna Be) Strangers" for
Merle Haggard and recorded a
few hits herself during the
sixties. She also provided her
equestrian daughter with her
first hit, "Ride, Ride, Ride"
(1966). But Lynn's break-
through didn't come until she
recorded Joe South's "Rose
Garden"—regarded as a
"man's song" until her version
topped both the pop and
country charts in 1971.*

Lang calls her band the Reclines (get it?) and performs a torrid "Three Cigarettes in an Ashtray" as a salute to her vocal idol. Pam Tillis recreates Kitty's "Amigo's Guitar" onstage. Rosie Flores draws on both legendary ladies for inspiration.

Kitty Wells and Patsy Cline mark the beginning of the modern tradition for women in country music. After their breakthroughs, there was no going back to the "and-now-for-a-religious-number-from-our-girl-singer" attitude. After they proved that women country stylists could sell records and concert tickets, the woman was no longer relegated to the role of a decorative afterthought on all-male bills. Radio programmers ceased to view records by women as airplay suicide.

Today, when we hear Emmylou Harris sing "Making Believe," we are hearing the profound influence of Kitty Wells. When we tell tales of Tanya Tucker's wild behavior, we are hearing echoes of Patsy Cline's kick-up-your-heels spunk. Patsy's legacy is in the millions of records sold by Crystal Gayle, Linda Ronstadt,

Above
*Sammi Smith acquired a
reputation as a distaff Outlaw
with her million-selling version
of Kris Kristofferson's "Help
Me Make It Through the Night"
(1971). Though she moved to
Austin, no more Outlaw songs
came her way. Here she is
during her Nashville days (ca.
1966), well within the law.*

*Jeanne Pruett first came to
Nashville in 1956 with her
husband, Jack Pruett, a
guitarist in Marty Robbins's
band. She began recording with
RCA in 1963, but initially had
more success as a songwriter,
landing songs with Robbins,
Tammy Wynette, and Conway
Twitty. Ironically, her
breakthrough hit, "Satin
Sheets" (1973), was written by a
man, John Volinkaty.*

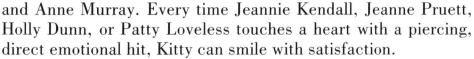

and Anne Murray. Every time Jeannie Kendall, Jeanne Pruett,
Holly Dunn, or Patty Loveless touches a heart with a piercing,
direct emotional hit, Kitty can smile with satisfaction.

And somewhere in the world, this very minute, some hopeful
young country gal is probably listening to the voices of the two
performers who remain the most overwhelming, influential, and
inspirational women in country music. God didn't make honky-
tonk angels. Sweet dreams, indeed.

11

SOUNDTRACK OF THE SOUTH: A FAN'S VIEW OF COUNTRY

Paul Hemphill

Beware of all enterprises that require new clothes.
—Henry David Thoreau, *Walden*, 1854

My passage into the world of country music, or at least into that world according to God and Hank Williams, began at dusk on a steamy June evening in 1948 as the cicadas cranked up for another night of serenading the sooty working-class neighborhood of Birmingham, Alabama, where I had just entered my twelfth year. Daddy was in his prime then, a leathery thirty-six-year-old long-distance trucker with his own rig and a taste for cowboy boots, aviator glasses, and El Producto cigars, a spirited "independent leased operator" who would never in his life join a union or go on somebody's payroll. He had been pretty much a mystical King of the Road for me all through the war years as he hauled stuff back and forth across America, returning from Oakland, Lubbock, Brooklyn, and Mobile with stories of wrecks on the highway and all-night truck stops and outwitting the highway patrol. All I knew of that life was what he had told me at the supper table on nights when he returned. But now, as school let out for the summer of '48, the time had come at last for me to ride along and see it all for myself.

The Grand Ole Opry, ca. 1936, when it was headquartered in the Dixie Tabernacle. See page 349.

Lonnie Glosson is best remembered for his bluesy harmonica-playing. Around 1938, he teamed up with Wayne Raney for harmonica duets. A decade later, Glosson provided harmonica back-up for Raney's hit "Why Don't You Haul Off and Love Me."

Wayne Raney did all right by his harmonica. During the late forties, he backed the Delmore Brothers on some of their classics for King Records, including "Freight Train Boogie" and "Blues Stay Away from Me." In turn, they backed him on his #1 hit "Why Don't You Haul Off and Love Me" (1949).

We rode at dusk, after stowing a week's worth of clean clothes in the cab of the freshly washed, blood-red, four-ton Dodge and fending off Mama's admonition that I not return with plans to be a truck driver ("It's good enough for me," he told her, "and I notice you ain't starving"). Soon enough, as night fell and a full moon followed us up and into the southern Appalachians on the twisting route to Cumberland, Maryland, I entered my father's world. "Call that Jew Overdrive," he would crack, over the whistling wind and roaring engine, as he slipped into neutral for a seventy-mile-per-hour free-fall down the other side of a mountain. The cab was littered with wrinkled road maps and cigar butts and beer bottles and oily rags and wrenches and, taped to the roof, a calendar pin-up of Rita Hayworth. *There goes Chattanooga.* The silver warehouse of a trailer, loaded with giant spools of cotton twine headed for the tire plant, rocked behind us. "I seen this waitress one time that had a face so ugly it had already wore out two bodies." *Knoxville at midnight.* Air brakes wheezing, tires squealing, lights blinking, air-horn wailing through the valleys. "Watermelons grow so fast in Texas, the bottoms wear off before they can pick 'em." *Wytheville, Roanoke, Lynchburg.* Hank Williams on the radio: "Came in last night at half past ten, that baby of mine wouldn't let me in—So move it on over . . ."

From the old Motorola dangling out of the dashboard, the signals weaving in and out as the rig worked its way northeastward from valley to valley, there came the soundtrack for all of this. *XERF in Villa Acuna, Mexico . . . And now, here's ol' Ernest Tubb . . . That's one thousand baby chicks, folks, sex not guaranteed . . . WCKY in Cincinnati . . . Lonnie Glosson and Wayne Raney . . . The All-Night Trucker's Show . . . Write Post Office Box Twelve, Del Rio, Texas, for your Magic Prayer Cloth . . . WWVA in Wheeling . . . For as long as He makes this offer possible . . . The singing governor, Jimmie Davis . . .* Suddenly, after midnight, the airwaves were alive with country music, not no damned Hollywood cowboys singing to their horses but this real stuff about whiskey and women and prison and moving on, like Merle Travis doing "Nine Pound Hammer"—

Roll on, buddy, don't you roll so slow.
How can I roll when the wheels won't go?
Roll on, buddy, pull a load of coal.
How can I pull when the wheels won't go?

—and I knew then, even with what little perspicacity a twelve-year-old towheaded son of an Alabama trucker can bring to such

344

Dave Dudley on the set of "Star Route," ca. 1964. A washed-up baseball player from Wisconsin, Dudley had been bouncing across the Midwest from one radio station job to another when he recorded "Six Days on the Road" in 1963. It became a trucker's anthem, giving the rough-hewn Dudley an image and an audience.

Merle Travis had established a reputation as a guitar picker par excellence *in 1947, when he brought a sketch for this electric guitar to his friend, mechanic Paul Bigsby. Bigsby built the instrument by hand to Travis's specifications. It became the first commercially successful solid-body electric.*

matters, that I had found the background music, the orchestration, for my father's life. He would listen to the *words* of those songs. Maybe there would be a song about some fellow who had come home from working in the mine all day and found that his wife had taken the car and left him with the kids and the mortgage. After playing with his cigar and mulling over the situation my father would say, as though he had just heard the Evening News, "Hell of a thing to do to some old boy, ain't it?"

I miss that. A lot of things have happened since then to me and to my father, not to mention to country music and to the South from which much of it sprang, and I'm not so sure that it has all been for the good. As the twentieth century began to wind down, finding America locked into another kind of war with Japan (this one over technological wizardry of a different sort), the South had become barely distinguishable from the rest of the nation. It wasn't even called the South anymore, in fact, having been absorbed by something called the Sun Belt, an appellation accorded any lands lying south of a line drawn from Washington to Oklahoma City to Los Angeles; and its young hardly noticed or even cared. The glass-and-concrete skyline of Atlanta looked precisely like that of Detroit. Television, the great homogenizer, had these new Sun Belters wearing the same clothes, eating the same processed food and speaking the same tongue, worshiping the same idols, and living in the same houses as their counterparts in Denver and Seattle. Ticky-tacky boxes, all in a row.

345

Merle Travis, late forties. The man responsible for such classics as "Sixteen Tons" and "Dark as a Dungeon" was the #1 fan of Mose Rager, a Kentucky coal miner who taught him how to play. Though Travis's guitar would eventually take him to network radio, Hollywood movies, and the top of the record charts, he always credited Rager for getting him started.

During the early 1960s, when this photo was made, Ohio-born Bobby Bare gave voice to displaced Southerners everywhere with records like "Detroit City" (1963), "500 Miles Away from Home" (1963), and "Streets of Baltimore" (1966).

Microwave ovens. Cable TV. McDonald's. I-85, I-75, I-20, I-95, World's Busiest Airport, World's Tallest Hotel. "You from Georgia? What exit?" Yuppies and electronic evangelists, designer jeans and designer ice cream.

Let there be no argument that much of the bad was swept out as the South cleaned up its act and joined the rest of the Union during the sixties and seventies. Pressure from the North and the East, along with the South's urgent desire for "respectability," meant that homogenization was inevitable. There would be no more of this blatant racism, not after network television turned its cameras on Eugene "Bull" Connor of Birmingham. There would be no more of these mill-town economies ("I owe my soul to the company store") once the unions came. There would be no more of this defiant provincialism and inbreeding and anti-intellectualism ("The South may not always be right," the comic Brother Dave Gardner would preach to the yahoos, "but by God, we ain't never *wrong*") once the first wave of Southerners went off to college. Gone, too, due to a general enlightenment brought about by television, investments, and even the interstate highway system, were the sad symbols of the South's isolation and poverty: sharecropper shacks, outhouses, unpaved roads, backyard family cemeteries, Ku Klux Klan billboards "welcoming" visitors to dying small towns; and the sight along those roads, especially on the edge of communities in the mined-out southern Appalachians, of southern boys hitching rides to Ohio and Michigan where they would live (and sometimes die) in

an alien "briarhopper" ghetto, listening to Bobby Bare tell their life story in "Detroit City": *By day I make the cars, by night I make the bars . . .*

And yet this progress, as was inevitable, also took away the very heart and soul of what was the South. I am reminded of Stephen Vincent Benet's lamentation in "John Brown's Body":

> *But when the last moonshiner buys his radio*
> *And the last, lost wild-rabbit of a girl is civilized*
> * with a mail order dress*
> *Something will pass that was American*
> *And the movies will not bring it back.*

True, all true, and let no man deny that there was a certain laid-back sensuousness—an *élan*—about the pre-television South, before the good old boys were tamed and the farms died and the front porches rotted and the train depots closed and K-mart replaced Briley's Five & Dime, which will not pass this way again. Never again will we see a Georgia governor on the hustings at a piney-woods barbecue, snapping his suspenders and rolling up his sleeves and fanning away gnats with a funeral-parlor fan all at once, audaciously promising the people in the grass that they have "three friends in this world: God, Sears & Roebuck, and Eugene Talmadge." Never again will we see a

Hank Snow, early 1960s. Now a grand old man of the Opry, the Canadian-born Snow had struggled since the mid forties to make it in the U.S. "I'm Movin' On" (1950)—a song his producer, Steve Sholes, originally rejected—was the watershed. After that, the hits just kept on coming: "Golden Rocket" (1950), "Rhumba Boogie" (1951), "I Don't Hurt Anymore" (1954), "I've Been Everywhere" (1962), "Hello Love" (1974).

mountain moonshiner *cum* stock-car driver named Lloyd Seay, stopped for doing seventy miles per hour through a town square and "payin' in advance" the fine for the return trip because "I'm gonna be in a hurry comin' back, too." Gone, or at least almost gone, are all of those exotic rascals of the sprawling southern outback who made the place a nation within a nation. Rainmakers. Tent revivalists. Snake-handlers. Hadacol salesmen. Shell-game operators fleecing the Yankees out on U.S. 1. Speed-trap sheriffs ("You in a heap o' trouble, boy"). "Madame Olga" reading palms and "Seminole Billie" wrestling alligators and "FiFi LaFourche" smoking a cigarette in a most peculiar way. Gone, all gone, replaced by more respectable rascals.

As the South underwent its wrenching changes during the latter half of the twentieth century so would its music, in all facets, undergo changes no less wrenching. Only the purists complained when the Grand Ole Opry was transplanted from the quaint historic ex-tabernacle Ryman Auditorium, in what had become seedy downtown Nashville, to the cushy air-conditioned comfort of a new auditorium anchoring a hokey "family amusement park" called Opryland USA. Only the purists complained when the entertainers moth-balled their fantastic sequined "suits of light." Only the purists complained about string sections and horns and electrified instruments and lip-gloss and elocution lessons and digital mixing and hybrid "crossover" pop-country songs. To most Southerners, weary of being called "quaint" and "tacky" and "hillbilly," this whole new glossy plasticized world of music that had lost its "country" was an affirmation that they had been accepted. Anyway, they could argue, how could you write an honest country song about, say, an extended farm family sitting on the front porch, eating homemade ice cream, making their own music, listening to train whistles echoing through the hills, wondering if Bubba got a job in Detroit yet, when none of that exists anymore?

It was two or three years later, after countless other junkets in my father's rig to places like Mobile, Pittsburgh, and Tampa, that he finally made a proposition over the supper table. "Why don't we just get in the car and go up to see the Opry," he said between mouthfuls of cornbread and pinto beans. By then I had two passions, baseball and country music, and my bedroom in the rear of our frame shotgun house was a shrine to both: one wall was papered with portraits from *Sport* magazine of Ted Williams, Stan Musial, and Nellie Fox; my Sears student desk was littered with 45 rpm's of Hank Williams, Ernest Tubb, and Carl Smith. My bedside Motorola stayed tuned at night to KMOX

Roy Acuff & the Smoky Mountain Boys play to a capacity crowd of about 2,300 during a Grand Ole Opry broadcast from War Memorial Auditorium (ca. 1940), the Opry's home from July 1939 until June 1943—when the Opry was asked to leave because fans left too much gum beneath their seats.

The Dixie Tabernacle, Fatherland Street, East Nasvhille, ca. 1936. The home of the Grand Ole Opry from 1936 to 1939, this Pentecostal Church building seated about a thousand.

Program for Grand Ole Opry --

American Ace Coffee—7:30 to 8:00
★ Roy Acuff—Low and Lonely
Tommy Magness—Black Mountain Rag
Dot & Smokey—Blue Eyes Crying in the Rain
Jimmy Riddle—Dill Pickle Rag
Roy andl Oswald—Eye From on High ✓
★ Uncle Dave Macon and Dorris—Take Me Back to My Old Carolina Home
Jug Band—Johnson's Old Grey Mule
Roy Acuff—Unclouded Day ✓
Joe Zinkas—12th Street Rag
Dot & Smokey—Are You Tired of Me Darling
Rachel & Oswald—Jesse James

Purina Show—8:00 to 8:30
★ Cowboy Copas—Dolly Dear
Uncle Dave Macon—Chewing Gum
★ George Morgan—Candy Kisses
Fruit Jar Drinkers—Girl I Left Behind Me
Cowboy Copas—Careless Hands
Lazy Jim Day—Singing The News
George Morgan—Rainbow in My Heart
Robert Lunn—Talking Blues
Hank Garland—Short Creek Shuffe
Cowboy Copas—One Step More

Prince Albert—8:30 to 9:00
★ Red Foley—Tennessee Polka
Tommy Wakeley—Try To Understand
Fowler Quartet—Ole Blind Barte nus
Red Foley—Just A Closer Walk With Thee
★ Jimmy Wakeley—Someday You'll Call My Name and I Won't Answer
Old Hickory Quartet—In The Good Ole Summertime
Red Foley—I'm Throwing Rice at the Girl I Love
Square Dance—Stony Point

Royal Crown Cola—9:00 to 9:30
Possum Hunters—Widow McGraw
Roy Acuff—Tennessee Central Number 9
Jamup & Honey—Jokes
Jimmy Riddle—Wabash Blues
★ Jimmy Dickens—Cold Tater
Jug Band—Uncle Noah's Ark
★ Lonzo & Oscar—I wish I Had a Nickle
Rachel & Oswald—Rabbit in the Log
Roy Acuff—Waiting For My Call To Glory
Bradley Kinkaid—Won't You Come Over To My House
Tommy Magness—Leather Britches

Warren Paint—9:30 to 10:00
Lew Childre—My Mammy
★ Ernest Tubb—Biting My Finger Nails and Thinking of You
★ Bill Monroe—To be Announced
★ Hank Williams—Lovesick Blues
Crook Brothers—Old Joe Clark
Ernest Tubb—Daddy When is Mommy Coming Home

Opry program, June 11, 1949. Those who were there that night will never forget it. During the 9:30 to 10:00 segment sponsored by Warren Paint, a skinny twenty-five-year-old from Alabama stepped up to the mike to sing his current #1 hit. Since it was his first appearance on the Opry, few recognized him. But by the end of "Lovesick Blues," the crowd couldn't get enough, calling Hank Williams back for half a dozen encores.

Opposite, top
Hawkshaw Hawkins and Little Jimmy Dickens, 1955. The six-foot-five veteran of WWVA had recently joined the Opry at the time of this photo (Dickens, at four-eleven, had been a member since 1948). He could have been a contender: just as his career was just picking up momentum, he perished in the March 1963 plane crash that also took the lives of Patsy Cline and Cowboy Copas.

in St. Louis (for Harry Caray's Cardinals broadcasts) and to WSM in Nashville (for the Opry). And now—*my God!*—we were actually going to see the Opry. Mama and my sister, four years younger than I, made up fried chicken, potato salad, and beans on the night before, and all during the five-hour ride to Nashville the next day in our new Dodge Coronet sedan—over twisting asphalt backroads my father knew like the back of his hand, up into the undulating heart of Middle Tennessee, Daddy keeping

String Beans—Cross Eyed Gal
Mel & Stan—I'll Gladly Take You Back Again
Bill Monroe—To Be Announced
Ernest Tubb—I Hung My Head And Cried

Wallrite—10:00 to 10:15
Bill Monroe—Kitty Clyde
Bradley Kinkaid—When I Was A Boy From The Mountains
Blue Grass Quartet—A Beautiful Life
Bill Monroe—Goodbye Old Pal
Shenandoah Valley—Live and Let Live

Gaylark—10:15 to 10:30
Milton Estes—John Henry
Jimmy Dickens—Bible On The Table
Jimmy Selph—A Petal From A Faded Rose
Milton Estes—Build Me A Cabin In Glory

Royal Flour—10:30 to 10:45
Roy Acuff—Coming From The Ball ✓
Uncle Dave Macon & Dorris—Kissing On The Sly
Roy Acuff—Poem
Roy and Gang—Farther Along ✓
Tommy Magness—Cackling Hen

Dr. Le Gear—10:45 to 11:00
Cowboy Copas—Package of Lies Tied in Blue
Mel & Stan—Two Little Rose Buds
Lazy Jim Day—Singing The News
Cowboy Copas—Waltzing With Tears in My Eyes
Red Herron—Sally Goodin

Allen Manufacturing Co.—11:00 to 11:15
George Morgan—Need You
Hank Williams—Mind Your Own Business ←
Velma—That Little Kid Sister of Mine
George Morgan—Put All Your Love In A Cookie Jar
Gully Jumpers—Going Cross The Sea

Sustaining—11:15 to 11:30
Ernest Tubb—Don't Rob Another Man's Castle
Lew & String Bean—Darling Nelly Grey
Butter Ball—I Can't Go For That
Ernest Tubb—Frankie & Johnny

Sustaining—11:30 to 11:45
Jimmy Dickens—The Rose From The Brides Bouquet
Lonzo & Oscar—Sour Wood Mountain
Crook Brothers—Ida Red
Jimmy Dickens—Pennies For Papa
Zeb Turner—Git It And Get

Sustaining—11:45 to 12:00
★Wally Fowler—Lead Me To That Rock
Robert Lunn—Corina
Fruit Jar Drinkers—Alabama Jubilee
Wally Fowler—May The Circle Be Unbroken
Fruit Jar Drinkers—Leather Britches
Wally Fowler—Get On Board

Minnie Pearl, mid 1940s. Sarah Ophelia Colley was a struggling actress and drama teacher when she first put together a comedy routine based on a man-hungry, small-town gossip she named Minnie Pearl. In November 1940, at age twenty-eight, she got her first chance to appear on the Opry and drew more than three hundred cards and letters. Today, next to Roy Acuff, she is the Opry's most visible symbol.

the car radio tuned to country stations so as to heighten the anticipation—I tingled. *Wonder who'll be there. Hank? Naw, they had to fire him for something. Little Jimmy Dickens really that little? Boy, what if Carl Smith's there! "I Overlooked an Orchid While Searching for a Rose." Wish I had an autograph book.* Now and then my father would catch my eye in the rear view mirror and would say, taking the El Producto from his mouth, "How-*dee*! Just so proud to be *hyar*." Minnie Pearl.

351

JIM ED BROWN, star of the Grand Ole Opry, international recording artist for RCA Victor, exclusive management: Hubert Long Talent Agency, 806- 16th Ave., Nashville, Tennessee.

Hello my good friend and Loyal Fans Just wanted to let you know that things are looking good for my TV Show. We start taping June 23rd and hope it won't be long before you will be seeing the "Gems" and me, with our special guest, in your home. We are looking forward to all this, and would be very happy to hear comments from you.
Your Friend,

28745-C

It's not unusual for country stars to respond personally to fan mail, sometimes even maintaining a regular correspondence with devoted followers. Twenty years after Jim Ed Brown sent this postcard, he and the little girl he sent it to (now grown, married, and working for the Country Music Foundation) still greet each other on a first-name basis.

The Wilburn Brothers joined the Opry in 1940 as part of Wilburn Family group, but had to leave because of child labor laws (Teddy was nine and Doyle was ten). Thirteen years later they returned. Their Decca hits ranged from old-time duets ("Knoxville Girl," 1959) to contemporary country ("Hurt Her Once for Me," 1966). By the time of this 1964 photo, the Wilburns had their own very popular syndicated TV show.

W. L. S. BARN DANCE
JULY 22, 1933 CHICAGO, ILL.

*Outside the Eighth Street
Theatre, Chicago, July 22,
1933. Inside: the most popular
radio show in town, possibly
the country—the WLS
"National Barn Dance,"
broadcast every Saturday night
from eight to nine over the NBC
network.*

That imposing shrine of fierce red brick that is the Ryman
Auditorium might as well have been Yankee Stadium when I
first spied it in the midday sun. It seemed as if a carnival was in
on the corner of Fifth and Broadway—cars and trucks from
everywhere in the parking lots, country music being piped from
record-and-souvenir shops, scores of people already queuing up
on the broad steps to buy tickets for the night's performance—
and soon we were a part of it. We took the picnic basket out of
the trunk of the car and ate in the parking lot catty-corner from
the Ryman, next to a family of six in a station wagon with Arkansas license plates, and when we finished dinner the women wan-
dered toward the shops while my father and I got in line for
tickets. We were in luck. Tickets were still available and we saw
that many of our favorites would be there that night. Toward

353

Opry sweethearts: June Carter and Carl Smith, about the time of their marriage, July 1952. Five years later, Smith married Goldie Hill; Carter married Johnny Cash in 1968.

Pilgrims' progress: Saturday night in downtown Nashville, 1960s.

nightfall, when the creaky double-doors were swung open to the stained-glass turn-of-the-century tabernacle Cap'n Tom Ryman had built for the evangelist who saved his soul, the four of us rushed down the boarded aisle for seats on the fourth pew from that hallowed stage.

Lord, Lord. For the better part of the night I sat there mesmerized, undeterred by the stultifying heat and blinded by rhinestones as one by one my radio heroes meandered front-and-center, larger than life. Here came Roy Acuff yo-yoing and balancing a fiddle on his nose and singing "Great Speckled Bird," Little Jimmy Dickens shouting "Sleepin' at the Foot of the Bed" while standing on an apple crate, big old raw-boned Martha Carson whapping out a gospel boogie called "Satisfied" on a guitar bigger than Dickens, Carl Smith (little Junebug Carter's husband, everybody knew that) with a powder-blue western-cut suit and pompadour hair crooning "Am I the One?" And Ernest Tubb and Webb Pierce and Faron Young and Hank Snow, who had my father singing along when he did "Movin' On," all of them moving in and out of the spotlights as the huge canvas backdrops were raised and lowered every fifteen minutes to denote that segment's sponsor (Brown Mule Tobacco, Martha White Flour, Goo Goo Candy Bars). It was the music of the people, by the people and for the people. When we got back home to Birmingham around four o'clock on Sunday morning, I (having slumbered in the back of the car with a rolled-up Opry program) had plans to check out the prices on steel guitars like the one used by the guy in Ernest Tubb's Texas Troubadours.

By the time I could afford a steel guitar, I didn't want one. Those were prosperous times for my father, so busy that he bought a second rig and hired a succession of drivers to run it, and within a year after that visit to the Opry he was buying our first television set. That black-and-white nineteen-inch screen brought promises of another world into our living room in Birmingham—California beaches, New York skyscrapers, Yankee Stadium, Chicago's Loop, the Rockies (much more imposing

than our Appalachians), Times Square on New Year's Eve, the World Series (so why go watch the Birmingham Barons play?), Kansas's amber waves of grain—and for the next twenty years I would try to cover up my roots and engage in a quixotic search for those promises. The specter of another way of life, where people live in airy California houses and speak like Dave Garroway and dress like Boston lawyers and sing like Perry Como, was too alluring to be denied. I became, in short, ashamed of my father and all he represented.

It went on like that for nearly twenty years. Elvis and rock 'n' roll came along as I was finishing high school, just in time to give me a comfortable alternative to Tubb, Acuff, Carl Smith, and all of those other ex-heroes who no longer suited my new sensibilities, so I embraced him and Kay Starr and Peggy Lee and Buddy Holly and anybody else deemed acceptable by the rest of America. During a summer of playing baseball in Missouri, unmercifully chided by teammates from places like Chicago, Ohio, Pennsylvania, and other exotic destinations, I began eliminating "y'all" from my vocabulary and firmly reinstated the the final letter *g* in all my gerunds and participles. As the first of our Hemphills to go off to college—albeit *Auburn,* derided as the "cow college" of Alabama—I was embarrassed to learn that pretty girls liked boys who had convertibles, nice clothes, good elocution, Dave Brubeck records, and rich daddies; not boys who said "ain't y'all" and liked cigars and boots and baseball and Hank Williams and had daddies who drove trucks. Consequently, when I finally got one to marry me, I owned a new Volkswagen (the rage then), a pair of wing-tip shoes, a Borsolino hat, and had a great collection of Peggy Lee and Andy Williams albums.

It took a year at Harvard, of all places, to bring me back full-circle to my senses. I spent the last year of the sixties there as a Nieman Fellow, one of a dozen newspapermen from around the country selected to spend a year in Cambridge, Massachusetts, pursuing whatever we wanted to pursue. I was thirty-three, a

When Ernest Tubb sang "Thanks a Lot," he meant it; his rapport with his fans was legendary. He had the back of his guitar inscribed with this message so he could flash it, along with his smile, at the end of his concerts.

*Jan Howard, Bill Anderson &
the Po' Boys on TV, 1969.
During the sixties, Anderson's
success as a solo act and in
duets with Howard led to his
popular syndicated TV show.
When the hits dried up in the
late seventies, he became known
to millions more through his
appearances on TV soap operas
and game shows.*

trucker's son from Alabama thrown among Yalies, *New York Times*men, Californians, and other worldly sorts, a heathen loose in the temple, and it was early on that I discovered what I perceived to be a great and comforting truth. *Hell,* I remember thinking one night while a Pulitzer-winning reporter went on about the vagaries of women, *Hank already said that.* Hank Williams had said it even clearer, in fact, out of all his south Alabama sensibilities. *The tears come down like fallin' rain . . . I'm so lonesome I could cry . . . I'll never get out of this world alive . . . Your cold, cold heart.* And so it was that I began work on my first book while there at Harvard, a thousand miles away from home, and that book was not about molecular theory.

It was fortuitous timing to proceed with a book on country music in 1969 because just then Nashville was poised on the brink of radical change. Following my outline, looking for the things I had loved as a younger man, I had no difficulty finding the vignettes to support the premise that no music in America had such a tap-root following as country music. In an isolated cabin in the north Georgia mountains I visited an old fellow who still listened to the Opry on a battery-powered radio and entertained himself by playing the fiddle he had made. In Dayton, Ohio, one afternoon I found an Appalachian migrant (a "briarhopper"), finished with his shift at the Frigidaire plant, getting drunk and dancing with the saloon jukebox as it played Bobby Bare's "Detroit City" over and over again. At Bradley's Barn outside of Nashville I saw Kitty Wells slap together a whole album of nasal, hard-country songs in three hours before trudging out to the bus for an extended tour of one-night performances in small-town auditoriums and gymnasiums. I went on the road for a week with Bill Anderson and the Po' Boys, riding through the January snow from Newark to Boston, hearing them play steel-guitar country for transplanted Southerners aching to hear a Georgia drawl. I hung out plenty in Nashville, at Tootsie's Orchid Lounge and backstage at the Ryman and in the decrepit houses along Sixteenth Avenue South ("Music Row") where the agents, writers, and song publishers conducted their business, and I made it to Bakersfield, California, one weekend night to hear Merle Haggard sing his baleful tunes of whiskey and prison and Okies to the homefolks in the high school gymnasium. There was plenty of evidence there to support the thesis that country music, as my father and I had known it twenty years earlier on that night in the truck, was alive and well.

But then I began to hear another tune being sung. "Keeping up with the times" was the recurring refrain I heard as I lunched with the general manager of the Opry and saw the grandiose plans for moving out of Ryman ("It's just an old firetrap") and into Opryland USA ("People want air conditioning and carpet these days"). The bulldozers were poised out there in the suburbs and on Music Row, which was about to be leveled in favor of a glassy tree-lined parkway, and about the only concession to the memory of Hank Williams was to take along a chunk of the Ryman stage where he first sang "Lovesick Blues" to be implanted in the new one at Opryland. Television production outfits were renting space on Music Row. Violinists from the Nashville Symphony were staying busy playing background on the "smoother" new music being recorded. Hank Snow, Ernest Tubb, Kitty Wells, Webb Pierce, and Faron Young weren't selling so well anymore, the void being filled by people like Glen Campbell, who had tried the "fightin' and dancin' clubs" but found them lacking and were now opting for a hybrid crossover music that the promoters and record moguls were beginning to call the Nashville Sound.

By the late seventies the remodeling job had been completed. The Country Music Association could flash irrefutable data— record sales, number of "country" radio stations in America, attendance figures for "country" stage shows, gate receipts from Opryland, Nielsen ratings for prime-time television specials—to prove that "country" music was enjoying its greatest popularity. It was no longer news when a Nashville performer worked Carnegie Hall or signed for a network television show or sold a million records. Every weekend in Nashville the tour buses

Tootsie's Orchid Lounge. Hattie Louise "Tootsie" Bess opened her bar in 1960 just across the alley from the Ryman, and it quickly became the favorite watering hole of Opry stars and such struggling hopefuls as Willie Nelson, Roger Miller, Tom T. Hall, and Kris Kristofferson. Tootsie, who had been something of a den mother to her patrons, passed away in 1978. The bar fell on hard times when the Opry moved in 1974—but it's still open.

Kitty Wells, Johnnie Wright, and son Bobby Wright, 1970s. After twenty-two Top Ten singles, MCA Records terminated a "lifetime" contract with Kitty in the mid seventies. It made no difference: she and husband Johnnie continued to play more than 150 dates a year for loyal fans.

The Grand Ole Opry House, home of the Opry since March 1974, seats 4,400 in climate-controlled comfort. Performers and fans alike say that something was gained and something was lost when the Opry moved from downtown Nashville out to the suburban Opryland theme park. As Loretta Lynn once put it, "When I go onstage at the new Opry, I ain't even nervous anymore."

clogged Music Row and Opryland, unloading thousands of people who had formerly regarded country music as tacky. Suddenly it was impossible for some old boy to ride into town on a Trailways from Oklahoma, a guitar slung around his neck, and knock on the doors of Music Row to hum-and-strum a few bars in order to get a recording contract, because, for starters, the imposing oak doors of the publishing houses on Music Square East and Music Square West were equipped with peepholes and remote-control locks to keep the riff-raff out. Ryman Auditorium had become a seldom-visited dollar-a-head museum amid the glisten-

THE OLD-TIMERS

While diehard fans argue about the current state and future of country music, a smaller, but equally avid group of music enthusiasts listens to and plays what they refer to as "old-time," "old-timey," or "mountain" music. Devotees of this earliest form of country music, tagged "hillbilly" by record companies in the 1920s and 1930s, pay little heed to the shifting winds of musical fashion blowing through Nashville.

Old-time music refers to the repertoire—mostly instrumental—current among rural American musicians in the early part of the twentieth century. Some of the lively, strange, and wonderful tunes were preserved when record companies like the Victor Talking Machine Company, Gennett, Vocalion, and Brunswick recorded them. Groups with colorful, expressive names like Gid Tanner & the Skillet Lickers, Hoyt Ming & His Pep Steppers, Da Costa Woltz's Southern Broadcasters, and the Red Fox Chasers, to name but a few, belong to an era regarded by today's old-time musicians as a golden age, when life, entertainment, and recording technology were less complex.

Interest in old-time music still runs high for a dedicated group of enthusiasts. Record labels like Rounder, County, Arhoolie, Shanachie, Flying Fish, and the cassette-only Marimac keep the oldest recordings in print while issuing new recordings by revivalist old-time groups like the Highwoods String Band, the Red Clay Ramblers, the Chicken Chokers, the Tompkins County Horseflies, and Major Contay & the Canebrake Rattlers. These modern groups assemble their repertoires from a mixture of old-time tunes, original composi-

The New Lost City Ramblers, ca. 1959. John Cohen (on guitar), Mike Seeger (on fiddle), and Tom Paley (on banjo) were among the first college-educated folk music fans to take up and popularize old-time country music.

tions, and adaptations of selections from other genres. To overcome the problem of distributing their specialized records to a scattered constituency, the independent labels have set up mail-order operations like County Sales, Roundup Records, and Down Home Music.

Journals and magazines like *Old Time Music*, *JEMF Quarterly*, *Record Roundup*, *County Sales Newsletter*, and *Old Time Herald* link the community of old-time enthusiasts through historical feature articles, record reviews, discographies, and concert and festival listings. Fiddling enthusiasts, a group that overlaps with the old-time music crowd, share information in publications like *Devil's Box*, *Idaho Fiddler*, *National Old Time Fiddler*, *Texas Fiddler*, and *Missouri State Old Time Fiddler Newsletter*. Though they serve a broader audience, *Frets*, *Banjo Newsletter*, *Sing Out!*, and *Bluegrass Unlimited* often run articles of interest to old-time enthusiasts.

Old-time musicians have a variety of opportunities to play their music, including private family and community social functions (Saturday night suppers, parties), public appearances (dances, performances in nightclubs that feature acoustic music), and annual gatherings of the clan (fiddle contests, music festivals). Most events welcome participation by inexperienced amateurs, and dancing plays an important part in the proceedings because old-time music is first and foremost dance music. Major annual events include fiddle contests at Galax, Virginia, Mount Airy, North Carolina, Union Grove, North Carolina, and the Brandywine folk-music festival held in Fair Hill, Maryland.

Controlled chaos: the Grand Ole Opry in full swing, early 1950s. At center stage, Minnie Pearl fronts a group of musicians, with host Carl Smith ambling to her left. Meanwhile, stage right, the Opry dancers do-si-do, as producer Jack Stapp and announcer Grant Turner work the audience for more applause, stage left.

Tuxedos and gowns at the Ryman, 1954: when Wagnerian opera star Helen Traubel visited the Grand Ole Opry, Nashville investment banker J. C. Bradford, National Life president E. B. Stevenson, and their wives showed up in formal attire more suited to Mozart than Minnie.

The Ryman Auditorium, home of the Opry from 1943 to 1974. The "Mother Church of Country Music" was, in fact, built in 1892 by riverboat owner Tom Ryman as a Christian tabernacle. Five years later, the Confederate Veterans reunion congregated at the Ryman, and a special balcony was added for their meetings. The pews seated 3,574.

ing new skyscrapers of refurbished downtown Nashville, and Tootsie's Orchid Lounge, where once the stars in all their glitter had ducked across the alley for a beer between numbers, hadn't been the same since the move to Opryland and the subsequent death of Tootsie Bess. The Grand Ole Opry could still be heard across the land every Saturday night, and Roy Acuff still opened

362

it with his yo-yo and balancing-fiddle act and "Great Speckled Bird," but the show was little more than a reminder of the past. Most Southerners seemed to agree, now, that the Opry was an amusing sideshow.

In 1987, on the occasion of my father's seventy-sixth birthday, I drove from my place in Atlanta to my parents' house in Birmingham. Five years earlier, when my sister and I were laying on a golden wedding anniversary party for them, I had tracked him down at an air base in Texas, where at seventy-one he was rolling five-hundred-pound surplus aircraft tires up a ramp into the trailer of a semi rig, to remind him of the party ("Tell Mama I'll be there when I get there"). But now, after a stroke, he was only a shadow of himself. The house was going to hell, but he didn't much care; for soon he and Mama would be moving into a new brick "retirement home" nearby. He spent most of his time in the darkened den, hardly knowing whether it was daytime or night, aimlessly watching the Nashville Network on the big color television that dominated the room.

Mama was asleep in the back room, and he was watching the parade of new Nashville stars—only the occasional refrain of a steel guitar over the cultured pop voice of a bewigged and lip-glossed female singer would give anyone cause to call this *country* music—as we visited. He had badgered Country Boy Eddie, a local early-morning country television performer, into acknowl-

Freddie Hart finally found an audience in 1971 after nearly twenty years of trying. Having failed to make much of an impression with records for Capitol, Columbia, Monument, and Kapp, he was down to his last album for Capitol (who had taken a chance on him again) when the track "Easy Loving" caught on in Atlanta and then became his first #1 country single, a pop hit, and the CMA Song of the Year for 1971 and 1972.

Webb Pierce & His Wondering Boys, "Louisiana Hayride," ca. 1951. Webb never enjoyed the wide recognition of a Hank Williams—beyond the pale of country music—but in the years immediately following Hank's death, country fans recognized Webb as the heir apparent to the honky-tonk throne.

Each June, some 20,000 country music fans arrive at Nashville's Tennessee State Fairgrounds to collect autographs, take pictures, and meet the stars at a week-long convention known as Fan Fair, begun in 1972 and sponsored by the CMA. Aiming to please in these early 1980s shots are Randy Owen, Earl Thomas Conley, and Marty Robbins.

Despite its resemblance to a concrete barn, the Country Music Hall of Fame & Museum has a reputation for treating the music with respect. Opened in 1967 and accredited by the American Association of Museums, the Hall of Fame draws 400,000 visitors annually. Underneath the museum are the offices and archives of the Country Music Foundation—operators of the museum and compilers of this book.

edging his birthday on the show that morning, he said. "Mama says Country Boy's tacky, but I don't care," he said. "He's country, and he don't care who knows it."

"Well, it's pretty hard to stay country these days."

"Ain't that the truth. I don't know what got into some of 'em."

"Come on outside," I said. "I got a truck."

"You? Got a truck?"

"Well, sort of."

We went outside so I could show him my new toy. After years of driving patched-up relics, the latest having been a classic '70 Olds Cutlass that ran when the weather was right (I had dubbed it "Detroit" in the belief that it was the last great American automobile), I had finally gone into hock for a trendy little putt-putt All-Purpose Vehicle called a Chevy Blazer. I called it a YupTruck, just right for Young Urban Professionals and Urban Cowboys, with air conditioning, four big tires, a good stereo radio system.

"Ain't much of a truck, is it?" he said.

"Kind of the *hint* of one, anyway. You got to admit that."

"Guess it is." He wasn't interested in driving it. "Radio any good?"

"Great radio. Got AM, FM, four speakers."

"Will it pick up country music?"

"Of course it will. What do you mean, 'Will it pick up country music?' It'll pick up anything that's on the air."

"If it'll pick up country music these days," my father said, "it's about the damnedest radio in America."

366

AT THE OPRY
By Garrison Keillor

The first musician to arrive for the last show at Ryman was Harold Weakley, drummer in the WSM staff band, which backs up singers who don't bring their own. He walked onstage an hour before show time while two stagehands were still setting up: three floor microphones (with guitar mikes attached) up front, and microphones for the piano, the snare drum, the guitar amplifiers, the announcer's podium, and the Four Guys, the staff vocal backup group. While they worked, the guards opened the front doors, and in filed the people who had been waiting for more than an hour already, lined up on the sidewalk in both directions from the entrance. A family took seats in the front row and opened a brown sack full of sandwiches. We all watched the stagehands. And then the backstage crowd arrived and spilled out onto the stage: musicians and their families, people who looked liked musicians but wore street clothes, people who looked like newspaper or magazine writers or public-relations men or Opryland executives, and one man in a plaid sports jacket who, even from the balcony, where I was sitting, looked to be the definite Roy Acuff.

The writers and photographers took up positions at both ends of the stage, behind iron railings that had been erected to keep them from wandering into the middle of the show. A stagehand untied a rope at the hitching rail and lowered the red barn. A man carrying a large suitcase walked through the barn door leading a little girl by the hand. He knelt at the front of the stage,

opened the case, and assembled the legs and pedals of his pedal steel guitar. He was joined by a fiddler and a piano player. From the stage and backstage came the sounds of the first tentative chords and runs, the fiddler tuning to the piano, and the steel man tuning to himself.

Even before the curtain closed and opened and the last show began, the attention that the audience directed at the stage was intense. By the time Bill Anderson and the Po' Boys came on and the first notes came out and Grant Turner raised his arms for applause, it seemed as if the show, which looked small compared with what you'd imagined at home as you lis-

While country music grew up, Tennessee farmers Sam & Kirk McGee kept playing the old favorites that had gotten them their start on the Opry in 1926. By the sixties, with a little help from the folk revival, a whole new generation was eager to hear their lively mix of vintage gospel, blues, and pop tunes.

Billy Grammer, 1960s. The former lead guitarist for Clyde Moody and Jimmy Dean scored a hit with his first release on the Monument label, the million-selling "Gotta Travel On" (1958). It got him a berth on the Opry and staked him to his own guitar company.

tened to the radio, couldn't bear up under this scrutiny, would sink from view under all the passengers onstage. Photographers worked the show from four sides: they squeezed under the railings to get in among the musicians, they came in through the barn door, they crept along the footlights. Television news cameras worked the audience as well, switching on brilliant floodlights to sweep a section of the crowd (filming the reaction of the crowd, which was stunned by the light); and, crowded up to the railings, the stage audience of reporters and important people (who, I found out later, couldn't hear the show very well) peered at the outer audience, which looked at them. Young children had been brought to see this and were told to remember it; all of us knew it was something we'd always remember, yet the harder we looked, the more it slipped away.

I will always remember: a father patiently explaining to a boy about five why the stage was so crowded, why this show was so different; Brother Oswald coming up to the balcony to see the show (people reached for his hand and brought children over to meet him), then going back down to put on bib overalls and play dobro on "Wabash Cannonball," sung by Roy Acuff; musicians coming and going between songs, checking the lineup sheet tacked to the back of the piano, talking and tuning up off-mike, then, when the moment was nigh, getting right in place and playing instantly; Joe Edwards, fiddler and sometimes lead guitarist on the staff band, jumping in on a moment's notice and playing as cleanly as if he'd been rehearsing all afternoon; the Four Guys, huddled around a floor mike behind the piano, improvising vocal harmony; Hank Locklin singing "Goodbye, Good-*bye*, dear ole *Ry*-man." But

every time the floodlights came on, every time a photographer angled right up to a scene and stuck his camera into it, I felt the show receding from memory even as we watched it; and I got up and went downstairs, backstage.

I was walking across the stage, behind the barn, heading for the control booth, when I spotted an old man standing alone at the back wall, out of the traffic. He smiled, and suddenly I knew him from a picture in a country music history book which had showed the same lopsided smile on the face of a young man with a fiddle in 1926. It was Fiddling Sid Harkreader, who had played with Uncle Dave. Mr. Harkreader was glad to talk to me, because he was eager to clear up a point of history to anyone who would listen. "It has been reported in the newspapers," he said dryly, "that I claim to be the first fiddler who ever played on the Grand Ole Opry. That is not true. Uncle Jimmy Thompson was. What I said was—and you take this down—I *said* that I was the first fiddler to play on *WSM*. That was shortly before Judge Hay started the Opry, on November 28, 1925." He looked to make sure I had it right so far. "I was also the first country musician from Tennessee to make a commercial recording in New York. Along with Uncle Dave Macon. That was on July 12, 1924. We made eighteen sides for Vocalion. Uncle Dave and me were also the first country musicians to play here in the Ryman Auditorium. We played here on December 19, 1925."

I asked Mr. Harkreader if it had been fun playing with Uncle Dave.

"Uncle Dave was always fun," he said. "We had a *lot* of fun. I remember him singing, 'When my sugar walks down the street,/ All the little birdies go tweet, tweet, tweet.' "

"The music is a lot louder now than it used to be, isn't it," I remarked, apropos of nothing in particular.

"Sometimes it is *too* loud," Mr. Harkreader said. He was looking for a reporter who had misquoted him on Monday, he told me. "He was standing just as close to me as you are now," he said, "and he goes and writes I was the first fiddler on the Opry. Well, I'm going to put him *straight*."

Take care of yourself, Mr. Harkreader, it was good talking with you.

Before the show, Gordon Evans, a WSM engineer, had invited me to visit the control booth. When I got there, after talking with Mr. Harkreader, Jim Hall, Evans's co-engineer, had just finished a half-hour shift at the controls; Evans sat in a close space between high equipment racks, adjusting volume levels on a desk-sized control board in front of him and watching the stage through a double-pane window to see which musicians would be playing on the next song. I counted thirty sliding volume knobs (called "pots," or potentiometers) that appeared to be in use. For each song, Evans adjusted at least six or seven of them, conferring occasionally with the announcer, Grant Turner or Hairl Hensley, over an intercom, talking over the telephone to an engineer in a sound truck in the alley who was recording the show for Opryland Records, or talking over a second telephone to an engineer at the WSM studios. Out of the monitor above his head came Jim and Jesse McReynolds singing, in high bluegrass harmony, John Prine's song "Paradise" ("When I was a *child*, my *fam*ily would travel/Down to *west*ern Kentucky, where my *par*ents were born"). With his right hand, Evans brought up the volume on the fiddle and bass, turned down the drummer, faded the applause mike, and picked up the telephone to the sound truck; his left hand had

already adjusted two dials on the equipment rack, and now, as he told the recording engineer to expect a steel guitar on the next song, it was waving in time to the music; when the chorus came ("And Daddy won't *take* me back to *Muhl*enburg County,/Down *by* the Green River where *Pa*radise lay"), he was in it, humming bass.

The best place to see the Opry that night, I decided, was in the booth with my eyes shut, leaning against the back wall, the music coming out of the speaker just like radio, that good old AM mono sound. The room smelled of hot radio tubes, and, closing my eyes, I could see the stage as clearly as when I was a kid lying in front of our giant Zenith console. I'd seen a photograph of the Opry stage in a magazine back then, and, believe me, one is all you need. So it was good to let the Opry go out the same way it had first come to me, through the air in the dark. After the show, it was raining hard, and the last Opry crowd to leave Ryman ran.

The first President to visit the Grand Ole Opry, Mr. Richard Nixon, was scheduled to touch down at 6 P.M. Saturday, ride to Opryland, watch a little bit of the first show in the new Opry House, unveil a plaque, speak, play the piano, ride to the airport, and take off shortly after eight. (He kept close to schedule.)

As I awoke, slowly, Saturday morning, it dawned on me that I didn't know where Opryland was, or how to get there, or whether I wanted to go. By midafternoon, I knew that Opryland was eight miles from the hotel by freeway and six by river, either way as practical as the other. There was no bus to Opryland; a rented car could be returned on a Sunday only at the airport, and I was leaving on the Sunday train;

Hank Locklin had reason to hold his guitar firmly: at age ten, he lost his first one when he couldn't make the payments. After middling success on the Decca and 4 Star labels, RCA singles like "Geisha Girl" (1957), "Send Me the Pillow You Dream On" (1958), and "Please Help Me, I'm Falling" (1960) put him on top of the charts—and in the mayor's office in his hometown of McClellan, Florida.

369

President Nixon regales the Opry audience and cast with "God Bless America," "My Wild Irish Rose," and "Happy Birthday" (for his wife), March 16, 1974.

the ultimate in modern electronics, acoustics, lighting, and audiovisual equipment," all described in an Opry brochure. This was nothing but plain prudery, and priggishness, and ordinary low-grade snobbishness on my part; I was ashamed of it, and I intend to correct it, but hadn't the time to correct it right then, and I left the hotel lest somebody call and offer me a ride.

I bought a green transistor radio for $6.95 in a pawnshop across the street from Linebaugh's. After dinner, I walked around looking at the old warehouses on Second Avenue North, also on my list of sights, got back to the hotel around five-thirty, took a long bath, and climbed into bed and turned on my radio. The Saturday-night Opry had just begun, with Roy Acuff singing "Wabash Cannonball," and he followed it with "You Are My Sunshine." Wilma Lee and Stoney Cooper did "Midnight Special." There was a minute of dead air, then long, long applause for the Nixons as they entered and took their seats. The President's appearance at the Opry didn't sit quite right with me, but Roy Drusky, who was the next performer in this alphabetical show, put it right with a heart-felt rendition of "Satisfied Mind":

the route by road was not direct, one would have to hitch two or three rides to get there; and my boots weren't made for walking. My dad's cousin Harold, the only Nashvillian I knew well enough to ask if I could borrow a car, was out of town for the weekend. So it was more than prudishness that kept me from Opryland, but I was relieved not to be able to go and not to have to see the President introduced by Roy Acuff, or to sit in the "specially designed contoured pew-type benches covered in burnt orange colored carpeting," or to lay eyes on this "vibrant and viable" building that "conveys a feeling of intimacy, informality, warmth and charm . . . yet contains

How many times have you heard someone say
"If I had his money I'd do things my way."
But little do they know that it's so hard to find
One rich man in ten with a satisfied mind.

The Crook Brothers, Herman and Lewis, played a dance tune for the President, and Billy Grammer (who had sung at rallies for Wallace for President) and Stonewall Jackson sang. Then the President. Another standing ovation. (The President is considered a patron of country music, because he has invited Merle Haggard, Johnny Cash, and Roy Acuff to perform at White House functions, and earlier in the week I had been surprised to find, in a morning of research, no country songs about him. I found two about Watergate—"At the Watergate the Truth Come Pourin' Out," by Joan Wile and Alan Thomas, and "Senator Sam," by C. Hicks and C. Burt —and several about Governor Wallace, including "Man from Alabama," by Ray King and W. Morris, and "The Solid Man," by Tommy Howard. But "Man from San Clemente" and "President Dick" remain unwritten.) The WSM staff band brought Mr. Nixon onstage with a lilting "Hail to the Chief," played like an Irish fiddle tune, which it probably is. The President's selections on the piano were "Happy Birthday" (for his wife on her birthday), "My Wild Irish Rose," and "God Bless America." "He is a real trouper, as well as one of our greatest Presidents," Mr. Acuff said. Mr. Nixon spoke. He said country music comes from the heart of America, it speaks of family and religion, and it radiates a love of country that is much needed today.

Most of this was done in the name of Mrs. Grissom's Salads and Rudy's Farm Country Sausage. After the President left, on the Goo Goo Cluster candy portion of the Opry, Jim and Jesse McReynolds sang "Freight Train" and Hank Locklin "Danny Boy." Hank Snow gave us "I'm Moving On," his all-time great hit, and Ernest Tubb did his, "Walking the Floor Over You." Dottie West sang "Country Sunshine" for Stephens Workwear, Western Jeans and Slacks, and the Wilburn Brothers did "Arkansas." And then —then—the moment I'd been waiting for. Sam and Kirk McGee from sunny Tennessee played "San Antonio Rose." It was the acoustic mo-

ment of the show, when the skies cleared and the weeping steels were silent and out of the clear blue came a little ole guitar duet. Stunning and simple, and so good after all the *sound* I'd heard that week—the sweetest "Rose" this side of Texas. I turned out the light, turned off the radio, and went to sleep on it.

In the morning, the radio was on the floor, its plastic cover cracked. I believe it would still work, but I will never play it again. It is my only Opry souvenir. Inside it, the McGee brothers are still picking and will forever, Minnie Pearl cackles, the Crooks are dancing, Jim and Jesse ascend into heavenly harmony, and the Great Acuff rides the Wabash Cannonball to the lakes of Minnesota, where the rippling waters fall.

Excerpted from "At the Opry," originally published in the *New Yorker*, May 6, 1974. © 1974 by Garrison Keillor. Reprinted by permission of Garrison Keillor.

President Richard Nixon was feeling the heat from the Watergate scandal on March 16, 1974, when he joined Roy Acuff onstage for the opening-night festivities at the new home of the Opry. "I'll stay here and learn the yo-yo," said Nixon to Acuff, "and you go to Washington and be President."

Contemporary Country Coast to Coast

12

9 TO 5: HOW WILLIE NELSON AND DOLLY PARTON QUALIFIED FOR "LIFESTYLES OF THE RICH AND FAMOUS"

Ken Tucker

People who don't know anything about country music know Dolly Parton and Willie Nelson—such is the way we measure their pop-cultural prominence. Together, the careers of Parton and Nelson describe the movement that country music made into the American mainstream over the course of the last two decades.

The rise of country music performers as mass-media pop stars was a slow but inevitable one. While urban audiences have proved capable of rejecting country music as hick entertainment, the show-biz centers of Los Angeles and New York have long cooperated with the Nashville-based industry to polish country stars' images and music.

By the time Willie Nelson and Dolly Parton came along, there were all sorts of precedents for their multimedia superstardom, but most of these were tied to the urban stereotype of the affable hick. Whether it was Buck Owens and Roy Clark cracking corny jokes and ogling busty Daisy Maes on "Hee Haw" or Minnie Pearl hollering "How-deee!" from an illuminated box on "Hollywood Squares," country performers were, before Nelson and

Dolly Parton offered a pleasing paradox: a curvaceous sex symbol who embodied the conservative virtues of family, marriage, and down-home music.

375

Yesterday, when I was young: Roy Clark, ca. 1960. Once a teenage national banjo champion, Clark developed into that rare picker who delights in the spotlight. Though blessed with only modest vocal abilities, his showman's touch and his flair for comedy earned him early exposure on syndicated country TV shows before he joined "Hee Haw" in 1969. One of country music's most telegenic personalities, he was named CMA Entertainer of the Year for 1973.

Like Willie Nelson, Roger Miller started out writing songs for stars and working as a sideman. His break came in 1964 when quirky records like "Dang Me" and "Chug-a-Lug" became huge hits. Riding the crossover success of "King of the Road" (1965) and an unprecedented eleven Grammy Awards in two years, he took on an NBC variety show in 1966. When his songs dried up, he drifted out of the limelight, only to reappear in 1985 with the songs for the Broadway musical Big River.

Parton, supposed to remain goofy-grinning good guys 'n' gals—Gomer Pyles with pedal-steel accompaniment.

There was a certain amount of country-to-pop crossover in the fifties and early sixties. Patsy Cline, Jim Reeves, Eddy Arnold, and Tennessee Ernie Ford, roughly to descend in quality, all recorded tunes that made the pop charts, but for one reason or another (in these cases, untimely deaths for the first two and simple mediocrity for the second pair), these country stars did not succeed in making country music a mass phenomenon. The music remained a sub-genre of American popular music that stood as far outside the media mainstream as, say, gospel or Dixieland jazz. Its impact was felt primarily in novelty hits that suddenly appeared on pop radio stations, flickered across the consciousness of most Americans, and then disappeared.

By the advent of the sixties, however, the growing big business of country music was exerting more of an influence on popular music at large, and the music's increasing appeal just happened to coincide with the new, pervasive popularity of television. Television, with its unslakable thirst for new programming, was entirely willing to see whether country music would attract viewers beyond its immediate record-buying public. The first notable example of this was "Ozark Jubilee," the country variety show that received network exposure on ABC beginning in 1955.

Hosted by Red Foley, "Ozark Jubilee" set the tone for all country music TV shows: easygoing host, cornball comedians, and, oh yes, country singers. This was as true of the late-1960s "Hee-Haw" ("Laugh-In" set in a barnyard) and "The Glen Campbell Goodtime Hour" (a "Smothers Brothers Show" spin-off without the political edge) as it was of "The Barbara Mandrell Show" (the King Sisters with a twang) a decade and a half later. Johnny Cash hosted his own TV show, one widely esteemed for its adventurous country, rock, folk, and jazz guest line-up; Cash attempted a rock-country-folk synthesis with Bob Dylan on the latter's *Nashville Skyline* album—but for one reason or another either failed to sustain it or never quite achieved the same degree of recognition.

Of the relatively few country music artists who achieved mainstream media success, Dolly Parton and Willie Nelson were the

On camera: Tennessee Ernie Ford hams it up with Minnie Pearl. For ten years (1955–65), Ford hosted country-style variety shows on TV, first with NBC and, later, ABC. He was so well-received, in fact, that during the 1956–57 season, he had two network variety shows going— one Monday through Friday during the day and the other Thursday nights. As Ol' Ern used to say, "Bless your pea pickin' hearts."

Jimmy Dean, late sixties. With help from promoter Connie B. Gay (who discovered the Texan in Washington, D.C.) Dean landed his first CBS-TV series in 1957, while still a virtual unknown. In the wake of million-sellers "Big Bad John" (1961) and "P. T. 109" (1962), Dean picked up a prime-time variety series on ABC in 1963. For three seasons, it was a top-rated show, staking Dean to his present business in eponymous breakfast sausage.

Rowlf the Muppet plays straight man for Jimmy Dean. The producers of Dean's 1963–66 ABC variety show added the Jim Henson puppet in hopes of broadening the program's appeal —and perhaps also to counteract hayseed garb and stone-country guests like George Jones and Ernest Tubb. The Nashville Network resurrected the puppet idea twenty years later with the popular Shotgun Red (created by Steve Hall).

Willie Nelson, probably the only person who will ever record songs by the likes of Lefty Frizzell, Kurt Weill, and the Allman Brothers —and score a Top Twenty country hit with each.

most odd and interesting. Although separated in age by a decade (Nelson was born in 1933, Parton in 1946), they came to national prominence at about the same time, in the mid-1970s. But in every other way, their public images are the opposites of each other—Nelson gruff, serious, and rough-edged; Parton sweet, playful, and smooth. What unites them is that they became mainstream stars by confounding the clichés of country artists who attempt to "cross over."

Parton, like so many other country stars, was a product of grinding poverty; virtually any interview she has given through-out her career is studded with anecdotes about her family's lack of everything from education to toilets. Unlike so many celebrities' tales of up-from-poverty triumph, however, Parton's were never rosy, romanticized public-relations statements; they contained the same hard-headed, common-sense details that, with an artist's decoration, informed her early songwriting successes such as "Joshua," "Coat of Many Colors," "To Daddy," and "In the Good Old Days (When Times Were Bad)."

Country summit: Glen Campbell makes a guest appearance on Johnny Cash's ABC-TV show, 1969. At the time, Campbell hosted his own "Glen Campbell Goodtime Hour" on CBS. A former session guitarist who had worked with the Beach Boys, Jan & Dean, and Rick Nelson, Campbell parlayed hits like "Gentle on My Mind" (1967) and "By the Time I Get to Phoenix" (1968) into TV and then movie semi-stardom.

Bob Dylan and Johnny Cash sing "Girl from the North Country" on the very first broadcast of Cash's ABC-TV series, June 7, 1969. At Cash's insistence, the series featured a wide spectrum of guests—Pete Seeger, Linda Ronstadt, James Taylor, Louis Armstrong, Mahalia Jackson, and the Who in addition to country stars like Merle Haggard and Roy Acuff. Like its host, the show was hip in an easy-going way.

The house that Porter built: "The Porter Wagoner Show," early sixties. Long before anyone had heard of Dolly, Porter Wagoner was a star with the top-rated country music TV show in syndication, year after year. Here's the cast before Dolly arrived: steel guitarist Don Warden, fiddler Mac McGaha, Porter, singer Norma Jean Beasler (whom Dolly replaced), guitarist George McCormick, and banjo player Buck Trent.

Dolly Parton and Porter Wagoner, late sixties. Joining Porter Wagoner's road show and syndicated television series in 1967 placed Dolly in the spotlight, where she thrived. Together, the two collected CMA duet honors three times (1968, 1970, 1971). Eventually chafing under Porter's tight rein, Dolly left his show in 1974, although he continued to produce her records until 1976.

While she never made her early years sound agonizing, there can be little doubt that escaping from home was a major reason Parton was singing on Cas Walker's Knoxville television variety show by the time she was only ten years old. Five years later, she'd performed on the Grand Ole Opry. She was also recording

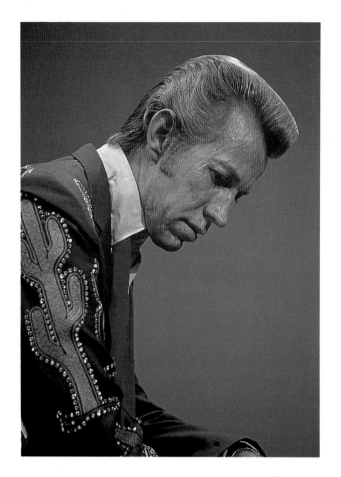

Satisfied mind: Porter Wagoner, 1960s. Though some may have dismissed his fiddle-and-steel sound, sequined costumes, and folksy mannerisms as antiquated, Porter Wagoner never sweated it. He knew his audience. By 1970 his syndicated TV show was airing in 100 cities, with 4 million fans watching every week.

Stand by your man: George Jones & Tammy Wynette, 1970s. Country's most-watched couple of the seventies married in 1969 and scored their first duet hit two years later. In song, they were a country fan's dream duo, but their life together was, by all accounts, a nightmare. Within two years of their #1 hit "We're Gonna Hold On" (1973), they had divorced.

during this time, but Parton first came to prominence as the singing partner of Porter Wagoner, the epitome of the sort of country music star she would soon come to supplant.

By the time Parton replaced his former partner, Norma Jean, Wagoner was a twenty-year veteran of country music, as well known for his blindingly gaudy Nudie suits and short temper as for his vinegary voice and old-fashioned country singing style. Porter and Dolly, as they were invariably known to their fans, were one of those mismatched pairs-made-in-heaven, a surly beanpole and a plump angel who made beautiful music together. They recorded a series of duets in the early seventies that provided Wagoner with his biggest commercial successes. And don't think Parton didn't know it.

"The years I worked with Porter, I worked for $300 a night," she told *Playboy* magazine. "Which is one reason I needed to get out on my own: I needed to make more money." Realizing that both her voice and her songwriting were invaluable ingredients in the Porter-and-Dolly success, Parton decided to take a chance and see whether the public would accept Dolly-as-Dolly. She commenced a solo career in 1974 and never looked back.

Now, there is no doubt that the major reason non-country fans initially took an interest in Parton was the outer package—"Peo-

ple will always talk and make jokes about my bosom," was the way she once put it with typical forthrightness. This, combined with her Frederick's of Hollywood high heels ("It's the only place I can find shoes high enough and sexy enough to suit me") and cartoonish hairpieces ("You'd be amazed how expensive it is to make a wig look this cheap"), transformed Parton into the country version of Mae West, and made her a highly telegenic figure amid the comparatively sedate female singers that surrounded her in 1970s country music.

But, while enjoying the sight of Parton as much as the next couch potato did, the knowledgeable country-music fan was aware that underneath that prodigious bust was the soul of a gifted songwriter. Like Willie Nelson, her closest parallel in the artist-turned-superstar category, Parton had firmly established herself as a composer able to create vivid, highly original songs. It was by no means unprecedented for women to write the sort of precisely detailed songs of rural life that Parton did, but hers were exceptionally strong examples of the genre—songs rooted in first-hand working-class experience, such as "In The Good Old Days (When Times Were Bad)" and "To Daddy." Moreover, it was a revelation to hear them sung in Parton's deceptively fragile, airy soprano voice. It was also entirely in keeping with the perky Parton persona to pass off such songwriting skill as nothing much: "I've written more than most writers do," she told one interviewer. "It's just so easy. I've got hundreds and

THE LAST LAUGH

You've got to hand it to Buck Owens, Roy Clark, and the gang; they smelled a winner amid all those barnyard jokes and corny cartoon characters. After twenty years, "Hee Haw" is still going strong, while the show that inspired it, "Rowan & Martin's Laugh-In," is gone with the trends.

"Hee Haw" premiered a week after "The Johnny Cash Show," in June 1969. Billed as country music's answer to "Rowan & Martin's Laugh-In," it began as CBS's summer replacement for the "Smothers Brothers Comedy Hour" on Sunday nights and became a weekly fixture in December 1969. With a cast of thirty regulars, "Hee Haw" brought to the screen the best of country music and the corniest of humor. The show ranked sixteenth in the Nielsen ratings when CBS purged it in July 1971 along with such other rural comedies as "The Beverly Hillbillies" and "Green Acres." "Hee Haw" refused to go away quietly, however. The show went into syndication the following fall and before long appeared on more stations than it had during its CBS days. By 1977, "Hee Haw" ranked as the number one non-network television program, and today its popularity continues. Despite the retirement of longtime

co-host Buck Owens in 1986, "Hee Haw" appears headed for a third decade.

But no one could have foreseen such success in the summer of 1969. Here's what Time (August 8, 1969) had to say about "Hee Haw":

The Corn Is Still Green

When the cast of the new CBS summer series, "Hee Haw"—a hillbilly version of "Laugh-In"—arrived at the train station to start taping in Nashville last May, the performers were paraded ceremoniously through town atop mule-drawn hay wagons. "We felt like such goddam fools riding down the main streets," recalls co-producer Frank Peppiatt. "We thought there would be throngs to meet us, but we ended up waving to each other."

If the response to "Hee Haw" seemed ho-hum in Nashville—the holy see of Grand Ole Opry and country show biz—then it seemed likely that the cast would be greeted anywhere else in America by bags of chicken feathers and cauldrons of tar. In a TV summer season stolen by [lunar-landing astronauts Neil] Armstrong and [Buzz] Aldrin, the show's only acknowledgement of the moon was the crescent-shaped opening in its prime prop—an outhouse. Had the public outgrown that sort of thing? And would TV viewers be turned off by the program's shameless plagiarism of their No. 1 favorite, "Laugh-In"?

The answer to both questions was no. In Nielsen audience figures published last week, "Hee Haw" finished first with a Sunday night average of 27.3 million viewers.

Candy Farmer. Like so much of TV, "Hee Haw" is a show that nobody likes—except the viewers. Newspaper critics reacted as if it were good reason to pull the plug on rural electrification. CBS, with unaccustomed humor, is running promotion spots replaying the show's most outrageous vignettes, with a kicker: "The critics are unanimous about 'Hee Haw'—but watch anyway!"

What the public is watching is gags lifted from tales as old as the "Arkansas Traveller" (ca. 1860) but spliced together with production as new as "Laugh-In." On "Hee Haw," the graffiti adorn not bikini-clad boogaloo dancers but Burma-Shave signs, and the routines occur not at cocktail parties but in cornfields. That is their natural habitat. One of the company announces, "I'm a farmer in a candy factory." "Whaddaya do?" asks a chorus of rural voices. "I milk chocolate." In another rib cracker, the straight man wonders: "Hey, Junior, how come I saw you eating with a knife at supper?" Junior: "My fork leaked." After the worst lines—not that any of them are good—an off-stage hand socks it to the culprit with a rubber chicken. Or an animated donkey pops up and chortles: "Wouldn't that sop your gravy?" To the relief of CBS, "Hee Haw," which has taken over the "Smothers Brothers'" time slot, never gets more controversial than: "What's the difference between a horse race and a political race?" "In a horse race, they use the whole horse."

Many viewers presumably tune in not for the comedy but for the country-and-western songs that fill up nearly one-third of "Hee Haw's" air time. There are top-name guests, and the hosts themselves are no slouches. Roy Clark—the one who looks like a heftier Sander Vanocur —was twice the national banjo champion. Guitarist-composer Buck Owens—the cross between Andy Griffith and George Segal—is a leading country recording artist.

Extraordinary Nielsen. Emerging as the real stars of "Hee Haw" are some of the previously unknown supporting players, who are less polished rustics. Stringbean, the emaciated chap who appears with the puppet crow on his shoulder, can barely read, according to friends, and has to be taught lines by his wife. Junior Samples, the fat man (275 lbs.), professed to have nothing to wear but his "Sunday overalls" at a CBS celebration party. Introduced to a key network executive—"Junior, this is the vice president"—Junior ingenuously responded: "Hello, Mr. Agnew."

The CBS party was a bit uncomfortable for Junior, but despite "The trouble with some of the words I'd never heered before," he says, "I'd like to do it again some time." Undoubtedly, he will get the chance. As a summer substitute, "Hee Haw" will go off the air Sept. 7, but its extraordinary Nielsen rating makes the show a likely CBS replacement for January dropouts. Apparently, many American viewers are fed up with the "crisis of the cities" programming that fills the TV news, and are seeking solace in the eternal verities—and inanities —of the country.

Like Roy Orbison, for whom he once worked as a sideman, Bobby Goldsboro has been associated with both pop and country music. After a few minor pop hits in the early sixties, he acquired the Midas touch in country with sentimental favorites like "Honey" (1968), "Watching Scotty Grow" (1971), and "And I Love You So" (1971).

hundreds of songs. . . . It's like, most people will sit down and smoke a pipe, but I just sit down and pick up a piece of paper. . . ."

Parton has always made much of the bonds of family life—most obviously, she toured for the early years of her solo career with the Traveling Family Band, which did indeed consist of numerous Partons. In this, too, she was like Willie Nelson, whose own traveling "family" included his sister Bobbie Lee. The invocation of family is an emotional button that country stars like to push—it seems to produce immediate sympathy among tradition-minded fans.

This was the pleasing paradox of Dolly Parton. On the one hand, she offered herself as a curvaceous cartoon, a genially exaggerated sex symbol; on the other, she embodied strong conservative virtues of family, marriage (Parton invariably took pains to portray her own, to construction contractor Carl Dean, as a strong one), and old-fashioned country music.

Much of this changed when Parton recorded "Here You Come Again" in 1977 and made her initial moves toward a mainstream show-business career. "Here You Come Again," written by veteran New York pop songwriters Barry Mann and Cynthia Weill, became a #3 pop hit and drew a line across Parton's career. She may have been trying to allay her old fans' fears in recording this sort of pop—"I'm not leaving country; I'm taking it with me," she said in numerous interviews during this time. To be precise, where she was "taking it" was to the savvy West Coast manage-

386

During the fifties and sixties, smooth-singing Jim Ed Brown recorded mostly with his sisters Bonnie and Maxine. He began charting as a solo singer in 1965, but "Pop a Top" (1967) was his only substantial hit for quite some time. Teaming with Helen Cornelius rejuvenated his career in the mid seventies, and the #1 "I Don't Want to Have to Marry You" landed them 1977's CMA Vocal Duo of the Year award.

Go figure: Dolly Parton, 1975. Two years after this photo, the CMA's Female Vocalist of the Year for 1975 and 1976 made her stretch for the pop charts and wider appeal. By the end of 1978, she had her first pop hit and the best-known set of curves since Marilyn Monroe.

ment firm of Katz, Gallin and Morey, which steered her toward MOR pop and used its influence to line up guest shots on TV talk and variety shows. Thus it was that Parton became more than a vaguely smutty joke in Johnny Carson's monologue—she became a flesh-and-blood joker seated at Johnny's right hand.

In a way, Parton's transition from country to pop was the opposite of a prevailing trend, the pop-to-country moves of singers such as Olivia Newton-John and John Denver. Before Parton's pop move took effect, folkie Denver had been crowing, "Thank God, I'm a Country Boy" and pining imploringly, "Take Me Home, Country Roads." Even more shamelessly, Australian Newton-John was putting bouncy pop-country ditties like "Let Me Be There" and "If You Love Me (Let Me Know)" at the top of the charts. The sort of country purveyed by Denver and Newton-John was an imported last-gasp version of the countrypolitan, Nashville Sound movement that by the early seventies was pretty much spent as an aggressive commercial strategy. Nevertheless, while hardcore country pros grumbled with understandable bitterness, the Nashville establishment showered Newton-John and Denver—or, more precisely, their big sales

"AND THE WINNER IS . . ."

By 1968 the country music industry felt it finally had come far enough uptown to to be taken seriously by folks in the big city. Smooth-singing Glen Campbell had been making regular appearances on the pop charts and, beginning that summer, introduced himself to prime-time viewers through his stint hosting "The Summer Smothers Brothers Show"—the prelude to "The Glen Campbell Goodtime Hour." Bobbie Gentry's "Ode to Billie Joe" had topped the pop charts the previous year, and "Harper Valley PTA," sung by Jeannie C. Riley, climbed to #1 that September. The time was right for the Country Music Association to gain some valuable exposure for country.

The vehicle was the CMA Awards Show, which made its television debut on NBC's "Kraft Music Hall," November 20, 1968, at 9 P.M. (Eastern). (The first CMA Awards presentation, held in 1967, was not televised.) Taped at the Grand Ole Opry's Ryman Auditorium on October 18, the show was hosted by Roy Rogers and Dale Evans, who were sure to be familiar faces to most of middle America. Indeed, the broadcast fared well in the Nielsen ratings, ranking thirtieth among programs aired that week. Besides the CMA and sponsor Kraft Foods, the evening's biggest winners were Glen Campbell (Male Vocalist, Entertainer of the Year), Tammy Wynette (Female Vocalist), and Porter Wagoner & Dolly Parton (Vocal Group, Vocal Duo).

What follows is the first few pages of the script for that first televised award show. Although brief, this segment of stage directions, cues, and dialogue reveals much about how the CMA intended country music to be portrayed.

Thank God I'm a Country Boy: Chet Atkins beholds what the Nashville Sound hath wrought as pop-folk singer John Denver clasps one of his CMA awards for Song ("Back Home Again") and Entertainer of the Year, 1975.

[NBC] PEACOCK [LOGO]/OPENING TITLES & BILLBOARD

(*FILM*: COLOR PEACOCK)

(*MUSIC*: KRAFT THEME)

(OPEN ON EXTREME WIDE SHOT, OPRY INTERIOR; SUPER-[IMPOSE] MUSIC HALL TITLES)

ED HERLIHY: (V[oice] O[ver])
From the home of the world-renowned "Grand Ole Opry" in Nashville, Tennessee . . . the Kraft Music Hall presents—the second annual Country Music Awards!

(SUPER NAME CRAWL)

With guest stars, Roy Acuff . . .
Chet Atkins . . .
Pat Boone . . .
Glen Campbell . . .
Johnny Cash . . .
Jimmy Dean . . .
Bobby Goldsboro . . .
Roger Miller . . .
Jeannie C. Riley . . .
Tex Ritter . . .
And—Tammy Wynette!

(BEAT)

And starring your hosts—the king and queen of the West—Roy Rogers and Dale Evans!

(SUPER KRAFT LOGO)

All brought to you by Kraft . . . Kraft for good food and good food ideas.

(*INTO*: COMMERCIAL #1)

ROY & DALE OPENING MEDLEY INTRO—ED HERLIHY

(OPEN W/ WIDE SHOT, OPRY STAGE)

(*MUSIC*: TYMPS [tympani roll])

ED HERLIHY: (VO)
And now, your hosts for the evening, Roy Rogers and Dale Evans!

(ROY AND DALE ENTER TO AP-PLAUSE AND TYMPS; SEGUE TO OPENING MEDLEY)

ROY AND DALE OPENING TALK

(ON APPLAUSE AT CONCLUSION OF MEDLEY, ROY AND DALE MOVE TO "HOME BASE" PODIUM)

ROY:
Thank you very much. It's a great honor to be here in Nashville tonight as the country music industry honors its brightest stars.

DALE:
And what a thrill it is to be standing here on the Grand Ole Opry stage. Just think, Roy, the greats from Patsy Cline to Hank Williams . . . and from Eddy Arnold to Minnie Pearl . . . have been heard, from this stage, by millions of listeners.

ROY:
And tonight, Dale, this old stage will be the setting for the Second Annual Country Music Awards. There are ten award categories, and earlier this year the artists, writers, producers, broadcasters, and executives who make up the Country Music Association . . . received a ballot with more than five hundred names. After that first-round voting the list of nominees was reduced to fifty—five in each category. Then, there was another vote to select tonight's winners.

DALE:
All of the balloting was supervised by the accounting firm of Price Water-house and Company, and the names of the winners are in sealed envelopes.

(PRICE WATERHOUSE REPRESEN-TATIVES ON STAGE WITH ALL TEN ENVELOPES; GOES TO "AWARDS PODIUM"—AND PLACES *ALL* THE ENVELOPES IN HOLDER ON PODIUM)

Those ten envelopes are being placed now on the awards podium by Mr. Char-lie Walker of Price Waterhouse. And, until our presenters open them, only the Price Waterhouse representatives know the names of the winners.

ROY:
And those fellows really know how to keep a secret. Why, for years now they've kept it a secret from Lassie that she's a boy.

DALE:
And I guess there was no way to keep that pun a secret.

ROY:
Nope, none. And before the evening is out, so will another big secret.

DALE:
What's that?

ROY:
The name of the newest member of the Country Music Hall of Fame.

DALE:
Well, Roy, let's end some of the tension and get to the first award. To present it is a record company executive, and a truly outstanding guitarist. Here is Mr. Nashville himself—Chet Atkins!

Within days of signing to Capitol Records, Bobbie Gentry recorded her "Ode to Billy Joe." The sultry, mysterious tale of a backwoods suicide topped both the pop and country charts during the summer of 1967, making an instant star of the Mississippi girl who had studied philosophy at UCLA and music theory at the Los Angeles Conservatory. After a couple of duet hits with Glen Campbell, she married rich and left the business.

Crystal Gayle, ca. 1970. That the CMA voted the torchy singer of "Don't It Make My Brown Eyes Blue" the Female Vocalist of the Year for 1977 and 1978 speaks volumes about country music in the late seventies. To hear her or to look at her, few would guess that she's Loretta Lynn's youngest sister, Brenda Gail Webb. Loretta, in fact, suggested the name change, taking "Crystal" from the Krystal fast-food chain.

figures—with numerous country awards and encouraged these cheerful carpetbaggers to serve as the most visible symbols of new, "young" country music.

Dolly Parton's abandonment of country music—for despite her sincere protestations, that is what it was—robbed the genre of its most colorful female star, and the story of women in 1970s country music is an aimless, not very thrilling tale. During this decade, hits were scored by new faces as various as Crystal Gayle, Donna Fargo, Tanya Tucker, and Janie Fricke; established pros such as Tammy Wynette, Loretta Lynn, and Lynn Anderson continued to work the same territory that had made them stars the decade before. In this atmosphere, an experienced performer like Barbara Mandrell was able to invent a canny synthesis of both musical styles and performing personae; Mandrell was at once middle-of-the-road authentic ("I Was Country When Country Wasn't Cool," for example, was probably the least country-sounding hit ever to invoke the word "country" in its title) and attempted to be sexy in the perky way that was acceptable to the sternest country fan.

Tanya Tucker grew up in the spotlight, notching her first Top Ten, "Delta Dawn" (1972), at age thirteen. For better or for worse, her rough-and-ready voice and racy material—like "Would You Lay with Me (in a Field of Stone)"—saddled her almost from the beginning with a reputation as a precocious "bad girl." This shot dates from the late seventies, when Tanya flirted briefly with rock before turning back to mainstream country.

Barbara Mandrell was made for TV: she looks like a million bucks, plays a passel of instruments, sings music that fits comfortably between country and pop, dances like a born hoofer, and reads cue cards with utter sincerity.

Movie stars: Jane Fonda, Lily Tomlin, and Dolly Parton, 1980. Fans and critics alike had high hopes for Dolly's movie career after her spunky debut in 9 to 5. The film proved a smashing success at the box office, while Dolly's title song topped both the pop and country charts—the biggest hit she's ever had. Unfortunately, as of mid 1988, her comic talent has been obscured in a series of lackluster pictures.

The Statler Brothers: Don Reid, Harold Reid, Phil Balsley, and Lew DeWitt, ca. 1965. These four chums from Staunton, Virginia, endeared themselves to country music's silent majority, singing good-humored, nostalgic material well-suited to their gospel quartet roots. They took their group name from Statler tissues, which gives some idea of their sense of humor. In 1982, Lew DeWitt left the group, replaced by Jimmy Fortune.

One reason it was even a possibility for Dolly Parton to pursue a movie career was that there had occurred over the course of the sixties and early seventies a gradual change in the mass media's attitude toward the music. This was particularly true in the movie industry. The movies had always treated country music as low-comedy, B-grade, rube stuff; Marty Robbins warbling while ramming a stock car into a bale of hay was practically New Wave sophistication compared to the slapstick scenarios to which country music was submitted in most country-music movies.

In 1975, *Nashville*, directed by Robert Altman, offered something new: the chance for country music to be used as a setting for a serio-comic plot that tried to avoid condescending to its subject. "Tried" is the important word here, for as sincere as he seemed to be, Altman had very little feeling for the music—his selection of folkie-manqué Keith Carradine to purvey well-wrought country was patently absurd. But the film's portrayal of an earnest, neurotic female country star on the verge of a breakdown was more interesting. This thinly disguised composite of Loretta Lynn and/or Tammy Wynette and/or You-Name-It, as played by singer-actress Ronee Blakely, was complex, unsparing, and sympathetic; it revealed the dark side of country stardom that the music industry itself rarely allowed for public consumption, and which only Daryl Duke's *Payday* (1973), featuring Rip Torn in a magnificent portrayal of an out-of-control Hank Williams disciple, had heretofore suggested on the screen.

Parton, to be sure, wasn't out to present a searingly realistic picture of the country music life to her fans; she wanted, in the jargon of the time, to stretch herself, to "grow" as an artist. She wanted to make *9 to 5*.

9 to 5 (1980) placed Parton alongside Lily Tomlin and Jane Fonda in a hit comedy that traded on the singer's va-va-voom appearance and sweet demeanor to create a beguiling screen persona. As uneven as the movie was, it offered a perfect translation of Parton's charm to the screen; the title song, which Parton sang and wrote, was a silly ditty that nonetheless went to #1 on the pop charts and probably confirmed to Parton that she'd made the right move in leaving country music behind.

The two movies Parton made after this, *The Best Little Whorehouse in Texas* and *Rhinestone*, were sorry affairs aesthetically. *Whorehouse*, however, turned a handsome profit—primarily, many film-industry observers said, because of Parton's amusing performance, not co-star Burt Reynolds's sodden one.

Willie Nelson attracted attention at the beginning of his career for the same thing Parton had: his songwriting. Born in Abbot,

Jerry Reed strikes a James Dean pose back when nobody knew he could act, ca. 1962. Now a bonafide movie star, Jerry Reed Hubbard earned his keep during the sixties as a Nashville session guitarist and songwriter. The author of Elvis Presley's "U.S. Male" and "Guitar Man" later recorded hits of his own—"Amos Moses" (1970) and "When You're Hot, You're Hot" (1971)—that showed off his fast-talking, fast-picking theatrical sense of style.

Texas, raised by his grandparents, he'd planned to become a college graduate and farmer before an early marriage and child forced him into a succession of salesman jobs, hawking everything from Bibles to vacuum cleaners while writing songs on the side. The vacuum cleaners didn't seem to inspire him very much, but he got an awfully good song out of the Good Book, "Family Bible." Working as the bass guitarist for Ray Price's

Cherokee Cowboys in the early sixties, Nelson established himself as a presence in Nashville with such compositions as "Crazy" (a hit for Patsy Cline), "Hello, Walls" (Faron Young), "Night Life" (Ray Price), and "Funny How Time Slips Away" (Billy Walker). In the mid-sixties, Nelson launched a solo performing career that met with moderate success, but he felt hemmed in by the formal show-business attitudes of the country industry and developed interests in many of the same things that were preoccupying sixties' youth, from Kahlil Gibran to dope.

Moving back to Texas in the early seventies, Nelson started hanging out with a motley collection of musicians, rockers as well as country players, and began performing in front of younger, more rock-oriented audiences than he'd encountered during his Nashville stay. There was already a significant rock audience for tradition-minded country music, as the country and bluegrass-influenced work of Gram Parsons and the Byrds had proven in the late sixties.

With his freshly grown long hair and increasingly rowdy following, Nelson had positioned himself as an outsider in the country-music world, with unusual ambitions to match. In 1974, he recorded *Phases and Stages*, one of the first concept albums in country music, its songs combining to tell a reasonably coherent story over the course of the record. He followed it up with another sprawling story, *Red Headed Stranger* (1975), which yielded his first #1 country single, "Blue Eyes Crying in the Rain." The album went all the way to #1 on the country charts and, significantly, cracked the pop-music Top Forty. Hot on its heels was one of those pop-culture coincidences that irrevocably alters an artist's career. RCA Records released *Wanted! The Outlaws*, a compilation of old tracks the company had lying around by Nelson, Waylon Jennings, Tompall Glaser, and Jessi Colter. Credit the marketing more than the material, which was, for the most part, pretty mediocre: the term "Outlaws" suddenly became the label of choice for the media when discussing the long-haired, rough-around-the-edges presentation of Nelson and Jennings—who, in turn, were soon referred to by their devoted following in the quickly slurred phrase "Willie-and-Waylon."

Once *Wanted! The Outlaws* sold a million copies, suddenly everyone, especially the Nashville establishment, began discussing the Outlaw Movement and What It All Meant. Before you knew it, self-styled disreputable types like David Allan Coe and Billy Joe Shaver had been signed to brand-new recording contracts to pursue their eccentricities unhindered, and heretofore mannerly country performers rushed to prove their hip credentials.

Willie Nelson, ca. 1966. Before he grew his hair long and donned jeans and sneakers, the one-time bass player for Ray Price looked like most Nashville songwriters and sidemen. Except, of course, when he wore something as faddish as this Nehru jacket, which seems to suit him about as well as the Nashville Sound did.

THE TOP FIFTY COUNTRY CROSSOVERS

Country music has never existed in a musical vacuum, but, from its beginnings, has been influenced by and has influenced other music. The term *crossover* is usually used to describe a country recording that hits big in the wider pop market, or else to describe a pop record that scores some success with a country audience. Examples of the latter include Dorothy Shays's "Feudin' and Fighting" (1947), Patti Page's "Tennessee Waltz" (1951), or Burl Ives's "A Little Bitty Tear" (1962).

The penetration of country into broader markets has actually been far more common and can probably be traced as far back as Vernon Dalhart's "The Prisoner's Song"/"The Wreck of the Old 97," a 1924 Victor release that clearly reached a wide national audience. Jimmie Rodgers's best sellers, Gene Autry's "That Silver Haired Daddy of Mine," Jimmie Davis's "Nobody's Darling but Mine" and "You Are My Sunshine," and Bob Wills's "New San Antonio Rose" likewise achieved early national popularity.

In 1940, *Billboard* magazine began tracking the nation's top popular recordings week by week, and since then it's been easier to verify which country records have crossed over. What follows is a list of fifty of the most popular country discs to hit the pop charts and the pop positions they attained.

Sign of the times: the Bellamy Brothers. Having written Jim Stafford's million-selling crossover hit "Spiders and Snakes" (1974), David Bellamy (right) and brother Howard got their own shot at the country and pop charts with "Let Your Love Flow" in 1976. Here they appear on the syndicated TV show "Pop Goes the Country"—an apt description for their subsequent country hits like "Lovers Live Longer" and "Old Hippie."

Pistol Packin' Mama	Al Dexter	#1	1943
Smoke! Smoke! Smoke! (That Cigarette)	Tex Williams	#1	1947
Chattanoogie Shoeshine Boy	Red Foley	#1	1950
Slow Poke	Pee Wee King	#3	1951
Sixteen Tons	Tennessee Ernie Ford	#1	1955
Young Love	Sonny James	#1	1956
A White Sport Coat	Marty Robbins	#2	1957
Gone	Ferlin Husky	#4	1957
El Paso	Marty Robbins	#1	1959
The Battle of New Orleans	Johnny Horton	#1	1959
He'll Have to Go	Jim Reeves	#2	1959
Waterloo	Stonewall Jackson	#4	1959
Gotta Travel On	Billy Grammer	#4	1959
Last Date	Floyd Cramer	#2	1960
Don't Worry	Marty Robbins	#3	1961
On the Rebound	Floyd Cramer	#4	1961
Walk on By	Leroy Van Dyke	#5	1961
The End of the World	Skeeter Davis	#2	1963
King of the Road	Roger Miller	#4	1965
Ballad of the Green Berets	Ssgt. Barry Sadler	#1	1966
Flowers on the Wall	Statler Brothers	#4	1966
Ode to Billie Joe	Bobbie Gentry	#1	1967
Harper Valley P.T.A.	Jeannie C. Riley	#1	1968
Honey	Bobby Goldsboro	#1	1968
Wichita Lineman	Glen Campbell	#3	1968
A Boy Named Sue	Johnny Cash	#2	1969
Galveston	Glen Campbell	#4	1969
Rose Garden	Lynn Anderson	#3	1970
Funny Face	Donna Fargo	#5	1972
The Most Beautiful Girl	Charlie Rich	#1	1973
Dueling Banjos	Eric Weissberg & Steve Mandell	#2	1973
The Streak	Ray Stevens	#1	1974
Before the Next Teardrop Falls	Freddy Fender	#1	1975
Rhinestone Cowboy	Glen Campbell	#1	1975
Convoy	C. W. McCall	#1	1976
Let Your Love Flow	Bellamy Brothers	#1	1976
Southern Nights	Glen Campbell	#1	1977
Don't It Make My Brown Eyes Blue	Crystal Gayle	#2	1977
Here You Come Again	Dolly Parton	#3	1977
You Needed Me	Anne Murray	#1	1978
She Believes in Me	Kenny Rogers	#5	1979
9 to 5	Dolly Parton	#1	1980
Coward of the County	Kenny Rogers	#3	1980
Looking for Love	Johnny Lee	#5	1980
Drivin' My Life Away	Eddie Rabbitt	#5	1980
I Love a Rainy Night	Eddie Rabbitt	#1	1981
Step by Step	Eddie Rabbitt	#5	1981
There's No Gettin' Over Me	Ronnie Milsap	#5	1981
Islands in the Stream	Dolly Parton & Kenny Rogers	#1	1983
To All the Girls I've Loved Before	Willie Nelson & Julio Iglesias	#5	1984

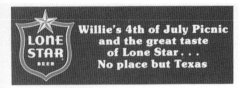

Agriculture meets counter-culture: beginning in 1972, Willie Nelson's Fourth of July picnics united farmers and freaks and folks of widely disparate habits and tastes.

Night life: after moving to Austin in 1970, Willie Nelson was no longer singing the honky-tonk blues. There, playing to young fans of folk and country-rock, he stumbled upon the audience he had been searching for during the preceding decade.

"I been stutterin'. . . all my life—thirty years p-p-p-profession-ally." Mel Tillis was doing pretty well as a Nashville songwriter, turning out hits like "Detroit City" for Bobby Bare and "Ruby, Don't Take Your Love to Town" for Kenny Rogers. But he didn't become a household name until he made his stutter a comic trademark. During the seventies, the CMA's 1976 Entertainer of the Year had twenty-six Top Ten country records.

The Outlaws phenomenon yielded two interesting results, one within the country industry and one without. The commercial triumph of Willie-and-Waylon made the veteran makers of hard-core country music cool again—what, for example, were Merle Haggard and George Jones if not the grandaddies of the Outlaws? When Nelson recorded a 1977 tribute album to Lefty Frizzell (*To Lefty From Willie*), he was legitimizing once more the stripped-down honky-tonk music that had been rejected by the Nashville Sound movement a decade earlier.

To the mass audience outside of country music, this Outlaw stuff was novel indeed. Here, for the first time in many people's

Who was country's top singles artist of 1980–81? Eddie Rabbitt could point to three singles in the pop Top Five during that period —"Drivin' My Life Away," "I Love a Rainy Night," and "Step by Step." Before he became a headliner, this Brooklyn-born son of Irish immigrants had written "Kentucky Rain" for Elvis Presley and "Pure Love" for Ronnie Milsap.

Robert Redford as Sonny Steele and Willie Nelson as his manager, Wendell, in The Electric Horseman *(1979). Redford once described his movie-making experience with the Buddha of country music as "comfortable . . . like working with your favorite shoe."*

memory, were country musicians who weren't acting like affable rubes, who were making music that went beyond the drinkin' and cheatin' clichés that pop audiences assumed comprised the entirety of country music. Here, in short, were country stars who behaved like rock stars, but who were making music that was more tuneful, more rooted in tradition than your average heavy-metal howler. The result was a mystique that the pop audience could become interested in, and suddenly the readers of main-stream mags like *People* wanted to hear those tales of Waylon's substance-abuse battles and rocky-but-right marriage to Jessi. For perhaps the first time in the genre's history, country music became common knowledge in pop-culture circles.

As in any other popular genre, however, this kind of thing goes in waves, and Nelson's sort of Outlaw country music took a beating in the wake of the *Urban Cowboy* phenomenon that com-menced in 1980. The only pop trend ever to be centered around a mechanical bull, *Urban Cowboy* tied together a mainstream movie star (John Travolta, made a star by *Saturday Night Fever* and eager to shed his disco image), a novelty (the bull), and a nightclub (Gilley's, the Texas tourist trap). Unaccountably, it worked—the movie was a hit, perhaps more for Debra Winger's lubricious ride on the bull than for the plot. For the country music industry, however, it proved there was life in compro-mised pop-country after all: Johnny Lee's "Lookin' For Love" topped the country music charts and surged up to #5 on the pop charts, an amazing feat for so studiously trivial a song. The soundtrack album to *Urban Cowboy*, padded out with perfor-

Allen Reynolds, Susan Taylor, and Don Williams visit the record-pressing plant to see Williams's debut country single, "Don't You Believe," June 1972. This one wasn't a hit, but the next one, "The Shelter of Your Eyes," broke into the country Top Twenty. With Reynolds as producer, Williams developed a relaxed, mellow style that accounted for thirteen #1s during the next ten years. (Taylor had been a member with Williams in a folk trio, the Pozo-Seco Singers.)

Freddy Fender cradles plaques commemorating the #1 status of "Before the Next Teardrop Falls" and "Wasted Days and Wasted Nights," 1975. Country's hottest newcomer that year was born Baldemar Huerta, the son of migrant Texas farmers. After struggling as an r&b singer, he had three country #1s in a row ("Secret Love" was the third). The hit formula of plaintively singing alternating verses of English and Spanish lyrics never worked quite so well for him again.

Opposite, bottom
Comedian Jerry Clower welcomes B. J. Thomas to the Opry stage, ca. 1981. The million-selling "Raindrops Keep Fallin' on My Head" (1969) remains Thomas's signature song; like several pop stars, however, he revived a flagging career during the seventies by turning to country music. Which, in turn, gave him a chance to rub shoulders with the likes of Clower, a former Mississippi fertilizer salesman.

Top left
The Gatlin Brothers: Steve, Larry, and Rudy, early eighties. Signed as a songwriter by Dottie West while still in college, Larry Gatlin put aside short stories to work on his new career. A recording contract with Monument Records soon followed. Backed by his brothers' harmonies, Gatlin's hits include "Broken Lady" (1976), "I Just Wish You Were Someone I Love" (1977), and "All the Gold in California" (1979).

Top right
BMI's Frances Preston and Joe Moscheo present Mac Davis with one of the many BMI citations his songs have earned for extensive radio and TV airplay, 1981. Before he became Hollywood's idea of a country star, Davis wrote songs to retire on—"In the Ghetto" for Elvis Presley, "Watching Scotty Grow" for Bobby Goldsboro, plus "I Believe in Music" (1971) and "Baby, Don't Get Hooked on Me" (1972) for himself.

mances by non-country artists such as the Eagles and Bonnie Raitt, sold millions of copies.

Willie Nelson had his own movie plans. His hardboiled mien and laconic voice made him an intriguing screen presence, and his deadpan delivery helped to establish him as an interesting actor, whether as the sidekick to Robert Redford in *The Electric Horseman* or the star around which the moody, elegaic western *Barbarosa* was built.

Guided by producer Billy Sherrill, Charlie Rich became an international star in 1973 with the million-selling "Behind Closed Doors." Unfortunately, the newfound reputation as a countrypolitan crooner didn't sit easily with the talented blues and jazz stylist. Showing up drunk for the 1975 CMA awards telecast, he announced John Denver as his successor to the Entertainer of the Year award, and set fire to the envelope.

Canadian Anne Murray has never claimed to be country, but her husky alto has brought her a devoted country following nonetheless. Despite her penchant for remaking Beatles songs and her recent move from an acoustic sound to synthesizers, Murray has remained a staple of country radio with soothing tunes like "Snowbird" (1970), "Danny's Song" (1973), and "You Needed Me" (1978).

Neither Nelson nor Parton was without a share of commercial and aesthetic failures. As good a movie as *Barbarosa* was, it didn't fare well at the box office; neither did *Honeysuckle Rose* or the Nelson-produced film adaptation *Red Headed Stranger*. Nelson indulged his superstar recording status with a series of duets with musicians as various as Leon Russell, Roger Miller, Webb Pierce, Ray Price, and Julio Iglesias. The collaboration with Pierce, "In the Jailhouse Now," was little short of magnificent, but only "To All the Girls I've Loved Before," a single recorded with Iglesias, was a commercial smash. No, in the post-Outlaws period of his career, the most influential recording Nelson made was *Stardust*, his 1978 collection of pop-song standards that revealed him to be a first-rate interpreter of pop without sacrificing his country integrity.

Parton's *Rhinestone* has already been mentioned as her most notable film bomb, but her recording career was more wayward. Drawn more and more to rock songs, she made a series of mediocre albums that failed to match her style with the material. Her biggest hit during her superstar period was "Islands in the Stream," a rote pop ballad duet with Kenny Rogers in 1983.

At this writing in early 1988, Parton was continuing to pursue an acting career while making at least one significant stab at reconnecting with her roots: *Trio* (1987), a collaboration with Linda Ronstadt and Emmylou Harris, was filled with the sort of country music—and Parton songwriting—that Dolly hadn't deigned to do in years. It was significant that, at precisely the moment when Parton had probably transcended the country-artist label, she chose to remind her public of it.

In the fall of 1987, Parton attempted to revive the fading variety-show format on television with "Dolly." She signed a two-year contract with ABC—an exceptional commitment to television for a movie star of her box-office caliber—and announced, "I'm good at television; I come across real well in people's living rooms." But Parton's drastic, if flattering, weight loss attracted more attention than her singing on the show, which on one occasion included a surrealistic version of Hank Williams's "Hey, Good Lookin' " sung with . . . Pee-wee Herman. Plagued by mediocre ratings and an aimless aesthetic, "Dolly" symbolized Parton's mass-culture problem: her audience wanted her to remain a giggly, corn-pone sex-bomb even as her own ambitions were telling her to do something different.

Nelson, too, sought to broaden his audience by recording more Willie-ized versions of pop-music standards and by turning himself into a movie star on his own terms. A paradigm of this effort is the movie version of *Red Headed Stranger*, in which Nelson

Kenny Rogers: boyhood friend of Mickey Gilley; former rockabilly, jazzman, folk singer, and rock 'n' roller; duet partner of Dottie West, Kim Carnes, Sheena Easton, and Dolly Parton; star of three TV movies based on his 1978 hit "The Gambler"; published photographer; millionaire. This stage shot dates from the late seventies, before he'd done it all.

That's entertainment: Dolly Parton joins in the applause for Willie Nelson at the 1979 CMA Awards show. After years of being told he was wrong by the Nashville Establishment, being named Entertainer of the Year that night was a moment of sweet vindication for Willie. Doubtless, Dolly knew the feeling, having received the honor in 1978, following accusations of abandoning country music for pop.

The $44 million dollar woman: Dolly Parton tapes a musical routine for her TV variety show "Dolly." That's how much money the ABC network spent trying to turn the series into a hit. After a dismal showing in the ratings for the 1987–88 season, ABC paid Dolly $11 million so they wouldn't have to fulfill her two-year contract and suffer through a second season.

Johnny Rodriguez and Charly McClain blend voices onstage, October 1979, as they did on their hit of that year "I Hate the Way I Love It." With his smoldering good looks and Tex-Mex style, Rodriguez was a very hot commodity in the early seventies; McClain had not yet recorded her radio hits "Sleeping with the Radio On" (1981) and "Radio Heart" (1985).

starred and presumably oversaw through the script-writing stage with his chum Bud Shrake. The movie was a commercial failure that contained yet another quietly powerful, if by now rather repetitive, Nelson performance.

In all of this, the careers of Parton and Nelson define the limits of country music stardom, the risks that must be taken and the compromises that must be made to cultivate the sort of widespread acceptance that is the greatest measure of success to people working in the popular arts. Parton and Nelson are so much a part of their times, so responsive to the era in which they create and perform, that it's often impossible to assess their recordings or their career decisions with anything approaching objectivity. It may well be that, years from now, it will be possible to see that each of these singers created a unified body of work. Certainly, the best music created by Dolly and Willie will withstand the occasional bad album, bad movie, or bad TV show to take its place among the strongest work that modern country music has yet offered.

RCA-H-122-2

13

THE BOTTOM LINE: BUSINESS PRACTICES THAT SHAPED COUNTRY MUSIC

Bill Ivey

THE UNTOLD STORY

Think about this as a definition of country music: a country record is any record a radio station that calls itself "country" will play and any record that a consumer who considers himself a "country fan" will buy. That's it—no fiddles, steel guitars, high lonesome harmonies, or rhinestone suits required.

And consider this: Chet Atkins, asked to define the Nashville Sound, puts his right hand in his pants pocket and gently jingles the change. "That," says Chet, "is the Nashville Sound."

Chet's gesture speaks to the obvious; we are all aware that country music can be a money-making enterprise. But perhaps the money-making aspect is in fact its essence, taking us further toward an understanding of country music than any scholarly dissertation on country style ever could. Of course, rock, rhythm & blues, jazz, and other pop music forms are just as commercial as country, but critical writing about country has ignored this essential detail and has nearly always treated country music as a free-floating art form, subject only to the ebb and flow of musical style and cross-influence—as if business were something *outside* the music, rather than the music's reason for being.

Let's return to our definition for a moment: country music is any record country radio will play and country fans will buy.

Elvis Presley signs with RCA. See page 433.

407

912

Associated Radio Co

Here in Person!
Eddy Arnold

NOW!

WALLY FOWLER

ASSOCIATED

GRAND OLE OPRY STARS! TUE. MAY 28
MUNICIPAL AUDITORIUM WED. MAY 29

Colonel Tom Parker (far left) proudly surveys the hoopla surrounding his star attraction of the moment, Eddy Arnold (center), ca. 1947. Under Parker's guidance, Arnold left the Grand Ole Opry in 1948 for more lucrative pursuits, such as big-city tours and his own radio shows. Managing Arnold proved a fine warm-up for Parker's life's work: Elvis Presley.

This description has two virtues. It works by actually encompassing the universe generally thought of as "country" without exception, and it places the weight of our definition where it belongs, in the two media that deliver the music: records and radio. Country music is any music that works in this system. And, ultimately, the system is concerned with financial results —sales, royalties, shipments, collections, and such. Thus, even though the country music business employs many individuals who are deeply committed to particular artists and musical styles, the business itself is incapable of such loyalty.

Though the country music industry frequently claims to be a victim of public taste, it actually possesses considerable control over which songs, artists, and records succeed. After all, the players in each segment of this system invent each day their sense of public taste and then act on that invention, choosing those songs, artists, and records to be blessed with the endorsement of the business. For a publisher, record executive, or radio programmer to be radically and continuously out of step with popular taste produces observable failure—and, eventually, turnover. Popular taste is generous, however, and many, many songs and records fall within its broad limits of what is acceptable. The power of the business occurs in selecting and promoting alternatives within this pool of acceptable work.

It was business acumen that first saw the value of hillbilly singers and the country song, and it was a change in the collection and payment of royalties that made the country music busi-

When promoter J. L. Frank began booking Gene Autry out of Chicago in the early thirties, Autry was making only $50 a week. In the late thirties, Frank moved to Nashville and brought son-in-law Pee Wee King (for whom he designed the snazzy poster) and Roy Acuff to the Grand Ole Opry. It was Frank who first took Opry performers from small-time schoolhouse shows to big-city auditoriums during the forties and early fifties.

ness truly profitable. Radio, insurance, and music publishing conspired to create that most peculiar phenomenon, the "third coast" recording center in an average Mid-South city. And names like Peer, Acuff-Rose, National Life, the CMA, and BMI were responsible for carrying country music from its rural, amateur roots to a place of prominence in the international entertainment industry.

RALPH PEER'S GREATEST DISCOVERY

From the moment electrical recording met American rural and ethnic music, the eventual appearance of rock 'n' roll—and the subsequent transformation of popular music across the world—was inevitable. Recordings provided these musical styles with the opportunity to evolve in a manner unknown even in the classical tradition. The permanence and portability that informal music gained from the disc recording made certain that by the 1980s the vast majority of music consumed in the world would be rock, pop, rhythm & blues, and country music—derived not from the pens of schooled composers nor performed by the trained voice, but based instead on this folk stuff discovered in the 1920s.

Enter Eck Robertson, a middle-aged Southerner who made what are now considered to be the first country music recordings after marching uninvited into Victor's New York studios in June 1922. His versions of the old-time fiddle tunes "Sallie Gooden" and "Arkansaw Traveler," released in April 1923, beat Okeh's initial Fiddlin' John Carson recordings to the market by several months.

These early country music recordings—and the ones that quickly followed—captured the unschooled talents of folk musicians for all to hear. The vocal styles were harsh and nasal, and the instrumental accompaniment was sparse, often just a fiddle, banjo, or guitar. The repertory was mixed: nineteenth-century popular songs, gospel tunes, the blues of rural blacks, and folk songs with roots in the British Isles. Naturally, the records were popular with rural residents familiar with the music, but city dwellers of southern extraction formed an audience of considerable potential.

Despite Victor's early entry into the hillbilly field—and some encouraging success—the company made no immediate commitment to the music. In fact, Okeh, Columbia, and Vocalion

The first to make a country record: Eck Robertson. Aged twenty-four, Robertson and fellow fiddler Henry Gilliland had just played at a Confederate veterans' reunion, when they made the extraordinary decision to take their act to Victor's New York studios. Victor recorded them in late June and early July 1922, finally releasing Robertson's solo record in April 1923. It was, by all accounts, country music's first release as well.

signed most of the early country artists. Victor did have considerable success by adapting the talents of seasoned professional singers like Vernon Dalhart ("The Prisoner's Song") and Carl T. Sprague ("When the Work's All Done This Fall") to hillbilly and cowboy material, but neither singer was the real McCoy—that is, a genuine amateur folk talent from the rural South.

Record executive Ralph Peer was eager to exploit this largely untapped reservoir of amateur talent, and in striving to do so he developed some of the key business relationships that allowed the early growth of the country music business. Peer had worked for Columbia in the teens, served in the Navy during World War I, and returned to the record business at Columbia's Kansas City office. He left Columbia to serve as assistant to Okeh's director of production. While with Okeh, Peer came in contact with singers like Mamie Smith (in 1920) and country harmonica player Henry Whitter (1923). In June 1923, Peer and Polk Brockman—

Pop session, Bradley Studios, 1959. The Anita Kerr Singers, a harmony group who supplied smooth background vocals to dozens of country and pop sessions held in Nashville, make some pop records of their own. This session was one of the first to use such a large string section, recruited from Nashville's symphony orchestra. Before long, string sections of this size would become standard on country records as well.

411

Following in Ralph Peer's footsteps, Eli Oberstein supervised country recording sessions for RCA Victor for much of the 1930s. Making regular trips to such regional recording centers as Charlotte, Atlanta, and Dallas, he did essential early legwork for RCA in the country market before working with big-band greats like Benny Goodman and Tommy Dorsey.

Jack Kapp became president of Decca's American operation with its founding in 1934. Through low-priced record lines, marketed heavily to jukeboxes, Decca helped country music flourish during the Great Depression. Kapp's brother, David, served as an important A&R man, working with Jimmie Davis and, later, Ernest Tubb.

an Atlanta record distributor and furniture dealer—recorded Fiddlin' John Carson for what has generally been considered the first country record to be marketed as such. Peer went on to a long career as a record producer and has been noted for his efforts as a collector of American folk music (though, clearly, he was looking for profit and, just as clearly, he exhibited little rapport with these rural entertainers). It was in music publishing, though, that Peer made his most lasting contribution to the business of country music.

As Peer's experience with the hillbilly business grew, he realized that recordings of popular standards had little appeal, particularly when recorded by twangy hillbillies with their somewhat limited potential audience (i.e., folks who sounded just like they did and weren't ashamed of it). New songs were the thing, new songs combined with consumer loyalty to a single artist. So Peer sought out those singers who could also write, and he signed them to writing agreements. He did not buy the copyright, as was common practice in the era, but insisted instead on a publisher's share of all royalties. This innovation established an ongoing relationship with these hillbilly music makers, something scarcely possible when songs were purchased outright. To this day, the royalty agreement and the continual demand for new material from singer-songwriters remain cornerstones of the country music business.

So confident was Peer of these untried business principles that he went to work for Victor at no salary, insisting only that he be allowed to control the copyrights he saw as so valuable. On this basis he built the Southern Music Publishing Company, one of the largest country-oriented firms in the history of the entertainment business.

THE BMI REVOLUTION

Peer's publishing discovery proved to be a gold mine for him and other canny businessmen, but it didn't make many hillbillies rich. During the 1920s and 1930s there were precious few sources of income for those singer-songwriters who recorded country music. Frequently record companies failed to pay performers their rightful royalties, and many record executives continued to buy performances outright, with only a flat fee paid for recordings that could go on to generate thousands of dollars in sales. As it was, the royalties paid to writers for each record sold (mechanical royalties) were meager—as little as $.005 per disc.

NBC - WLW - WLS - KDKA - WTAM - WSM - WSB - WHAS - WAVE - WOWO - WWVA - CBS

FORM 2620 5M SETS 4-39 U P & S. CO.

DECCA RECORDS, INC.
621 WEST 54TH STREET
NEW YORK CITY

Month ___May, 1939___

Check No. ___74806 - 6/1___

Vo. No.___A/C___

Amt. ___$565.00___

STATEMENT OF REMITTANCE

The attached check is in full settlement of the following:

Clayton Mc Michens
Georgia Wild Cats

6/1/39..............$565.00

But there was another potential source of income for composers —known as the performance royalty—which was truly significant and generally unavailable to country writers.

The performance royalty accrues to a copyright whenever a song is performed in public: in a club, concert hall, on radio and, more recently, on television. Through the early days of recording, the American Society of Composers, Authors, and Publishers (ASCAP) collected and paid out performance royalties to songwriters. Membership in ASCAP was competitive and restricted, however; in the pop field it was generally limited to established Tin Pan Alley writers, who were working in a respected, European tradition of song. Even if they had known about it, the generally unsophisticated country and blues songwriters were almost uniformly barred from joining ASCAP, and thus they received no performance money at all, just the pittance earned by their record sales.

By 1939, the time had come for a reckoning. ASCAP had been charging radio stations fees based upon the stations' rates for radio advertising; those stations with higher ad rates paid a higher flat fee, for which they could play any selection licensed by ASCAP. Faced with a substantial ASCAP rate hike in 1939, the broadcasters rebeled, forming their own licensing organization, Broadcast Music, Inc. (BMI). It was, in effect, a strike, and for a time, no ASCAP material was played on the air. Broadcasters could, of course, play nineteenth-century standards no longer protected by copyright, or they could seek out those writers who were not yet affiliated with any licensing organization.

As this remittance statement reveals, hillbilly recording artists often settled for flat session fees instead of long-term royalty agreements in the early days. During the Great Depression, many performers were more than happy to take the bird-in-the-hand.

413

THE INDEPENDENTS

Since the early 1920s, so-called major record companies have dominated the country music field through extensive distribution networks, large promotion budgets, and corporate ties to broadcasting or motion-picture conglomerates. Three major firms—RCA-Victor, Columbia, and Decca—virtually monopolized country record sales until the end of World War II. But as the demand for country records increased right along with the burgeoning postwar economy, a host of new independent labels entered the country market. The major labels still claim the lion's share of country retail record sales, but over the years the independents have given many a country entertainer valuable commercial and artistic opportunities. Here are some of the most important independents of the last five decades:

KING, Cincinnati. Founded by Syd Nathan, ca. 1943. Artists: Cowboy Copas, Grandpa Jones, Paul Howard, Clyde Moody, the Delmore Brothers as well as r & b artists like James Brown. Eventually merged with Starday. Now owned by Gusto.

MERCURY, Chicago. Founded in 1945. Artists: Rex Allen, Flatt & Scruggs, the Carlisles, pop artist Patti Page, who recorded "Tennessee Waltz." Now owned by Poly-Gram.

4 STAR, California. Bought by Bill McCall, 1945. Artists: T. Texas Tyler, Smokey Rogers, the Maddox Brothers & Rose. Sporadically active since 1960s. Now based in Nashville.

VOGUE, Detroit. Founded by manufacturer Tom Saffady, 1946. Specialized in colorful, romantically illustrated picture discs of pop and country acts. Artists: Patsy Montana, Lulu Belle & Scotty, Nancy Lee & the Hilltoppers. High production costs and fierce competition put the label out of business within a few years.

BULLET, Nashville. Founded by former WSM announcer Jim Bulleit, 1945. Artists: Pee Wee King, Sheb Wooley, Johnnie Lee Wills, Zeke and Zeb Turner; responsible for "Near You," a million-selling pop record in 1947 by Nashville's own Francis Craig Orchestra. Last releases in the early 1950s.

STERLING, New York. Founded by Al Middleman, 1946. First commercial recordings by Hank Williams. Other artists: Jimmy Wakely, the Willis Brothers. Operation folded during American Federation of Musicians' ban on recording in 1948.

RICH-R-TONE, Johnson City, Tennessee. Founded by businessman Jim Stanton, 1947. Artists: the Stanley Brothers, Wilma Lee & Stoney Cooper. Stanton let the label fade, then revived it in Nashville in the 1970s.

IMPERIAL, West Coast. Founded in 1948. Artists: Adolph Hofner, Slim Whitman, Ricky Nelson. Releases continued into the 1960s. Now owned by Capitol-EMI.

DOT, Gallatin, Tennessee. Founded by record store owner Randy Wood, 1950. Artists: Mac Wiseman, Tommy Jackson, Lonzo & Oscar, Jimmy Newman, Pat Boone, the Hilltoppers. Eventually moved to the West Coast and merged with ABC-Paramount, which was later

absorbed by MCA. Revived as a subsidiary label by MCA in 1986.

ABBOTT, California. Founded by entrepreneur Fabor Robison, 1951. Artists: Jim Reeves, Mitchell Torok, Floyd Cramer. Companion label, mostly pop, was Fabor Records. Robison eventually sold his rights to various parties.

STARDAY, Texas. Founded by Jack Starnes and H. W. "Pappy" Daily, ca. 1953. Artists: George Jones, Arleigh Duff. Moved to Nashville in late 1950s, temporarily merging with Mercury. Merged with King in 1960s. Now owned by Gusto Records.

SUN, Memphis. Founded by Sam Phillips, 1952. Artists: Elvis Presley, Johnny Cash, Carl Perkins, Jerry Lee Lewis, Roy Orbison, Charlie Rich. Purchased in 1969 by Shelby Singleton, who subsequently formed the Sun International Corporation to reissue the classic Sun recordings.

HICKORY, Nashville. Founded by music publishing magnates Roy Acuff, Fred Rose, and Wesley Rose, 1954. An outlet for Acuff-Rose artists who did not record on major labels. Artists: Al Terry, Rusty & Doug Kershaw, Wilma Lee & Stoney Cooper, Ernie Ashworth. Label virtually defunct by 1970s. Now owned by Gaylord Publishing Company.

MONUMENT, Nashville. Founded by Fred Foster, 1958. Artists: Roy Orbison, Billy Grammer, Larry Gatlin, Dolly Parton, Kris Kristofferson. Bankrupt by mid-1980s.

COUNTY, Founded by Dave Freeman, 1964. Now part of Freeman's larger organization, which includes the County Sales mail-order operation, the Rebel label, and the County label. Artists: Kenny Baker, the Stanley Brothers, Tommy Jarrell (new recordings and reissues).

REBEL, Mt. Ranier, Maryland. Founded by entrepreneur Dick Freeland in mid-1960s. Artists: the Country Gentlemen, the Seldom Scene. Purchased by County in 1980.

ROUNDER, Cambridge, Massachusetts. Founded by Ken Irwin, Marian Leighton, and Bill Nowlin, 1970. Recording and mail-order operation similar to County. Artists: Riders in the Sky, the Johnson Mountain Boys, Ricky Skaggs.

FLYING FISH, Chicago. Founded by Bruce Kaplan, ca. 1974. Artists: John Hartford, Doc Watson, Vassar Clements, Hot Rize.

SUGAR HILL, Durham, North Carolina. Founded by Barry Poss, formerly of County, 1978. Artists: Ricky Skaggs, the Whites, Chris Hillman, New Grass Revival, Seldom Scene.

Fred Rose and Roy Acuff, ca. 1943. Rose knew songs, having written instant standards for pop star Sophie Tucker and western king Gene Autry before signing on as staff pianist at Nashville's WSM in 1942. Acuff, then the Opry's rising star, could sing the fire out of them. In 1942, they teamed up to form Acuff-Rose Publications, within ten years one of the most successful music-publishing houses anywhere.

So stations played the standards to mark time, and an enthusiastic BMI staff set about signing country and blues songwriters, who had been ignored by ASCAP.

No other event in the history of American music did so much to aid country music's commercial success. Though BMI had an obvious financial stake in the success of these unaffiliated writers, the organization also possessed a dedicated staff (based in New York) who had a genuine sympathy for indigenous American music. Radio suddenly opened up to blues, jazz, and country, and BMI collected millions of dollars in performance royalties for the songwriters, with the result that country songwriting and recording gained immensely in financial and professional stature. Much as recordings had provided the technological means to give folk-based music the permanence once reserved for the manuscripts of classical compositions, BMI provided the radio exposure and the payment structure to establish country songwriting and publishing as thoroughly professional activities. With the additional boost of radio stations dedicated to the country sound (country format radio), the time was ripe for the rise of a new, independent center for country recording and publishing.

THE RISE OF MUSIC CITY

The story of Nashville as a center for the country music business is entirely a post–World War II narrative. Though the Grand Ole Opry gave the city a musical reputation in the twenties and thirties, Nashville was then merely one of a dozen cities routinely broadcasting live country-oriented radio shows. It was the formation of Acuff-Rose Publications in 1942 that provided Nashville with its first commercial music business independent of WSM and the Grand Ole Opry. Acuff-Rose set the tone for future music ventures in what would one day be known as Music City, U.S.A.

Fred Rose was an accomplished piano player and pop songwriter, responsible for such country hits as "Blue Eyes Crying in the Rain" and "Fire Ball Mail." His partner, Roy Acuff, had quickly established himself as a major Grand Ole Opry star after joining the show's cast in 1938. Their joint publishing venture took advantage of BMI's presence and provided a channel through which earnings could flow to Opry-connected songwriters. Significantly, these funds stayed in Nashville, in the

Acuff-Rose's first team, late fifties: Wesley Rose, the Everly Brothers, and Boudleaux Bryant. Early in the decade, Fred Rose had filled the company coffers by pitching the songs of Hank Williams to Mitch Miller's Columbia pop stars. Five years later, son Wesley found a comparable goldmine in the Everlys, who vaulted from the Opry to the top of the pop charts on the strength of songs by Bryant and his wife, Felice.

Cindy Walker, 1940s. This fiercely determined young Texan took Los Angeles by storm in the early forties, landing a Decca recording contract and successfully pitching songs to Bing Crosby, Bob Wills, and other hot West Coast acts. Eventually, she concentrated solely on songwriting, creating some of country music's most enduring classics—"Bubbles in My Beer," "You Don't Know Me," "In the Misty Moonlight," "Warm, Red Wine."

John D. Loudermilk was still in school at Campbell College in North Carolina in 1956, when George Hamilton IV had a smash hit with his "Rose and a Baby Ruth," the melody of which was inspired by a Crisco Shortening commercial. After that the hits just kept on coming: "Waterloo" (1959) for Stonewall Jackson, "Ebony Eyes" (1961) for the Everly Brothers, "Abilene" (1963) for Hamilton, and "Tobacco Road" (1964) for the Nashville Teens.

While Mel Foree was still in the service during World War II, Fred Rose recruited him for the new Acuff-Rose publishing operation. To enhance Foree's effectiveness as a future song plugger, Rose helped him polish "No One Will Ever Know" and convinced Roy Acuff to record the song in 1945. After his discharge, Foree signed on with Acuff-Rose and promoted the company's songs for the next forty years.

Boudleaux & Felice Bryant, 1950s. Mr. and Mrs. Bryant chalked up their first success with "Country Boy," a Top Ten hit for Little Jimmy Dickens in 1949. But they're best remembered for the hits they provided the Everly Brothers (and Acuff-Rose)—"Bye, Bye Love," "Wake Up, Little Susie," "All I Have to Do Is Dream," "Love Hurts," and more. They wrote "Rocky Top," a 1968 hit for the Osborne Brothers and now a standard, in fifteen minutes.

hands of local writers and in the coffers of Acuff-Rose. Publishing money, beginning in those years, became Nashville's largest source of locally controlled music capital, fueling the growth of Nashville as a music center.

Within a few years following the formation of Acuff-Rose, the company fashioned several important alliances. In 1945, Fred lured his son Wesley from an accounting job with the Standard Oil Company in Chicago. The younger Rose's presence brought needed business discipline, expertise, and aggressiveness to bear upon the artistic endeavors of the elder Rose. Meanwhile, Fred Rose, who had made many connections during his two decades in the pop music field, kept in touch with industry leaders in New York. Fred's rapport with New York pop record executives soon proved crucial to the expansion of Nashville's influence within the national music industry.

The single most important alliance for the newly formed publishing company was, in fact, a creative one. In the summer of 1946, Fred Rose signed a young Alabama songwriter, Hank Williams, to an Acuff-Rose writing contract. Hank's career would last only another seven years, but his songs proved timeless—and enormously lucrative. With occasional, though uncredited, songwriting assistance from Fred Rose, Williams wrote and recorded a string of hits that dominated the country charts from 1949 to 1953. But Acuff-Rose wasn't content with Hank's unprecedented country triumphs: they had their eyes on the rich pop market.

Both Fred and Wesley Rose realized that country songs could be easily adapted from one musical genre to another. More important, Fred Rose also had the ability to recognize pop and country hits, and the skills to polish basically good songs into

By the time Hank Cochran arrived from the West Coast, in 1960, Nashville had become a mecca for hundreds of aspiring singers and songwriters like him. Cochran came out head-and-shoulders above the pack, writing and co-writing such classics as "I Fall to Pieces" for Patsy Cline and "Make the World Go Away" for Eddy Arnold.

Bill Anderson in 1961, when he was probably country music's hottest new singer-songwriter. The ex-DJ and newspaper reporter from Georgia joined the Opry that year on the strength of a 1958 hit for Ray Price, "City Lights," and one of his own, "Tip of My Fingers" (1960). "Po' Folks" was breaking into the charts just as he entered the Opry cast; "Mama Sang a Song" (1962), "Still" (1963), and numerous others were yet to come.

Annie Lou & Danny Dill, early fifties. Following several years performing on the road and on radio with wife Annie Lou, Danny Dill found his true calling as a songwriter. In 1959, he and Marijohn Wilkin collaborated on "Long Black Veil," which Dill has since described as an "instant folk song" capitalizing on the folk music boom. Four years later, he and Mel Tillis turned out the classic "Detroit City."

Overleaf, top
Born in Kentucky, songwriter Harlan Howard was holding down a factory job in Los Angeles when his songs first appeared on record. With hits like the #1 "Pick Me Up on Your Way Down" (Charlie Walker, 1958) under his belt, he set up shop in Nashville early in the sixties. Since then, he's made more than two million dollars with such classics as "Heartaches by the Number," "I Fall to Pieces," "Busted," and "I've Got a Tiger by the Tail."

421

Tuxedo junction: "Sunday Down South," ca. 1950. WSM stood for more than country. The Opry station produced this pop program for a regional radio network assembled by the sponsor, Lion Oil, during the forties and early fifties. Here Snooky Lanson (right), who later became a national TV star on "Your Hit Parade," does the crooning, while Owen Bradley, announcer Jud Collins, and guest Rod Brasfield gather center stage.

greatness. All that remained was to get these sure-fire hits into the hands of pop artists. Fred Rose's main connection here was Mitch Miller, then head of A&R for Columbia Records. Miller was an accomplished record producer who achieved a measure of acclaim as an artist for his *Sing Along with Mitch* albums and subsequent televison series. It was he who encouraged Columbia's pop artists to cut songs like "Cold, Cold Heart" (a #1 pop hit for Tony Bennett), "Half as Much" (#2, Rosemary Clooney), "Jambalaya" (#3, Jo Stafford), and other Williams favorites. It was also Miller who was responsible for Patti Page's #1 pop recording of "Tennessee Waltz," another Acuff-Rose copyright, penned by Pee Wee King and Redd Stewart. Fred Rose's ability to place Acuff-Rose material with pop artists contributed mightily to the impact of these (and other) Acuff-Rose copyrights. These copyrights, in turn, led the way to Nashville's conspicuous emergence as a music center.

The Grand Ole Opry, of course, played a continuing, and now accelerating, role in Nashville's fortunes. Though the radio broadcast had been merely one among many such country barn

Pipe in hand, Bing Crosby makes a Nashville appearance for a special WSM show during the forties. Accompanying him are pianist Owen Bradley, and drummer Farris Coursey, all pop musicians at heart who doubled as country session players. WSM orchestra leader Beasley Smith (second from left), with help from Bradley and WSM colleague Marvin Hughes, wrote the Roy Acuff hit "Night Train to Memphis" in 1942.

dances in the twenties and thirties, the years following World War II began to reveal important ways in which the show was unique.

Red Foley & the Andrews Sisters, 1950s. Pairing country and pop acts was a handy way to draw on two audiences at once, or so thought record execs of the 1950s. Foley recorded several times with the Andrews Sisters between 1951 and 1954. Likewise, George Morgan teamed with Rosemary Clooney, and Tennessee Ernie Ford with Kay Starr. Most successful of all were Jimmy Wakely and pop singer Margaret Whiting, whose "Slipping Around" sold nearly two million copies in 1950.

The Grand Ole Opry was never just a radio program. It was, in fact, a major promotional and marketing vehicle for the National Life and Accident Insurance Company, its parent. The Opry's enormous popularity with rural audiences meant, among other things, that it had value far in excess of its independent ability to generate revenue; after all, it sold countless insurance policies, which meant that even as other live radio broadcasts succumbed to the competition of television and record-playing radio, the Opry could endure as the down-home voice of an affluent insurance company. Inevitably, in the late 1940s and early 1950s, the Opry began to attract the best: the greatest

424

artists, the most talented sidemen, the sharpest executives. It was as if the Opry and the city of Nashville had become magnets, attracting the performers cast away by radio shows that could no longer afford to compete.

National Life offered Nashville another advantage as a music center. The Grand Ole Opry was one of many live shows produced by WSM radio, the broadcasting affiliate of National Life. The Opry itself, and certainly the station as a whole, did much more than feature country performances. WSM produced a full range of entertainment—big-band shows, news, comedy—for the NBC network. Thus, the total pool of talent available through the WSM family far exceeded the resources of the Opry alone.

We must remember that the successes of Acuff-Rose and the rise to preeminence of the Grand Ole Opry had, as a backdrop, changes in the record and broadcast industries of the most far-reaching sort. The establishment of BMI, the rise of independent radio and small record labels, the demise of both live music on radio and sheet-music sales, the growth of television, even improvements in amplified musical instruments and sound systems —all of these were inverting the long-established structure of the New York-based music industry. With a strong pool of talent and a fledgling publishing industry, Nashville was uniquely poised to benefit from these changes in the shape of the music industry. It required only the intervention of a handful of far-sighted musicians and businessmen to add recording to the activities current in town.

David Stone (Harry's brother) joined WSM as an announcer early in the 1930s and soon replaced the ailing Judge Hay as head of the station's Artist Service, or booking department. During Hay's protracted absences, the Stones hired Pee Wee King (1937) and Roy Acuff (1938) for the Opry in their continuing effort to find singing stars who could outshine the show's semiprofessional, old-timey string bands.

Efficient and calculating, Harry Stone became WSM's assistant manager in 1928 and gradually eased manager George D. Hay aside as the Opry founder's health failed. During Stone's tenure as station manager (1932–50), he began selling Opry airtime to sponsors, lined up the lucrative R. J. Reynolds account for the Opry's half-hour NBC network show, and recruited pop-influenced vocal groups to augment the old-time string-band sound Hay preferred.

A NASHVILLE SOUND

A disc from Nashville's first major independent studio, Castle Recording Laboratory. Taking their name and logo from the WSM slogan "Air Castle of the South," WSM engineers Aaron Shelton, Carl Jenkins, and George Reynolds conducted sessions at the radio station for a year and a half before setting up studios of their own in 1947 at the nearby Tulane Hotel.

Opposite
The stars come out for the formal opening of Jim Denny's Cedarwood Publishing Company, June 26, 1954. At the time, Denny (far right) worked full-time as the Opry's manager and head of WSM's booking agency. Two years later, he ran afoul of the station's management for operating Cedarwood, a partnership with singer Webb Pierce (seated at desk). Without missing a beat, Denny left WSM to run the publishing company and set up his own booking agency.

Nashville hardly mattered at all in the recording of country music before World War II. Ralph Peer and his Victor field recording unit stopped off briefly on their way back from Memphis in the fall of 1928 and recorded a few Opry acts, but that was an isolated instance. It would be sixteen years before Victor returned to the city for a session. Although Nashville-based musicians and singers often participated in recording sessions, they did so in other cities. Opry artists, such as Eddy Arnold and Pee Wee King, frequently traveled to Chicago to record; and Cincinnati—in particular the Herzog studio—was also a popular recording site during the late forties for artists such as Red Foley and Hank Williams.

Commercial recording really began in Nashville when WSM engineers Aaron Shelton, Carl Jenkins, and George Reynolds established the Castle Studio in the downtown Tulane Hotel in 1947. Shelton, Jenkins, and Reynolds had conducted their company's first sessions at WSM, but the station's management was uncomfortable with their free-lance work, so they ventured off on their own. (This was to be a repeated pattern in the relationship between WSM, National Life, the Opry, and Nashville's fledgling music industry. Many early industry leaders either resigned or were fired from WSM positions when their independent, free-lance work appeared to be in conflict with their duties at the radio station. Manager-publisher Jim Denny and publisher Jack Stapp are among many who parted sharply with WSM but remained to lead the music community.)

With the founding of Castle, it became possible to conduct full-fledged recording sessions in Nashville. Paul Cohen, an A&R director for Decca, was one of the first record executives to make use of the Castle Studio. Fred Rose, Columbia's Art Satherley and Don Law, Capitol's Ken Nelson and Lee Gillette, and Mercury's Murray Nash soon brought their artists in as well. Once the required facilities were available, the convenience of recording Opry stars right in Nashville—including access to the Opry-WSM pool of sidemen—made the growth of this segment of Nashville's music industry inevitable.

Just as the Mitch Miller–Fred Rose connection was central to Nashville's early success as a publishing center, so other partnerships boosted Nashville to prominence in recording as well. Steve Sholes, A&R director for RCA Victor, had signed guitarist Chet Atkins to the label in 1947. Atkins, who had first achieved recognition as a radio sideman in the years after World War II,

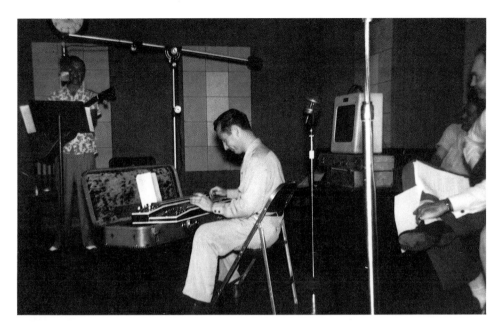

Country session, forties style. In the foreground, Little Roy Wiggins plays the tinkling steel guitar that became a hallmark of Eddy Arnold's early sound. Many fans bought Arnold's records as much to hear Wiggins as the star singer (on Roy's left). If Wiggins couldn't make an Arnold session, A&R men would instruct other steel players to duplicate the Wiggins style.

HOW CHET ATKINS
DID IT: 1957–74

When I came on at RCA, I struggled for a while because I was kind of afraid to spend money. I came from real poor beginnings, so thrift meant a lot to me. But I realized finally that I was gonna have to spend some money and make some hits, or I'd be out of a job.

The first guy I signed after I came on was Don Gibson. I remember I called my superior, Steve Sholes, and told him I wanted to sign Don. He said, "You know, he's been on RCA once, plus Columbia and MGM—two or three labels." But I'd been working with Don and I knew he was writing some great songs, powerhouse songs. So I said, "I want to try him. I like him and I think he can make hits." As always, Wesley Rose [Gibson's publisher] was giving his opinion, and he did that with Don Gibson, saying, "Let's keep it country." So we went in and made a session with fiddles and steels. Didn't sell a one. And I said, "OK, let's do it my way this time, Wesley." Don sent me a demo from Knoxville, a little old tape, and it had two songs he'd written in one afternoon—"Oh Lonesome Me" and "I Can't Stop Loving You." He had made "Oh Lonesome Me" in a small, live room, and the bass drum was going [makes a *whop-a-whop whop-a-whop* sound with his hand]. So I called him and said, "Who's that drummer?" And he said, "That's Troy Hatcher." Well, I knew Troy. I'd known him when I worked in Knoxville. Young guy over there. So I said, "Bring him over." Because I realized this was a different sound. So we got in the studio and did it my way, and thank

goodness, it was just a smash. It was a wonderful feeling—I just got all kinds of confidence.

The record was different because we miked the bass drum, and I don't think that had ever been done before; I never had heard it, if it had. Back in those days, everybody'd just gang around the mike. You know, we had an engineer, Jeff Miller, who would just put one of those old condenser mikes in the middle of the floor and put the bass, drums, rhythm guitar, and everything on it. Actually, I think he had left when I made "Oh Lonesome Me," because I don't think we ever made a hit together. He was fortyish and was set in his ways to some extent, and he'd always say, "Well, we did it this way in New York." I remember it was impossible to get an intimate sound because he wouldn't let any singer get up too close to the mike—he was afraid they'd "pop a *p*." And of course, if you popped a *p* it made the record skip and and so on. But as I said, we put a mike on the bass drum, and E-Q'd it [balanced the treble and bass]. It was a new sound, so fresh and different for the time.

After I'd had a couple hits, I would just draw on chord changes I'd learned in jazz and things I'd heard in gospel and classical music —bass lines, chords, and such. And I'd just add those influences when I felt like it. No one knew the difference, and sometimes we got some great sounds that way.

After I made those hits with Jim Reeves and Don, I had a lot of luck. I think that every artist that was at RCA then eventually had a hit, if

The picker who became a record executive: Chet Atkins with his first love, early 1950s.

they stayed on long enough. I usually had about thirty-five to forty artists that I recorded myself. Of course, we'd make an album back then in one day—just go in and make twelve sides, four songs on a session. All of the artwork was done in New York, and Steve took care of all the financial matters. For a long time, I didn't have to worry about budgets or anything like that. I just made the records; I was good at it, too. But eventually the company started piling paperwork on me, asking, "What are your goals for this year? What do you expect of this employee or that employee?" And I'd feel silly filling out those reports. So I started backing away and finally was out of producing altogether—my preference.

(Transcribed and edited from remarks made at the Country Music Foundation, April 20, 1987.)

429

Jimmie Skinner and Eddy Arnold at Jimmie Skinner's Music Center in Cincinnati, ca. 1953. During country's late-fifties recession, Skinner's record shop and mail-order operation served many Midwesterners starving for bluegrass and hard-country. Also a singer, Skinner's small successes on record were far outstripped by some of the songs he wrote, including "Doin' My Time" and "You Don't Know My Mind," which have become bluegrass standards.

Four of the hottest session cats around: bassist-guitarist Louis Innis, guitarist Zeke Turner, fiddler Tommy Jackson, and steel guitarist Jerry Byrd. During the forties and fifties, these four pickers were not only mainstays of country recording sessions in Cincinnati and Nashville, but also worked frequently on radio, playing Cincinnati's "Midwestern Hayride" and the Grand Ole Opry.

began his association with RCA by making records as a singer (it was intended that he would compete with Capitol's Merle Travis, then a highly popular singer, guitarist, and songwriter). Though the records were not successful, they formed the basis of a friendship between Atkins and Sholes. As Sholes soon dis-

covered, Chet was not just another hot guitar picker; in his own quiet but confident way, he was a born leader. Or, as Chet has sometimes put it: "Right away, I started telling everybody else in the sessions what to do. I've always been that way, because most of the time I knew four chords and the other guys knew three. I guess Steve Sholes saw something in me." Thus, when RCA Victor began to conduct regular sessions in Nashville in 1955, it was only natural for Sholes to call on Chet as a sideman, session leader, and as a local coordinator for Victor's Nashville recordings. Gradually, Chet eased into the role of making key production decisions during the recording process. By the time Sholes could commit RCA to the creation of a Nashville office, in 1957, it was certain he would select Chet to head it.

Owen Bradley played a similar role for Decca's Paul Cohen beginning in the late forties. For several years, Bradley had been a staff pianist and bandleader for WSM. Like Atkins, Bradley had been exposed to a wide spectrum of popular music, including country. Because Cohen worked out of Decca's New York

Don Gibson had failed with four different record labels and was just scraping by in a Knoxville trailer park when he wrote two sorrowful songs one day in 1957. Later that year, after Chet Atkins had signed him to RCA, Gibson recorded both tunes for his first single. "Oh, Lonesome Me" hit both the country and the pop charts; the flip side, "I Can't Stop Loving You," has become a country standard.

431

Decca A&R man Paul Cohen and his assistant Owen Bradley, 1950s. Cohen (right) began to hold recording sessions in Nashville around 1947. Since Cohen worked out of New York, Bradley, a sharp young WSM staff pianist, helped organize and run the Nashville record sessions. When Cohen moved on in 1958, Bradley was the logical choice as his replacement.

headquarters, he relied on Bradley to hire musicians for Decca Nashville sessions. Like Atkins, Bradley gradually assumed the role of producer. Thus, when Cohen left Decca to become head of Coral Records in 1958, it was hardly surprising that Bradley took over Cohen's old job as A&R director for Decca's Nashville operation.

Cohen and Sholes clearly shared a commitment to Nashville. Of course, they both realized that Nashville was home to an emerging music industry and that the city's artistic resources were impressive. Each also preferred, however, to be away from home for very personal reasons. Persistent and believable rumors that Paul Cohen carried on a long-term love affair with a Nashville woman help explain his interest in the city. Sholes was himself fleeing a thoroughly unhappy marriage to which he was

432

Slim Whitman reaches for a high note in a Nashville session, 1950s. With expert players like violinist Lillian Vann Hunt, bassist Bob Moore, and pianist Owen Bradley (in the background), the trip north to Opry country was well worth the time and money to the reigning star of the "Louisiana Hayride"— and, more importantly, to his Los Angeles record label, Imperial.

Steve Sholes lands the big fish, November 1955. Sholes had been supervising RCA's country and r&b sessions for about ten years when he found the singer who combined both music styles in a volatile package. Sholes's signing of Elvis generated untold millions for RCA and clinched the company's decision to expand its Nashville operation.

just as thoroughly committed—both by the mores of the era and by personal inclination. Though never accused of infidelity, he clearly enjoyed the respite brought on by his travels south. However they happened, the connections between Sholes and Atkins, and Cohen and Bradley, provided Nashville with an advantage possessed by no other heartland music community— a trusted link to the record-label headquarters in New York. These relationships provided the final nudge needed to push the city into a unique place in American entertainment.

THE ROCK 'N' ROLL CRISIS

The future for both country music and Nashville looked uncommonly bright in 1954. Despite Hank Williams's death the year before, Nashville was making a substantial impact on the pop music charts, and the possibilities for growing involvement in the embryonic television industry seemed certain. The advent of rock 'n' roll changed all that. Its impact on country music has been much discussed in numerous books and journals, but it is important to note that rock affected segments of the country music business unequally. For example, Nashville's record in-

dustry participated in rock's success with relative ease: it was, in fact, RCA's signing of Elvis Presley that enabled Steve Sholes to commit the label to the creation of a Nashville office. By 1957 Elvis, Gene Vincent, and other rock 'n' rollers were recording in Nashville. In contrast, country music publishers and country radio suffered. Wesley Rose has said that rock 'n' roll hurt business at Acuff-Rose to such an extent that, at one disastrous point, the company spent only half-days in the office, with the entire staff adjourning to softball games every afternoon during the summer of 1957.

Performance royalties for radio airplay had helped bankroll country music's rise to financial success, but as one station after another deserted country records in favor of rock, money from performances quickly dried up. Mechanical royalties suffered the same fate, as country record sales quickly went the way of airplay. The solid revenue base that Nashville established during the early 1950s disappeared virtually overnight.

Eventually, the cataclysm affected the entire established pop music industry. The drop-off in royalties and business activity was felt in New York and Los Angeles as much as in Nashville. Indeed, in the long run, the formal pop music associated with Tin Pan Alley suffered the most at the hands of rock 'n' roll. In the short term, the whole pop industry was affected, and every segment of the industry responded in self-defense to rock's chal-

Left
Bobby Helms was Cashbox's *pick as country's top singer of 1957— and no wonder: "Fraulein" hit the country charts in March and remained there for a year, having peaked at #1. "My Special Angel" topped the country charts that fall, reaching the #7 slot on the pop charts. He finished up 1957 with "Jingle Bell Rock," a #6 pop hit that's now a holiday standard. Though he had several more country hits, he never had another year like this.*

Above
Smooth singers like Leroy Van Dyke spearheaded the CMA's expansion drive during the early sixties. On CMA sales presentation shows staged in New York, Chicago, and Detroit, his good looks and fresh, contemporary sound helped sell country music to big-city advertisers and broadcasters who didn't cotton to hillbillies. His biggest record, "Walk on By," crossed over to the pop charts in 1961.

lenge. It should surprise no one that the Recording Industry Association of America (RIAA), the National Academy of Recording Arts and Sciences (NARAS), and the Country Music Association (CMA) were each formed between 1957 and 1958. Every segment of the music business, if it was not already organized, circled the wagons to fend off the assault from rock 'n' roll.

Of the various responses, the organization of the CMA achieved the most notable, and certainly the most visible, success. The story of the CMA and of the rise of Nashville's country music industry from the late fifties forward is, in fact, one of the great success stories of American business.

With country music publishing crippled and country radio virtually destroyed by rock, the straggling remnants of the Country

435

Connie B. Gay helped bring small-town music to the big city. Raised in tiny Lizard Lick, North Carolina, he set up shop in Washington, D.C., where he built a country music empire during the fifties and sixties. In addition to promoting hillbilly stage shows, he produced syndicated radio and TV shows —appropriately titled "Town and Country Time"—for the rapidly urbanizing country music market.

Wesley Rose, 1950s. Old timers say that tongues wagged in Nashville when Fred Rose brought his son Wesley down from Chicago to become general manager of Acuff-Rose, in 1945. What did a twenty-seven-year-old accountant know about country songs? Not much. But he knew business, and he soon learned enough to sign John D. Loudermilk, Don Gibson, the Everlys, and Mickey Newbury to the firm after Fred died in 1954.

Music Disc Jockey Association met in Naples, Florida, in 1958. It is significant that two men, Wesley Rose and Connie B. Gay, both claim credit for the initial action required to convert what was left of the CMDJA into the Country Music Association. Rose, of course, was Nashville's preeminent publisher. Gay was nearly the equivalent in country broadcasting, having pioneered country radio in the Washington, D.C., area with a string of broadcasting successes. The two men—perpetual rivals within the CMA—symbolized the union of publishing and radio that would fuel the growth of country music throughout the 1960s and 1970s.

BMI had in fact opened a small Nashville office in 1958. BMI's presence linked the licensing organization with the fledgling Nashville music industry and symbolized an authentic commitment to the city. The office was a point of contact, but it also advanced funds against anticipated earnings of publishers and songwriters. Through the "advance," Nashville-based publishers acquired the capital necessary for operations in the period before actual royalty income exceeded expenses—a transition that took several years in some cases. By the early 1960s, the venerable Acuff-Rose was joined by Tree and by Cedarwood—formed by former WSM executives Jack Stapp and Jim Denny, respectively—and by a host of smaller but still profitable Nashville-owned publishing companies. BMI encouragement and the clout of the advance against earnings underwrote this growth.

It was more difficult for record labels to get on board the CMA bandwagon. Large companies, of course, were able to capitalize on rock's popularity nearly as effectively as on the popularity of

436

Jack Stapp with Opry star Ferlin Husky (right) and his manager Bob Ferguson (left), 1950s. Like Jim Denny, Stapp had organized a publishing company—Tree Music (1951)—while working at WSM. When station management decided that Stapp's work at Tree constituted a conflict of interest, he left WSM after eighteen years as program director (1939–57).

Capitol Records producer Ken Nelson coaches Sonny James during a recording session, ca. 1960. Though he had grown up singing and playing in pop dance bands, Nelson became a staunch supporter of country music and the CMA. One of his most consistent hitmakers during the rock onslaught was James, who first topped the charts in 1956 with "Young Love." Between 1967 and 1971, he had sixteen consecutive #1 hits.

other forms of music (though rock did, briefly, favor the independent labels that had sprung up after the war). Nashville record labels were really just branch offices in the late 1950s, lacking the discretionary funds necessary to assist the CMA's early efforts. Significantly, the two record executives who joined the collective fight early on were not based in Nashville. RCA's Steve Sholes, operating out of New York, and Capitol's Ken Nelson, in Los Angeles, committed their organizations to the collective promotion of country music through the CMA. Each was well positioned to bring his label into the fight, something virtually impossible for Nashville-based record men of the era. With Capitol and RCA on board, CMA had created an alliance among publishing, record, and radio interests that could affect the financial well-being of the country music industry. That alliance remained in effect for more than twenty years.

Country Music on Broadway *(1964) masqueraded as the documentary of a country extravaganza playing the Great White Way, when the filming (and lip-synching) really took place in Nashville. Nevertheless, the feature film served notice that country's popularity was growing. And besides, the cast was wonderful.*

The CMA attempted to influence radio programmers, radio and television advertisers, and the ad agencies that represented those advertisers. The CMA conducted research to profile the country fan and presented concerts featuring major country artists in New York and Chicago. *"Country music is popular. It will sell your product. People will listen to your station if it is country. An endorsement by a country artist will sell laundry soap . . ."* Repeated again and again, the message began to take effect. Full-time country stations, numbering a pitiful 81 in 1961, were some 600 strong just eight years later. By the late 1960s, country music in Nashville, borne on the shoulders of country radio, was entering its second era of prosperity.

Artistic trends within the music aided this accelerating popularity. As a natural outgrowth of their musical sophistication, Chet Atkins and Owen Bradley had created a pop-country amalgam that came to be known as the Nashville Sound. The success of artists associated with that sound (Jim Reeves, Eddy Arnold, Patsy Cline, Marty Robbins), combined with the quirky crossover success of acts like Roger Miller, resulted in records with a broad appeal that reinforced every argument the CMA could make about the popularity of country music.

Nashville was (and is) uniquely structured for activities of this kind. The Nashville entertainment community has always been large in relation to the size of the city itself. Indeed, an eight-square-block area known as Music Row has encompassed nearly the entire music industry since the mid fifties. Little wonder, then, that it is easier for the leadership of Nashville's music industry to get together than it is in New York or Los Angeles. Add to proximity a strong sense of common purpose—an "us-

Maxine, Bonnie, and Jim Edward Brown at the Opry, early sixties. Like Jim Reeves, who recommended the brother-sister act to RCA's Chet Atkins, the Browns were a country act who could sound city slick. In 1959, Chet and the Browns gave the uptown Nashville Sound a new twist when they recorded "The Three Bells." Few fans realized that this pop and country #1 had previously been popularized in France by chanteuse Edith Piaf.

Marty Robbins, suitably attired to promote "A White Sportcoat (and a Pink Carnation)," 1957. Aiming squarely at the pop market, Columbia had Robbins record the song in New York, with production by Mitch Miller and backing by Ray Coniff's orchestra. It shot to #2 on the pop charts. The versatile Opry star ultimately placed twenty-four songs on the pop charts, including the western classic "El Paso" (1959) and the bluesy "Don't Worry" (1960).

439

against-them" attitude nurtured by generations of regional defensiveness—and the success of CMA's promotional efforts should come as no surprise.

BOOM TOWN—AND BUST

Through the 1960s, the overall success of country music corresponded, more or less, to the growth of country radio. Format radio had emerged as the only effective vehicle for promoting records, and it was radio that, through performance fees, paid the writers and publishers who were the bedrock of the Nashville music business.

If we can say that the sixties belonged to music publishers and country radio, then someday we will probably look back on the

440

Country session, seventies style: David Houston and Barbara Mandrell record in Nashville, ca. 1971. Houston was the bigger star at the time, having won two Grammy awards in 1967 for "Almost Persuaded." Mandrell was his second duet partner (Tammy Wynette being the first); the Houston-Mandrell team connected with "After Closing Time" in 1970.

seventies as the period when Nashville's record labels came of age. Crossover hits like "King of the Road," "A Boy Named Sue," and "Harper Valley P.T.A." produced unprecedented sales for the country divisions of major labels. The trend continued as the songs of Kris Kristofferson ("Help Me Make It Through the Night," "Sunday Morning Coming Down," "Me and Bobby McGee") provided a sophisticated country literature capable of attracting an urban audience. Well-publicized recording sessions by Bob Dylan, Joan Baez, and other non-country performers further enhanced Nashville's image as a recording center. During the seventies, one artist after another broke the barriers separating pop from country, and as Kenny Rogers, Anne Murray, and Willie Nelson achieved pop success, Nashville label offices enjoyed the prosperity reserved for writers and publishers in the previous decade.

Record label profits mostly ended up in New York and Los Angeles, of course, for the colonial status of Nashville's record divisions has never been seriously challenged. Nevertheless, Nashville branches found that economic success led to greater independence and control, if not to increased dollars in town. Nashville offices got bigger as well. Columbia, which had nine staffers in Nashville in 1971, employed thirty-three in those departments of the country division by 1981. RCA and MCA (formerly Decca) followed similar patterns.

In the past, the various New York headquarters had allowed their Nashville record divisions precious little autonomy; it was standard practice, for instance, for New York to dictate album

From back-up to front office: Buddy Killen was a studio bassman when Tree Music president Jack Stapp brought him into the publishing company, around 1953. Stapp later made Killen co-owner and president, with Stapp moving up to the chairmanship in 1975. After Stapp died in 1980, Killen became sole owner and one of the industry's most powerful executives.

cover art and liner notes. Even more galling, in the early days, New York A&R staff frequently altered the equalization and the mix of session tapes sent up from Nashville, with the result that a Nashville producer couldn't be certain that his latest record would retain the treble and bass response he'd intended or that the drums wouldn't drown out the guitars when the final product arrived in the record stores. No more: by the mid-seventies strong record sales had earned Nashville offices the final say in matters of album mix, cover art, artist development, signings, special retail campaigns—in short, everything it takes to make a product and sell it.

Unfortunately, in the same decade, serious weaknesses in the structure of the Nashville music business began to appear. Both major music licensing organizations, BMI and ASCAP, had become involved in protracted legal battles over the legitimacy of the "blanket license," which allowed the collection of flat fees from broadcasters and live music venues for distribution to writers and publishers. Both BMI and ASCAP used these legal actions and the underlying threat to their collections policies to justify the elimination of writer and publisher advances that had been so crucial to Nashville's growth in the sixties. The licensing firms had really been banks during that decade, advancing enormous sums against future royalty earnings to allow publishers to begin operation or to expand, and to allow struggling writers, in some cases, even to eat and pay rent. Because of intense competition between the licensing firms, the practice of advancing against royalties was open to abuse by writers and publishers willing to play one organization against the other. Though both BMI and ASCAP no doubt breathed easier as advances left the scene, an important source of financial backing for publishing had disappeared. By the early 1980s, publishing companies that might have relied on advances for capital turned instead to the sale of all or portions of their song catalogs to acquire funds for operations. As a result, by the mid eighties, there were virtually no major independent publishers in the city: Hallnote Music was acquired by the Welk Group (Lawrence Welk is a giant in the music publishing field); Combine Music (home of Kris Kristofferson's lucrative songs) was sold; so were Cedarwood and even the venerable Acuff-Rose. Of the Nashville giants, only Tree Publishing remained locally owned. Thus, the largest single financially independent component of the country music business had come under the control of corporations based outside Nashville.

Meanwhile, radio had determined that it didn't much need new songs at all. Marketing studies had shown that old hits had more appeal for the older, more affluent targets of country radio

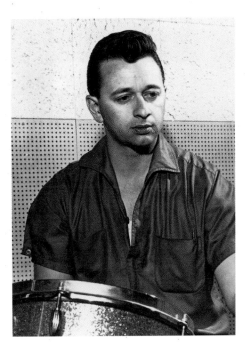

Ray Edenton—a dead ringer for Boris Karloff in this ca. 1964 snapshot. A rhythm guitarist in Nashville sessions for more than thirty years, Edenton also tried his hand at solo recording and songwriting, helping to compose "You're Running Wild," a hit in 1956 for the Louvin Brothers.

Buddy Harman had been playing drums with big bands when—in a bold move for the time—Carl Smith hired Harman to play in his band in 1954. Murrey Harman, Jr., soon became one of Nashville's most frequently used studio drummers, though he had to make his debut on the Opry hidden behind a curtain, playing just a snare drum, with brushes.

Charlie McCoy can play guitar (and other instruments), but he made his reputation as Nashville's standout session harmonica player of the past thirty years. He's often credited with singlehandedly reviving country's interest in the harmonica.

than unfamiliar new material. Much to the dismay of record manufacturers, radio was offering them short playlists open only to established artists and partly filled with old material that had outlived its salability on record or tape years ago.

Music publishers, of course, are paid for performances whether a song is new or old. Because of BMI's (and, later, ASCAP's) aggressive actions in the country field, performance royalties had long ago outstripped mechanicals as the major source of money for writers and publishers. Naturally, publishers were not as distressed by tight playlists and oldies formats as were the record companies.

By the mid 1980s, records and radio were at loggerheads. The labels held that radio stations had an obligation to present new material and new artists; radio executives claimed a right to assemble merely the most appealing and profitable format possible, relying on established acts and past hits. Publishers, who could benefit from either approach, sided with neither radio nor records in this dispute. As the financial interests of the major players in the country music game diverged, it became impossible for the CMA to mount the unified collective actions that had succeeded in the 1960s.

The early 1980s produced another source of financial pressure on Nashville's country record divisions. By that time it was clear that the unprecedented boom in country music seen in the late 1970s had been the result of a short-lived fad. The *Urban Cowboy* phenomenon (named for the movie that glorified an imagined late twentieth-century honky-tonk cowboy life-style) spread not only country music, but cowboy dress, pickup trucks, mechanical

443

Bob Moore, dean of Nashville bassists, studiously lays down a beat during one of his countless sessions, ca. 1964.

Buddy Emmons worked as a sideman for some of country's biggest stars, including Little Jimmy Dickens, Ernest Tubb, and Ray Price, while also making a name for himself as a session player and solo instrumentalist with a jazzy touch. An innovator in pedal steel design and tuning, Emmons collaborated with Shot Jackson on the Sho-Bud line of steel guitars. Here, in 1964, he plays a steel guitar stamped with his own brand name.

For a few brief years, Hank Garland was a star among Nashville's session pickers. His hot, jazzy playing on Red Foley's 1949 hit "Sugarfoot Rag" earned him a label credit: "With guitar solo by Hank 'Sugarfoot' Garland." He went on to play countless Nashville sessions, eventually stepping out as an influential solo jazz artist. Head injuries sustained in a near-fatal 1961 car crash cut short his brilliant career at age thirty.

bulls, and a slew of other symbols of country living into an urban society long thought immune to the charms of rural culture. The boom produced talk show appearances for Loretta Lynn, Dolly Parton, and Willie Nelson, and generated a spate of dramatic films (some fine, some laughable) that featured these stars. Country record sales, in particular, benefitted from all this exposure.

Inevitably, the record labels increased budgets and expanded staffs to handle what at the time appeared to be more than an ephemeral trend. More significantly, recording artists took note of their increased importance and popularity, and, through their managers, did their best to commit labels contractually to appropriate royalty arrangements. Some very expensive deals were cut in those years, deals that generally called for large advances and for significant guaranteed payments when the artists completed a new album. Sadly, many of these agreements outlived by years the business climate in which actual sales would come close to earning back advances and guarantees. Something would have to give—and it wouldn't be the record companies. Big-name artists with long-standing label relationships found themselves (albeit sometimes briefly) without contracts. Dolly Parton, Waylon Jennings, and Johnny Cash all switched labels when management passed on their terms for renewal. Kenny Rogers slipped under the wire, signing a giant contract with RCA just before the softness of the late-seventies boom became apparent (Rogers has since moved to Warner Brothers).

For the country divisions of record labels, the year 1985 marked a new period of painful retrenchment. Although everyone was quick to point out that sales still exceeded those of the

444

pre-*Urban Cowboy* days, it was small consolation. Throughout the 1970s, country music's share of total record sales had varied little, hovering between 10.5 percent and 12 percent. The *Urban Cowboy* fad gave country music a temporary boost, and for a time country accounted for nearly 15 percent of all records sold. But, by 1986, the take had fallen back to 9 percent, though of a greatly expanded total volume of records and dollars. Country sales in that year totaled more than $415 million.

BACK TO THE BOTTOM LINE

The retrenchment of 1985–86 accelerated the decline of major stars of the sixties and seventies, because it made deals typical of the end of that era nearly unacceptable to country record divisions. Instead, a new generation of artists was ushered in, artists whose sights were set not too low, but at least at targets attainable in these tougher times. Not only were younger artists more realistic in their demands of record labels, but the pared-down A&R staffs were more open to fresh musical approaches than they might have been in an earlier era. The emphasis was now on the entire label roster, not just a flagship superstar or two. With RCA and Warner Brothers leading the way, traditional and country-rock acts viewed as antique or exotic in the seventies found themselves with major label deals.

Today, a new generation of Nashville record executives is calling the shots. Some of these division heads have come from the artistic production side of the business, others from marketing.

During the sixties, Pete Drake once provided the steel guitar licks for three-quarters of the records appearing on Billboard's country chart. He also founded a publishing company, ran a recording studio, and worked as a producer. Yet he'll probably go down in history as the "Talking Steel Guitar Man" for his instrumental hit "Forever," on which he "speaks" with the voice of a steel guitar, using a plastic tube connecting his amplifier to his mouth.

Harold Bradley, 1960s. Until he spent a summer playing guitar for Ernest Tubb on tour, Owen Bradley's kid brother thought country music was corny. The tour with Tubb changed the seventeen-year-old jazz fan's mind, and soon he joined Owen in the Nashville studios, contributing guitar, six-string bass, and banjo licks to innumerable records.

445

THE NASHVILLE NETWORK

One that got away: Bobby Bare interviews Lacy J. Dalton for the pilot episode of "Bobby Bare and Friends," 1983. Despite strong critical response, the Nashville Network dropped this fine program of conversations with songwriters in 1985.

The Nashville Network, commonly known by its acronym, TNN, made its debut on March 7, 1983. Created as part of the entertainment complex that operates the Grand Ole Opry, Opryland, and WSM Radio, TNN began as cable TV's first all-country network, with an eighteen-hour daily schedule of programming. Obviously, those responsible for TNN's creation knew that there was a market for what they were trying to do: TNN premiered with the largest audience of any cable network up to that point, some 21 million viewers, and TNN has repeatedly ranked as America's most-watched cable network, with the total number of subscribers now approaching 30 million.

One reason for its popularity is its great variety. The top show, Ralph Emery's "Nashville Now," presents live music from the industry's brightest stars each weeknight. Nothing less than the "Tonight Show" of country music, "Nashville Now" is run four times daily, once live and three times on tape. "New Country," which airs immediately after the live broadcast of "Nashville Now," showcases the newer stars performing tracks from their recent LPs. TNN viewers also enjoy

a live half-hour of the Grand Ole Opry each Saturday night, preceded by backstage chats with the stars. Buffs of the classic singing western movies get a double helping on TNN: they can watch Roy Rogers & Dale Evans hosting "Happy Trails Theater," and Gene Autry and Pat Buttram on "Melody Ranch Theater." "Country Clips" meets the burgeoning demand for music videos, while country news and feature stories are the fare on "Crook and Chase" and "This Week in Country Music," both hosted by Lorianne Crook and Charlie Chase. Bill Anderson hosts "Fandango," the world's first country music TV quiz show (which has lately broadened its question-base to include other music as well). Cooking, recreation, travel, and sports are the subjects of

an increasing number of TNN programs, such as "Country Kitchen" and "Wish You Were Here."

Sadly, some of the better TNN programs are already broadcast history. Among those shows no longer in production are Teddy Bart's "Inside Nashville," an interview program; the late Archie Campbell's "Yesteryear in Nashville," an interview and clips show spotlighting performances from the past; "Tumbleweed Theater," a western movie show hosted by Riders in the Sky; "Bobby Bare and Friends," offering relaxed, informative conversations between Bare and top country songwriters; and "Country Notes," a fine news and feature program. In spite of the shows that failed to catch on, TNN has been a remarkable success story.

Country music's "Tonight Show": host Ralph Emery wades into the studio audience of "Nashville Now," 1986. That year, Cable Guide *magazine named the veteran WSM announcer the most popular personality on cable television.*

447

Marvin Hughes, 1940s. A WSM staff pianist and music director for many years, Hughes often worked the Opry's "Prince Albert Show" in addition to doing session work. For much of the sixties, he ran Capitol Records' Nashville office.

Hargus "Pig" Robbins, 1963. So frequently has this blind pianist appeared on sessions that some record company files simply give his name as Pig among the list of musicians. In Robert Altman's 1975 movie Nashville, *star singer Haven Hamilton (played by Henry Gibson) kicks a bumbling piano player (named "Frog") out of a session, angrily telling the producer, "Now you get me Pig, and then we'll be ready to record this here tune!"*

After years of backing up stars like Ernest Tubb and Carl Smith, Hal and Velma Smith made a brief bid for the spotlight in the fifties. Ultimately, they had much more success remaining behind the scenes: Hal organized the Pamper Music publishing house, eventually working in TV production and artist management; Velma became a studio guitarist, whose rhythm playing found particular favor with Chet Atkins.

They share an ability to mix artistic and business judgment with a sophistication unheard of in Nashville little more than a decade ago. These bottom-line-conscious executives learned how to profit once again from sales of a few hundred thousand albums, and promotion and marketing specialists explored every avenue that might lead to increased income. Country songs appeared in movie soundtracks, and labels and managers encouraged corporate sponsorship of tours. Labels even cooperated in the development of artist-oriented exhibits at the Country Music Hall of Fame. Details bypassed as irrelevant in the years of *Urban Cowboy* prosperity now separated success from failure. A record industry motivated by a touch of apprehension now exploits every opportunity. And it was working: more new acts (twenty-three) appeared on the charts in *Billboard* during 1986 than ever had before. To an even greater extent than during the Outlaw years, the business declines of the early 1980s produced a spirit of experimentation and openness toward alternative musical styles and new acts. MCA reactivated Dot Records as a creative budget line and tried a special series devoted to New Age instrumental recordings. Not all of this has worked, but enough has.

Floyd Cramer, 1960s. The session veteran already had a modest pop hit with his 1958 piano tune "Flip, Flop, and Bop" when Chet Atkins asked him to duplicate the "slip-note" technique of New York songwriter Don Robertson for a Hank Locklin session. When Locklin's record went to #1, Cramer recorded "Last Date" (1960) in the new style, launching a series of crossover hits and making the "slip-note" sound synonymous with country music.

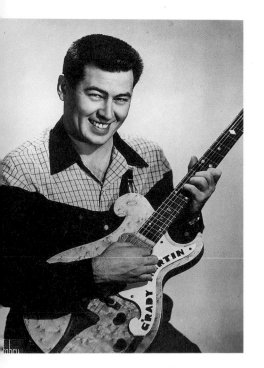

Grady Martin, early fifties. A professional fiddler-guitarist at age fifteen, he worked for several Opry artists before settling in as one of Nashville's leading session guitarists. His licks provided the hooks for Red Foley's "Chattanoogie Shoeshine Boy" (1950), Marty Robbins's "El Paso" (1959), and Roy Orbison's "Oh, Pretty Woman" (1964). In the eighties, he joined Willie Nelson's band.

Jerry Byrd, early great of the steel guitar, 1949. Much in demand at Cincinnati and Nashville sessions for his pure melodic style, Byrd also recorded instrumentals like "Steelin' the Blues" (1949). In the mid fifties, when the pedal steel supplanted his older, lap-steel sound, he refused to follow the trend. Eventually, he left Nashville for Hawaii— birthplace of the steel guitar.

Perhaps most importantly, the rift between country record companies and country radio is gradually closing. Movement has come from both sides, with broadcasters increasingly aware that they require the continuing output of a healthy industry to compete in a cutthroat radio environment, while record companies have done a better and better job of providing contemporary music that lures programmers away from long-established acts and oldies.

The institutional base of Nashville's country music industry remains strong and is in fact growing. The CMA remains a leading trade association. The Country Music Foundation reaches hundreds of thousands of fans and Nashville visitors through the Country Music Hall of Fame & Museum and the Foundation's other programs. Cable television's Nashville Network was pro-

450

Veteran dobro player Harold "Shot" Jackson recorded as a featured instrumentalist, but he's better known as a session man and for his work as a sideman with the Bailes Brothers and, later, Johnnie & Jack, during the forties and fifties. For many years, Jackson and steel guitar player Buddy Emmons were partners in the famous Sho-Bud steel guitar company.

Bud Isaacs wasn't the first to play the pedal steel guitar, but he made it sound indispensable. Webb Pierce's "Slowly," released in January 1954, distinctly featured Isaac's new sound, and the #1 hit drove pickers into a frenzy trying to figure out how Isaacs was able to change pitch in mid-note. His mastery of the instrument's complicated pedals and knee levers rendered regular steel guitars obsolete overnight.

moting the city and country music in more than 35 million homes by the end of 1987, and the full promotional potential of that unique cable network has yet to be fully realized. Nashville and its country music industry seem well positioned for another era of growth. A brief weakness in the pop-rock business, an emerging crossover superstar, or a Nashville-based writer whose work crosses genre lines—any of these could start a boom. The structure to support such success is already in place.

Nashville's country music community is the anomalous product of accident, business design, and entrepreneurial leadership. As early as the 1960s, Nashville had defined its role as a cliquish, quirky recording and publishing center capable of effective collective action that consistently outstripped and astonished other entertainment communities. In the late 1980s, spurred by its own, private recession, Nashville bounced back and restored to the town a solid feeling of success. The labels were again doing well, a couple of new independent publishers opened offices, and the two largest licensing organizations were hinting that old-style advances might soon be back. Just as Ralph Peer's innovation and BMI's aggressive advocacy had reshaped country music's creative environment generations ago, Nashville's new bottom-line orientation retained the city's independence and seems to have paved the way for yet another period of artistic growth and economic prosperity.

WANTED!

THE OUTLAWS

Waylon Jennings, Willie Nelson, Jessi Colter, Tompall Glaser

REWARD REWARD

Waylon Jennings

Willie Nelson

Jessi Colter

Tompall Glaser

RCA

APL1-1321

14

FROM THE BUMP-BUMP ROOM TO THE BARRICADES: WAYLON, TOMPALL, AND THE OUTLAW REVOLUTION

Chet Flippo

Revolution and counterrevolution may seem to be the most un-likely topics ever to be associated with country music, but the tendency to rebel is ingrained in humans, it seems, and it certainly is imbedded in the persons most likely to be prominent in country music: white, southern males of modest education, little or no formal music training, considerable ego, and virtually no sense of an enduring musical tradition. The history of country music is not a long one but neither is it especially tranquil.

Any conflict, though, was always carefully kept behind the scenes during country's first few decades. That was easily done because of the paternalistic nature of the country music structure, which was effectively run by a handful of men: the song publishers, the record company heads (who also controlled the producing of records), the Grand Ole Opry hierarchy, the few booking agents, and those who controlled the big country radio stations. The artists had virtually no say in anything (and, significantly, had no inkling whatsoever that they could ever have a say in anything approaching self-determination). Most evolution

Wanted! The Outlaws *(1976) became country music's first platinum album, despite consisting of previously released tracks and outtakes that hardly represented the singers' best work. It was a triumph of packaging and marketing.*

453

in country music came about from the top down, rather than the reverse, and came about for commercial, rather than artistic, reasons. (One distinction must be made here: rebellion by country artists has inevitably been over life-style, for want of a better term, rather than over music. The classic example was Hank Williams, whose musical force could not be denied, but whose pathetic rebellion was rooted in the paranoia of an insular upbringing, alcohol, and drugs.)

Without going into great detail, even a casual reading of country music's history shows a cyclical pattern of action and reaction, based on commercial factors—on what the Nashville movers and shakers thought would sell. As a conservative business, country music may safely be said to have always preferred to follow, rather than to anticipate, trends. Rockabilly is a classic example. It was imposed upon Nashville by outside influences—from just down the road, in Memphis, at Sun Records—and could not be ignored after Elvis Presley's success. The country music industry initially tried to ignore it and keep selling honky-tonk music, deliberately disregarding the social forces behind the changes in musical tastes. But there was such a groundswell for the new music—particularly by artists—it became clear that it was a future that could not be swept away. RCA farsightedly signed Elvis and thereby guaranteed its commercial future.

At the time, the present and future titans of Nashville labored, with mixed successes, to make rockabilly work in the marketplace. Owen Bradley at Decca scored with Brenda Lee, but he completely misread and misunderstood Buddy Holly in a disastrous studio recording session in Nashville. Similarly, his studio work with Johnny Burnette's Rock 'n' Roll Trio was quickly forgotten. (Johnny Cash, who had been one of the great hopes at Sun Records, along with Elvis, later said that his rockabilly past was held against him by power shakers in Nashville, and Opry manager Jim Denny was one person he named.) At RCA, Chet Atkins, the wunderkind guitar picker who had worked with Hank Williams, now found himself in the studio trying to guide the likes of Presley and the Everly Brothers. And the reason is of the course the reason why record companies exist: to sell records and make money.

As rockabilly waned and—not coincidentally—country moved closer to pop music, Bradley and Atkins brought forth what came to be known as the Nashville Sound. In another age, it might have been called "Lite Country." What it was was carefully formulated, inoffensive music designed to appeal to fans of pop music while still retaining enough of a country identity to make it on jukeboxes in the honky-tonks, even though the fiddles had been replaced by violins. With Bradley, the Sound peaked with his production of Patsy Cline ("Crazy," "I Fall to Pieces,"

Hank Williams onstage at the Opry, ca. 1951. Though his rebellion had more to do with drink than self-determination, Hank remains, in the eyes of many, the original Outlaw. Backing him here are bassist Ernie Newton and WSM staff guitarist Chet Atkins, who would soon work with rockabillies, only to find himself squared off against Outlaws in twenty years' time.

Jim Reeves at the mike, early 1960s. Together Reeves and producer Chet Atkins strove for a relaxed, intimate approach to country music that could compete with pop music on pop's terms. Crossover hits like Reeves's "He'll Have to Go" (1959) did just that—and sounded about as country as Mantovani to Outlaw ears.

Waylon Jennings & the Waylors, 1960s. Not until 1973 was Waylon finally able to bring his own band into the studio to play on his records.

"Sweet Dreams"). The Nashville Sound itself was more closely identified with Atkins and his best-known pickers: saxophonist Boots Randolph, pianist Floyd Cramer, and guitarists Hank Garland and Grady Martin (the latter would later join Willie Nelson's band). If you'd like one example, Jim Reeves's "He'll Have to Go" is perfect: country sentiments with a pop presentation. An airport lounge honky-tonk song.

The producer was truly king with the Nashville Sound in operation. He chose the songs, the pickers, the arrangements, the album cover, the strings and vocal backing used to "sweeten" the whole package. The singer was almost an afterthought. A lot of singers resented that, but there was nothing they could do about it. The record companies were selling records, not individual careers. In the past, country songs had crossed over to pop audiences mostly when covered by pop singers (as Tony Bennett did with Hank Williams's "Cold, Cold Heart"). Elvis changed all that, and the pop possibility became tantalizing.

It was into such a pop-country quagmire that a young generation of country singer-songwriters such as Willie Nelson and Waylon Jennings came in the sixties. Nashville had tried to ignore the Beatles and all that they represented—the whole youth culture, pop culture, counterculture. Country music seemed fixed in a death frieze, epitomized by the Opry and its aging,

456

Waylon pays a visit to "The Porter Wagoner Show," back when Porter was the star and Waylon wasn't, 1960s.

rural, loyal-to-Roy Acuff audience on the one hand, and the younger, moved-to-the-city country blue-collar crowd that wasn't satisfied by Danny Davis & the Nashville Brass. The Nashville Sound had moved to middle-of-the-road music and lost whatever country identity it had had. Meanwhile, audiences were no longer isolated or segregated: even in rural areas, younger people listened to the latest Top Forty pop and rock hits, and, as they did so, they began to ask more of country music.

But Nashville wasn't listening. Albums were still recorded quickly on a nickel-and-dime budget and often featured a hit single surrounded by a lot of dross; country stage shows were often bare-bones affairs—music, but scarce else. For the artists, expectations were worse: sales of a hundred thousand for a record were wonderful (compare this with pop acts' frequent sales of over one million); bookings were still into the Crab Orchard circuit; and playing the Opry on Saturday night (for union scale) was still the ideal. It's easy to see in hindsight that there was a ceiling over Nashville: there was no notion that things could be bigger or better or even different. Country was a small-time game, played for small-time stakes. What sold was what was recorded, and what was recorded was what sold.

During this time (the sixties going into the early seventies) there were many factors that came to change country music drastically and forever. I would like to concentrate on one that was basically fostered by singers caught up in the Nashville Sound. There came to be a broad-based revolution spawned by the non-power brokers—the writers and singers—that was as

457

The man who packaged the Outlaws: Jerry Bradley (right) with RCA producer Norro Wilson, 1970s.

Outlaw's best friend: Bobby Bare, 1970s. By the time the Outlaws came along, Bare had already blazed a trail for them, gaining creative control of his records in the early seventies. Meanwhile, he consistently recorded songs by unheralded songwriters—Kris Kristofferson, Shel Silverstein, Billy Joe Shaver, Guy Clark, and Townes Van Zandt. And he was the one who recommended Waylon to Chet Atkins.

much influenced by the Beatles as Bob Dylan, as much by the Vietnam War as by country star Johnny Cash (who had been a one-man phenomenon). It was called the "Outlaw" movement, a glib publicity term, but it came to represent a genuine watershed in country music history.

It sprang from a back-alley rendezvous in Nashville between kindred spirits who liked to stay up late and carouse around town before getting down to business with some music. But it came to represent a real determination by a handful of artists to bring country music into line with the rest of the music world—artistically as well as financially. By the time it ran its course, the Outlaw movement had changed the face of country music forever. The producer as king—that feudal notion was shattered. Country artists gained control over their own record sessions, their own booking, their record production, everything else related to their careers, including the right to make their own mistakes. It was a major shift in country music. It also brought country artists into the million-dollar stratosphere of pop and rock artists and also, of course, into their cocaine- and marijuana-laced decadence.

It's not often that one movement can coalesce around one event, but, conveniently, the whole Outlaw upheaval came to define itself by the release of one record album that was also the first platinum-selling (one million copies plus) in Nashville history.

The album—*Wanted! The Outlaws*—itself was not really anything spectacular, even by modest Nashville standards. RCA producer Jerry Bradley (Owen's son) conceded that, but knew he had hit upon what could become the biggest marketing coup of his life. For once, Nashville was selling a concept, rather than just peddling records. Bradley, in fact, said just that when he called me in 1975 to ask me to write liner notes for the *Outlaws* album. "I'll send you tapes on it," he told me, "but I'll bet you've heard most of it before. What I'm doing is putting Willie and Waylon and Tompall [with Waylon's wife, Jessi Colter] together as the Outlaws, because that's the way they are regarded here in town. This is a package, a total package that I'm looking to break outside the country market. That's why I'd like you to do the notes: you know the music and the musicians, but you're not a cheerleader like the writers here in town. You're definitely not considered part of the establishment."

Well, I had to admit that that was certainly true enough. One of Nashville's two daily newspapers had recently run a lengthy article attacking me for my views on the state of country music, in pieces published in *Rolling Stone* magazine. And I had re-

458

Chet Atkins and Waylon Jennings, 1960s. Waylon liked all kinds of music—rock, folk, pop—but the smooth Nashville Sound never suited his rough and rowdy ways. "I couldn't go pop with a mouthful of firecrackers," he's reported to have said. Still, under Chet's direction, Waylon covered a song that had been a pop hit for actor Richard Harris, "MacArthur Park" (1969), complete with strings and chorus vocals. It won a Grammy but never cracked the country Top Twenty.

ceived quite a bit of hate mail, most of it from Nashville. So, in a sense, I had to be flattered to be considered, even tangentially, an outlaw in Nashville.

Bradley, of course, had his own motives. Always in his father's shadow, he longed to make his mark in the industry. Even though he had nominally taken over RCA's Nashville reins from Chet Atkins, the latter's presence was still formidable within the company. And, with this album, Bradley was not going out on a limb so much as he was dealing with a relatively safe proposition. In all but name, the Outlaw business was pretty much in place and fairly successful long before the *Outlaws* album appeared, in 1976. The term itself had surfaced with Waylon's 1972 hit song and album of the same name, "Ladies Love Outlaws." The song, written by Lee Clayton, one of the junior Outlaws in Waylon's orbit, was intended, Clayton said, more or less tongue-in-cheek. But it quickly caught on as a sort of anthem.

And as far as the Outlaw business being a genuine rebellion against Nashville, it was at heart the inevitable revolt of sons against fathers. But even more so, it was a true declaration of independence by those involved. Willie had never been served well by the Nashville system and simply wanted to be left alone to pursue his musical visions. If he had to go to Texas to do so, so be it. (Ironically, a year before the *Outlaws* was released, Willie went up to a little studio in Garland, Texas, with his band

459

Jessi Colter, early 1970s. Singer-songwriter Miriam Johnson took her stage name from a genuine outlaw: her great-great-great uncle Jesse Colter, a member of the notorious James Gang. Married to Waylon Jennings since 1970, she was inspired to write her signature hit, "I'm Not Lisa" (1975), when Waylon accidentally called her by the name of an old flame.

Nashville Rebel (1967) put Waylon onscreen long before Willie and Kris. Reportedly, Waylon fell asleep during the filming of one of his love scenes with co-star Mary Frann (who now plays the wife of Bob Newhart in his CBS television series "Newhart"), foreshadowing audience reactions everywhere. Today the best place to catch this B-grade effort is Waylon's Music Row curio shop.

and recorded his true breakthrough album, *Red Headed Stranger.* When CBS Records' Billy Sherrill balked at releasing the sparsely arranged record, Willie won the test of wills.) Waylon had felt ill-served by the system for years, and rightly so. He mainly wanted a little freedom: to record with his road band and to record what songs he wanted to, when he wanted to, without a producer who had been assigned by Atkins, and especially

460

where he wanted to. It was this last wish that led to his alignment with Tompall Glaser and the formation of Outlaw Headquarters at Hillbilly Central, Tompall's studio on Nineteenth Avenue South in Nashville. Under terms of his RCA contract, Waylon was required to record at RCA if he was within two hundred miles of Nashville. Waylon had long chafed under RCA's heavy hand and had made his first move for independence in 1972 when Neil Reshen, his New York City manager (whom Waylon often referred to as his "mad dog on a leash"), discovered that, technically, RCA had not automatically picked up Waylon's option to re-sign with the company. Reshen soon had Columbia, Atlantic, Capitol, and Mercury wooing Waylon, to the great dismay of Chet Atkins and Jerry Bradley. After tense negotiations, RCA

Waylon Jennings, late 1970s. The former DJ and one-time bass player for Buddy Holly was nearly forty years old when, suddenly, after a decade of unfulfilled potential, he became a country music superstar.

461

Just good friends: Waylon's erstwhile manager Neil Reshen, producer Billy Sherrill, Willie Nelson, Tammy Wynette, and CBS execs Tony Martell and Ron Alexenburg.

Billy Joe Shaver and Bobby Bare flank CBS executive Roy Wunsch, early eighties. Shaver (left) had all but given up on making it as a songwriter in Nashville when Bare recorded a Shaver tune and signed him to his publishing company. Since then, the Texan's poetic way with honky-tonk has been heard on the records of Kris Kristofferson, Tom T. Hall, Jerry Reed, and John Anderson. In 1973, Waylon's Honky Tonk Heroes *album featured all Shaver songs save one.*

462

Smooth operator: Columbia's Billy Sherrill, 1960s. During the rise of the Outlaws, Nashville's hottest producer (Tammy Wynette, Charlie Rich, Tanya Tucker) acquired a reputation for excess, because his records typically featured a lush orchestral sound. Nevertheless, when the harder Outlaw style became chic, he turned around and produced records for David Allan Coe and Johnny Paycheck that fit right in.

eventually re-signed Waylon, but gave him the greatest artistic freedom of any of its country artists. Atkins complained that his own contract with RCA held no such freedom. Waylon was pretty much left in control of his records—not something he really expected right away and certainly not something he was accustomed to. The freedom was also a muscle he himself would have to flex; RCA obviously was not going to spell out to him all the ways he could supplant what the label had been doing.

His music didn't change immediately, but his records did—especially the 1973 album that became the quintessential Outlaw work: *Honky Tonk Heroes*. It also set the formula for what became known as Outlaw music: sparsely accompanied and highly personal songs; a cowboy's diary set to a driving beat, as it were. This was Waylon Jennings working at full-bore, finally able to do what he wanted to, capturing his lusty, gritty vision. Nine of the ten songs on *Honky Tonk Heroes* were written by another Texas Outlaw, Billy Joe Shaver, a gifted poet who was determined to try Nashville because of his idols, Willie and Waylon. Billy Joe hitchhiked to Nashville on the back of a truck loaded with cantaloupes, naive in his belief that such songs as "Black Rose"— about a black-white romance—could make it in Nashville. They did, although they could not have five years earlier or five years later. The Outlaw window was open, however briefly. Even though the credits say the album *Honky Tonk Heroes* was recorded at RCA, the bulk of it was cut at Tompall Glaser's Hillbilly Central studio, with Waylon and Tompall producing.

Of all the y-clept "Outlaws," Tompall was the most outspoken in his reaction to the status quo in country music and in Nash-

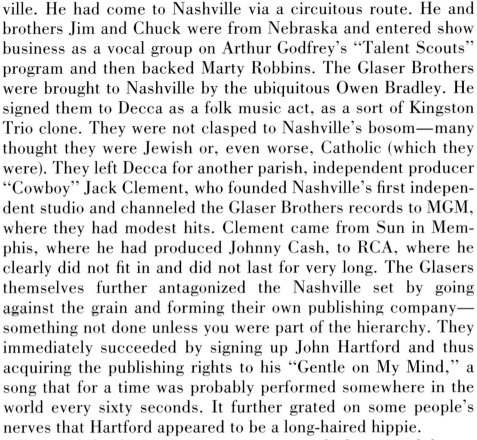

Jack Clement, jack-of-all-trades and visionary, about the time he was producing the Glasers, early 1960s. With a resumé that included playing bluegrass with Buzz Busby, writing and orchestrating pop crossovers for Johnny Cash at Sun, and launching the career of Charley Pride, he was the right man to produce Waylon's 1975 declaration of independence, Dreaming My Dreams.

ville. He had come to Nashville via a circuitous route. He and brothers Jim and Chuck were from Nebraska and entered show business as a vocal group on Arthur Godfrey's "Talent Scouts" program and then backed Marty Robbins. The Glaser Brothers were brought to Nashville by the ubiquitous Owen Bradley. He signed them to Decca as a folk music act, as a sort of Kingston Trio clone. They were not clasped to Nashville's bosom—many thought they were Jewish or, even worse, Catholic (which they were). They left Decca for another parish, independent producer "Cowboy" Jack Clement, who founded Nashville's first independent studio and channeled the Glaser Brothers records to MGM, where they had modest hits. Clement came from Sun in Memphis, where he had produced Johnny Cash, to RCA, where he clearly did not fit in and did not last for very long. The Glasers themselves further antagonized the Nashville set by going against the grain and forming their own publishing company—something not done unless you were part of the hierarchy. They immediately succeeded by signing up John Hartford and thus acquiring the publishing rights to his "Gentle on My Mind," a song that for a time was probably performed somewhere in the world every sixty seconds. It further grated on some people's nerves that Hartford appeared to be a long-haired hippie.

Some of the Glasers' money went into a little state-of-the-art recording studio in a turn-of-the-century house on Nineteenth Avenue South, well off of Music Row. The brothers divorced as a musical act in 1972, and Tompall emerged as the nascent solo performer, cutting the introspective 1973 album *Charlie*. He also was the Glaser-in-residence at the comfortable studio, which quickly became known as Hillbilly Central, and which was a magnet for anyone in Nashville who was non-Nashville-establishment. It became, especially after dark, the clubhouse for the Outlaws, or those fancied to be one of their number. Waylon and Tompall, after a chance meeting, took a liking to each other. There are striking similarities: both are strong individuals, loners, shy to the point of painfulness, distrustful of strangers, both had been burned in the music business, both were by nature trusting persons, and each held fierce and unwavering notions as to what their music ought to be. And especially what it ought not to be. And—perhaps most important of all—Waylon and Tompall were pinball nuts. They loved nothing better than to lean their lanky frames into a pinball machine and ride those flippers all night.

At the time, the area between Nineteenth Avenue and Vanderbilt University was a regular warren of cheap clubs, murky dives, hooch joints, raucous drive-ins, and beer-milk-bread con-

Left
Guy Clark, who once worked for the Dopyera family in California making dobros, moved to Nashville in 1971 and crafted songs—"Desperadoes Waiting for a Train," "L.A. Freeway"— widely admired by fellow Outlaws and songwriters. In 1981, Ricky Skaggs took his song "Heartbroke" to the top of the charts.

Top right
John Hartford, ca. 1968. This devotee of Earl Scruggs was never tagged an Outlaw, but he could have been. "Gentle on My Mind," his hobo song for the counterculture, put Glen Campbell in touch with the youth market in 1967 and gave Hartford's publishers, the Glasers, the money they needed to operate independently in Nashville. Appearing regularly on the Smothers Brothers' TV series didn't endear him to Nashville's old guard, either.

Opposite, bottom
The Glaser Brothers as clean-cut folk singers, fresh from their Nebraska farm and ready to take on the world, 1957. From top to bottom: Chuck, Tompall, and Jim.

venience stores—each of which had at least one pinball machine. And these machines paid off. In real money. Waylon and Tompall sometimes would collect a couple of hundred bucks each for a few hours' work on the flippers.

I was privileged to spend more than a few nights on the pinball circuit with them, and I was to find that that was where they conducted a lot of their business—making decisions, meeting songwriters and being pitched songs and keeping up with who was writing what, doing a little songwriting themselves as they sent that little silver ball spinning. Their favorite joint was a dubious establishment called the Bump-Bump Room, and the Bump-Bump became—almost as much as Hillbilly Central—the

Tompall Glaser, reading the fine print at Hillbilly Central, 1970s. His music has never gotten much airplay, but his methods made a big impression on Waylon.

nerve center of the Outlaw movement. An earlier generation had Tootsie's Orchid Lounge, next to the Opry. The Outlaws had the Bump-Bump Room (and they of course had no use for the Opry at all). They were, in effect, creating an alternative and parallel world distinct and separate from the Nashville establishment— no mean feat in a town as small as Nashville. In Hillbilly Central, Waylon finally found what he had not had at RCA's studios: a private outpost where he could come and go at any hour and do whatever he pleased, no questions asked. And he was surrounded by kindred folk. Very often, recording would not begin until Waylon and Tompall and whoever had cruised the pinball joints until they were ready to go to work. Then they would retire to Nineteenth, crack open the bottles of Black Jack, tune up the guitars and turn on the tape. It was an unregimented life they were seeking, one completely removed from the Nashville system, which actually was still patriarchal in nature, in which the producers and label heads, intentionally or not, treated the artists as dim-witted children or indentured servants. (Jennings still rankles over directives he received from RCA which began:

466

"Dear Artist.") Glaser was even more vitriolic than Jennings, and his published comments about what he called a corrupt system seemed to guarantee that he would be frozen out by the system, which ultimately proved to be the case.

An astonishing thing was that, until Waylon in particular began to receive exposure in the rock press and success with rock audiences and became aware of how things were done in rock, the Outlaws—as well as most artists in Nashville—didn't realize that having artistic freedom in the recording studio was a given outside Nashville. You could record what you wanted and record it with your road band, you could pick the cover of your album, you could try to find a booking agent capable of putting you into places better than the blood-and-guts honky-tonks. You could pick a manager from Los Angeles or New York or anywhere else, and it could be someone who wasn't part of the tiny Nashville old-boy network. And—the biggest heresy—you could

Mickey Newbury was among the leaders in a new generation of songwriters who hit Nashville in the late sixties and early seventies. Instead of writing catchy phrases, Newbury distilled emotion and experience in such songs as "Sweet Memories" and "Why You Been Gone So Long"—though he also wrote Kenny Rogers & the First Edition's trendy stab at psychedelia, "Just Dropped in (to See What Condition My Condition Was In)."

Townes Van Zandt is revered among critics and Texas songwriters for his introspective, carefully crafted songs. Though he has made records since the late sixties, he remains best-known for "Pancho and Lefty," recorded as a duet by Willie Nelson and Merle Haggard. Says Steve Earle: "Townes Van Zandt is the best songwriter in the whole world, and I'll stand on Bob Dylan's coffee table in my cowboy boots and say that."

467

One of the few Austin Outlaws to reach the wider pop market: Michael Murphey, 1970s. At a time when sensitive singer-songwriter types were dominating the pop charts, he eased into the big time in 1975 with country-tinged acoustic numbers like "Wildfire" and "Carolina in the Pines." These days, he goes by the name Michael Martin Murphey and records mainstream country in Nashville.

Kinky Friedman was the wackiest Outlaw of them all: the son of a University of Texas professor, a former Peace Corps volunteer who claims to have introduced the Frisbee to Borneo, leader of the Austin-based Texas Jewboys, writer of "Get Your Biscuits in the Oven (and Your Buns in the Bed)," one-time candidate for mayor of Kerrville (Texas), and, lately, the author of two comic detective novels.

control your own publishing, which had always been Nashville's darkest little secret and of course was always where the real money was. You could even pick your own producer and not have to sign over half the publishing to him, which had been commonplace in Nashville. In short, that was the crux of the Outlaw movement; it had nothing to do with long hair or wearing black leather or smoking dope or any other such trivial sideshow issues. It was actually a fairly sober attempt at gaining self-determination and independence—not such a rare thing for creative people to seek. I can remember being touched by what I considered Waylon's naiveté when—after he started opening for such rock bands as the Grateful Dead—he was literally flabbergasted to learn that such groups could actually put riders into their contracts calling for specific food and drink to be served them in their dressing room. It was almost like watching a barefoot kid discover shoes.

For quite a while, the so-called Outlaws didn't really realize the power they were accruing and the impact they were making. Until their efforts translated into money—which is, after all, what the system really understands and appreciates—they were laboring in the wilderness, as it were. One of the most concrete and telling examples of their clout was an unprecedented concert presented as an alternative to the usual stuffy Disc Jockeys Convention in Nashville. The DJ convention was run by the major labels, with staid concerts and interview sessions and the like. But in 1973, Waylon decided to put on an independent show.

Shel Silverstein with Dr. Hook, 1975. The bald hipster who drew cartoons for Playboy *and wrote children's books seemed at first an unlikely country songwriter. Yet he provided memorable, offbeat country hits for Johnny Cash ("A Boy Named Sue"), Bobby Bare ("Marie Laveau"), and Tompall Glaser ("Put Another Log on the Fire"), among others. He also wrote "The Cover of the Rolling Stone" for the rock band Dr. Hook, which explains this photo.*

Austin's favorite rowdy: Jerry Jeff Walker, 1970s. Born and raised in upstate New York, Walker traveled the country playing folk songs during the sixties, eventually settling in Austin. There, his good-time approach to folk, rock, and country found an immediate and loyal audience.

Almost three thousand people jammed a ballroom at the Sheraton to see Troy Seals, Sammi Smith, Willie Nelson, and Waylon kick out all the jams in what was perhaps the one transcendent event of the whole Outlaw business. I was there, and the notes I took tell me that it was one of the most authoritative, self-confident musical evenings I have ever witnessed, that the music soared and the audience took off with it, and that in the early morning hours, as the show shut down, the heady, almost giddy feeling in the ballroom was contagious. There was a very real and spoken conviction that the old guard of country music was crumbling and the Huns were at the gate, starting to batter it down, and would not be denied. Their time had come.

What they did not yet have to effectuate real change in the Nashville music hierarchy was big record sales. Sales, anywhere in the music business, equaled money, and money equaled power. The more of everything, the better. Getting music writers from *Rolling Stone* to rave about an Outlaw concert at the Sheraton was one thing, but moving those albums out of the stores—that was the kicker, that would certify whether or not this little "movement" that Nashville seemed to have on its hands would amount to anything more than a temper tantrum being thrown by some talented, if immature, youngsters who had not yet learned the tribal ways. Jerry Bradley knew that. He knew, he thought, just how to fix all that with his big Concept Album.

What the album turned out to be was this: *Wanted! The Outlaws* had only Waylon's name on the spine (because he was the

Waylon Jennings with two of Nashville's top songwriters—Bobby Braddock (left) and Bob McDill, 1977. In addition to penning "Good Ole Boys Like Me," McDill supplied Waylon with "Amanda," earlier a hit for Don Williams. With Curly Putman, Braddock wrote "D-I-V-O-R-C-E" for Tammy Wynette and "He Stopped Loving Her Today" for George Jones.

For most, "Outlaw" was just an image; for ex-convict David Allan Coe, it was the real thing. Despite recording for CBS since the early seventies and having written two huge hits—"Would You Lay with Me (In a Field of Stone)" and "Take This Job and Shove It"—he has remained an outsider in Nashville, ostracized for such eccentricities as tattoos, a bevy of common-law wives, and having recorded the occasional X-rated album.

only one of the four Outlaws under contract to RCA at the time). Jerry Bradley decreed that there be a burnt-at-the-edges wanted-poster look to the cover of the thing, with Waylon's picture front and center, to be flanked by Willie, Tompall, and Jessi, with my liner notes on the back, in the form of a poster or broadside. The cuts on the record were unremarkable. Side one was made up of Waylon's "My Heroes Have Always Been Cowboys" and "Honky Tonk Heroes," Jessi's "I'm Looking for Blue Eyes" and "You Mean to Say," and "Suspicious Minds" by Waylon and Jessi. Side two opened with Willie and Waylon singing "Good Hearted Woman" and "Heaven or Hell," Willie's rendition of "Me and Paul" and "Yesterday's Wine." It ended with Tompall's "T for Texas" and "Put Another Log on the Fire." Not exactly a song line-up to draw the angels' hosannas. Yet, this *Outlaws* album was the first platinum album in country music history. There have been many answers advanced to explain that and, I suspect, the most nearly correct one is that the timing of the album was perfect. Two spectacular albums from 1975—Willie's *Red Headed Stranger* and Waylon's *Dreaming My Dreams*—primed the Outlaw audience. Had it been released even six months earlier or six months later, its impact might have been negligible. As it was, its fallout was considerable.

Outlaws was released on January 12, 1976, amid great hoopla by RCA. It soon crossed over to the pop charts, was certified

470

IT'S UNFORTUNATE THAT THERE STILL HAS TO BE A SAMPLER, OR PRIMER, OR GOLDEN BOOK OF SOME OF THE BEST SINGERS WORKING ANYWHERE, BUT APPARENTLY NOT EVERYONE HAS GOTTEN THE MESSAGE YET. MAYBE THIS ALBUM CAN INTRODUCE YOU TO SOME PEOPLE YOU WOULD HAVE LIKED TO HAVE KNOWN SOONER BUT JUST DIDN'T HAVE THE OPPORTUNITY TO MEET.

THESE ARE SOME SPECIAL PEOPLE, VERY SPECIAL. THEY'VE BEEN WAITING IN THE WINGS FOR YEARS TOO MANY YEARS, TO ASSUME THEIR PROPER PLACES IN THE STRUCTURE OF AMERICAN MUSIC. WHEN IT BECAME APPARENT TO THEM THAT THEIR PROPER PLACES WERE PERHAPS BEING UNDULY DELAYED BECAUSE OF CERTAIN RESENTMENTS HARBORED AGAINST THEM BECAUSE OF THEIR REAL AND IMAGINED UNCONVENTIONALITY, THEY — BY GOD — DECIDED TO TAKE MATTERS IN THEIR OWN HANDS. THERE RESULTED A RATHER DIFFICULT PERIOD OF FIGURATIVE DOORS BEING SMASHED AND GENERAL CONFUSION AND NAMECALLING IN NASHVILLE. WHEN THE SMOKE CLEARED AND THE FALLOUT RETURNED TO EARTH THERE WAS EFFECTED A MAJOR SHIFT IN COUNTRY MUSIC. "PROGRESSIVE COUNTRY"(FOR WANT OF A BETTER TERM) WAS ON THE MAP WAS HERE FOR GOOD. AND THESE ARE THE PEOPLE RESPONSIBLE FOR THAT. CALL THEM OUTLAWS, CALL THEM INNOVATORS, CALL THEM REVOLUTIONARIES, CALL THEM WHAT YOU WILL, THEY'RE JUST SOME DAMNED FINE PEOPLE WHO ARE ALSO SOME OF THE MOST GIFTED SONGWRITERS AND SINGERS ANYWHERE.

THEY ARE MUSICAL REBELS, IN ONE SENSE, IN THAT THEY CHALLENGED THE ACCEPTED WAY OF DOING THINGS. LIKE ALL PIONEERS, THEY WERE CRITICIZED FOR THAT BUT TIME HAS VINDICATED THEM.

TOMPALL GLASER WAS ONE OF THE FIRST IN NASHVILLE TO CHART HIS OWN MUSICAL COURSE AND IT WAS LONELY FOR HIM FOR YEARS, BUT, NOW HE IS BEGINNING TO RECEIVE THE RECOGNITION DUE HIM.

WAYLON JENNINGS, AS THE MOST VISIBLE OF THE PROGRESSIVE COUNTRY PACK, HAS BEEN QUIETLY FIGHTING FOR YEARS IN HIS OWN WAY FOR ACCEPTANCE. BOTH HE AND JESSI COLTER (WHO COINCIDENTALLY, IS ALSO KNOWN AS MRS. WAYLON JENNINGS) WERE AUTHENTICALLY AHEAD OF THEIR TIME. NOW, THE TIMES HAVE CAUGHT UP WITH THEM.

THAT STREAK OF RUGGED INDIVIDUALISM THAT IS THE UNIFYING BOND FOR THESE MUSICAL OUTLAWS IS NOWHERE MORE EVIDENT THAN IN WILLIE NELSON'S LIFE AND TIMES. UNQUESTIONABLY ONE OF THE FINEST SONGWRITERS WHO EVER LIVED, WILLIE WAS KNOWN FOR YEARS ONLY TO OTHER WRITERS AND TO A SLOWLY GROWING CULT OF FOLLOWERS. ALL THAT HAS CHANGED NOW. "MIRACLES APPEAR IN THE STRANGEST OF PLACES, WILLIE SINGS IN "YESTERDAY'S WINE, ONE OF MY FAVORITES FROM HIS COLLECTION OF REMARKABLE SONGS. AND THAT'S TRUE. WHEN I FIRST STARTED KEEPING TRACK OF WILLIE AND WAYLON AND JESSI AND TOMPALL, I (ALONG WITH THEIR OTHER CULT FOLLOWERS) FELT ALMOST RESPONSIBLE FOR THEM SINCE THEY WEREN'T THAT WELL KNOWN TO THE PUBLIC AND THE MUSIC INDUSTRY AS A WHOLE DIDN'T LIKE TO ACKNOWLEDGE THEM. THEY DIDN'T WEAR NUDIE SUITS AND THEIR MUSIC DIDN'T CONFORM TO THE COUNTRY NORM OF SONGS OF DIVORCE AND ALCOHOL AND LIFE'S OTHER LITTLE MISERIES. THE ONLY THING THAT WORRIED ME WAS THAT I KNEW THESE PEOPLE WERE BORN SCRAPPERS AND REALLY LOVED FIGHTING FOR ACCEPTANCE. WHAT WOULD HAPPEN TO THEM, I WONDERED, WHEN THEY INEVITABLY WON (AS I KNEW THEY WOULD)? WOULD THEY LIKE SO MANY WHO STRUGGLE JUST FOR THE SAKE OF THE STRUGGLE, GROW FAT AND LAZY WHEN THEY GREW SUCCESSFUL?

THERE WAS NO NEED TO WORRY. THIS PAST YEAR, EACH OF THEM HAS GOTTEN BETTER, WRITING BETTER, AND SINGING WITH BREATHTAKING CONFIDENCE.

THEY'RE THE CUTTING EDGE OF A BRAND OF AMERICAN MUSIC THAT I FIND THE MOST SATISFYING DEVELOPMENT IN POPULAR MUSIC IN THE PAST DECADE. IT'S NOT COUNTRY AND IT'S NOT COUNTRY-ROCK, BUT THERE'S NO REAL NEED TO WORRY ABOUT LABELING IT. IT'S JUST DAMNED GOOD MUSIC THAT'S TRUE AND HONEST AND YOU CAN'T ASK FOR MORE THAN THAT.

Chet Flippo.

ASSOCIATE EDITOR
ROLLING STONE

471

George Jones and Johnny Paycheck, ca. 1980. About this time, Jones finally began receiving his due as country's finest stylist. Meanwhile, Paycheck—a former sideman who owed his break as a headliner to Jones—gained Outlaw status in 1978 with "Take This Job and Shove It." The image got out of hand in 1986 when Paycheck was convicted of shooting a man in an Ohio tavern. Paycheck's T-shirt reads: "Nashville Can't Take a Joke."

gold by the beginning of April, and became country's first platinum-selling album by December. Country music was no longer just a singles market: it now was an album market and thus could rival the sales of rock releases. Willie and Waylon virtually became household names. Their albums began selling gold (500,000 copies) on their own strengths. They were invited to the White House by President Carter in 1978 (Willie and Jessi went; Waylon declined). Their names were more often in *Rolling Stone* than in *Music City News*. Jessi, who had never been overly ambitious and who had a new son at home, stayed in the background. Tompall Glaser, who had been between record labels at the time of the *Outlaws* release (and thus had no albums out to ride the *Outlaws* coattails) had a falling-out with Jennings. His

As Edwin Bruce, he was a teenage rockabilly who made a couple of records for Sun. Two decades later, Ed Bruce was an honorary Outlaw, having written Waylon & Willie's hit "Mamas, Don't Let Your Babies Grow Up to Be Cowboys" with his wife, Patsy. In this photo, he brings his Memphis cowboy touch to the set of "Hee Haw."

solo career was static and he reunited with his brothers for a time.

Meanwhile, Outlaw-clone music inundated Nashville, and Willie and Waylon clones flooded the South and Southwest. In Texas, particularly, the Outlaw look became an everyday uniform, and that led right into the "Texas Chic" trend which itself directly spawned the whole *Urban Cowboy* business. Willie and Waylon soon declared themselves sick of the Outlaw moniker, but they were more or less stuck with it. In 1978, Waylon felt moved to write and record the song "Don't You Think This Outlaw Bit's Done Got Out of Hand," and he doesn't write all that much.

The excesses performed in the name of Outlaw, by musicians and fans alike, were legion. A backlash was inevitable, especially after other performers began to see the amount of success (and money) that accrued to Willie and Waylon. Their records and concerts were scrutinized and criticized to a degree neither had thought possible. They were directly blamed for the basically sleazy *Urban Cowboy* craze that briefly touched country music. They were probably responsible for the New Traditionalists, who responded against the new commercialization of Urban Cowboyism (Nashville Sound as filtered through Gilley's in Pasadena, Texas, and then by the Eagles in California) by returning to a stripped-down, no-frills, back-to-the-basics hard-country music. White hat country, rescued by the likes of George Strait and Reba McEntire. It was not so different from what the Outlaws had started with, in their own revolt against

473

Outlaw reunion: Ten years after the Outlaw business, Willie Nelson, Waylon Jennings, Kris Kristofferson, and Johnny Cash got together to record a hit single called "The Highwayman" and an album by the same title. Here these gentlemen of leisure put on a show for the fans.

Waylon and Willie's first duet, "Good Hearted Woman" (1975), had been a piece of studio trickery, which RCA put together by overdubbing Willie's vocal on an old live concert tape of Jennings. However, their 1978 album, Waylon & Willie, did contain five legitimate duets, including the #1 hit "Mamas, Don't Let Your Babies Grow Up to Be Cowboys."

Nashville Sound I. The fact that that revolt was effectively co-opted by commerical forces was not overlooked. (Even as the Outlaw surge was being effectively swamped by the excesses of Urban Cowboyism, Jerry Bradley was out there trying to conjure up an Outlaws II; but by then Waylon and Tompall had fallen out. What Bradley ended up with was the *Waylon and Willie* album in 1978. That was not a landmark record, in any sense.)

Oddly, what may have been the biggest legacy of the Outlaws was scarcely recognized. In effectively challenging and then shattering Nashville's feudal system, the Outlaw movement opened the doors of artistic freedom wide—perhaps a shade too wide for some. Country music (and its new pop audience and attendant prosperity) not only had made room now for a Joe Ely or a Rosanne Cash or a Ricky Skaggs, it also had room (too much, some said) for a Kenny Rogers.

Joe Ely rose to prominence in Austin just as Outlaws were giving way to Urban Cowboys. Though rock critics have championed his country-rock albums since the late seventies, his songs have rarely played on country radio. It's unlikely that most country fans outside of Texas have ever heard of him.

475

15

WILL THE CIRCLE BE UNBROKEN: THE CHANGING IMAGE OF COUNTRY MUSIC

Patrick Carr

THIS YEAR'S MODEL

As one views the parade of new country artists through the past couple of years, catching each frame of Nashville's vision of its future as it flickers past, the images don't so much blur as collide, fracture, ricochet; their components careen away randomly, hurtling across musico-social space to connect somewhere out there in America in a whole culture's worth of belief, perception, prejudice, and preference.

Here's a rail-thin, moody young fellow in a funked-up fifties retro Nudie jacket and custom-kneeholed faded Levi's singing pure 1940s honky-tonk music; his image and pose, somewhere just *so* between arrogance and boredom, is the perfect picture of urban 1980s SoHo-Western chic. He's very popular among teenage urban roots revivalists, middle-aged ex-hippies still pining for the "alternative country" of their youth, and any kind of hardcore country fan who feels like he's reached home when he hears a pedal steel guitar.

Here's another, a somewhat older young man who looks like the slightly paunched, worn-out, could-have-been-a-contender feller holding down the stool next to you in a depressed steeltown tavern; his speciality is a big, low-bottom, Luther Perkins–style

Eighties lady: K. T. Oslin, 1987. A former Broadway chorus girl, jingle singer, actress in denture and hemorrhoid commercials, and folkie in a trio with songwriter Guy Clark, Kay Toinette Oslin has been around. She was forty-five years old and living in Manhattan when "80's Ladies" made her the idol of America's grown-up single women.

T. Graham Brown's brand of country owes more to Soul Brother #1 James than to Jim Ed or Hylo—which he is the first to admit. Eschewing western wear, "His T-Ness" prefers sunglasses, tiger-print sportcoats, and casual beachwear—all the while exuding an attitude that suggests he's got all the angles covered.

Texan Lyle Lovett maintains his home state's penchant for grand gesture by piling his hair as high as he can balance it and by employing enough musicians to justify calling his jazzy back-up group the Large Band. His songwriting frequently leans toward biting satire, as in "An Acceptable Level of Ecstasy" and "She's No Lady." And he's the kind of guy who'll close his shows with "Stand by Your Man" just for the hell of it.

rockabilly guitar sound behind songs of risk and loss and a soured American Dream. Rockabilly fans and folks who like some social meat in their lyrics love him to death.

And here's another, real nice and friendly, the kind of ultra-presentable, open-faced, all-country boy you'd just love to see young Mandi dating. You might have some serious doubts about such a union if you hadn't actually seen the boy's picture or videos or award show appearances—his voice sounds so quint-essentially hardcore honky-tonk country, so well smoked and 80-proof cured, that you'd have thought he spent the last thirty years showing George Jones how to acquire hard luck and trouble. But as it is, it's okay; he's sort of a miracle, a genuine sage of white man's blues with a fully functioning liver, a ready smile, and most of a life still ahead of him. So, naturally, just about everybody thinks this boy's the one to beat.

And my, they just keep coming, men and women too, their images entirely up-front and uncoordinated, with room for anybody and anything.

Here's a lusty, lascivious lounge lizard in a loud jacket and a skinny tie, applying sixties r&b saxophone licks to cunningly hooked eighties country-pop tunes. Here's a woman looking like a bridesmaid several hours into a Mexican wedding reception, sounding like Janis Joplin interpreting Patsy Cline for a mob of pogoing Anglopunks. Here's another, a southern-born refugee from the New York advertising business, proclaiming that she's the "Woman of the Eighties" in the style of Carly Simon or Carol Bayer Sager. Here's an eraser-headed, earnestly folkie fellow, obviously very sensitive indeed, and a girl up from Austin,

K.D. Lang openly acknowledges the weird niche she fills, saying country "was way overdue to have an androgynous singer." With a voice at times reminiscent of Patsy Cline and a look best described as boyish, the kooky Canadian has made more headway so far with young rock fans than country. Nevertheless, Owen Bradley believes in her, having come out of retirement in 1988 to produce her second album, a collection of torch songs.

Texas, singing morally impeccable rad/lib material in a linen peasant blouse.

It just goes on and on. Here's a spiky-haired little guy in a brocaded Jimi Hendrix military uniform jacket, picking pure incredible dancing bluegrass on an amplified mandolin, deep dramatic rock on a scarlet Fender Telecaster. He gives way to a trio of females from Buffalo Bill's Wild West Show, five bouncing baggy-panted boys from Barnum & Bailey, four sweet sisters from a suburban prayer meeting, two exceptionally clean Key West hippies, a nurse and her daughter, a Wrangler male model, a beach bum, a Johnny Rotten impersonator, a young Minnie Pearl, and several future TV game show hosts.

What's going on here?

In a purely businesslike sense, Nashville is operating intelligently. The shotgun offense is in effect. Multiple loads of product and image—any kind of pop/rock/folk/country product, any image found attractive anywhere in America save, perhaps, its

479

Emmylou Harris, Dolly Parton, Linda Ronstadt, 1987. Mutual admirers and friends since the early seventies, these three began collaborating on each other's records a decade ago. Their work together led to Trio, *a million-selling 1987 album. (The costumes are courtesy of western tailor Manuel.)*

inner-city ghettos—is being scattered all over the map, pumped out there more or less willy-nilly on the theory that when one load connects with an audience of sufficient substance, more precise promotional weaponry can be employed to saturate the target thus revealed.

This is a sensible approach to industry growth, the mark of a mature enterprise. It bespeaks, among other things, confidence: a certain security, a belief in the producer's ability to respond efficiently to forces within its own captive market and, when the opportunity presents itself through an unusually solid hit, to

It's only rock 'n' roll: Sawyer Brown, 1987. Taking their name from a West Nashville street, this group roared into the national spotlight in 1983 on "Star Search," the national TV talent contest hosted by Ed McMahon, and signed to Capitol Records' Nashville division soon after. As their costumes suggest, they perform with an energy and flamboyance more typical of rock 'n' roll than country.

Marty Stuart's look is a fair approximation of his sound: traditional country with a rock 'n' roll attitude. Having apprenticed in the bands of Lester Flatt and father-in-law Johnny Cash, Stuart can quote hillbilly scripture chapter and verse—and he is a connoisseur of country memorabilia. But he's still waiting to shake loose with a big hit.

Literary and sensitive, Austin-born Nanci Griffith could be described as contemporary country's egghead. She's come up with her own term, "folkabilly," to describe her music, and she frequently poses clutching her latest good read. A mainstay of the songwriter-dominated Kerrville (Texas) Folk Festival, Griffith has also supplied hits to other artists, including Kathy Mattea's "Love at the Five and Dime."

compete equally with other national and international producers on wider turf.

But how, pray, can such a bewildering array of disparate musical styles and characters possibly be lumped together, somehow incorporated into any stylistic definition of a "country" image?

The answer is that they can't; for these days a "country" act is defined not by any connection with rurality in either music or appearance, but by point of origin in the overall popular-music marketing apparatus (Nashville or another recording center feeding into the country divisions of the major record companies), and by target audience (the staggeringly diverse demographic of listeners to radio stations identifying themselves as "country"). Therefore, modern country music must be defined as whatever the recording and radio industries choose to market under a "country" label, and whatever the "country" radio audience and record buyers will accept.

Or perhaps that last point should be restated as "whatever other radio and record audiences *won't* accept." For today, thanks to the relentless format specialization of the American

Foursquare: the Forester Sisters, 1987. Mr. Forester's daughters were up on Lookout Mountain when Warner Bros. records went looking for a female harmony group to compete with the Judds. Their warm harmonies, refined through years of singing in church and at social gatherings around their Georgia home, have brought Kathy, June, Kim, and Christy several Top Ten country hits, beginning with 1985's "(That's What You Do) When You're in Love."

commercial radio industry since the late 1950s—an unprecedentedly rigid segregation of broadcast content into talk or music, youth or adult, black or white, oldies or newies, and so on—country stations have ended up as purveyors not only of country material clearly defined as such by specific stylistic elements, but also of other popular music that isn't clearly identifiable as hard rock, new wave, new age, blues, rap, rhythm & blues, jazz, classical, big-band nostalgia, whatever.

Where radio goes, there goes the recording industry, and so Music Row today is not so much a specialist production unit as a kind of muscial refugee center with a specialist core. Certainly it's where you go if you want to make music in one of the many clearly rural musical traditions, but it's also where you go if you can't, or don't want to, get slotted into some other pigeonhole.

This is by no means a negative tactic, because your potential audience is vast. You have, in effect, joined the ranks of music makers communicating not with an audience that thinks of itself as separate in some way—more fashionable or sophisticated or alienated than others—but with people who consider themselves to be swimming in the mainstream of American life. They're not

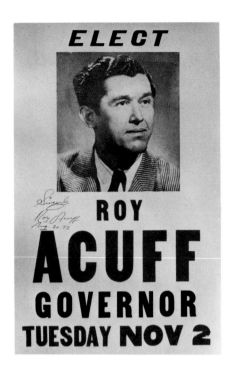

So popular was Roy Acuff during the forties that Tennessee's Republican Party offered him the gubernatorial nomination twice (1944 and 1946) before he finally accepted in 1948. He ran against his friend Gordon Browning and lost big. On the bright side, though, he didn't have to trade his hundred-thousand-dollar-a-year earnings as an entertainer for the governor's $8,000 salary.

Roy Acuff in a still from Smoky Mountain Melody (1948). Then at the height of his popularity, Acuff appeared in eight feature films between 1940 and 1949. Unlike Ernest Tubb and Jimmie Davis, Roy flatly refused to play a cowboy onscreen.

necessarily average, or unexceptional, or even conventional, but —well—normal. A kind of apolitical Silent Majority, if you will. For, partly by accident and partly by design, those are the people the country music industry now considers its own.

So while the image of country music today still contains plentiful lures for groups and individuals who wish to identify themselves with specific rural values and traditions, it also offers a much broader, all-American kind of invitation: *Quit trying to be different. Relax. Come, be normal. There's room for everybody in here.*

Not too long ago to "be country" meant that you had been cast by a geo-socio-economic accident of birth into an almost automatically adversarial relationship with the dominant urban/suburban culture; in effect, you belonged in a cultural ghetto. Now it's a simple matter of free consumer choice. Anybody can make the choice, no questions asked, no attitudes implied.

ARE YOU READY FOR THE COUNTRY?

Any analysis of country music's image must at some point dwell on the obvious: that historically in America (and indeed in most other industrialized nations) the rural working class has been the object of prejudice, of stereotyping amounting to contempt, on the part of the urban population.

Jimmie Davis appeared in several movies during the forties without incident, but caused a ruckus back home when he took time off from his job as Louisiana's governor to star in a dramatized version of his life story, Louisiana *(1947). He soon quieted the opposition, though, and got back to business.*

Such prejudice is expressed in cultural terms as mockery of country ignorance and backwardness, but its driving forces are at heart socioeconomic. For the very elements that created pride and shared identity within the country community—passionate loyalty to tradition, historical continuity, small social scale, a belief in cyclical rather than progressive relationships between people and their environment, and cooperation between individuals and groups in the struggle for survival—are in direct opposition to the values of the American Dream: relentless growth and progress on all fronts, and competitive socioeconomic dominance over one's fellow citizen.

The Dream does not brook disagreement, and implicit in its urban-capitalist vision of society—the official ideology of government, industry, and the dominant media—is the clear understanding that anybody who doesn't buy it, any class of people content to stay where they are, must be lacking in savvy, get-up-and-go, ambition. Therefore they must be unsophisticated, unintelligent. They must be hicks, rubes; they must be not just different, but dumb.

When this is the basic attitude of urbanites toward ruralites (occasionally it isn't, but more on that anon), the urban view of country culture, specifically the music of country people, is that while such activity may perhaps be mildly fascinating in a *National Geographic* kind of way, or even startling in its rude beauty, basically it's primitive, not the kind of art capable of

485

JEANNE-GORDON, Photographers

Grand opera comes to the Grand Ole Opry: Helen Traubel, star of the Metropolitan Opera, visits the Opry's "Prince Albert Show," March 27, 1954. The half-hour "Prince Albert" segment of the Opry was then drawing an audience of 10 million every Saturday night—certainly more than Traubel had ever played to before. Joining her are Rod Brasfield, George Morgan, and Grant Turner, among others.

sustaining the interest with which a sophisticated consumer approaches urban creativity.

Consider, for example, a 1926 description of white southern rural folk and their music in the show business weekly *Variety*. It voices an attitude you can still find floating in the cultural ambience today, the quick "they sing through their noses and cry in their beer" dismissal voiced by (often older) people who obviously haven't checked in with their local radio station lately.

"The 'hill-billy' is a North Carolina or Tennessee and adjacent mountaineer type of illiterate white whose creed and allegience are to the Bible, the chautauqua, and the phonograph," the *Variety* writer explained, adding that such people had "the intelligence of morons" and amused themselves with "sing-song, nasal-twanging vocalizing."

An anonymous copywriter for a 1925 Victor song catalog had been somewhat kinder in his pitch for two of Vernon Dalhart's "hill-billy" performances. His job being to sell the tunes, he had gone so far as to find redeeming social value in them. The songs were not "productions of, or for, the cabaret or the vaudeville stage, but for the roundhouse, the watertank, the caboose, or the village fire-station. . . . These songs are more than things for passing amusement; they are chronicles of the time, by unlettered and never self-conscious chroniclers."

486

As it happened, Vernon Dalhart was far from an "unlettered and never self-conscious chronicler." This transplanted Texan was in fact a sophisticated veteran of the New York stage who, after specializing for a while in "coon songs," had made a conscious decision to concentrate instead on the newly lucrative, underexploited hillbilly market. Which turned out to have been an astute move; Dalhart had a long string of very successful hits in the twenties, among them the first million-selling country record, "The Prisoner's Song," a folksy tearjerker cooked up in New York by his Tin Pan Alley creative team.

That, however, is not the most important point. A much larger issue revolves around the fact that were country music strictly a family affair, a folk-art form confined to the folk from whom it sprang, the attitudes of outsiders such as that unknown copywriter would be essentially irrelevant.

But that's not how the history goes. Almost as soon as the technology of recording and radio made it possible, people began trying to sell the music of the country culture beyond its natural boundaries. And at that point, the approval of outsiders began to matter very much indeed. If you were a member of the country community who had committed yourself to making a living by selling your music (and thus, incidentally, buying into a particularly competitive division of the American Dream crapshoot), the

Louis Marshall Jones got the nickname "Grandpa" from Bradley Kincaid, because Jones always sounded so grouchy when they worked together on early-morning shows at Boston's WBZ, during the 1930s. The name fit Jones's old-time brand of music and stuck, even though Grandpa was still in his twenties. These two shots date from the 1940s, when the "Hee Haw" star had to wear makeup to look the part.

487

question of how best to present yourself—what maintainable image to adopt in the cause of maximum popularity—became crucial to your economic future.

THE HOME FOLKS AND THE PRODIGAL SON

The dynamics of image making were revealed early in the commercial life of country music by the fortunes of two very different musical acts discovered by Victor field recordist/producer/entrepreneur Ralph Peer in 1927: Jimmie Rodgers and the Carter Family.

Look at the Carters. There they stand, straight-backed and serious: good, traditional, respectable, God-fearing people dressed in their Sunday best, linked to each other by blood and to their Appalachian culture by their music, which they perform with a highly conscious intent of preservation and dissemination. A. P. Carter, the leader of the group, is a folklorist as much as an entertainer; his family represents the people of the rural Southeast, linking their history to the future of a wider America through the technology of record and radio. The Carters and their music clearly project the old country values of harmony, tradition, and continuity. They are home folks.

So how do they go over? As it turns out, their music does indeed live forever. The songs they write or popularize have been recorded again and again by hundreds of performers in the thirties, forties, fifties, sixties, seventies, eighties, and most likely will continue to be, and their music paves the way for a long, rich tradition of country-folk recording that parallels the commercial mainstream of the country music industry throughout its subsequent growth. That tradition will produce its own stars (Woody Guthrie, Pete Seeger, Doc Watson) and one great commercial explosion (the folk music boom of the 1960s), but its mostly young, middle-class, urban-liberal audience will be almost entirely separate from that at which the major commercial country production centers aim their product, and most of its personnel will be semi-professionals; their world will be one of small clubs, low-budget independent record labels, and fees that sometimes leave a little something after the expenses, sometimes don't.

As the tradition grows, so it begins. In their career as working musicians, the Carters don't even make a living; A. P. has to take sabbaticals from the group to earn money as a carpenter.

Good country people: the Carter Family—Sara, A. P., and Maybelle—when they were performing over Mexican border radio stations, ca. 1941.

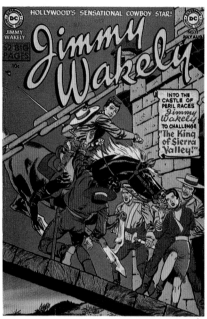

During the heyday of the singing cowboy, some performers, like Gene Autry, became the subjects of children's adventure novels. Jimmy Wakely, however, was one of the few to star in his own comic book. This issue dates from the summer of 1951.

Yodeling cowboy: before western get-ups were fashionable for country singers, even Jimmie Rodgers tried them out. They served as good publicity for the handful of cowboy tunes he released, such as "Cowhand's Last Ride."

Now look at Jimmie Rodgers. Here we have a man who is obviously on the loose. Intentionally adrift on the open road, his home and family somewhere far behind him, he sings about a world in motion from wherever he happens to be: a railroad boxcar, a low-rent roadhouse, a New York hotel room, or a New Orleans jail cell. His music is something new—he is the first white recording artist to borrow freely from the black blues tradition, and as his short career progresses he will add elements of jazz and other urban pop forms to his basic mixture of blues and Anglo-Appalachian folk music—and he is very much in tune with the times. This is a reckless, expanding, rapidly changing, technology-driven era in which mobility and adventurism pervade the popular imagination.

Rodgers has created a new kind of popular music, and part of his success in selling it is his care not to be typecast as a country

Jimmie Rodgers, outfitted as Ralph Peer had recommended: snappy, sharp in a casual kind of way, ca. 1929. This publicity photo made its way into many posters and newspaper ads that year.

Landing gear retracted, "Jumping" Bill Carlisle mugs for the camera while the Carlisles maintain that essential rhythm. In 1953, about the time of this photo, this Opry group put three novelty tunes into the Top Ten: "Knothole," "No Help Wanted," and "Is Zat You, Myrtle?" Such loony tunes helped keep Bill's manic stage energy at a fever pitch.

boy. Ralph Peer advises him in this area: it is Peer who coins the culturally neutral "Blue Yodeler" title, suggests the sharply contemporary bowtie-and-straw-boater outfit in which Rodgers poses for his publicity pictures, steers his artist directly toward an urbane image. Not snobby-sophisticated, not elitist, but snappy, sharp in a casual kind of way.

The combination of music and image works very well. Rodgers is accepted across the board, in the city and in the country, in the North and in the South. He becomes the first recording artist to parlay authentic, rurally grounded music into genuine big-league national stardom.

Rodgers is a populist star, a friend of working people throughout America, but there is one aspect of his music, a haunting edge found also in some of the Carters' songs, that is quite specifically country. Basically it's a sense of things lost or given up to progress and mobility.

In Rodgers's case it's personal; amid the songs of rambling and mischief, his recording persona sometimes sings very poignantly and nostalgically about the country home he's left behind. And that strikes a deep chord out there in the uprooted America of the boom-and-depression 1920s and 1930s; while it is possible to imagine him (and for his listeners to imagine themselves) one day completing the cycle of the Prodigal Son, returning to the old ways, it is clear that this possibility is remote, and

490

THE CHANGING IMAGE OF COUNTRY MUSIC

so the feeling communicated and shared is one of sorrow, of a yearning for comfort and familiarity that can't be fulfilled. The expression of this feeling is one of the legacies Rodgers leaves to country music when, after living too fast in a too-fast world, he dies of tuberculosis in 1933, at the age of thirty-five.

And that is another legacy. Jimmie Rodgers is country's first honky-tonk wanderer, its first edge-dweller and outlaw (not a bad man, but a good man lost in a bad world), and ultimately its first tragic hero.

These personae qualify as images—like the home-folks stance of the Carters, they are personal identification points available to those who feel some kinship with them—but they are not images in the way the term is most often used in the modern world; they are not items from a menu to be chosen, assembled, and customized in the cause of attracting customers. They are real. They are true reflections of the troubled side of the country soul. They will appear again throughout country music's history.

GIDDY-UP

Jimmie Rodgers had been, essentially, a voice of reality—a persona dealing in one way or another with the vicissitudes of life in the times he occupied. By so doing, he had brought some relief to people suffering the violent turmoil of the Depression years; he was going through it with them.

His approach didn't exactly die with him, but gradually country music shifted away from realism toward escapism. On one front, the increasingly popular radio barn dance shows and "Hillbilly Hours," catering specifically to rural audiences all over the nation, dove headlong into often highly exaggerated hillbilly humor and nostalgia, benevolent harmless insiders' lampoons, and caricatures and celebrations designed to amplify rather than obscure the folksy side of rural music and culture. The names of some of the star acts say it all: Dr. Humphrey Bate & His Possum Hunters, Gid Tanner & the Skillet Lickers, Roy Acuff & His Crazy Tennesseans, Arkie the Woodchopper, Homer & Jethro, Mainer's Mountaineers.

Meanwhile, chiefly in the Southwest, dance bands like Bob Wills's Texas Playboys created a whole new version of urban big-band jazz for the country folks' forget-your-troubles Saturday nights. And on the wider front—the turf onto which country musicians set out to compete with urban musicians for the attention of a genuinely mass audience—a brand new image grew.

Will the real cowboy please stand up? Among the notables showing off their fancy western duds in this ca. 1947 shot are Hank Snow, Tex Ritter, Merle Travis, Ray Whitley, and T. Texas Tyler. Meanwhile, on the right side, Roy Acuff wears his usual suit and tie, demonstrating that good taste is timeless.

It was a purely escapist image, built on and out of fantasy. True, the occasional real cowboy of the real American West had indeed entertained his partners around campfires with the old folk songs, but he certainly wasn't the charming, golden-throated singin' sophisticate of the Hollywood B-movie western who fiddled his way through a warm, benevolent, heroically simple and utterly unreal America while the nation burned, courted revolution, and then involved itself in global war. That enormously popular matinee idol was a dream.

But no matter. The cowboy image, which got its start on record with California vocal outfits like the Sons of the Pioneers before connecting with its true fantasy vehicle in Tinseltown, was a godsend for all manner of country musicians who might otherwise have had to limit themselves to the radio barn dance circuit. At the time, the cowboy music of the westerns had more in common with New York's Tin Pan Alley and Hollywood back-

How the West was won: Gene Autry strums amid his impressive western wardrobe, 1940s. Within a few years, such cowboy trappings would be standard issue for all country singers.

Ladies love outlaws, as Waylon once sang, but kids love cowboys. Kenny Roberts, a yodeler from New England who had worked Fort Wayne's "Hoosier Hop" in the forties, found an appreciative new audience right under his nose in the early years of the baby boom. During the fifties, he hosted several children's shows on Cincinnati's WLW and other Ohio TV stations.

LIKE A RHINESTONE COWBOY

Country music owes its most distinctive visual symbol—the brightly colored (some might say gaudy), spangled stage costume—to a diminutive Jewish ex-boxer by the unlikely name of Nudie. Raised in Brooklyn, the son of a cobbler, Nudie Cohen began traveling the country shortly after World War I, finding work, by turns, as a freelance flyweight boxer ("at stag parties $1 for three rounds," he once told *People* magazine), as an extra in Hollywood, and as a struggling tailor.

In the early 1940s, after bouncing back and forth between the coasts for nearly three decades and with little to show for it except his experience in making costumes for strip-tease acts, Nudie was in Los Angeles, nearly broke, gamely trying to establish himself as a tailor. Somehow he befriended Tex Williams and convinced the popular western singer that he could smartly outfit Tex and his band. Even though the job was a near disaster—with some band members' costumes ending up too small, others too long, and all having to be fixed at the last minute—Williams liked Nudie's style. He kept buying costumes and plugged the tailor's work at show dates and over the radio. It was like manna from heaven: as word spread on the West Coast, Gene Autry, Roy Rogers, and Rex Allen all came into Nudie's shop for a new suit. Within months, a genuine Nudie costume became *haute couture* for the well-dressed cowboy singer. Nudie's business thrived, eventually expanding to include twenty-one tailors working under his direction.

Although in the beginning a Nudie suit was simply a western version of clothing styles that were fashionable in the 1940s and 1950s, over time the costumes became more and more colorful—and outlandish. Frequently, Nudie and his tailors customized costumes with gimmicks inspired by the singer's name or image. Thus, Porter Wagoner often had suits decorated with wagon wheels, Ferlin Husky had his husky dogs, and Jimmy C. Newman ("Alligator Man") had alligators. In 1957, Nudie reached the height (or depth) of excess when, for $10,000, he designed a twenty-five-carat gold lamé tuxedo for Elvis Presley.

By the late 1950s, the rhinestone Nudie suit had become synonymous with steel guitars. But within a few years, as country labored to acquire a sophisticated look to go with its smooth Nashville Sound, country costumes toned down; dinner jackets and formals replaced the rhinestones. During the 1970s, the country image changed yet again as Waylon, Willie, and the Outlaws donned T-shirts and blue jeans, just like rock stars of the day.

Today, with the return to music styles of the forties and fifties led by artists like Emmylou Harris, Dwight Yoakam, and Randy Travis, the costumes are beginning to sparkle again. No one is more surprised by the revival of the rhinestone than Manuel of Manuel's Western Wear in North Hollywood, California. A protégé of the late Mr. Cohen (who died in 1984), Manuel is carrying on the rhinestone tradition.

Manuel began working for Nudie in the late 1950s, and during his tenure there he designed costumes for many of country music's biggest stars, including Kitty Wells, Dolly Parton, Little Jimmy Dickens, Por-

ter Wagoner, and Hank Snow. In 1957 he made Hank Williams, Jr.'s first cowboy suit—and continues to design for him today. In 1970, he made the trend-setting white jumpsuit that Elvis wore for his Las Vegas debut.

It was around this time that Gram Parsons first came to Manuel after having seen some T-shirts the tailor had embroidered for Mick Jagger and Keith Richards. Parsons wanted a visual symbol for his new band, the Flying Burrito Brothers—a symbol that would simultaneously evoke Music Row and Haight-Ashbury. He suggested a Nudie suit embroidered with marijuana leaves and poppies. Although Manuel and Parsons worked on the costume together, Manuel is quick to point out that the idea of featuring illegal substances was entirely Gram's. Since then, many other rock performers have sought out Manuel's artistry, including David Crosby, Neil Young, and Elton John.

Although his clientele and musical tastes vary, Manuel says he enjoys working with country artists most. As he puts it, "Country music is my hometown, where I pull up my chair and sit back." Nudie couldn't have said it any better.

495

lots than with the country music of the rural Southeast. But that didn't deter those country musicians of the forties in the least: they realized that the cowboy image could plug them into America's mainstream current; it certainly beat being labeled as backward dolts from the hills. And even though the singing-cowboy goldmine found itself played out by the end of World War II, it established a link of image between country people and cowboys that survives to this day.

The country-cowboy connection is still very strong—it is only in the last decade, after all, that the qualifier "& western" has begun to disappear from the term "country"—but it is absolutely artificial. There is no substantial reason on God's earth why American rural working people anywhere but in real cow country should think it perfectly natural to dude themselves up like the Cisco Kid come Saturday night. It's not their tradition at all; it grew under the hothouse studio lights of Hollywood from a seed planted when a few young musicians were smitten by a bright idea.

Arkie the Arkansas Woodchopper (Luther Ossenbrink) actually came from Missouri. His typical outfit—consisting of cowboy hat, lumberjack shirt, riding breeches, and high-topped boots—reflected the musical variety of the WLS "National Barn Dance," long a showcase for his singing, square-dance calling, and master-of-ceremonies work. This publicity shot dates from the 1930s.

THE REAL THING

But so what, hoss? There's no denying the cowboy image is truly sharp and truly American. It also does a nice job of showing where your basic cultural affiliation lies; *cowboy* means *country*, now doesn't it? And if anyone questions you on that point (an unlikely occurrence, but let's pretend it might happen anyway), all you have to do is direct them to the nearest photograph of the man who more than anyone before or since defined the essential image of country music: Hank.

Hank Williams, that is. A very nicely tailored, subtly decorated, western-cut suit for which he must have paid Nudie the Tailor a sizable strip off the roll of hundred dollar bills he always carried with him. It's not gaudy at all, but on the other hand it's nothing remotely like your average Sunday best—plus the boots (hand-tooled, of course; one-of-a-kind, of course), the shirt, the hand-painted tie, and the top-of-the-line five-gallon Stetson. Also a band called the Drifting Cowboys, who likewise dress the part.

But Hank doesn't sing a word about little dogies or lonesome nights on the old prairie. In fact the element of fantasy, western or otherwise, is almost entirely lacking in his music. In a sense, the duds are irrelevant, unimportant window dressing, for in Hank's case it's the music and the personality that rocket him to

Family man: Hank Williams takes a break from the lost highway, ca. 1950. With Hank in his Franklin Road home are step-daughter Lycretia, son Randall Hank, and wife Audrey.

stardom. And what we have in that area is the very reverse of escapism. In a much more direct, explicit, sentimental, and ultimately chilling rekindling of Jimmie Rodgers's initiative, Hank is singing about *his real life.*

Basically, that life is a nightmare relieved only by bouts of hardcore honky-tonking. His missus, whom he loves with an all-consuming passion, doesn't reciprocate. She fools around, so he fools around, and it makes him crazy so he drinks, he gambles, he fights, he honks and tonks to beat the band. Some of this stuff might actually be fun, mind you, the kind of thing any red-blooded American has a right to enjoy from time to time, but in Hank's case, that's not what's happening. The bottom line is that the poor sonofabitch is beating his brains against the wall and tearing his heart out because when it comes right down to it, all he really wants out of life is a good, happy, loving Christian home and family. And he just isn't going to get it.

497

Happy birthday, baby: Lycretia Williams (in the dark party dress) celebrates her birthday in the Williams family home, with entertainment courtesy of friendly neighborhood songsters Fred Rose and Hank Williams, ca. 1951.

Today a singing persona like that, real or fake, is unlikely to achieve Hank's kind of megastardom, but in the late 1940s, a place full of men and women brutalized by war and cheated by peace to the point where the incidence of alcoholism and divorce and suicide was higher than at any previous point in American history (and climbing fast), it hit the spot with a vengeance. An awful lot of people from all sorts of social backgrounds could relate very directly to ol' Hank; crying in your beer was pretty much a national pastime.

Talk about striking reverberant chords; Hank hit the mother of them all. His kind of personal-confessional songs and lean, stripped-down five-piece hillbilly band sound became the new trademark of Nashville music, and for a while honky-tonk country competed very successfully with the blander, less involving pop forms of the time.

Today the years of Hank's reign are often called the Golden Era of country music. Partly this is because in Hank, the country recording industry had finally found its Great Communicator, an artist whose songs were capable of moving anybody, anywhere. *Despite* being recorded and presented without either exaggeration or obscuration, they were universal. And that revelation was liberating. It meant that the route to success lay not in the imaging of the music—cornpone, sophisticate, western, whatever—but in the emotional power of the music itself. And so for an

Merle Travis entertains the boys in the barracks with "Reenlistment Blues" in From Here to Eternity *(1953). While appearing in the Academy-award-winning film, Travis met the English actress Deborah Kerr. She professed to be a big fan of Travis's, tuning in faithfully every Saturday to watch him on Los Angeles's top TV barn dance, "Town Hall Party."*

intensely creative while in Nashville, country self-consciousness disappeared. It is no accident that the best of the resulting songs and records, which created the stylistic pool from which every great contemporary hard-country artist continues to draw, sound just as powerful today as they did in '49 or '52.

The high time, however, was brief. Hank's death on the first day of 1953 did nothing to erode his personal popularity among committed country fans, but the loss of the Great Communicator (and a kind of national recovery from the postwar blues) did erode the power of honky-tonk music in the larger society. This fact was recognized in Nashville, and record producers and marketing men were starting to wonder what they might do about it when, suddenly, catastrophically, a whole new image burst on them from nowhere.

Well, not nowhere. It came from distressingly close to home, from Memphis just a couple of hundred miles to the west, and moreover it was something they should perhaps have figured out for themselves. The seeds of it had been there in some of Hank's work as well as in the occasional record of lesser contemporary lights, and further back the central notion—musical miscegenation—had been Jimmie Rodgers's breakthrough move.

This was rockabilly music, the grafting of black folk music to white to create a quantum leap in novelty, energy, sexuality, and rhythmic power. Producer Sam Phillips was the mad scientist,

*Sheb Wooley (right) and pals
discuss how they'll have the
laugh on Gary Cooper in* High
Noon *(1952). In addition to
playing in dozens of westerns,
the singer also starred as Pete
Nolan in the TV series
"Rawhide." In 1968, he won the
CMA's Comedian of the Year
award for the novelty songs he
recorded in the guise of his alter
ego, Ben Colder.*

Opposite
*Independence Day: Elvis Presley
at Memphis's Russwood Park,
1956. Elvis grafted black folk
music onto white, making a
quantum leap in novelty, energy,
sexuality, and rhythmic power.
Pop music—and country music,
for that matter—would never be
the same.*

Elvis Presley the guinea pig. They cooked up the musical brew
together, but Elvis himself went further; he adopted the black
image.

In pure musical terms, American blacks and whites had never
been very far apart, and American musicians had never been as
culturally or socially segregated as the larger society. (The debt
of almost all forms of white American music to black American
influence and even inspiration is as enormous as it is generally
unacknowledged.) But Elvis's initiative was new. The hot-pink
suit, the sexual abandon of his performances, the pure funk
power he'd experienced in black Memphis clubs and which he
now projected as his own—none of it had been seen by white
audiences before.

And, of course, BINGO! Rebellion! Party time! TEEN CUL-
TURE! The kids didn't want to moan when they could scream,
waltz when they could boogie!

One aspect of the industry's response was predictable and
immediate: the rockabillification of its product and artists more
or less across the board. Nashville-trademark steel guitars and
fiddles all but disappeared; former balladeers and honky-tonkers, chroniclers of adult life's pains and passions, were transformed into teenage hepcats, party animals, rebels without a
cause. Image reigned once again over substance.

But it didn't work. Nashville's rockabilly music was relatively
tame, tending toward the coy rather than the provocative—

500

All gussied up: Del Wood, early fifties. For much of its early history, country music looked to the movies for inspiration on how best to photograph its performers. Thus, even a barrelhouse ragtime piano player like Opry star Del Wood got the Hollywood touch. She had this photo made shortly after selling a million copies of her 1951 instrumental "Down Yonder."

Hank Jr. as matinée idol, ca. 1964. It's hard to believe that this suave young sophisticate would someday make a living with songs like "A Country Boy Can Survive" and "Buck Naked." Randall Hank Williams was about fourteen when this photo was made.

a thoroughly predictable phenomenon, given the exquisitely calculated, two-steps-back-from-contemporary-frontline-urban-mores sense of taboo that was (and is) country music's instinctive yardstick for acceptable lyrical content—and the kids could tell. They much preferred the genuine article spewing from the gusher in Memphis, where Sam Phillips had cornered the market on real rockabillies—Jerry Lee Lewis, Carl Perkins, Charlie Rich, Johnny Cash—who might otherwise have been there when Nashville needed them (they all ended up there eventually, of course, but only when the kids didn't want them anymore).

Nashville's other response was, basically, one of surrender. There being no perceived growth potential in classic straight honky-tonk music and precious little reward in trying to compete on the youth front, the means of production were turned toward a new target. Nashville's future, it was felt, lay in providing music for the flip side of the youth rebellion: the relatively ma-

The late fifties were dark days indeed for country music. In order to compete with rock 'n' roll, country performers not only banded together in package shows like this, they also stooped occasionally to adopt the moniker "rock 'n' roll," even when—as in this case—it hardly applied.

ture, conservative, conventional urban-surburban middle-class population whose material advancement through the postwar years had provided the affluence that made a teenage consumer culture possible in the first place.

The existing musical tastes of such people ran in the direction of softness, mellifluousness, a certain cocktail-hour suaveté; some tickling of the ivories, some sweeping strings, perhaps a judicious touch of brass, a vocal with some moonlight and money in it. And hence the infamous Nashville Sound.

SANITIZED FOR YOUR PROTECTION

Basically, the Nashville Sound (a term popularized by a 1963 *Time* magazine story) was a shotgun wedding of inherently sentimental country melodies and pop-jazzy production technique, the package dressed up in evening wear and sanitized, as much as possible, of rural odor.

And much was indeed possible. Surveying the album covers and publicity photographs of the Nashville Sound era, it is difficult to imagine the singers as anything more rural than, say, discreet gentlemen and lady farmers, persons with a fine eye for

503

Boots Randolph and Chet Atkins, showing the world that Nashville can be-bop with the best of them, 1966. At the time, Atkins and Randolph ("Yakety Sax," 1963) often performed in concert with pianist Floyd Cramer.

During the sixties, George Hamilton IV successfully combined folk songs, country music, and Ivy League wardrobe. Starting out as a nineteen-year-old pop star, he sold a million records with John D. Loudermilk's "Rose and a Baby Ruth" in 1956. By the time he recorded another Loudermilk tune, "Abilene" (1963), he had joined the Opry and was considered just as country as the next fellow.

horseflesh and good English tweed. They could never have been born in shacks, worked the cottonfields, or won a wild back-country fiddle contest, and it was impossible to conceive of them dying alone of alcoholism and drug addiction and hillbilly heart-break in the back seat of a Cadillac, as Hank had done, in the middle of the night, on the blacktop to nowhere. They could, and would, go down in appropriately sophisticated fashion, conveyed to the life beyond by private aircraft (notably the Beechcraft Bonanza, then as now a distinctly upscale machine known among pilots as "the Doctor Killer").

The Nashville Sound was successful. Record sales achieved a life-saving level quite quickly and rose steadily to respectable and even healthy proportions over the next fifteen years. But the dream of full assimilation, economic and social equality with the Tony Bennetts and Andy Williamses of this world, proved elusive.

One bottom line, it seems in retrospect, is that the whole idea didn't have much potential to begin with; the primary demographic target of Nashville Sound music, eventually defined to a tee by producer Billy Sherrill as "the housewife washing dishes at 10 A.M. in Topeka, Kansas," just didn't buy many records. Another is that in the same way the rock 'n' roll kids had been able to tell a genuine hepcat from a possum in tiger-striped sharkskin, that housewife knew that no Nashville smoothie—not

504

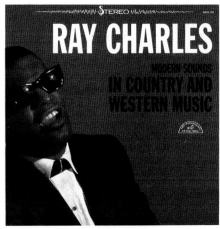

Recording this 1962 album of country songs came naturally to r&b great Ray Charles, since he grew up listening to the Grand Ole Opry. It proved so successful, with Charles's version of "I Can't Stop Loving You" selling over three million copies, that he recorded a sequel LP, released in 1963. In 1965, he returned once more to the well, recording Buck Owens's "Cryin' Time," landing yet another hit in the pop Top Ten.

Welcome to my world: Jim Reeves on the loose, early sixties. The Texan who got his first big break filling in for an absent Hank Williams on the "Louisiana Hayride" ultimately became the smoothest crooner the Nashville Sound ever produced. Here, not long before his fatal 1964 plane crash, he looks every inch the urban swinger—then Music City's ideal of a country star.

one of them in the long line from Gentleman Jim Reeves to Roger Miller to Charlie Rich, the Silver Fox—would ever golf regularly with Mel Tormé. The image was a fake.

The image also made industry personnel uncomfortable, for throughout the Nashville Sound era, which lasted well into the 1970s, there was in country music a constant feeling of walking on eggshells.

On the social front, this feeling was apparent in the industry's exaggerated concern with its image in Nashville itself. Prior to this period of attempted sophistication, the disdain in which the social elite of "The Athens of the South" held the white-trash music business in their midst had never been much more than vaguely irritating. Now it mattered a lot. It really hurt the executives of the country recording industry that while the nation at

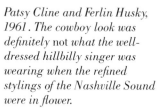

Patsy Cline and Ferlin Husky, 1961. The cowboy look was definitely not what the well-dressed hillbilly singer was wearing when the refined stylings of the Nashville Sound were in flower.

Johnny Cash plays host to Mickey Dolenz, Mike Nesmith, and Davey Jones of the Monkees, on his ABC-TV series, 1969. Cash was a country original; the Monkees were a pop group manufactured for TV. Here, on national television, they somehow find common ground.

Enjoying the fruits of his labors, Eddy Arnold sits at Johnny Carson's right hand, mid sixties. Boosted by such crossover hits as "Make the World Go Away" (1965), Eddy became one of the first country stars to appear on "The Tonight Show."

large seemed truly impressed by the achievements the Country Music Association was trumpeting all over the press—Just *look* at those consumer median-income figures, those big-city coun-trypolitan radio demographics, those suavely colorful Major En-tertainers exchanging urbane early-morning banter with the talking heads of all three national TV networks! Watch the Pres-

*Honky-tonk men, ca. 1965:
Eddy Arnold meets Rolling
Stones Charlie Watts and Keith
Richards. As host of Kraft Music
Hall specials, Eddy Arnold had
to make the acquaintance of all
manner of folk.*

ident of the United States himself open the amazingly expensive,
tasteful, ultrasuburban brand new Opry complex!—the folks
who mattered in the social arrangement of their own home town
just didn't seem to get the message. Nashville's city fathers
didn't even see fit to extend a simple little courtesy like renaming
the hub streets of the country music industry as "Music Square"
until the mid-1970s; in the meantime, for all those years, music
industry personnel continued to squirm in their social ghetto,
paying the psychological price of attempted upward mobility
everywhere they turned as they tried harder and harder to distance themselves from their roots. God only knows how much of
the music's conscious image manipulation in the sixties and seventies was motivated not by economics, but by the simple crav-
ing for full acceptance in Nashville's better country clubs.

Charley Pride, late sixties. RCA released his first single "Snakes Crawl at Night" (1965) without publicity photos. The ploy worked in part because Pride's voice was so thoroughly country that no one suspected he could be black. It didn't hurt, either, that Pride has never made an issue of race, preferring instead to let the music do the talking. His reward: more than twenty million records sold and the CMA's Entertainer of the Year award for 1971.

On the musical front, the mood was even more fragile. In the cause of pandering to that imaginary housewife's sense of musical and social propriety, far too many things couldn't be done: sounds not made, songs not sung, stories not told, fun not had, chances not taken. The honky-tonk blues, the hillbilly fever, the rockabilly fire—all core ingredients of the country musician's most powerful creative reality—couldn't be allowed to show in public. And so they went underground. The very qualities that had made Hank Williams a world-class all-time star were exercised only in musicians' homes, in little late-night clubs, and occasionally out on the road amid the real country fans, the Great Unwashed who didn't give a damn what the neighbors might think.

All of which meant that the country music industry of the sixties and early seventies qualified quite nicely for description by an adjective achieving a certain popularity at the time: *uptight*.

WHEN COUNTRY WASN'T COOL

Uptight. The word doesn't mean much more than "upset" now, but in the sixties and early seventies it meant a lot: white, old, rich, square, redneck, military-industrial, Republican, Fascist, dangerous—the enemy.

The enemy of whom? The blacks, the young, the poor, the women, the hip, the peace-and-brotherhood revolutionaries, the free lovers, the stoned. And despite the fact that an alternative vision of Nashville was available—the city of the Lovin' Spoonful's "Nashville Cats" and Bob Dylan's *Nashville Skyline*, the place where Dylan made *Blonde on Blonde* and Kris Kristofferson did all his early work, the home of the "pure" old-timey and bluegrass music college kids had always loved to the point of worship—the new tribes of affluent middle-class young revolutionaries chose to view Music Row in the black-or-white light of ideology. To them, country music was epitomized by Merle Haggard's "Okie from Muskogee," Barry Sadler's "Ballad of the Green Berets," and Tammy Wynette's "Stand by Your Man." And even though "Okie," for instance, was recorded in California, the conclusion was inevitable: Nashville was quite obviously where the enemy was concentrated. It was the home and castle of the squares.

508

Nashville's answer to Herb Alpert: Danny Davis & the Nashville Brass, 1970s. A former trumpet player in the big bands of Gene Krupa and Bob Crosby (among others), Davis had worked in A&R for several years before joining Chet Atkins's staff in Nashville. Sensing a trend in the mid sixties, he applied horns to country music and for a while made a very good living at it. Some folks even considered his records country.

Attention: Staff Sergeant Barry Sadler, U.S. Army Special Forces. He wasn't a country star, but the patriotic song that he and army buddy Robin Moore wrote, "Ballad of the Green Berets" (1966), hit country music in the guts, selling more than seven million records. Along with "Okie from Muskogee" (1969), it gave the counterculture an idea of where country stood.

In many ways it was. The industry's commitment to rural political conservatism on the one hand and suburban social convention on the other was strong, and the new youth values threatened those loyalties. So Nashville, despite some serious misgivings about the economic wisdom of such a course in some parts of town, generally resisted liaison with the hippies. When a new approach to its own music began to emerge from California—the folk-harmony initiative of Crosby, Stills, Nash and Young, the redefined acoustic traditionalism of the Grateful Dead's albums *Workingman's Dead* and *American Beauty*, and most significantly the achingly beautiful, ultra-country work of Georgia boy Gram Parsons with the Byrds and the Flying Burrito Brothers and Emmylou Harris—Music Row closed its ears. The hippies' country music remained the hippies' alone; there was almost no crossover into the rural market from that first California wave.

It wasn't for want of trying, either. Parsons in particular often spoke of trying to break into the Nashville family. He was a country boy, never very comfortable in the rock 'n' roll world, and he longed for his music to be accepted on its home ground, by the people for whom and about whom it was made.

In some ways Parsons was another Jimmie Rodgers—a new creative bridge between urban-rural and folk-pop musical forms,

509

I hope from year to year this will bring you fond memories of the Merle Haggard visit.

I have written a special poem to help you recall

Thanks

Sincerly, Hag

Today is somebody's birthday
Some mother's child was born
Some will remember
Some will forget
Some will be tootin' their horn

The older you are
The more it means
'Cause the more you have to recall
Today is somebody's birthday
And may it be the greatest of all

Poet of the common man
Merle Haggard March 17, 1973

Merle Haggard had endeared himself to President Richard Nixon with the resolutely patriotic anthem "Okie from Muskogee" (1969). Later, when Haggard visited the White House for a command performance on March 17, 1973, he brought this self-penned birthday card for First Lady Pat Nixon.

Finger-lickin' good: the Opry's Billy Walker and Kentucky Fried Chicken founder Colonel Harlan Sanders compare drivers and drumsticks, September 1966. The two were publicizing the Music City Pro-Celebrity Golf Invitational. By this point, country music's influence in Nashville was such that Colonel Sanders made a point of catering the affair.

Hot burrito to go: Gram Parsons, not long for this world, ca. 1973. Born Cecil Connor and raised in a wealthy Georgia home, Parsons dropped out of Harvard to play music. His fusion of country and rock—which he called "cosmic American music"—influenced musicians in both camps, beginning with his work on the Byrds' Sweetheart of the Rodeo (1968) album. He died five years later of a drug overdose at the age of twenty-six.

an edge dweller, an artist intimately familiar with the prodigal son themes of loss and longing and infinitely skilled in their expression. But in the crucial area of image he had none of Rodgers's skills or resources. He had long hair, and he wore marijuana leaves emblazoned on his Nudie suit, and those symbols boxed him in; the image that brought him acceptance by the hippies condemned him in the country.

Had he lived longer, long enough to wait out the ideology wars that raged in his path, Parsons might have been accepted eventually; his partner Emmylou Harris was, and so was Linda Ronstadt, and so were many of the other folk-to-rock-to-country

The Flying Burrito Brothers, wearing the Nudie suits designed to evoke visions of Music Row and Haight-Ashbury, 1969: Sneaky Pete Kleinow, Chris Ethridge, Gram Parsons, and Chris Hillman with two lost souls.

travelers who began their popular careers in the light of his vision. But as it was, though his death robbed the music of a creative energy every bit as potent as Hank's had been, almost nobody in the country community realized it. Gram Parsons died like Hank under the curse of too much hillbilly soul, of loneliness and exhaustion and substance abuse on the honky-tonk road. But the event was interpreted as a rock 'n' roll affair—just another screwed-up rich hippie paying the price for his kicks.

ARE YOU READY FOR THE COUNTRY?, Part 2

The missed musical connections of the sixties and early seventies between Nashville and the California country hippies belong in the realm of ideology and image, specifically the highly charged meeting ground that lies between urban and rural America. Basically it is an area of contention; the urbanrural relationship is usually adversarial. From time to time, however, as happened in the environmental/organic/communal back to-the-earth movement of the sixties, a peculiar factor disrupts the normal patterns of cultural prejudice.

The peculiar factor is the self-doubt of the urbanites. It is there all the time, a nagging subtheme suggesting uncomfortable

512

questions about the true emotional value of sophistication and the morality of individual socioeconomic supercompetitiveness, and periodically it grows into a kind of national crescendo.

At such times country values, or at least an idealized perception of them, become fashionable in the urban culture. Farmers and hillbillies and the like are lauded for their simplicity, their directness, their honest naiveté, their harmonious relationship with nature, and urbanites go to some lengths to identify themselves with those qualities.

This process, historically expressed in art, music, literature, and the mass media, has happened again and again in America. Its minor fluctuations are too numerous to list, but its major eruptions are obvious. Country life became a public ideal during the first great immigrant-swollen expansion of the cities during the mid-nineteenth century; following the horrific ravages of the Civil War, the nation's first taste of full-scale industrialized mayhem; during the Great Depression, when the assumptions of the

The two faces of Ray Stevens: the madcap musical comedian responsible for "Ahab the Arab" (1962), "Gitarzan" (1969), "The Streak" (1974), and "Mississippi Squirrel Revival" (1985) also wrote and recorded the socially conscious "Mr. Businessman" (1968) and the feel-good anthem "Everything Is Beautiful" (1970).

The album that bridged a generation gap in country, thanks to the Nitty Gritty Dirt Band and the veterans who joined them for this historic three-record set.

American Dream shattered with lethal force; and again, most recently and relevantly, in the massive national identity crisis sparked by the Baby Boom's opposition to the Vietnam War and the uban-military-industrial American way of life in general.

But these periodic pastoral romances don't last. Usually the well-intentioned foolishness persists until a) whatever upheaval first prompted the retreat from urbanity dies down, or b) it dawns on the dreamers that in reality, country people are not at all simple, direct, naive, or engaged in a pastoral idyll. They are in fact just as ambivalent, subtle, and sophisticated in their relationship to the rural environment as city people are to the urban landscape. Moreover, that environment is every bit as potentially hostile as its urban antithesis. It also becomes plain that in general, country people are reactionary. They don't like change, and they *really* don't like the kind of changes that accompany a flood of urbanites invading their communities and carpetbagging their culture.

These realizations come as a great disillusionment, the kind of rude awakening that must be suppressed rather than assimilated into a genuinely sophisticated worldview, and thus urban

514

Will the Circle Be Unbroken:
*Randy Scruggs, Doc Watson,
Earl Scruggs, and Merle Travis.*

*Mother Maybelle Carter, Randy
Scruggs (Earl's son), and Doc
Watson.*

*Producer Bill McEuen, Roy
Acuff, and Earl Scruggs.*

COUNTRY COMEDY

Comedy has always been an important part of country music. Many singers and musicians, from Fiddlin' John Carson and Uncle Dave Macon to Homer & Jethro and Ray Stevens, have made humor a cornerstone of their acts. Likewise, country music has always had a special place for those comedians, like Minnie Pearl, Whitey Ford (the Duke of Paducah), and Archie Campbell, who are not musicians but specialize in stand-up comedy and comic skits.

As writer-musician Doug Green has noted, comedy became entwined with country music back in the nineteenth century through the rural phenomenon known as the

medicine show. To sell their nostrums and potions, traveling quack doctors hired on teams of struggling young talents, who played music, acted in skits, mugged in blackface—in short, did anything necessary to bring folks out to the medicine wagon. Many of country music's greats—from Roy Acuff to Gene Autry to Bob Wills—got their starts in such traveling shows. Later, when these performers became popular enough to headline their own road shows, it was only natural that they would fall back on the tried and true entertainment formulas they had learned apprenticing in the medicine shows. So their bands featured musicians who often doubled as comedians.

Vaudeville, too, had a considerable influence on country humor. In the 1920s and 1930s, as vaudeville shows were displaced from one theater after another by motion pictures, many acts from the vaudeville circuits—Jamup & Honey and the Duke of Paducah, for example—found a new home on radio barn dances, thus perpetuating many routines. The outlandish costumes (ill-fitting coats and pants, funny hats, loud ties) worn by country comedians like Minnie Pearl, Rod Brasfield, Stringbean, and the Duke of Paducah were legacies from the clowns of vaudeville.

Just as country music grew out of American folk music, the country comedy routines passed down through the medicine shows and vaudeville originated in American folk humor. In fact, the themes, comic devices, and routines of such contemporary country comedians as Jerry Clower and Minnie Pearl are basically the same ones that have amused country folk for much of the last two centuries. From the beginning, country comedians have exploited the humor of rural stereotypes, such as the rube hillbilly or the ethnic immigrant. And they have portrayed rustic characters through exaggerated country accents and folksy patter.

One enduring source of country humor is the inevitable friction between the city slicker and the hayseed—though today's comedic vehicle may be the television show "Hee Haw" rather than a vaudeville skit or traveling minstrel show. Another continuing source of material is the conflict between authority and the good ol' boys: in the 1930s, Gid Tanner & the Skillet Lickers portrayed the standoff on record as a contest between moonshiners and revenuers; more recently, Jerry Reed and Burt Reynolds have expressed the same theme in their movies by pitting truck drivers against highway patrolmen.

Because it often depends on costumes, props, and gestures, country comedy has always been more plen-
tiful onstage than on record or radio. Unfortunately, thanks to the ongoing homogenization of culture, country comedy is no longer as plentiful as it once was. As Doug Green has suggested, corny humor often embarrasses youngsters growing up in the country, reminding them too much of their heritage, while it simply baffles city dwellers—or leaves them unduly smug.

Comedy is no longer an essential element of the country stage show. Nevertheless, through good ol' boy movies, the novelty songs of Ray Stevens and Pinkard & Bowden, television programs like "Hee Haw," and broadcasts of the Grand Ole Opry, country's comedic tradition continues. For every New York nightowl watching David Letterman, there's still someone in the heartland laughing at the crazy collision of country values with those of the urban world.

Archie Campbell's double-talk and spoonerisms were just what the doctor ordered to bring country comedy up to date in the days of the Nashville Sound. Not long after joining the Opry in 1958, he shocked WSM management by walking onstage in a business suit, rather than the standard rube garb—he got his way. Here he is on "Hee Haw," for whom he served as gag writer as well as comedian from 1969 until his death in 1987.

Lonzo & Oscar admire their million-selling comedy record for RCA Victor, "I'm My Own Grandpa" (1948). In the grand country tradition, Lonzo & Oscar could play hillbilly buffoons one minute, then race through tongue-twisting, brain-teasing songs the next. Here Ken Marvin is Lonzo and Rollin Sullivan (right) is Oscar; Rollin's brother Johnny eventually replaced Marvin.

517

"I'm goin' back to the wagon, boys; these shoes are killin' me!" Although Benjamin "Whitey" Ford's tag line and ill-fitting pea-green suit suggested a country rube out of place in town, his stage moniker—the Duke of Paducah—was truer to his more citified wisecracks. The former Opry star died in 1986, but his gags are still with us: in the seventies, he sold his file of 400,000 jokes to the producers of "Hee Haw."

Homer & Jethro, 1940s. Guitarist Henry "Homer" Haynes and Kenneth "Jethro" Burns were expert jazz players who made their living as country comedians, first on Knoxville radio in the thirties, then at Kentucky's Renfro Valley, and at Chicago's "National Barn Dance" after World War II.

perception cycles back to the dumb-rubes image of the rural population.

Thus it was almost inevitable that the farmers and the country-oriented hippies of the sixties could never be friends, and that Nashville could not function as an effective go-between. And so the hippies went their own country way, buying their Eagles and Linda Ronstadt records and attending "purist" folk-bluegrass festivals but resolutely refusing to listen to anyone who had Nashville's seal of approval, while Nashville continued to pursue its housewives.

And that perhaps is where we might still be today had it not been for the reemergence of that mythic image from the popular-fictional West, the cowboy. A cowboy, as we already know from the lesson of the thirties and forties, can be everybody's friend.

Lester "Roadhog" Moran & His
Cadillac Cowboys take a gander
at their first sales award: a
plywood record for their album
Alive at Johnny Mack Brown
High School, 1970s. Actually,
these stars of Rainbow Valley's
WEAK are the comedic alter
egos of the Statler Brothers, who
poke good-natured fun at one of
country's dearest traditions—
local amateur radio performers.

The Duke's coat of arms says it
all: the ill-fitting shoes, the
corny jokes—fresh off the hay
wagon.

GIDDY-UP, AGAIN

The new cowboys, Waylon and Willie and the boys, weren't the
golden-throated goody-goodies of yore. They were in fact a lot
like the bad guys of the B movies: shaggy, dirty, intemperate,
antisocial except among their own, and given to the public wearing of *dark*-colored cowboy clothes, notably a lot of black
leather. They were, in short, what they came to be called: Outlaws.

A wonderful image, that. It could mean so much, and so many
people could identify with it. On the widest front, the drug culture and the sexual revolution (let alone the various antiauthori-
tarian political movements of the sixties and seventies) had
moved a huge segment of the American population into psychological if not operational opposition to the law, to the point where
the crusading outlaw was in fact a more generally appealing
figure than the repressive lawman.

On the record-buying front, the image was likewise in synch
with the times. Rock 'n' rollers were outlaws—the life-style was
pretty much defined by the flouting of all sorts of legal and moral
rules—so a Rolling Stones fan could buy Waylon and Willie
records without feeling he was selling out to propriety. These
guys were also very specifically outlaws in Nashville, as their

Elvis Costello, Johnny Paycheck, and Greg Geller (left) listen for pearls of wisdom from Billy Sherrill (seated), 1981. Costello, an English New Wave rocker, came to Nashville to record an album of country songs, with Sherrill as producer. It didn't sell and was roundly criticized by many on Music Row. Of his countrypolitan producer, Costello has since said, "He's a complete and utter hack. Hasn't got an ounce of feeling in him."

The night shift: an armed guard and O.B. McClinton watch Stax engineer Larry Nix at work, February 1972. Recording for Stax, a Memphis soul label, O.B. placed a few hits on the country charts but never cracked the Top Twenty. However, shortly before his death in 1987, his recordings began selling well through telemarketing. In 1988, he was inducted posthumously into the Country Music Hall of Fame's Walkway of Stars.

hype proclaimed at length and in detail, and so your ideological anti-Nashvillian (your disgruntled hardcore country fan as well as your basic ex-hippie) could also shell out the bucks in all good conscience.

Add to the above the fact that in the middle 1970s both mainstream rock and mainstream country were creatively comatose, and you have the ideal set-up for a Major Movement. And of course the substance was there, not just the image. Nashville's

520

best songwriters and most powerful performers had been waiting nigh on twenty years for the opportunity to cut loose now provided by the Outlaws' rearrangement of power in favor of the artist, not the record company producer.

And so the uptight bubble burst, and the new music came forth in a torrent, and the hippie/country ideology wars began to recede into history. A thoroughly contemporary vision of the Texan-cowboy-outlaw West, a "Me Decade" landscape populated by hard-loving, blunt-talking individualists and tough stand-up persecuted artists (and cocaine dealers, bodyguards, loose women and other players in the traditional rock 'n' roll theater) united the urban boogie fiends and rural honky-tonkers of the nation under the rude bold flag of Outlaw chic.

It was quite a high, a creative explosion to equal that of Hank Williams and his peers in the forties (and commercially even more successful than Hank had been), but such a fierce fire couldn't last, and it didn't. Real musical revolution turned quite quickly into image cooptation, and by the time the fatuous, John Travolta-inspired *Urban Cowboy* fad found its way into the mens' and ladies' clothing departments at Bloomingdale's (Ah—Ethel Kennedy two-stepping with Gore Vidal in a $1500, fringed cowgirl vest at the Lone Star Cafe: cultural meltdown!), the creative energy of Outlaw music had flagged.

It had, however, accomplished something Nashville had never really thought possible. Quite apart from broadening the stylistic base of commercial country music to reincorporate the lost threads of blues and folk and rockabilly, it had penetrated the youth market. When the kids of the seventies thought of country music, they no longer saw images of deadhead middle-aged surburbanites or hippie-bashing rednecks or broken-hearted yokels moaning the shitkicker blues; they saw artists, real musicians, people with concerns and sensibilities something like their own.

And the kids of the seventies would become the adults of the eighties. They would grow to enjoy all sorts of pop music, and they would remember that Nashville was a supplier worthy of their consumer curiosity. Their local country station would be as fertile a source of socially appropriate music as any on their radio dial.

Cowgirl deluxe, revisited: Carlene Carter, in boots made for walking, 1980. The daughter of Carl Smith and June Carter, formerly married to English New Wave rocker Nick Lowe, released critically acclaimed country-rock LPs in the late seventies and early eighties but has remained on the country fringe nonetheless.

AND SO ON

After the Outlaws, it was all downhill, and the executives and public relations persons of the country music industry could stop worrying so much about the product's generic image.

Boxcar Willie, alias Lecil Martin, keeping the hobo tradition alive at the Opry, 1980s. A man who actually grew up riding the rails, Boxcar sold more than three million copies of his King of the Road *album without ever placing a song in the country Top Ten. Instead, the record sold through TV advertising. He took his stage name from the title of a song he'd written about a hobo who looked a little like Willie Nelson.*

Minor creative movements would influence a certain proportion of the product at any given time—an embrace of git-down electric amplification this year, a return to stone-country honky-tonking the next, a sudden plague of lounge lizards, a flurry of newgrass, a rockabilly reprise, an attack of social conscience—but it would be understood that these trendettes would conform to an approximately predictable cycle of relative popularity. So instead of being allowed to initiate general life-or-death stampedes in their stylistic direction, they would simply be added to the menu of existing fare.

And basically, as long as the menu could be kept both catholic and contemporary, an intriguing array of dear old favorites and the *au courant nouvelle*—Redneck Rock Bocephus, Lite Rock A la bama, Filet de Forties Skaggs, Texas Soul Strait, Pickled Liver Jones, Schmaltz Greenwood, Nostalgia Nelson, Apple Pie

522

No generation gap here: Lee Greenwood and Sylvia stand shoulder to shoulder with Pee Wee King, ca. 1982. King, of course, provided Nashville one of its biggest crossover hits ever when he co-wrote "The Tennessee Waltz" with bandmember Redd Stewart in 1947. Sylvia hit both the pop and country charts with "Nobody" in 1982. Greenwood's biggest crossover was "I.O.U." (1983).

Mandrell, Cheesecake Parton, Yoakam à la Mode, whatever—management need never worry about the restaurant going out of business. Significant numbers of somebodies out there would always be sure to pick the item most attractive to their particular palate, their personal image of where they fit in the world.

In its idle hours, management could ponder the conceivable benefits of a name change, a revamping of the overall image—would "American Music" not perhaps project a more contemporary, universal feel?—but really, it didn't matter. The product was home free.

523

16

DON'T GET ABOVE YOUR RAISIN': RICKY SKAGGS, ALABAMA, AND THEIR CONTEMPORARIES

David Gates

"There'll always be a honky-tonk somewhere," Nashville neotraditionalist Randy Travis sang in the concluding song of his 1986 debut album. It was apparently intended as an anthem, a country music counterpart to "Rock and Roll Will Never Die." But the Honky-Tonk of the Future, as seen by songwriters Johnny MacRae and Steve Clark was hardly a bustling place, "with a jukebox in the corner/and someone crying in their beer and one old hanger-on-er." And that lonesome "somewhere" suggested reduced expectations. By the mid eighties, neither MacRae and Clark nor anybody else was willing to predict that honky-tonks would be springing up like McDonald's stands. Still, country music did appear likely to survive—and for a while there, folks were beginning to wonder.

As the decade began, it seemed that there was a honky-tonk everywhere—complete with mechanical bull. 1980 was the year of *Urban Cowboy*, the looking-for-Mr.-Goodbeer film starring John Travolta, which for some reason prompted the types who had infested discos a year or two before to squeeze into tight-fitting jeans and onto crowded hardwood floors to attempt the Texas two-step and the cotton-eyed joe. Pseudo-kicker saloons appeared in New York, Boston, Chicago, and many smaller northern cities. Houston, home of the famous Gilley's, had about

Alabama made it to the top playing a brand of mountain music that leans more heavily on the Eagles than on the Carter Family. From left: Mark Herndon, Jeff Cook, Teddy Gentry, and Randy Owen.

The movie that put Gilley's on the map and revealed that John Travolta's dancing talent was not limited to disco. The soundtrack album—featuring songs by poppish country stars like Kenny Rogers and Charlie Daniels alongside countryish pop stars like Linda Ronstadt and the Eagles—went platinum.

At the height of the Urban Cowboy fever, Johnny Lee and Mickey Gilley (right) drink a promotional toast to their amazing success, 1981. Lee sang Urban Cowboy's theme song, "Looking for Love" (1980). In addition to being part-owner of the famous nightclub at the time, Gilley had compiled a dozen #1 hits, remaking pop ("True Love Ways"), soul ("Bring It on Home to Me"), and honky-tonk ("Window Up Above") oldies.

a dozen country-western clubs in 1975; in the early eighties, there were some three hundred.

The *Urban Cowboy* soundtrack album, which featured songs by poppish country stars like Kenny Rogers, Charlie Daniels, and Mickey Gilley alongside countryish pop stars like Linda Ronstadt and the Eagles, was the culmination of the crossover trend of the 1970s. Johnny Lee's hit single, "Lookin' for Love," the movie's theme song, created an association in the popular imagination of the singles-bar ethos with the sound of easy-rocking country music. One result: around $250 million worth of country record sales a year. By 1981, country had edged out pop as America's second-best-selling form of music after rock 'n' roll. The *New York Times'* Stephen Holden went so far as to claim that country had "supplanted rock for the time being as the dominant commercial mode" of popular music.

Five years later, the calico shirts were tucked away in the closet next to the Nehru jackets. In September 1985, a page-one story by the *Times'* Robert Palmer reported that country music audiences were "dwindling," record sales "plummeting," and that the Nashville Sound might soon be "as dated as the ukulele." Even Tammy Wynette, the First Lady of Country Music, warned that if things didn't change "we're all going to be out of business." The story was widely misread as an out-and-out obituary. Even people who should have known better missed Palmer's crucial point that the Nashville Sound, which sold so many records for Wynette in the sixties, was just one variety of country music. It was only natural that fashions would change over twenty years. Moreover, there was a whole world of country music that had little to do with the Nashville branches of the major record companies: a thriving festival scene for bluegrass and old-time music, thousands of hard-working bar bands across the country, legendary performers like Kitty Wells who still toured over a hundred days a year, and even the Grand Ole Opry itself, home base for veterans like Jean Shepard, Charlie Louvin, and Jack Greene who had been left behind by changing trends.

But the center of the country music industry was still on Music Row, in the Nashville operations of CBS, MCA, RCA, and Warner Brothers records—and their annual reports made scary reading. Record sales had slipped by $75 million a year, and a #1 country single—which had once meant sales of around 350,000 units—now sold an average of 100,000. Stars who had made lucrative deals during the *Urban Cowboy* craze were now failing to pull their fiscal weight. The Nashville establishment of the seventies—Conway Twitty, Crystal Gayle, Mickey Gilley, Barbara Mandrell, Johnny Cash—found their sales cut in half. Cash was even dropped from the CBS roster.

Ronnie McDowell's first country hit was "The King Is Gone" (1977), a tribute to the recently departed Elvis Presley done in the Presley style. Since then, McDowell has worked to establish an image of his own. Ironically, he recently remade "It's Only Make Believe" (1988), Conway Twitty's thirty-year-old Elvis impression.

Juice Newton, early eighties. Judy Kay Newton from Virginia Beach, Virginia, started out singing folk songs in California. In 1981, on the strength of three country and pop hits—"Angel of the Morning," "Queen of Hearts," "The Sweetest Thing" —she scored a platinum album. Though she married a polo player and took a short time off to have a baby, she's still a regular on the country charts.

527

Then, a year and a half after Palmer's piece, Stephen Holden
was back announcing in the *Times* that country music had suddenly "turned itself around" and "captured the ears of a new
audience"; sales were again above $200 million. Clearly some-
thing must have been going on during those lean years that was
now bearing fruit. In fact, two quite opposite things had been
going on. One was a hard-hitting new mix of rock and country—
the latest offspring of the interbreeding which had been going on
since rockabilly in the 1950s and which overpopulated Nashville
in the seventies. The other was a return to country traditions the
music industry had written off as outmoded—acoustic instruments, fiddles, steel guitars, and unabashedly southern accents.
As unlikely as it seemed at first, the purists were at least holding
their own with the progressives by mid decade. And each of
these new movements had produced a superstar act to rival Willie Nelson and Dolly Parton, the dominant figures of the seventies: Alabama, the new kings of crossover, and Ricky Skaggs,
the pope of purism.

Alabama has never been a critics' band. In everything from
music to politics, the best-selling group in country music is more

Cousins Randy Owen, Teddy Gentry, and Jeff Cook harmonize in the studio, early eighties. Despite the early hoopla about being a self-contained band, Alabama's main contribution to their records has been the vocals; they leave the picking mostly to seasoned studio hands.

popular than fashionable. "Godspeed, President Reagan," said drummer Mark Herndon at the 1986 Academy of Country Music Awards, shortly after the U.S. air strike on Libya. "I think you done the right thing." In New York, the writers groaned; at Knott's Berry Farm's Good Time Theatre, the thousands cheered. It's a critical commonplace to compare Alabama's sound to bubblegum rock. Holden of the *Times*, while conceding their "professionalism"—always a lefthanded compliment—has called their songs "shamelessly derivative and shallow," and the music itself "so homogenized and impersonal that there's often no difference between it and commercial jingles." Discussions of roots country music routinely trot out Alabama when it comes time to find a whipping boy.

Yet it would be hard to find contemporary country musicians with rootsier backgrounds than lead singer/rhythm guitarist Randy Owen, lead guitarist/fiddler Jeff Cook, and bassist Teddy Gentry, the three cousins who are Alabama's founding members. (Herndon, a rock 'n' roller from Massachusetts, is another story: he'd never even heard of Mel Tillis before joining the band.) Owen and Gentry grew up playing at snake-handling services at a Holiness church on Lookout Mountain up on the Georgia line. With Cook, from Fort Payne in the Alabama flatlands, they played beer joints, barn dances, VFW and American Legion halls, and, for three years, at an amusement park near Fort Payne, where they backed up visiting Grand Ole Opry stars like

Earl Thomas Conley began using his middle name in 1978 to avoid being confused with John Conlee and Con Hunley. He had already made a name for himself, however, as a Nashville songwriter, penning major hits for Mel Street ("Smokey Mountain Memories," 1975) and Conway Twitty ("This Time I Hurt Her More Than She Loves Me," 1975). ETC came into his own with the LP Don't Make It Easy for Me *(1983), which spawned four #1 singles.*

The Oak Ridge Boys: Duane Allen, William Lee Golden, Richard Sterban, and Joe Bonsall, ca. 1979. This top gospel quartet moved into mainstream country in 1976 and shortly afterwards began racking up Top Ten hits, culminating in their million-selling crossover "Elvira" (1981). Their group harmonies and rock-band backing prefigured the coming of country-rock groups like Alabama.

Gary Morris gives producer Jim Ed Norman his full attention, 1985. While Morris has been successful as a country singer, lately he's shown more interest elsewhere—appearing as a blind singer on ABC-TV's "The Colbys" in 1985–86 and taking leading roles in New York productions of La Bohème *(1984) and* Les Misérables *(1987). He told* Playboy *magazine: "I am not, never have been, nor have been purported to be a good ol' boy."*

Cal Smith and Jeanne Pruett. At a local talent contest, they won a trip to the Opry themselves and got to shake hands with Lester Flatt.

The cousins, with a series of drummers, spent summers playing for tips at a joint called the Bowery in Myrtle Beach, South Carolina, a resort where requests for country, rock, and soul music might all be shouted at the same bandstand. The band was then called Wildcountry: you named it, they played it. (These multimillionaires still fondly remember a woman who pulled a hundred-dollar bill out of her brassiere and called for "Roomful of Roses," a song from the forties recently covered by Mickey Gilley. Of course they knew it. Then she pulled out another. And another.) By 1977, they were a big deal in Myrtle Beach; they'd changed the group's name to Alabama and even had a single on a small label that got to #77 on the *Billboard* chart. Not to mention the three albums they'd paid for themselves and sold from the stage. In 1979, Herndon became their permanent drummer and they released a second single, "I Want to Come Over," on the Dallas-based MDJ label. The group spent some time shopping for a deal in Nashville, but the big labels claimed they weren't interested in groups.

They got interested in 1980. Another MDJ single, "My Home's in Alabama" hit the Top Twenty, and the band performed this song as well as the hit-to-be "Tennessee River" at a "new faces" show in Nashville. Record company executives were impressed by the band's flawless vocal harmonies, AOR (album-oriented rock) instrumental textures, and practiced showmanship. The offers started coming in, and Alabama signed with RCA—which, it turned out, had indeed been looking for a group to put up against MCA's Oak Ridge Boys and Mercury/PolyGram's Statler Brothers. Their first RCA album, *My Home's in Alabama*, was heavily promoted and became an almost immediate

Hank Williams, Jr.—who once seemed a pale imitation of his famous father, bound for an early grave—has emerged as one of country's most distinctive voices. Recovering from a near-fatal 500-foot plunge off a Montana mountain in 1975, he has come out on top, consistently selling his albums in the millions. In fact, in 1982 he placed nine albums on the charts simultaneously—a feat unequaled by any other country entertainer.

best-seller. Eventually it went double platinum—that is, it sold two million copies. So has every album since.

It seems perverse to argue that Alabama is more directly in the main line of country music tradition than a "neotraditionalist" like Ricky Skaggs; but, in fact, there's a pretty good case to be made. The great innovators of the past—Charlie Poole, the Skillet Lickers, Jimmie Rodgers, Bob Wills, even Ernest Tubb —were enthusiastic contaminators of "pure" country music, whatever that may be. Drums, electric guitars, and hot improvised solos, now commonplace, were once controversial. So were the influences of ragtime, blues, Tin Pan Alley pop, big-band jazz, and fifties rock 'n' roll. Wills's Glenn Miller-ish "Big Beaver" was at least as far from country music as Alabama's rocking "She and I"; Billy Byrd's jazzy guitar breaks on Ernest Tubb's records were as up-to-the-minute in their day as Jeff Cook's rock-and-rasp leads.

Alabama, in fact, is at its worst on its simplistic country-fiddle nostalgia numbers like "Mountain Music" and "If You Want to Play in Texas," on which Cook saws away with a maddeningly monotonous shuffle. The band is far more comfortable rocking

Feels so right: the boys from Fort Payne join the Mandrell Sisters and Glen Campbell for a musical interlude on NBC's "Barbara Mandrell and the Mandrell Sisters" TV show, 1981. From left: Teddy Gentry, Irlene Mandrell, Randy Owen, Barbara Mandrell, Campbell, Louise Mandrell, Jeff Cook; drummer Mark Herndon, who doesn't sing, is conspicuously absent.

Cut from the same cloth as Alabama, Exile scored a #1 pop hit in 1978 with "Kiss You All Over" before converting to country in 1983. The group already had country credentials, however, since they maintained a steady schedule of country studio work in Lexington, Kentucky, and since leader J. P. Pennington is the son of the late Lily May Ledford of the Coon Creek Girls.

Ronnie Milsap's first record, a double dose of r&b on the Scepter label, landed him gigs with acts like Bobby "Blue" Bland and the Miracles. Shifting to country early in the seventies, he signed a contract with RCA in 1973 and charted in the Top Ten with his first release, "I Hate You." Since then he has consistently turned oldies, soul numbers, ballads, and pop songs into country gold. In 1977 the CMA named him Entertainer of the Year.

out: Cook's guitar playing is fluid and inventive, and they can generate excitement comparable to that of the Eagles, Rush, or Bob Seger, whom they cite as their favorites. On their MOR (middle of the road) ballads, the vocal harmonies are more sophisticated than those of their gospel-based counterparts, the Oaks and the Statlers, and Owen's artfully hoarse lead singing has a rough edge missing from similar material by Kenny Rogers.

Still, all this is relatively faint praise. There is, finally, an important distinction between Alabama and innovators like Bob Wills: Wills, probably the most open-minded bandleader in country music history, opened up unexplored territory; Alabama merely relied on the country-rock formula already proven over and over again in the seventies by acts like the Eagles and the Charlie Daniels Band. Alabama has an uncanny knack for the hit song—twenty #1 singles by mid 1987—and an equally uncanny knack for avoiding the challenging and the profound. A George Jones performance like "Beneath Still Waters" packs more chills into three minutes than can be found in all of Alabama's *Greatest Hits* put together. Their music is too coldly accomplished ever to attain the radical simplicity and directness of Ernest Tubb, and too formulaic to risk Wills's sometimes wacky eclecticism.

Alabama's greatest contribution to country music is its popularity—and especially during the industry's lean years, 1982 to 1986, this was of the greatest importance. Alabama's profitability helped RCA to take chances on newer performers and to keep deserving but commercially shaky acts like Gail Davies on the roster. Moreover, Alabama brought many young listeners reared

Restless Heart, 1987. Something like a younger, more urbane version of RCA labelmates Alabama, these former session musicians make music for both the young professional and the four-wheel drive enthusiast. Their ballad "I'll Still Be Loving You" crossed over to #3 on the Adult Contemporary charts in 1987. From left: lead singer Larry Stewart, bassist Paul Gregg, keyboard player Dave Innis, guitarist Greg Jennings, and drummer John Dittrich.

Gail Davies has a reputation in Nashville for doing things her way—producing her own albums, raising her son by herself, and leading her own country-rock band, Wild Choir (1986). Although she has the respect of her peers, she's never had a #1 song.

on rock to country music: one function of popularized music is to build a bridge where there might have been a wall. In the early sixties, lightweight folk acts like the Kingston Trio and Peter, Paul & Mary opened the way to groups like the New Lost City Ramblers, who led on to the still deeper and more obscure pleasures of Roscoe Holcomb and Dock Boggs. In the 1980s, Alabama may have opened the way to Ricky Skaggs and on to George Jones. Most Americans, of course, will probably never be ready to go quite that deep into the country. What Alabama offers them isn't to be held in contempt, either: a catchy song on the radio to help get them through the day.

Since 1980, Alabamoid groups have become a country music subgenre. Exile, Sawyer Brown, Southern Pacific, and Restless Heart—as well as the still-popular Oaks—all laid dense vocal harmonies atop AOR guitars and keyboards and a heavy dance beat. Much of this music was fast food for the ears: cranked out according to formula with state-of-the-art technology, and instantly consumed. The influence of seventies California rock was also apparent in individual singers like Dan Seals. Outside the country music establishment, so-called "cowpunk" bands like Jason & the Scorchers, Lone Justice, Rank & File, and K. D. Lang & the Reclines combined an often superficial evocation of roots country with a slam-dance beat.

The problem with most eighties country-rock was its tendency to shortchange either one side of the hyphen or the other—or to wimp out on both. A welcome exception was Steve Earle. Earle's 1986 debut album, *Guitar Town*, coincided with the first albums of neotrads Randy Travis and Dwight Yoakam. At first Earle's

acoustic rhythm guitar, the pedal steel, and the references to hillbillies and good old boys led some listeners to conclude that all three were brothers in arms. In fact, Earle had as much in common with rock populists like Bruce Springsteen and John Cougar Mellencamp as with Travis and Yoakam. Unlike some country songwriters in the Reagan era, Earle doesn't sentimentalize small-town life. The characters to whom he gives voice ache above all to escape in their beat-up cars "made with union labor on American soil"; their one certainty is that they never will. Earle's music, with its snarling guitars and relentless backbeat, is appropriately rootsy—and appropriately devoid of conventional country comforts. John Anderson, a singer at least as passionate and mannered as Earle, has also managed to stay true to his hard-country roots without losing his hard-rock edge. He's sung Porter-and-Dolly duets with Emmylou Harris, and George-and-Melba duets with Delia Bell. And there are always a couple of steel-guitar-drenched weepers on his albums. But hits like "Swingin'," "Let Somebody Else Drive," and "Black Sheep" owed more to Chuck Berry or Little Richard than to Lefty Frizzell. Whatever Anderson's music is, it isn't for wimps. "I don't want to be in the middle of the road," he says. "Fella could get run over out there."

There are, of course, plenty of stars from the 1970s still working that amorphous middle—Kenny Rogers, Lee Greenwood,

Steve Earle says he sings hill-billy, country radio program-mers often call it rock, and the critics are divided. Earle's first Nashville recordings, done for Epic in 1983, were clearly in-tended as updated rockabilly, and they flopped. However, his 1986 debut album for MCA, Guitar Town, *won the support of critics as much for its eloquent tales of blue-collar life as for its rock-steady twang.*

Highway 101, 1987. Nitty Gritty Dirt Band manager Chuck Mor-ris organized this group around Minnesota farm girl Paulette Carlson, who first came to Nashville in 1981 and had pre-viously recorded minor country hits for RCA in 1983–84. Bassist Curtis Stone is the son of West Coast producer and publisher Cliffie Stone. Other members are drummer Scott "Cactus" Moser and guitarist Jack Daniels.

COUNTRY-ROCK

A contemporary of the Allman Brothers, the Marshall Tucker Band, and Lynyrd Skynyrd, Charlie Daniels has outlived all the southern rock bands of the seventies (and some of their unfortunate members). Since topping the country charts in 1979 with his sprightly rock-fiddle tune, "The Devil Went Down to Georgia," he has been accepted as a country artist.

Opposite, bottom
Country punks: Jason & the Scorchers, 1987. Formed in Nashville in 1981, this was one of the first bands to mix punk rock style with country twang. In the beginning, said guitarist Warner Hodges (center), "We used to do a set of Sex Pistols, a set of Hank Williams rocking, and a set of New York Dolls." Needless to say, country fans ignored them. Clockwise from Hodges: singer Jason Ringenberg, drummer Perry Baggs, bassist Jeff Johnson.

Country-rock could be said to date all the way back to the hybrid of hillbilly and blues music ("boogie") made popular in the late forties by white artists like the Delmore Brothers, Red Foley, Tennessee Ernie Ford, Moon Mullican, Arthur "Guitar Boogie" Smith, and the Maddox Brothers & Rose. And in the mid-fifties, another strain of country-rock—the rockabilly sound of Elvis Presley, Johnny Cash, Jerry Lee Lewis, Carl Perkins, and dozens of other revved-up country boys—was forged in the Memphis studios of Sam Phillips's Sun record label.

But when most folks use the term country-rock, they are referring to a phenomenon of the late sixties and seventies, a popular style in which the artistic pretensions of rock (as distinguished from rock 'n' roll), were combined with instruments, vocal harmonies, or lyrical themes more commonly associated with country music. Country-rock was largely a reaction to the heavily political, overbearing self-importance that rock had taken on. Blending rock with country's down-to-earth style seemed to afford an opportunity to simplify both the music and the message.

Many of the most visible country-rock groups came from California. But it was the Beatles who set the stage for the trend when, as early as 1964, the influential group released such country-flavored originals as "I'm a Loser" and "I Don't Want to Spoil the Party," and then a Buck Owens cover, "Act Naturally," in 1965.

With the Beatles pronouncing country cool, American rock musicians felt freer to let their own hillbilly heritage show. As social controversy over the Vietnam War

and the Civil Rights movement ebbed, the record-buying public responded to music that was more introspective and personal in character. Country-rock bridged the gap between the electric sixties and the sensitive seventies. The Byrds' *Notorious Byrd Brothers* and Bob Dylan's *John Wesley Harding*—both making nods to country—appeared on the charts early in 1968. In August, the Byrds' *Sweetheart of the Rodeo*, recorded in Nashville and featuring the work of newest member Gram Parsons, entered the charts. Although sales of *Sweetheart* were only moderate, the album exerted a tremendous influence on other musicians, opening the gates for a spate of country-rock releases.

Dylan's next work, *Nashville Skyline*, left no doubt about his enthusiasm for country music. Also recorded in Nashville, *Skyline* included a cameo appearance by Johnny Cash on "Girl from the North Country." The same week that *Skyline* entered the charts—May 3, 1969—the Flying Burrito Brothers, another influential group led by ex-Byrds Parsons and Chris Hillman, made their chart debut with *Gilded Palace of Sin*. Two months later, Poco's *Pickin' Up the Pieces*, with Rusty Young on pedal steel, appeared.

Linda Ronstadt and Neil Young made country-flavored albums in 1970. The following year brought another LP by the Burrito Brothers. Commander Cody and His Lost Planet Airmen and the New Riders of the Purple Sage (a Grateful Dead spinoff founded by Jerry Garcia) made their first appearances on the LP charts.

1972 was country-rock's breakthrough year: Parsons released his first solo LP; Ronstadt continued to explore country; Neil Young's *Harvest*, featuring hits "Heart of Gold" and "Old Man," came out; Michael Murphey (later known as Michael Martin Murphey) emerged from the Austin, Texas, scene with "Geronimo's Cadillac"; Rick Nelson's Stone Canyon Band scored a hit with "Garden Party"; the most commercially successful country-rock group of all, the Eagles, had a #12 hit with their first single, "Take It Easy"; and the Nitty Gritty Dirt Band enjoyed success with *Will the Circle Be Unbroken*, a collaboration with Nashville's old guard.

Although the movement's creative energies peaked around 1973, the resulting trend continued for several years on the strength of releases by John Fogerty (as the Blue Ridge Rangers); Parsons (posthumously); his protégée Emmylou Harris; the Souther, Hillman and Furay Band; Pure Prairie League; Firefall; Asleep at the Wheel; and the Eagles. In fact, the Eagles scored hits—albeit less and less country—into 1980, before disbanding in 1982.

To the east, southern musicians mixed roots and rock 'n' roll to produce variations on the country-rock theme. The Amazing Rhythm Aces, Tennessee natives, scored a pop hit (#14) with "Third Rate Romance" in 1975, which they followed with country hits "Amazing Grace (Used to Be Her Favorite Song)" and "The End Is Not in Sight." The success of the Marshall Tucker Band and the Charlie Daniels Band, both southern rock groups, paved the way for Alabama, who in 1980 became the first rock-style group to begin their career as country recording artists. After a near-fatal accident in 1975, Hank Williams, Jr., made a comeback by playing music that often hewed closely to the boogie of southern rockers like the All-man Brothers and Lynyrd Skynyrd.

Country music still provides inspiration for rock musicians. In 1981, English new wave pioneer Elvis Costello recorded a full album of country tunes, *Almost Blue*, working in Nashville with producer Billy Sherrill. In 1984, *Musician* magazine ran an article entitled "Country Punk: A Contemporary Marriage of Rural Honesty and Raw Passion Begets Cowpunk." Writer Rob Patterson cited Rank & File, Jason & the Scorchers, Lone Justice, the Screaming Sirens, the Last Roundup, and Blood on the Saddle, among others, as examples of young rock groups whose energetic music drew from country. And in the late eighties, as pop music charts reflected the popularity of big beat dance music, the Nashville record labels welcomed such rock 'n' roll-tinged performers as Steve Earle, Dwight Yoakam, K. D. Lang, Rosie Flores, Restless Heart, Foster & Lloyd, and the Desert Rose Band (led by Chris Hillman) as mainstays of their country rosters.

Above
Foster & Lloyd's first single, the rockabilly-styled "Crazy Over You," cracked the country Top Five in the summer of 1987. Radney Foster plays the rhythm guitar and sings lead; Bill Lloyd (who recorded a solo rock LP for Boston's Throbbing Lobster Records) provides the lead guitar and harmonies.

Anne Murray, Ronnie Milsap, T. G. Sheppard, Janie Fricke (who finally began spelling her name Frickie to clarify the pronunciation), Crystal Gayle, Mickey Gilley, Barbara Mandrell. And if the weekly charts are any indication, they're not getting run over. If critics have never paid more than obligatory attention to them, they don't seem to be losing any sleep over it. But the audience for their music—an undemanding mix of ballads, soft rock, sprightly uptempo ditties, and toned-down rock 'n' roll oldies—is increasingly the older listeners, and it's surely indicative that relatively few new singers of the eighties have followed their lead. One is Charly McClain, whose gentle voice is just country enough to keep things interesting, and whose close-harmony duets with husband Wayne Massey ("Just One Look in Your Eye") are invariably catchy. Another is Marie Osmond, wholesome child star belatedly turned country singer, whose 1985 duet with Dan Seals, "Meet Me in Montana," prevented a neotraditionalist sweep of that year's CMA awards.

The eighties' nearest equivalent to the mainstream stars of the seventies may be ex-Las Vegas lounge singer and card dealer Lee Greenwood, and John Conlee, a former disc jockey with a ripe baritone. Greenwood's repertoire ranges from soft rock ("You've Got a Good Love Coming") to soft country ("Dixie Road"). The gutsier Conlee's series of hits includes both medium-hard country songs (the 1978 "Rose-Colored Glasses") and

540

John Conlee labored for six years as a mortician before he got into the music business as a DJ. He was working for a Nashville station when he and a newsreader wrote "Rose Colored Glasses" (1978), the first of his many Top Ten hits. His ripe baritone sounds so country now it's hard to believe that he initially tried to be a rock singer.

Opposite, top left
Janie Fricke was a top jingle and session singer, first in Memphis and then in Nashville, before she began charting with her own records in the late seventies. Like all the best jingle singers, she can sing virtually any style well. A series of #1 singles between 1982 to 1984 earned her honors as the CMA's Female Vocalist of the Year for 1982 and 1983, a title she relinquished to Reba McEntire.

Opposite, top right
John Anderson helped shingle the roof of the new Opry House before he began climbing to the top of the country charts in the late seventies. Tagged as a traditionalist at first, he leaned a little toward rock after the enormous crossover success of "Swingin'" (1983) and fell from grace with country purists. Here he records at Nashville's Columbia Recording Studios before the fall, 1983.

Opposite, bottom
Lee Greenwood may be the Rodney Dangerfield of country music. Just as he was finally getting a little respect after years on the Las Vegas lounge circuit, country music turned away from his middle-of-the-road sound, and the critics pounced on him. For a couple of years, though, his rough-around-the-edges ballads were burning up the country charts. Here he accepts his second consecutive CMA Male Vocalist of the Year award, 1984.

perky paeans to the putative joys of everyday middle-American life (the 1983 "Common Man"). Like perennial superstar Conway Twitty, Conlee and Greenwood still sound a little too country for Adult Contemporary airplay, don't rock quite hard enough to suit most Alabama fans, and certainly aren't pure enough for the hardcore Randy Travis crowd.

Performers like Greenwood and Conlee, whose appeal is wider than it is deep, used to be the mainstays of the country music business, and still move—as they say in the trade—a lot of product. Where they'll be in the 1990s is anybody's guess. But

by the mid eighties they were being seriously crowded by a group of singers who seemed to appeal strongly both to record buyers in their teens and twenties and to old folks nostalgic for the days of Hank and Lefty: the much discussed new traditionalists.

In 1980, hardcore country music was dying in its own hometown. Nashville's recording industry, catering to an increasingly middle-class and suburbanized market, was encouraging few new singers in the uncompromisingly regional, uncompromisingly working-class tradition of Ernest Tubb, Hank Williams, Kitty Wells, Webb Pierce, George Jones, and Merle Haggard. Even Tubb himself, the father figure of hard-country music, had been dropped by MCA records (formerly Decca) after thirty-five years. Haggard and Jones still stuck to their guns and still sold records —some—but other hard-edge honky-tonkers, like Conway Twitty, were cutting back on the pedal steel. Wasn't *Urban Cowboy* the final vindication of the crossover revolution that had begun in RCA's Studio B in the 1950s?

A lot of country singers were more than happy to pay the price of a crossover hit: that corny fiddle-and-pedal-steel sound was okay for those fossils on the Opry, but these, after all, were modern times.

As Nashville lost interest in hard country, though, outsiders were discovering it. Some rock 'n' rollers, like the Beatles and the Rolling Stones, seemed mostly interested in country music's camp value: the Beatles' cover of Buck Owens's "Act Naturally" and the Rolling Stones' "Far Away Eyes" were little more than

542

She's a little bit country, he's a little bit rock 'n' roll: Marie Osmond and Dan Seals at Fan Fair, 1985. Marie's duet with Dan Seals, "Meet Me in Montana," was her first country #1 since "Paper Roses" (1973). The duet turned out to be the first of many country chart-toppers for Seals, who used to be one-half of pop duo England Dan & John Ford Coley.

Together again: George Jones and Tammy Wynette meet the press to announce a new album of duets, 1980. By this time, George and Tammy were divorced. Tammy's new husband, George Richey, keeps an eye on the proceedings.

dabbling. But musicians whose roots were in the folk-revival scene had a deeper understanding. Bob Dylan was recording with Nashville session players as early as *Blonde on Blonde* (1966). California folk-rockers like Jerry Garcia, Roger McGuinn, and Linda Ronstadt were profoundly influenced by country music. Still, late-sixties records like the Byrds' *Sweetheart of the Rodeo* and Gram Parsons's *International Submarine Band*, however authentic-sounding, were basically country music for hippies. The message of contemporaneous mainstream country records like Haggard's "Fightin' Side of Me" was No Hippies Allowed.

Michael Johnson, 1987. When asked by announcer Keith Bilbrey about his "transition from folk-rock, MOR ballads ['Bluer Than Blue,' 1978] to country, Michael Johnson correctly appraised the situation: "I don't think I've changed that much. I think the industry has come around to me." Who do you think Billboard's *top country singles artist of 1987 was? Randy Travis? George Strait? Nope. It was Michael Johnson.*

The voice of experience: Vern Gosdin, 1984. During his thirty years as a singer, Gosdin has seen it all: gospel radio in Alabama during the fifties; bluegrass in California with Chris Hillman and Don Parmley; modest success with his brother Rex in the Gosdin Brothers; and stints on Elektra, Cherry, AMI, Ovation, Compleat, and CBS as a solo act. In 1988, he was hitting the charts with pure honky-tonk.

A reconciliation between Nashville and these admiring outsiders was attempted by the Nitty Gritty Dirt Band, whose bestselling 1972 album *Will the Circle Be Unbroken?* showcased Roy Acuff, Mother Maybelle Carter, Pete "Bashful Brother Oswald" Kirby, and Merle Travis. But the most important transitional figure was Emmylou Harris, a folksinger discovered by Parsons and his Flying Burrito Brothers in Washington in 1971; she toured and recorded with Parsons until his death in 1973. In 1975 she released her first solo album, *Pieces of the Sky*, which contained pure and reverent—if sometimes over-delicate—versions of songs by Dolly Parton, Haggard, and the Louvin Brothers. It was a loving rebuke to Nashville's abandonment of its roots—her cover of the Louvins' "If I Could Only Win Your Love" went to #4 on the country charts—and it got the attention of rock fans who still felt it was declassé to be seen buying a Tammy Wynette record. On subsequent records, Harris's singing got tougher. She continued to lay on the fiddles, steel guitars, and close harmonies, and gradually she won over a Nashville establishment once inclined to be put off by her flower-child image. In 1980 she was named the CMA's Female Vocalist of the Year.

544

The godmother of the new traditionalists: Emmylou Harris, 1987. Plucked from obscurity in 1971 by Gram Parsons, Harris picked up where Parsons left off, taking hard-country music to a broader audience and inspiring younger musicians to maintain the flame. The list of graduates from her Hot Band reads like a who's who of contemporary country: Rodney Crowell, Ricky Skaggs, James Burton, Albert Lee, Emory Gordy, Tony Brown.

Mel McDaniel had pumped gas, worked in a motel, and written songs for other singers when he notched his first #1 in 1984—"Baby's Got Her Blue Jeans On." In 1986, he had a Top Twenty country hit with a Bruce Springsteen song, "Stand on It," done Jerry Lee Lewis-style.

By the mid 1980s neotraditionalism was solidly entrenched and Harris herself had become an establishment figure, as ready to host awards shows as John Denver or Mac Davis. And her indirect descendants were picking up most of the prizes: George Strait, Reba McEntire, Randy Travis, and the Judds. In one way or another, Harris had helped make the way for acts as diverse

545

With the door opened by Alabama, the Nitty Gritty Dirt Band came over to country music in 1983 after a decade and a half as a rock band with country sympathies. (They had recorded Will the Circle Be Unbroken *in 1971 before country-rock was fashionable.) In 1987, long-time member John McEuen left the band, replaced in 1988 by Bernie Leadon, former mainstay of the Eagles.*

Kathy Mattea grew up listening more to Joni Mitchell and Buffy St. Marie than to Loretta Lynn and Kitty Wells. Upon arriving in Nashville in 1978, she took a job as a tour guide at the Country Music Hall of Fame & Museum before moving on to work on demo and jingle sessions in Nashville studios. She's recently drawn comparisons to Anne Murray, as much for the country-folk sound of her records (courtesy of veteran producer Allen Reynolds) as for her mellow alto voice.

Steve Wariner broke into country music as a teenage bass player for Dottie West and then Bob Luman. Signing with RCA in 1978, he split time for a while between his solo singing career and playing bass for his idol, Chet Atkins. Though country fans now know him as the singer of such #1 hits as "Life's Highway" and "You Can Dream of Me," he's also become a distinctive lead guitarist, frequently picking on his own records.

Vince Gill wrote his 1988 hit "Everybody's Sweetheart" about his frustration over not getting to see his wife, Janis Gill, who is one half of Sweethearts of the Rodeo. Gill was a member of Bluegrass Alliance, Ricky Skaggs's Boone Creek, and Pure Prairie League before signing with RCA in 1983. Like Steve Wariner, Gill picks a mean guitar (and four other stringed instruments) in addition to singing.

547

Desert Rose Band, 1987. Leader Chris Hillman was a founding member of the Byrds and the Flying Burrito Brothers, the two most important country-rock bands in pop music history. The Desert Rose Band, the latest in this distinguished line, comprises a full quotient of California country-rock veterans, including Herb Pedersen, Steve Duncan, Bill Bryson, Jay Dee Maness, and John Jorgenson.

as Dwight Yoakam and the O'Kanes, Steve Earle and the Whites, John Anderson and Nanci Griffith. Some new performers, like Steve Wariner and Kathy Mattea, combined the spare acoustic sound of back-to-basics country with a slightly more pop sensibility. Others, like Ricky Van Shelton, Patty Loveless, and ex-Byrd Chris Hillman's Desert Rose Band, favored a more raucous honky-tonk sound. But the most successful of all these neotraditionalists, and the one whose career Harris influenced most directly, was a genial—and shrewd—young Kentuckian named Ricky Skaggs.

Ricky Skaggs may not have created back-to-basics country singlehanded, but his success certainly smoothed the way for everyone else. Between 1981 and mid 1987 Skaggs had four gold albums and eleven #1 singles, a powerful inducement to record companies to let country be country. He won assorted Grammys and CMA awards. Chet Atkins called him the man who saved country music—persuasive testimony, if a bit curious coming from the man who had run Studio B. *Esquire* magazine pronounced him, along with Meryl Streep, Apple computer mogul Stephen Wozniak, and Julius Erving, one of the "Men and Women Under Forty Who Are Changing America." Pretty fast company for a country boy; but Skaggs, who at the age of nine got up onstage with Bill Monroe and played the Master's own mandolin, was used to that.

Part of Skaggs's success is due to his cannily combining a country purist aesthetic—and born-again religious convictions—with a trendy sensibility. The video for his single "Country Boy," for example, featured the seventy-three-year-old Monroe

548

Ricky Skaggs performs at the 1983 CMA awards telecast. The CMA had named him Male Vocalist of the Year for 1982. Note the old-timey microphone, one of his trademarks.

capering in a subway car with a bunch of black breakdancers, and New York's Mayor Ed Koch lip-synching the words "I am just a country boy, country boy at heart." Skaggs enjoys reminding audiences that they're not in Kansas anymore: his stage patter may include a Three Stooges "nurk nurk nurk," or he may clown around with a mandolin version of the theme from *The Godfather*. He wears fashionably skinny ties, and his hair, which once flopped in casual Beatle bangs, has been sculpted by Nashville's Razz for Hair into a sort of new-wave dinosaur's crest.

Skaggs, born in Cordell, Kentucky, learned early on while playing festivals and colleges with a variety of bluegrass bands that city folks don't bite. He grew up in a musical family, learned to play at a tender age, and listened not only to bluegrass and

549

A former member of Emmylou Harris's Hot Band, Rodney Crowell has had songs recorded by Harris, Waylon Jennings, the Nitty Gritty Dirt Band, rock 'n' roller Bob Seger, and others. Meanwhile, he has served as producer for several artists, including his wife, Rosanne Cash. Despite a fine Orbison-esque tenor and strong solo recordings, Crowell remains Nashville's best-kept secret.

Rosanne Cash, 1987. Johnny Cash's daughter began to earn the respect of the country music industry when her song "Seven Year Ache" (1981) topped the country charts and registered #22 on the pop charts. With husband Rodney Crowell producing, her music often has a crisp rock edge that appeals to non-country audiences, although in 1988 she scored a #1 country hit with a straight country reading of her father's song "Tennessee Flat Top Box."

country music but also to the Beatles, the Rolling Stones, and the Hollies. Seeing the Stanley Brothers in concert changed his life. After Carter Stanley died in 1966, Skaggs joined Ralph Stanley's Clinch Mountain Boys as a mandolin player. At fifteen, he was not only a professional musician, but a member of a band second only to Bill Monroe's in the world of ultra-traditional bluegrass. (One colleague was guitarist Keith Whitley, who by 1987 had a couple of hits on RCA, and who sounded like the second coming of Lefty Frizzell—when he wasn't sounding like the second coming of Johnny Lee.) After three years, Skaggs moved to Washington, D.C., and played with more progressive bands like the Country Gentlemen and J. D. Crowe & the New South. His own band, Boone Creek, played a brand of "newgrass" at least as sophisticated as anything coming out of

Hot band: Emmylou Harris (guitar) with backing support from Sharon and Cheryl White, and Ricky Skaggs (partially obscured), late seventies. The two years Skaggs spent in Emmylou's Hot Band proved mutually beneficial—he served as her mandolinist, guitarist, fiddler, harmony singer, and bluegrass guru; she brought him into the mainstream.

Keith Whitley & Lorrie Morgan, ca. 1987. As a teenager, Whitley played bluegrass with Ricky Skaggs in Ralph Stanley's band. Now he sings mainstream country ("Don't Close Your Eyes," 1988) with a touch of honky-tonk. Wife Lorrie Morgan —daughter of the late Opry crooner George ("Candy Kisses") Morgan—leans more toward material in the style of Patsy Cline. Like Whitley, she records for RCA.

Nashville. It owed a lot to Stanley and Monroe, but a lot, too, to the European swing of Django Reinhardt and Stephane Grappelli.

In 1978 Skaggs, tired of driving a van and toting his own equipment, relocated to L.A. and spent two years with Emmylou Harris's Hot Band as mandolinist, guitarist, fiddler, harmony singer, and bluegrass guru. Harris and her band, in turn, introduced him to the world of drums, pedal steel, and Fender Telecasters. Harris's 1980 *Roses in the Snow*, which featured Skaggs heavily, anticipated his own *Don't Cheat in Our Hometown*, first released on North Carolina's Sugar Hill label the same year. (In 1983, it was rereleased on CBS with a couple of new tracks.) Like his subsequent records, it was a hybrid of the acoustic bluegrass he'd played most of his life—hot fiddle and mandolin solos and close vocal harmonies—and honky-tonk country, with drums, electric bass, and steel guitar.

A single, Skaggs's version of Carter Stanley's "I'll Take the Blame," became a local hit in Houston, the heart of Urban Cowboydom. CBS signed Skaggs, but most Nashville executives weren't overawed by the possibilities. This retro-sounding stuff had gotten Emmylou Harris her CMA award, but Kenny Rogers had the platinum albums and crossover singles: in 1980, "Lady" had stayed at #1 on the pop charts for six weeks. But the following year Skaggs's first CBS LP, *Waitin' for the Sun to Shine*, sold a more-than-respectable 400,000 copies and yielded two #1

Before they were known as the Whites: Buck White & the Down Home Folks, early seventies. At the time, the family group was playing bluegrass and old-time music on the festival circuit. About ten years later, the Whites brought an updated version of their traditional sound to the country radio with hits like "Hangin' Around" (1983). Shown here: father Buck, mother Pat, daughters Sharon (later to marry Ricky Skaggs) and Cheryl.

country singles. And when the *Urban Cowboy* craze had run its course, he suddenly found he was holding the hot hand.

Skaggs isn't in Haggard's or Jones's class as an interpreter of country songs, but his taste is impeccable, and his classic bluegrass tenor voice gives country standards like Jones's "The Window Up Above" and Webb Pierce's "I Don't Care" a new crispness and clarity. He records with his own road band (including ex-Monroe fiddler Bobby Hicks) rather than the usual Nashville studio musicians, and he produces the sessions himself. His records, consequently, have both an uncommon spareness and an uncommon warmth.

It would make little sense to hire rent-a-pickers anyway, since Skaggs himself is a studio-quality fiddler, mandolinist, acoustic guitarist and, more recently, electric lead guitarist. His live shows feature high-intensity extended jams—not to give the star a chance to rest his voice or change costume, but to show off a part of his music as important as his singing. Of all country singers, he's the least likely ever to put aside his guitar and stand in the spotlight romancing the microphone. Skaggs's competence and self-assurance sometimes seem boundless. But despite his ease on stage, his wife, singer Sharon White, had to talk him into taking over as his own lead guitarist when the intimidatingly gifted Ray Flacke left his band. "He just didn't think he could play well enough to handle the job," says White.

552

The face that launched a bunch of hits: George Strait, 1987. The former cattle rancher has become a bonafide country superstar, with million-selling LPs, sold-out arena shows, and even a full-length concert video that moves well in suburban video stores. His appeal comes partly from his clean-cut good looks, partly from his dedication to hot Texas dance and honky-tonk music, played by one of the best road bands in country music.

"And he was worried about bein' able to sing and play the guitar and the mandolin and do all the talkin', too. But he really is enjoyin' it now. I knew he would."

Except as an inspirational example, Ricky Skaggs was by no means an influence on most of the other back-to-basics acts that emerged in the 1980s. For Skaggs, the straight-ahead country of Haggard and Jones was the afterthought, bluegrass the well-spring. George Strait, on the other hand, was their direct descendant: he was playing Texas honky-tonks while Skaggs was playing festivals. By 1979, Strait, neither an Outlaw nor a country-rocker, was discouraged enough with the music business to accept a job in Uvalde, Texas, designing feedlots for cattle. At

553

the last minute—the company had even found him a house—he decided to give it one more year. A few weeks later, he recorded "Blame It on Mexico" and "Unwound," both of which ended up in the Top Ten. His 1983 LP *Right or Wrong*, with its #1 single "You Look So Good in Love," made him a superstar—and the closest thing in country music to a teen heartthrob.

In the 1940s, Strait, born in Pearsall, Texas, could have starred in Republic westerns. Onstage he wears a cowboy hat, a crisp white shirt with a small GS monogram, and blue jeans with a crease. His stage patter seldom goes so much beyond a laconic "thank you." And he still ekes out his own hits with Bob Wills, Hank Williams, and Merle Haggard numbers, as he did in the mid-seventies, when he and his Ace in the Hole Band played every bar and beer joint in south and central Texas. These influences, particularly Haggard's, are still eerily present in Strait's voice. Some of his more recent music, like 1987's "All My Exes Live in Texas," has leaned toward a high-gloss western swing— Haggard's 1970 Bob Wills tribute album was a major influence —and away from the honky-tonk sound of hits like "Does Fort

Like Patsy Cline, with whom she is often compared, Reba McEntire has deep country roots, but sings with a searching voice that can handle virtually any musical style. Her breakthrough came with straight country material in 1984; four years later she revealed that her kind of country includes remakes of old r&b songs like "Sunday Kind of Love" and Aretha Franklin's "Respect."

John Schneider has good looks, a warm country baritone, and eight years of country hits, but he still hasn't shaken his reputation as a TV actor (Bo Duke on "The Dukes of Hazzard") playing a country singer.

Like her friend and former roommate Janie Fricke, Judy Rodman began her professional career singing jingles and sessions in Memphis. She moved to Nashville in 1980, where she did more of the same. In 1985 her first album, Judy, *appeared on MTM Records. Fans and critics alike took notice when Bob Dylan complimented her records after the two met at the first Farm Aid benefit concert; she recorded Dylan's "I'll Be Your Baby Tonight" in 1987.*

Worth Ever Cross Your Mind?" Critics have begun to fault Strait for being bland and derivative. But at the very least he's derivative of the right sources—and to be the Tommy Duncan of the 1980s is not an unworthy achievement.

Reba McEntire had her first record deal in 1978, before Skaggs or Strait, but only after their successes did her hard-country voice—"lips," for example, are "leeups"—reach beyond a cult following. She put out an album a year for the next six years; two of her singles reached #1, but she wasn't getting rich. In 1984 she jumped from Mercury/PolyGram to MCA and recorded *Just a Little Love*, a dreary specimen of state-of-the-craft country pop, a miscalculation that disappointed her traditionalist following and didn't win over many Kenny and Dolly fans, either.

Her next album, the militantly titled *My Kind of Country*, was a complete turn-around: transcendently gloppy heart songs with pedal steel and sweetly aching overdubbed harmonies, and a touch of Texas swing, with fiddling by one-time Texas Playboy Johnny Gimble (who had also played George Strait's sessions). McEntire even changed her image to correspond. On the cover

For Father's Day, 1984, Holly Dunn sent her father, a San Antonio preacher, a demo of a song she had written especially for him. The next time he saw her he threw his arms around her and told her how much he loved her, something he'd never felt comfortable doing before. Later, he confessed that the song had brought tears to his eyes. When she recorded the song for MTM Records in 1986, "Daddy's Hands" became her first Top Ten hit.

Loretta Lynn's cousin Patty Loveless wrote country songs for Doyle and Teddy Wilburn's publishing company when she was only fifteen and still known as Patty Ramey. After marrying Wilburn's drummer Terry Lovelace, she dropped out of country to sing rock 'n' roll. Now a member of the Grand Ole Opry, this emotional, open-throated stylist could give Reba McEntire and Wynonna Judd a run for their money.

of *Just a Little Love* she was dressed in frilly white, gamely trying to impersonate a temptress; for the *My Kind of Country* cover she posed in blue jeans (and her outsized rodeo belt buckle), looking perkily unglamorous, with blue sky and mountains behind her. "Ricky and George," she says, "gave me the guts to do it." What worked for Ricky and George worked for Reba. *My Kind of Country* and its irreproachably country hit single "How Blue" made McEntire the CMA's 1984 Female Vocalist of the Year. The sequel, *Have I Got a Deal for You*, was even better—a hard-country masterpiece.

Since then, McEntire has moved—for better or worse—toward the middle of the road with hits like "Whoever's in New England." She's arguably the best female singer since Patsy Cline—an acknowledged influence—and indisputably the new queen of country. But her formidable technical skills and her ambition to reach the widest possible audience seem to have run away with her and the rigorous aesthetic of her best work is missing from her more recent albums. But while it's easy to make invidious comparisons between her later work and a staunchly purist record like Randy Travis's debut album, *Storms of Life*, McEntire has been making records for a long time. "How Blue" was a breakthrough; ten "How Blues," she was shrewd enough to recognize, would have become a dead end. Her solution may not please the purists, but it doesn't seem to bother the fans a bit.

McEntire's closest competitor among the new female singers is probably young Wynonna Judd. The Judds, Wynonna and her mother Naomi (whose real names turn out to be the considerably less folksy Christina and Diana), appeared in 1984 with a rags-to-riches story right out of Hollywood. In fact, the Judds *were* right out of Hollywood, where they had moved from their native Kentucky in 1968. After several rough years, they went back, in a deliberate return to roots. It was in Kentucky, in a house without telephone or television, that Wynonna learned to play guitar and began singing with her mother. In 1979 they moved to Nashville, and—at least according to legend—got their record contract by auditioning live in RCA's boardroom. Since 1984, they've had a series of hits—beginning with "Mama He's Crazy" and "Why Not Me?"—all heavy on acoustic guitar and close-harmony singing. Thanks to guitarist and arranger Don Potter, the Judds managed to achieve with stripped-down, folky instrumentation a sweet-and-funky energy usually produced only by electric bands. And Wynonna's remarkably expressive singing, perfectly complemented by Naomi's tart harmonies, became more assured with every record.

Like Dwight Yoakam, Rosie Flores came to Nashville's attention by playing in L.A. (in her case it was in rock bands) and appearing on a little-known but influential country compilation album called A Town South of Bakersfield *(1985). Her debut country album (1987), which teamed her with Yoakam's producer and lead guitarist Pete Anderson, twanged as hard as Yoakam but didn't sell like him.*

557

The Judds—mother Naomi and daughter Wynonna (on guitar) —as they appeared at a 1983 showcase performance and on the cover of their first LP in 1984. Weaned on the records of Bonnie Raitt and Joni Mitchell, Wynonna supplies the strong, soulful lead voice; Naomi adds the harmonies, stage sass, and the moxie that have made them a million-selling country act.

Sweethearts of the Rodeo— sisters Janis Gill and Kristine Arnold (right)—took their name from the Byrds' famous country-rock LP. They burst on the Nashville scene in 1986, the year after they won the Wrangler Country Showdown talent contest. Arnold's lead voice and Gill's harmony entwine with a tautness that has led some critics to dub them "the female Everlys." Janis, by the way, is married to country singer Vince Gill.

Strait, McEntire, and the Judds were in the first wave of post-Skaggs neotraditionalists. A second wave—the Travis-Earle-Yoakam invasion—soon followed. Randy Travis had put in years of club work in his native North Carolina before moving to Nashville. In 1985, he was finally discovered at a tourist bar near Opryland by Warner Bros. executives consciously scouting for a new Ricky Skaggs. His resonant, heartfelt, Haggard-like bari-

After signing with Warner Bros. Randy Travis (born Traywick) watched his first single stall at #67 on the charts. When a second release, "1982," went to #6 in early 1986, Warner's tried the first single again. "On the Other Hand" went to #1.

559

When CBS went looking for a traditional country singer to compete with Randy Travis, they found former pipe fitter Ricky Van Shelton, who had moved to Nashville from eastern Virginia in hopes of just such a break. On the strength of five hit singles, Shelton's debut album went gold in 1988. With his smooth, straight-ahead baritone and good looks, he promises to vie with Travis in the coming years for country sales and awards.

Act naturally: Larry Boone, 1988. Now a recognized name on the charts, with intimations of a budding movie career as well, Larry Boone once supported himself in Nashville singing for $20 a day, a meal, and tips at the Country Music Wax Museum. Some 2,000 fans have a collectible copy of the LP the traditional country singer financed himself and peddled to tourists.

tone is about an octave away from Skaggs's bluegrass tenor, but his devotion to tradition is equally absolute. His hit single "On the Other Hand" is a country classic on the order of Buck Owens's "Together Again," George Jones's "She Thinks I Still Care" or Mel Street's "Borrowed Angel": a perfect song perfectly performed. Travis is the kind of star Nashville dreams about: quiet and respectful, and reverential toward institutions like the Grand Ole Opry. Dwight Yoakam is the kind they don't know what to do with: a Kentuckian-turned-Californian who used to hang out with cowpunks like Lone Justice, who sometimes opens for rock bands like Hüsker Dü, who affects loud, Nudie-style duds with a camp flair, and who is openly contemptuous of the industry for betraying pure country music. In fact, Nashville would know exactly what to do with him if his records stopped selling. Yoakam's music is derived from rockabilly—his first hit was a cover of Johnny Horton's "Honky Tonk Man"—and the Bakersfield sound of Owens's Buckaroos. Compared to Travis, his singing seems oddly affectless—as if he were trying too hard to imitate a country singer. But, like Skaggs, he uses his own band in the studio, and he gets a raw country edge that's sometimes missing even from Travis's more slickly produced records. This slightly dangerous sound, coupled with Yoakam's hipper pose, has proved appealing to the more venturesome rock fans who buy records by Los Lobos or the L.A. cowpunks—and it hasn't hurt him with country fans, either.

560

The kind of star Nashville doesn't know what to do with: honky-tonk man Dwight Yoakam, 1987. Turned down by everyone when he first came to Music City in the late seventies, Yoakam tasted sweet revenge ten years later when his first album went gold and the second one followed suit. In 1988 Yoakam got the opportunity to record and tour with a country renegade from the past—his long-time idol, Buck Owens.

By 1987, there was yet another new wave in sight—not honky-tonk revivalists but more cerebral singer-songwriters whose roots were in acoustic folk music. Texan Lyle Lovett was writing complex, ironic songs like "God Will," somewhat in the manner of a country Tom Waits. Fellow Texan Nanci Griffith, who had played the coffeehouse circuit for years, suggested a country Joni Mitchell. Most interesting—and successful—of all were the O'Kanes, Nashville songwriters Jamie O'Hara (who wrote the Judds' hit "Grandpa") and Kieran Kane (who co-wrote Ala-

Songwriters Jamie O'Hara and Kieran Kane (right) joined forces as the O'Kanes after the demos they'd made in Kane's attic sounded better than expected. Following several months on the Nashville club circuit, the O'Kanes signed with CBS when the company invited them to assemble an album's worth of their austere arrangements— and didn't change a thing. Their first single, "Oh, Darlin'," cracked the country Top Ten in 1987.

bama's "Gonna Have a Party"). Their collaborative efforts, like "Oh Darlin'," deftly deconstructed the formal conventions of folk and country songs. Their mandolin-guitar duets and two-part harmonies evoked the great brother acts of the past, like the Monroes and the Louvins. And they created a wholly original —and wholly country—electric-acoustic band sound with fiddle, electric guitar, mandolin, accordion, bass fiddle, and drums. The O'Kanes' "Can't Stop My Heart from Loving You" was a #1 hit in 1987, but the long-range commercial potential of such laid-back music was still in doubt, especially on Top Forty country radio. Still, this latest wave showed that Music Row wasn't entirely closed to émigrés from the coffeehouse and festival scene, where country music's deepest folk roots had been preserved, however artificially, during the dark years.

The O'Kanes pointed to one possible way around the impasse that, sooner or later, every Nashville neotraditionalist has to face: how to keep it country yet make it new. For the country-rock crowd, the solution seemed simple: trot out the synthesizers, crank up the drums and the guitar feedback, and market your records out of Nashville. This was by no means always an aesthetic disaster, and many country-rockers were indifferent to what seemed to them the academic question of whether they were playing rock or country. Music was music, right? The dilemma was far keener for singers like Skaggs and Strait, who felt a genuine reverence for country tradition and a genuine calling to perpetuate it—and yet were not content with mere scholarly revivalism. Their solution was to recombine preexisting elements—in Skaggs's case, honky-tonk and bluegrass; in Strait's, honky-tonk and western swing—into a synthesis at least temporarily fresh. The O'Kanes' band sound was a more radical example of the same approach. Their music evoked the Louvin Brothers, the Blue Sky Boys, the Everly Brothers, Elvis Presley's Sun rockabilly band, even Pee Wee King's Golden West

Jo-El Sonnier and accordion, 1988. Born to sharecroppers in Rayne, Louisiana, Sonnier had his own fifteen-minute radio show at age six, but it was another thirty-five years before he cracked the country Top Ten with "No More One More Time" (1988). Overcoming a Cajun accent so thick he needed an interpreter, he marked time recording music for small independent labels—and even appeared as a biker in the movie Mask *(1985) starring Cher— before signing with RCA in 1987.*

Country music's answer to Debbie Gibson and Tiffany: Alison Krauss, 1988. She took her first violin lessons at age five, won her first fiddling championship at twelve, and signed with Rounder Records at fourteen. She also sings pure country, prompting critics to proclaim her a new star. Now a seventeen-year-old sophomore at the University of Illinois, she still takes time out from her studies to play dates with her band, Union Station.

Cowboys. The almost mystical simplicity of their songs also reflected their mix-and-match modernism: there were echoes of folk song and classic country, stripped down to their most abstract and elemental.

Yet even such a sophisticated solution has its theoretical limits. Where do you go—assuming it's necessary to go somewhere —once you've worked through all the permutations? No serious artist is content merely to do what's been done before: Arnold Schoenberg may have believed that there were great symphonies still to be written in the key of C, but he didn't seem eager to write them himself. Certainly the Nashville neotraditionalists made some of the freshest and most exciting country music of the 1980s. But there was something disquietingly self-conscious

564

Eddy Raven got his start in Nashville when fellow Cajun Jimmy C. Newman connected him with the Acuff-Rose publishing house in 1970. He landed hits with Don Gibson, Roy Clark, and Jerry Reed but also had to work for a while as a motel lounge singer. After ten years of modest success on several labels, he clicked with RCA and a calypso-style country song, "I Got Mexico" (1984), his first #1.

David Lynn Jones got his long-awaited break when Willie Nelson scored a #1 hit in 1986 with his song, "Living in the Promiseland." Rock and country critics alike endorsed his first LP, Hard Times on Easy Street, for its combination of hard-driving tunes and social conscience. It was produced by an unusual team—Jones, Mick Ronson (former guitarist for David Bowie), and Richie Albright (drummer for Waylon Jennings).

about much of their work—and that was almost entirely unprecedented in country music. Merle Haggard's affectionately didactic tribute albums to Jimmie Rodgers (1969) and Bob Wills (1970) were early warnings that the country music tradition was in need of conscious preservation: in other words, that it was becoming irrelevant. In the late 1940s, the notion of a tribute album to, say, Roy Acuff would never have occurred to Hank Williams: Hank was too busy trying to outsell him. When Loretta Lynn, in the fifties, dreamed of being the next Kitty Wells, she was

dreaming of supplanting an older but popular contemporary. When Ricky Skaggs dreamed of being the new Bill Monroe, it was a far more rarefied ambition.

Lynn grew up in an environment where country music was the norm. Her choice of a career ratified the aesthetic values of her community. But Skaggs, Lynn's fellow Kentuckian, came of age in a different world from Butcher Hollow, a world in which the Beatles had shouldered out the Stanley Brothers. For Skaggs

566

and his coevals, the decision to become a country singer was far more eccentric than for Loretta Lynn—and it involved some role-playing along with the role-modeling. The more thoughtful of today's country neotraditionalists can't help having a sense of watching themselves impersonate the great figures of the past—who lived and worked unself-consciously in the present. Country music has finally—take your pick—become decadent or achieved self-awareness.

But whether in a last bloom of decadence or in a new burst of vitality, country music was indisputably thriving again by the mid 1980s—thanks equally to its continuing fusion with the pop music mainstream and to its rediscovery of its own traditions. The tension between these two impulses had been around since the days of Vernon Dalhart and Fiddlin' John Carson, and the music business seemed to have no trouble accommodating both an Alabama and a Ricky Skaggs. The basic conceptual contradiction of country music remained: at the bleakest, the alternatives were commercial and aesthetic suicide by freezing a narrow and timebound regional tradition, and generic suicide by crossbreeding the music out of existence. But, as always, this was a problem for the individual artist to face. The individual listener was faced only with an ever-expanding range of alternatives—including the mass of important historical recordings respectfully remastered and reissued. At the very least, it seemed certain once again that there would always be a honky-tonk somewhere, with one hell of a jukebox in the corner.

The hottest country stars of 1988 are booked for the spring or fall Marlboro Country Music Tours, which the cigarette company has sponsored since 1983. To deflect possible criticism from anti-tobacco activists, Marlboro designates large sums from its gate receipts to various charitable causes. The line-up for 1988: Restless Heart, Alabama, the O'Kanes, George Strait, Kathy Mattea, Merle Haggard, the Judds, Ricky Van Shelton, K. T. Oslin, and Randy Travis.

COUNTRY MUSIC: A SELECTED DISCOGRAPHY

To understand country music, you've got to listen to it. Until you hear Jimmie Rodgers yodel a blues or James Burton pick the guitar, you won't understand why country fans are such a devoted lot. Organized in roughly chronological order, this discography describes a basic country collection, listing the best recordings *currently available* from a cross-section of artists and styles. (Issue numbers refer to LPs, although cassettes and compact discs are often available as well.) In many cases the discography names more than one selection for an artist or style, usually when both a hits sampler (appropriate for the new fan) and an exhaustive boxed set (for the confirmed devotee) are on the market.

But be warned: record companies (especially the major labels) frequently delete titles that have stopped selling, so don't assume that all the records listed here are still available. Sometimes it takes a little determination to locate country records—especially by artists who are no longer recording. Unless you live in a city with a specialty store for country fans, you may need to order your selections through the mail.

Fortunately, several mail-order operations do cater to country record buyers. County Sales, Roundup Records, Down Home Music, and Elderly Instruments all carry a mixture of new releases by current artists, newly reissued vintage recordings, and independent-label product. With the help of these firms, you can usually find the record you want (if it's still in print) at a reasonable price.

County, Roundup, and Down Home publish newsletter/catalogs that offer interesting and opinionated reviews of new releases. *County Sales Newsletter* sticks mainly to bluegrass, old-time, and traditional country music, but both *Record Roundup* and *Down Home Music Newsletter* also offer blues, gospel, jazz, new age, ethnic, folk, vintage rock 'n' roll, and more.

For out-of-print records, or in the event that none of the mail-order outlets above can come up with the disc you want, *Goldmine* magazine, subtitled "The Record Collector's Marketplace," offers the best hope. In addition to artist profiles and discographies, the bi-weekly tabloid publication runs dozens of ads and auction lists for used and hard-to-find records. If you're really desperate, you can mail inquiries ("want lists") to the collectors who publish auction lists in the magazine. Once you enter the network of hard-core collectors, virtually any recording can be had— for the right price.

County Sales
P.O. Box 191
Floyd, Virginia 24091
703-745-2001

Down Home Music
10341 San Pablo Avenue
El Cerrito, California 94530
415-525-1494

Elderly Instruments
1100 N. Washington
P.O. Box 14210
Lansing, Michigan 48901
517-372-7890

Roundup Records
P.O. Box 154
North Cambridge, Massachusetts 02140

Goldmine
Krause Publications
700 East State Street
Iola, Wisconsin 54945
715-445-2214

Jimmie Rodgers

Jimmie Rodgers: America's Blue Yodeler (Smithsonian Collection of Recordings DMM 2-0721). A three-album set with notes by Nolan Porterfield, Rodgers's biographer.

The Carter Family

A Collection of Favorites by the Carter Family (Stetson HAT 3022). A repackaging of 1930s Decca recordings.

The Carter Family on Border Radio (John Edwards Memorial Foundation JEMF 101). Drawn from prerecorded radio shows aired over Mexican border stations.

Bristol Sessions

The Bristol Sessions (Country Music Foundation CMF 011). Double-album sampling of famous July–August 1927 sessions conducted by Ralph Peer. Features the first recordings of Jimmie Rodgers, and the Carter Family. Twenty-one other acts. Album received 1987 Grammy nomination, as did notes by Charles Wolfe.

Old-Time String Bands

Old Time String Band Classics: Original Recordings from 1927–1933 (County 531). Reminders of the richly varied string-band tradition, which was then assimilating elements of jazz and blues.

Old-Time Fiddling
Old-Time Fiddle Classics (Vol. 1: County 507; Vol. 2: County 527). Two excellent anthologies showcasing Eck Robertson, Lowe Stokes, Clayton McMichen, Fiddlin' Arthur Smith, and other champion fiddlers.

Delmore Brothers
Brown's Ferry Blues: 1933–41 Recordings (County 402). A dozen classic duets, including the title cut and "Gonna Lay Down My Old Guitar."

Blue Sky Boys
The Sunny Side of Life (Rounder 1006). "Kentucky," "Alabama," "Turn Your Radio On," and thirteen other Depression-era tunes from the Bolick brothers, Bill and Earl.

Opry String Bands
Nashville String Bands (Vol. 1: County 541; Vol. 2: County 542). Representative selections by bands who helped launch the Opry during the 1920s and 1930s.

Uncle Dave Macon
Go 'Long Mule (County 545). Best reissue album of material by Macon. Supported by the Fruit Jar Drinkers.

Patsy Montana
Patsy Montana and the Prairie Ramblers (Columbia Historic Edition FC 38909). Of the dozen cuts, only five feature Patsy Montana. The rest are by the Ramblers, who recorded in their own right in addition to backing the famous cowgirl yodeler.

Bradley Kincaid
Mountain Ballads and Old Time Songs (Old Homestead OHCS 107). Sixteen favorites from the singer's native Kentucky hills, including "Barbara Allen" and "The Fatal Wedding."

Roy Acuff
Roy Acuff (Columbia Historic Edition FC 39998). ARC and CBS recordings from 1936 to 1951 that document Acuff's transition from string-band leader to one of country music's first star singers.

Cajun Music
Louisiana Cajun and Creole Music 1934: The Lomax Recordings (Swallow LP-8003-2). Double LP of field recordings supervised by John and Alan Lomax for the Library of Congress in 1934. Extensive notes by Alan Lomax and Cajun music authority Barry Jean Ancelet.

Louisiana Cajun Music, Vols. 1–7 (Old Timey). Series of historic recordings, issued by Chris Strachwitz's Old Timey Label. Strachwitz has also released new recordings by traditional Cajun acts on the Arhoolie label.

Gene Autry
Gene Autry (Columbia Historic Edition FC 37465). "Tumbling Tumbleweeds," "Don't Fence Me In," and eight more classics from the singing cowboy's recording heyday.

The Gene Autry Collection (Murray Hill M61072). A four-record boxed set covering the late 1920s through the early 1950s. (Note: Murray Hill M61072 is the same as Columbia P-107080-83.)

The Sons of the Pioneers
Sons of the Pioneers (John Edwards Memorial Foundation JEMF 102). Radio transcriptions from the 1930s, showcasing country music's foremost western harmony group.

Sons of the Pioneers (Columbia Historic Edition FC 37439). Notes include essential data on the band's changing personnel.

Tex Ritter
An American Legend (Capitol SKC-11241). This three-disc boxed set spans 1942–73. Tex introduces the selections with his own spoken annotations.

Cowboy Music
Back in the Saddle: American Cowboy Songs (New World NW 314/315). Two-disc overview of cowboy music, from traditional to contemporary. Twenty-eight artists represented, including Jules Verne Allen, Carl T. Sprague, and the Girls of the Golden West.

Bob Wills
Bob Wills Anthology (Columbia KG 32416). A collection of Wills's biggest hits, 1935–47. Two-record set.

The Golden Era (Columbia Historic Edition C2-40149). Notes by Wills expert Bob Pinson enhance this career overview. Two-record set.

Bob Wills Fiddle (Country Music Foundation CMF 010). Instrumentals from 1935–42, ranging from traditional fiddle tunes to jazz and blues. Twenty cuts, seven of them previously unissued.

Milton Brown
Pioneer Western Swing Band: 1935–1936 (MCA 1509). Decca material from one of western swing's seminal bands.

Spade Cooley
Spade Cooley (Columbia Historic Edition FC 37467). A sampler from the largest and flashiest western swing band.

Bill Monroe
Bill Monroe (Columbia Historic Edition FC 38904). Ten recordings from the formative 1945–47 period when Lester Flatt and Earl Scruggs helped to transform the Blue Grass Boys.

Bill Monroe with Lester Flatt and Earl Scruggs: The Original Bluegrass Band (Rounder Special Series SS-06). These Columbia recordings from 1946–47 marked the beginning of bluegrass as we now know it. Notes by Neil Rosenberg.

Country Music Hall of Fame (MCA 140). A great album of Monroe standards, released by Decca soon after Monroe's 1970 election to the Country Music Hall of Fame.

Flatt & Scruggs
Flatt and Scruggs (Columbia Historic Edition FC 37469). Ten excellent examples of the duo's finest work, recorded 1952–59.

Mercury Sessions (Vol. 1: Rounder Special Series SS 18/PolyGram Special Projects PSP 5003; Vol. 2: Rounder Special Series SS 19/PolyGram Special Projects PSP 5004). Flatt and Scruggs right after they left Monroe (1948–52): "Foggy Mountain Breakdown," "Roll in My Sweet Baby's Arms," and other classics.

The Stanley Brothers

The Stanley Brothers: The Starday Sessions (County CCS 106/107). A two-album set of late 1950s–early 1960s recordings, including "Little Maggie," "Rank Stranger," "If I Lose," and many more.

Stanley Series, Vol. 1, No. 1 (Copper Creek CCSS V1N1). First of a series featuring live albums made during the late 1950s and early 1960s. Eight records issued as of mid 1988.

Various Bluegrass Bands

Hills and Home: Thirty Years of Bluegrass (New World 225). Best anthology of bluegrass recordings, with excellent notes by Neil Rosenberg.

Eddy Arnold

All-Time Favorites (RCA Britain NL 90004). A re-release of Eddy's first 12-inch LP, recorded in 1956, *before* he'd met the Nashville Sound. These original recordings include steel guitar by Roy Wiggins.

Floyd Tillman

Floyd Tillman (Columbia Historic Edition FC 39996). Includes "Slippin' Around," "Drivin' Nails in My Coffin," and eight other influential honky-tonk hits.

Ernest Tubb

Honky-Tonk Classics (Rounder Special Series 14). Decca recordings (1940–54) that helped to define the honky-tonk style.

Ernest Tubb Favourites (Stetson HAT 3011). British reissue of a 1956 Decca album of Tubb's biggest hits, all recorded during the 1940s.

Red & Ernie (Stetson HAT 3000). Duets that Tubb recorded with Decca labelmate Red Foley during the 1940s and early 1950s.

Hank Williams

I Ain't Got Nothin' But Time (December 1946–April 1947) (Polydor 422-825 548-1 Y-2). First of eight two-album sets (all recommended) covering Hank's entire recording career in chronological order. Remastered in original mono and free from the posthumous overdubbing that marred many previous collections of Hank's hits. Compiled by Colin Escott and Hank Davis.

Forty Greatest Hits (Polydor 821 233-1 Y-2). For the budget minded, this two-record set is the best sampling of Hank's work. In mono, with only "Weary Blues from Waiting" overdubbed (as it was originally issued in 1953). Notes by Tony Byworth include country chart positions.

Just Me and My Guitar (Country Music Foundation CMF 006). Twelve previously unreleased demo recordings from Hank, with only his guitar as accompaniment.

The First Recordings (Country Music Foundation CMF 007). Hank's earliest recorded performances: twelve demo recordings (ca. 1946).

Lefty Frizzell

Lefty Goes to Nashville (Rounder Special Series SS 16/Columbia Special Products P16810). Earliest Columbia recordings, with album notes by Lefty's brother, David.

Treasures Untold: The Early Recordings of Lefty Frizzell (Rounder Special Series 11/ Columbia Special Products P15665). Includes "Always Late," "I'm An Old, Old Man," and other cuts from Lefty's heyday, 1950–53.

Lefty Frizzell: His Life—His Music (Bear Family BFX 15100). Fourteen-album set covering Frizzell's entire career, with notes by Charles Wolfe. Albums 1–11 are CBS Special Products 15452–15462.

Hank Thompson

Songs for Rounders (Stetson HAT 3052). Reissue of a 1959 Capitol album. Guitarist Merle Travis backs Hank on hard-core honky-tonk numbers.

Dance Ranch (Stetson HAT 3027). Reissue album of fifties gems from the Capitol vaults.

Webb Pierce

Webb! (Stetson HAT 3019). Reissue of a 1959 Decca LP.

Cross Country (Stetson HAT 3004). Reissue of a 1962 Decca LP.

Ray Price

The Honky Tonk Years (Rounder Special Series SS-22). Early Columbia material from Price's "Cherokee Cowboy" period.

Ray Price's Greatest Hits (Columbia CS 8866). "Crazy Arms," "City Lights," "Release Me," ten more.

Merle Travis

Back Home (Stetson HAT 3044). Capitol released many of these recordings in 1946 in an album of 78s and in 1956 on a 12-inch LP. Stetson's reissue of the 1956 LP keeps such Travis standards as "Nine Pound Hammer," "Dark as a Dungeon," "I Am a Pilgrim," and "Sixteen Tons" available.

Red Foley

Tennessee Saturday Night (Charly CR 30230). Rhythm & blues-tinged hits recorded for Decca between 1947 and 1958.

Beyond the Sunset (MCA 147). Country gospel material from a master of the form.

Louvin Brothers

Tragic Songs of Life (Stetson HAT 3043). Haunting duet harmonies, applied to the sad old tunes of the Blue Sky Boys, Karl & Harty, the Carter Family, and others. Reissue of a 1956 Capitol release.

Radio Favorites, '51–'57 (Country Music Foundation CMF 009). Fourteen previously unreleased live recordings; one side secular songs, the other gospel.

Hank Snow

20 of the Best (RCA International NL89422). Contains most of Hank's Top Ten country chartmakers, including "I'm Movin' On."

Elvis Presley

The Complete Sun Sessions (RCA 6414-1-R). Two-album set of thirty-three recordings Elvis made for Sun Records during 1954–55, including seventeen outtakes and alternate takes. Notes by Peter Guralnick.

Carl Perkins

Original Sun Greatest Hits (Rhino RNLP 70221). Fourteen tracks include "Blue Suede Shoes," "Honey Don't," and "Everybody's Trying to Be My Baby."

The Sun Years (Charly Sunbox 101). Three-disc boxed set of fifty-five recordings with accompanying booklet by Colin Escott and Martin Hawkins. Includes many previously unissued recordings and alternate takes.

Jerry Lee Lewis

Milestones (Rhino RNDA 1499). Two-disc set of twenty-five recordings, including three 1960s cuts for Smash and three 1970s cuts for Mercury, along with nineteen Sun recordings spanning the years 1956–61.

The Sun Years (Sun/Charly Sunbox 102). Twelve LPs containing 209 recordings, including many previously unissued cuts and alternate takes. Accompanying booklet by Colin Escott and Martin Hawkins.

Johnny Cash

The Vintage Years, 1955–1963 (Rhino RNLP 70229). Fourteen selections, spanning Johnny's Sun years (1955–58) and his early years with Columbia. Includes hits from "Hey Porter" to "Ring of Fire."

Columbia Records, 1958–1986 (Columbia C2 40637). Two-album set with a remarkable range of material, encompassing folk songs, love songs, and novelty tunes. Most recent cut actually recorded in 1983.

Johnny Cash and the Tennessee Two: The Sun Years (Sun/Charly Sunbox 103). Boxed set of eighty-two tracks on five albums, including seventeen alternate takes or previously unissued titles. This comprehensive package of Johnny's Sun recordings includes extensive biographical and discographical notes by Colin Escott and Martin Hawkins.

Sun Records

The Sun Story (Rhino RNDA 71103). Two-record, twenty-six track sampler. Every major Sun performer is represented (Presley, Perkins, Cash, Lewis, Orbison, Rich) as are several lesser lights (Billy Riley, Jackie Brenston, Carl Mann).

Kitty Wells

The Golden Years (1949–1957) (Bear Family BFX 15239). Rare RCA material and most of Kitty's early Decca recordings. Set of five discs comprises nearly 100 recordings. Includes notes by Charles Wolfe.

Kitty's Choice (Stetson HAT 3018). Reissue of an earlier Decca album of classic 1950s hits. Includes "It Wasn't God Who Made Honky-Tonk Angels."

Patsy Cline

Live at the Opry (MCA 42142). Hear Patsy as Grand Ole Opry fans heard her from 1956 to 1962.

The Patsy Cline Story (MCA 2-4038). Double LP of Patsy's big country and pop hits.

Jim Reeves

Live at the Opry (Country Music Foundation CMF 008). Twenty live Reeves performances from 1953–60.

Legendary Performer (RCA CPL1-1891). Some of Jim's best studio work.

Marty Robbins

A Lifetime of Song, 1951–1982 (Columbia C2 38870). Excellent compilation that spans the artist's career.

Gunfighter Ballads and Trail Songs (Columbia PC 8158). "El Paso," "Big Iron," and other western classics.

Loretta Lynn

Loretta Lynn's Greatest Hits (Vol. 1: MCA 935; Vol. 2: MCA 932). Chart hits of the sixties and seventies.

Conway Twitty

The Very Best of Conway Twitty (MCA 1485). The hits that built his career: "Hello Darlin'," "You've Never Been This Far Before," "It's Only Make Believe," and twelve others.

Number Ones (MCA 1488). Ten-song collection of more recent hits from the country singer with more #1 records than any other artist.

Buck Owens

Unfortunately, all of Owens's records are out of print. The Country Music Foundation is planning a reissue, however, of live recordings from a 1966 Carnegie Hall appearance.

Merle Haggard

The Best of Merle Haggard (Capitol SN-16054). The early hits: "I'm a Lonesome Fugitive," "Branded Man," "Strangers," seven more.

The Best of the Best of Merle Haggard (Capitol ST-11082). The hits that launched Hag to stardom: "Okie from Muskogee," "Hungry Eyes," "Workin' Man Blues," eight more.

George Jones

Burn the Honky Tonk Down (Rounder Special Series SS-15). A collection of tracks from Jones's years with the Musicor label (1965–71).

Anniversary: Ten Years of Hits (Epic KE2-38323). Jones hits of the seventies and eighties—every one of them great. Two-album set.

Tammy Wynette

Anniversary: 20 Years of Hits (Epic E2-40625). The best Tammy collection to date. Two-album set. Includes three duets with George Jones.

George & Tammy: Greatest Hits (Epic PE34716). Seventies hits that made George Jones and Tammy Wynette one of country music's leading duets.

The Statler Brothers

Country Music: Then and Now (Mercury SR 61367). This modest 1972 concept album is what the harmony quartet is all about: nostalgic hits ("The Class of '57"), some oldies, some gospel, and some good-natured, funny send-ups of small-town country radio.

Charley Pride

The Best of Charley Pride (Vol. 1: RCA AYL1-5148; Vol. 2: RCA AYL1-4832). Two good collections of sixties and seventies hits.

Dolly Parton

The Best of Dolly Parton (Vol. 1: RCA Victor AYL1-5146). Includes many of her best early songs, such as the autobiographical "Coat of Many Colors" and "My Tennessee Mountain Home."

Willie Nelson

Greatest Hits (& Some That Will Be) (Columbia KC2-37542). Double album consisting mostly of seventies and eighties hits.

Red Headed Stranger (Columbia KC-33482). The self-produced 1975 concept album that was Willie's breakthrough to stardom.

Stardust (Columbia FC-35305). Pop standards, produced by Quincy Jones. First appearing in 1978, the LP has stayed on the charts into the 1980s.

Waylon Jennings

Greatest Hits (RCA Victor AHL1-3378). Representative selection of hard-edged hits.

Waylon and Willie (RCA Victor AYL1-5134). Solos and duets by Waylon and Willie Nelson; most recorded during their Outlaw phase.

The Byrds

Sweetheart of the Rodeo (Columbia PC-9670). Sparked by bandmember Gram Parsons, this 1968 album helped inspire the country-rock movement of the late sixties and early seventies.

Gram Parsons

Grievous Angel (Reprise MS-2171). Harmonizing with Emmylou Harris. Includes original material and songs penned by Boudleaux Bryant and by the Louvin Brothers. Released 1974.

The Nitty Gritty Dirt Band

Will the Circle Be Unbroken (Liberty LWCL-51158). Landmark three-album set featuring Mother Maybelle Carter, Roy Acuff, Merle Travis, Jimmy Martin, Doc Watson, Earl Scruggs, and other country pickers. First released on United Artists in 1972.

Hank Williams, Jr.

Hank Williams, Jr. & Friends (PolyGram 831 575-1 Y-1). Re-release of a 1975 MGM album. Charlie Daniels, Marshall Tucker Band guitarist Toy Caldwell, and Allman Brothers' pianist Chuck Leavell join Hank on his first venture into southern rock.

Urban Cowboy

Urban Cowboy (Asylum DP-90002). Soundtrack from the 1980 motion picture. Two-disc set with pop-country songs by Johnny Lee, Anne Murray, the Charlie Daniels Band, Mickey Gilley, others.

Emmylou Harris

Blue Kentucky Girl (Warner Bros. BSK 3318). Influential 1979 LP features top-notch material from songwriters old (Leon Payne, the Louvin Brothers) and new (Rodney Crowell). Stellar supporting cast includes Crowell, Ricky Skaggs, and James Burton.

Alabama

Alabama's Greatest Hits (RCA AHL1-7170). Five years of hits from country's best-selling group. Released 1985.

John Conlee

John Conlee's Greatest Hits (MCA 5405). Down-to-earth songs about working-class life. Includes "Rose Colored Glasses," "Busted," "Back Side of Thirty," and seven more.

576

Ricky Skaggs
Waitin' for the Sun to Shine (Epic FE 37193). Self-produced 1981 album, his first for Epic. Includes the hits "Crying My Heart Out Over You," "Don't Get Above Your Raisin'," and "You May See Me Walkin'."

Comin' Home to Stay (Epic FE 40623). An appropriate title for this 1988 album, as Skaggs returns to the country roots sound that first propelled him to stardom.

John Anderson
Greatest Hits (Warner Brothers 1-25169). This 1984 collection contains many of Anderson's hard-core country hits, such as "Swingin'," "Wild and Blue," and "I Just Came Home to Count the Memories."

George Strait
George Strait's Greatest Hits (MCA 5567). Ten-song collection of solid honky-tonk tunes ("Let's Fall to Pieces Together") and beautiful love songs ("Unwound").

Greatest Hits Volume Two (MCA 42035). More of the same, plus a touch of western swing with "Am I Blue," "You're Something Special." Eight more.

Reba McEntire
My Kind of Country (MCA 5516). The Oklahoma cowgirl's 1984 breakthrough album. Includes hits "How Blue" and "Somebody Should Leave," with eight other cuts.

The Judds
Why Not Me (RCA Victor/Curb AHL1-5319). In addition to the title song, this 1984 album includes the #1 hits "Mama He's Crazy," "Love Is Alive," and "Girl's Night Out."

Randy Travis
Storms of Life (Warner Brothers 1-25435). Travis's million-selling 1986 debut includes the hits "On the Other Hand," "1982," "Diggin' Up Bones."

Steve Earle
Guitar Town (MCA 5713) Earle's first, self-penned album for MCA brought country-rock up to date. Released in 1986.

Dwight Yoakam
Guitars, Cadillacs, Etc., Etc. (Reprise 1-25372) Yoakam's major-label debut in 1986 was a repackaging of his six-song 1984 LP for Oak Records, plus four new tracks. A mix of old nuggets ("Honky-Tonk Man," "Ring of Fire") and originals, this LP earned a gold record.

The O'Kanes
The O'Kanes (Columbia C 40459). 1986 debut album from songwriting team of Jamie O'Hara and Kieran Kane. Includes their first hit, "Oh, Darlin'."

COUNTRY MUSIC: A SELECTED BIBLIOGRAPHY

In addition to their own firsthand knowledge, the authors relied upon the following works in writing the text. Some of the titles listed below, such as Joel Whitburn's compendiums of record chart information, are strictly reference works. And some of these books, especially the privately printed ones, are not available in the average bookstore. But a good many are eminently readable, easily available, and well worth seeking out. For those curious to learn more about country music—and popular music in general—they offer a wealth of information, insight, and entertainment.

Atkins, John, ed. *The Carter Family*. Old Time Booklet 1. London: Old Time Music, 1973.

Autry, Gene, with Mickey Herskowitz. *Back in the Saddle Again*. Garden City, New York: Doubleday & Company, 1978.

Bane, Michael. *The Outlaws: Revolution in Country Music*. Garden City, New York: Country Music Magazine Press/Doubleday/Dolphin, 1978.

Barnouw, Erik. *A History of Broadcasting in the United States*. 3 Vols. New York: Oxford University Press, 1966–70.

Bond, Johnny. *Reflections: The Autobiography of Johnny Bond*. Los Angeles: John Edwards Memorial Foundation, 1976.

———. *The Tex Ritter Story*. New York: Chappell & Company, 1976.

Cantwell, Robert. *Bluegrass Breakdown: The Making of the Old Southern Sound*. Urbana: University of Illinois Press, 1984.

Carr, Patrick, ed. *The Illustrated History of Country Music*. Garden City: Doubleday & Company, 1979.

Carter, Janette. *Living with Memories*. Hiltons, Virginia: Carter Family Memorial Music Center, 1983.

Dellar, Fred, Roy Thompson, and Douglas B. Green. *The Illustrated Encyclopedia of Country Music*. New York: Harmony Books, 1977.

Denisoff, R. Serge. *Waylon: A Biography*. Knoxville: University of Tennessee Press, 1983.

Escott, Colin, and Martin Hawkins. *Sun Records: The Brief History of the Legendary Record Label*. New York: Omnibus, 1980.

Flippo, Chet. *Your Cheatin' Heart: A Biography of Hank Williams*. New York: Simon and Schuster, 1981.

Gentry, Linnell. *A History and Encyclopedia of Folk, Country, Western and Gospel Music*. Nashville: privately printed, 1961.

Gillett, Charlie. *The Sound of the City*. New revised edition. New York: Pantheon, 1983.

Green, Douglas B. *Country Roots: The Origins of Country Music*. New York: Hawthorn Books, 1976.

Griffis, Ken. *Hear My Song: The Story of the Celebrated Sons of the Pioneers*. Camarillo, California: Norken, 1986.

Hall, Claude, and Barbara Hall. *This Business of Radio Programming*. New York: Billboard Publications, 1977.

Hemphill, Paul. *The Nashville Sound: Bright Lights and Country Music*. New York: Simon and Schuster, 1970.

Horstman, Dorothy. *Sing Your Heart Out, Country Boy*. Nashville: Country Music Foundation Press, 1986.

Hurst, Jack. *Grand Ole Opry*. New York: Harry N. Abrams, Inc., 1975.

Hurst, Richard Maurice. *Republic Studios: Between Poverty Row and the Majors*. Metuchen, New Jersey: The Scarecrow Press, 1979.

Lomax, John, III. *Nashville: Music City U.S.A.* New York: Harry N. Abrams, Inc., 1985.

Malone, Bill C. *Country Music, U.S.A..* Revised edition. Austin: University of Texas Press, 1985.

Malone, Bill C., and Judith McCulloh, eds. *Stars of Country Music*. Urbana: University of Illinois Press, 1975.

Marcus, Greil. *Mystery Train: Images of America in Rock & Roll Music*. New York: E. P. Dutton, 1975.

Mason, Michael, ed. *The Country Music Book*. New York: Scribner's, 1985.

Miller, Don. *Hollywood Corral*. New York: Popular Library, 1976.

Moore, Thurston, ed. and producer. *The Original Country Music Who's Who Annual for 1960*. Cincinnati: Cardinal Enterprises, 1959.

————, ed. and producer. *The Country Music Who's Who*, 1965 edition. Denver: Heather Publications, 1964.

Morthland, John. *The Best of Country Music*. Garden City: Doubleday/Dolphin, 1984.

Nassour, Ellis. *Patsy Cline*. New York: Tower Books, 1981.

Passman, Arnold. *The Deejays*. New York: MacMillan, 1971.

Pleasants, Henry. *The Great American Popular Singers*. New York: Simon and Schuster, 1974.

Porterfield, Nolan. *Jimmie Rodgers: The Life and Times of America's Blue Yodeler*. Urbana: University of Illinois Press, 1979.

Reid, Jan. *The Improbable Rise of Redneck Rock*. Austin: Heidelberg Publishers, 1974.

Rogers, Roy, and Dale Evans with Carlton Stowers. *Happy Trails*. Waco, Texas: Word Books, 1979.

Rosenberg, Neil V. *Bill Monroe and His Blue Grass Boys: An Illustrated Discography*. Nashville: Country Music Foundation Press, 1974.

————. *Bluegrass: A History*. Urbana: University of Illinois Press, 1985.

Rothel, David. *The Singing Cowboys*. South Brunswick: A. S. Barnes & Company, 1978.

Sheldon, Ruth. *Hubbin' It: The Life of Bob Wills*. Tulsa: privately printed, 1938.

Stambler, Irwin, and Grelun Landon. *The Encyclopedia of Folk, Country and Western Music*. First and revised editions. New York: St. Martin's Press, 1969, 1983.

Stricklin, Al, with Jon McConal. *My Years with Bob Wills*. San Antonio: The Naylor Press, 1976.

Townsend, Charles R. *San Antonio Rose: The Life and Music of Bob Wills*. Urbana: University of Illinois Press, 1976.

Tribe, Ivan M. *Mountaineer Jamboree: Country Music in West Virginia*. Lexington: University of Kentucky Press, 1984.

Tuska, Jon. *The Filming of the West*. Garden City: Doubleday & Company, 1976.

Tosches, Nick. *Country: The Biggest Music in America*. Revised edition. New York: Scribner's, 1985.

Vecsey, George, with Leonore Fleischer. *Sweet Dreams*, New York: St. Martin's Press, 1985.

Whitburn, Joel. *Joel Whitburn's Top Country and Western Records 1949–1971*. Menomonee Falls, Wisconsin: Record Research, 1972.

————. *Joel Whitburn's Top Country and Western Records 1972–1973*. Menomonee Falls, Wisconsin: Record Research, 1974.

————. *Top Country Singles and LPs 1981*. Menomonee Falls, Wisconsin: Record Research, 1982.

————. *Top Country Singles and LPs 1982*. Menomonee Falls, Wisconsin: Record Research, 1983.

————. *Billboard's Music Yearbook 1983*. Menomonee Falls, Wisconsin: Record Research, 1984.

————. *Billboard's Music Yearbook 1984*. Menomonee Falls, Wisconsin: Record Research, 1985.

————. *Billboard's Music Yearbook 1985*. Menomonee Falls, Wisconsin: Record Research, 1986.

————. *Billboard's Music Yearbook 1986*. Menomonee Falls, Wisconsin: Record Research, 1987.

Williams, Roger M. *Sing a Sad Song: The Life of Hank Williams*. Second edition. Urbana: University of Illinois Press, 1980.

Wolfe, Charles. *The Grand Ole Opry: The Early Years, 1925–35*. London: Old Time Music, 1975.

————. *Tennessee Strings: The Story of Country Music in Tennessee*. Knoxville: University of Tennessee, 1977.

————. *Kentucky Country: Folk and Country Music of Kentucky*. Lexington: University Press of Kentucky, 1982.

Wolfe, Charles, ed. *Truth Is Stranger Than Publicity: The Autobiography of Alton Delmore*. Nashville: Country Music Foundation Press, 1977.

INDEX

This index is designed to give readers—especially those newly acquainted with country music—a quick reference to persons or groups mentioned and pictured in the text. The names of artists, groups, and other creative personnel are followed (in parentheses) by a statement of the subject's most prominent **activities** in country music; in the case of individual performers, the **band** he or she is most closely associated with; and, wherever possible, approximate **working dates**. Limited space prevents listing every endeavor in which a person was—or is—involved. Page numbers in italic refer to illustrations.

589

593

Photo Credits

All photographs—with the exception of those listed below—have come from the archives of the Country Music Foundation. The CMF gratefully acknowledges the following contributions:

Tommy Allsup: 132 (Haggard); Capitol Records: 211, 402 (Murray), 478 (Brown), 481 (Sawyer Brown); Claude Casey: 75; CBS Records: 112 (Asleep at the Wheel), 180, 474 (top), 481 (Stuart), 528, 534 (Exile), 541, 544 (Gosdin), 550 (Crowell), 550 (Cash), 558 (Sweethearts of the Rodeo), 560 (Shelton), 562; Robert Dye: 301, 302, 329 (Jackson & Thompson), 351 (Hawkins & Dickens), 501; Colin Escott: 288, 298 (Rich), 299 (Feathers), 406/433 (Sholes & Presley); Leonard Kamsler: 454, 466; Louise Krauss/photo by Lou McClellan: 564; Alan Mayor: 447, 469 (Silverstein); MCA Records: 146 (Riders in the Sky), 478 (Lovett), 482, 537 (Earle), 548, 553, 554, 556 (Loveless); MTM Records: 555 (Rodman), 556 (Dunn); Mack Newberry/Solters Roskin Friedman: 404 (lower); Opryland/Donnie Beauchamp: 359; Bob Pinson: 16, 110, 112 (Ritter), 119 (Hi Flyers), 120, 122, 126 (lower), 145, 174 (Duff), 178 (Collins), 200, 235 (right), 267 (Texas Playboys), 270 (Texas Playboys), 342/349, 392 (Statlers), 484 (film poster), 485, 492; PolyGram Records: 546 (Mattea), 560 (Boone), 565 (Jones); RCA Records: 208 (Osbornes), 252, 279 (Snow), 279 (Hall), 291, 310, 329 (West), 372/398 (Nelson), 374, 378/jacket, 379 (left), 387 (Brown & Cornelius), 387/jacket (Parton), 402 (Rich), 449, 458 (Bare), 460 (Colter), 461, 476, 505 (Reeves), 508, 509 (Davis), 513, 524, 530 (Conley), 534 (Milsap), 535 (Restless Heart), 536, 539 (Foster & Lloyd), 544 (Johnson), 547 (Wariner), 547 (Gill), 558 (top left), 563, 565 (Raven); Renfro Valley Folks, Inc.: 56 (Barn Dance, Lair); Jon Riley: 566; Kenny Roberts: 493 (Roberts); Showtime Archive, Toronto: 295 (Riley), 295 (Cochran Brothers), 297 (Vincent), 300 (Rock 'n' Roll Trio); Jon Sievert: 10/51, 127 (steel guitar), 138 (both guitars), 142 (guitar), 177 (guitar), 228 (guitar), 237 (guitar), 345 (guitar); Chris Skinker: 194, 195, 352 (postcard); Gordon Stoker: 297 (Nelson); Warner Bros. Records: 479, 480/jacket, 483, 532, 537 (Highway 101), 545 (Harris), 546 (Nitty Gritty Dirt Band), 557, 559/jacket, 561.

Sidebar Credits

The following Country Music Foundation staff members researched and wrote the sidebars that accompany the book's major essays:

Ch. 1: "Strings in Numbers," Charlie Seemann; "He Was a Swell Guy, Yessir," Bob Pinson, Paul Kingsbury. *Ch. 2*: "Word from Home," Bob Pinson, Paul Kingsbury (statistics courtesy of Charles Wolfe); "Anatomy of a Barn Dance," John Rumble. *Ch. 3*: "What Happened to the Barn Dance Radio Shows?" John Rumble; "How the Record Charts Work," Jay Orr. *Ch. 4*: "Origins of Western Swing," Bob Pinson, Paul Kingsbury; "The Real Singing Cowboys," Charlie Seemann. *Ch. 5*: "On Location with Art Satherley," Bob Pinson, Paul Kingsbury; "Cajun Spice," Charlie Seemann; "Country Clubs," Ronnie Pugh. *Ch. 6*: "Festivals for the Faithful," John Rumble, Dean Crum; "Bluegrass's Western Front," Chris Skinker; "Leaves of Grass," Dean Crum, Paul Kingsbury. *Ch. 7*: "Honky-Tonk Pioneers," Ronnie Pugh; "Bakersfield's Honky-Tonkers," Ronnie Pugh. *Ch. 9*: "C'Mon Everybody," Jay Orr; "Whole Lotta Shakin'," Paul Kingsbury. *Ch. 10*: "Women's Work," Charlie Seemann; "Answer Songs," Ronnie Pugh. *Ch. 11*: "The Old Timers," Jay Orr. *Ch. 12*: "The Last Laugh," Paul Kingsbury; "And the Winner Is…," Paul Kingsbury; "The Top Fifty," Ronnie Pugh. *Ch. 13*: "The Nashville Network," Ronnie Pugh; "The Independents," John Rumble. *Ch. 15*: "Country Comedy," Charlie Seemann, Paul Kingsbury; "Like a Rhinestone Cowboy," Chris Skinker, Paul Kingsbury. *Ch. 16*: "Country-Rock," Jay Orr.